M000014540

FIELDING'S
KENYA

Fielding Titles

Fielding's Alaska Cruises and the Inside Passage
Fielding's America West
Fielding's Asia's Top Dive Sites
Fielding's Australia
Fielding's Bahamas
Fielding's Baja California
Fielding's Bermuda
Fielding's Best and Worst — The surprising results of the Plog Survey
Fielding's Birding Indonesia
Fielding's Borneo
Fielding's Budget Europe
Fielding's Caribbean
Fielding's Caribbean Cruises
Fielding's Caribbean on a Budget
Fielding's Diving Australia
Fielding's Diving Indonesia
Fielding's Eastern Caribbean
Fielding's England including Ireland, Scotland & Wales
Fielding's Europe
Fielding's Europe 50th Anniversary
Fielding's European Cruises
Fielding's Far East
Fielding's France
Fielding's France: Loire Valley, Burgundy & the Best of French Culture
Fielding's France: Normandy & Brittany
Fielding's France: Provence and the Mediterranean
Fielding's Freewheelin' USA
Fielding's Hawaii
Fielding's Hot Spots: Travel in Harm's Way
Fielding's Indiana Jones Adventure and Survival Guide™
Fielding's Italy
Fielding's Kenya
Fielding's Las Vegas Agenda
Fielding's London Agenda
Fielding's Los Angeles Agenda
Fielding's Mexico
Fielding's New Orleans Agenda
Fielding's New York Agenda
Fielding's New Zealand
Fielding's Paradors, Pousadas and Charming Villages of Spain and Portugal
Fielding's Paris Agenda
Fielding's Portugal
Fielding's Rome Agenda
Fielding's San Diego Agenda
Fielding's Southeast Asia
Fielding's Southern California Theme Parks
Fielding's Southern Vietnam on Two Wheels
Fielding's Spain
Fielding's Surfing Australia
Fielding's Surfing Indonesia
Fielding's Sydney Agenda
Fielding's Thailand, Cambodia, Laos and Myanmar
Fielding's Travel Tool™
Fielding's Vietnam, including Cambodia and Laos
Fielding's Walt Disney World and Orlando Area Theme Parks
Fielding's Western Caribbean
Fielding's The World's Most Dangerous Places™
Fielding's Worldwide Cruises

FIELDING'S
KENYA

By

Bridget Glenday

Susan Southwick

and

Joan Westley

Fielding Worldwide, Inc.

308 South Catalina Avenue

Redondo Beach, California 90277 U.S.A.

Fielding's Guide to Kenya

Published by Fielding Worldwide, Inc.

Text Copyright ©1997 Fielding Worldwide, Inc.

Icons & Illustrations Copyright ©1997 FWI

Photo Copyrights ©1997 to Individual Photographers

FIELDING WORLDWIDE INC.

PUBLISHER AND CEO	**Robert Young Pelton**
GENERAL MANAGER	**John Guillebeaux**
MARKETING DIRECTOR	**Paul T. Snapp**
OPERATIONS DIRECTOR	**George Posanke**
ELECTRONIC PUBLISHING DIRECTOR	**Larry E. Hart**
PUBLIC RELATIONS DIRECTOR	**Beverly Riess**
ACCOUNT SERVICES MANAGER	**Cindy Henrichon**
PROJECT MANAGER	**Chris Snyder**
MANAGING EDITOR	**Amanda K. Knoles**

PRODUCTION

Martin Mancha   **Ramses Reynoso**

Craig South

COVER DESIGNED BY	**Digital Artists, Inc.**
COVER PHOTOGRAPHERS — Front Cover	**Manoi Shah/Tony Stone Images**
Back Cover	**Robert Young Pelton/Westlight**
INSIDE PHOTOS	**David Anderson, Bruce Coleman, Inc.,**
	Robert Young Pelton/Westlight
ILLUSTRATIONS	**Tuula Sotamaa, Pam Toh, Elizabeth Washburn**

Inquiries should be addressed to: Fielding Worldwide, Inc., 308 South Catalina Ave., Redonc
Beach, California 90277 U.S.A., ☎ (310) 372-4474, Facsimile (310) 376-8064, 8:30 a.m.
5:30 p.m. Pacific Standard Time.
Website: http://www.fieldingtravel.com
e-mail: fielding@fieldingtravel.com

ISBN 1-56952-146-8

Printed in the United States of America

Letter from the Publisher

World travelers Bridget Glenday, Susan Southwick and Joan Westley have ved in and traveled throughout Kenya for four years. During their four-heel drive, hot air balloon and camel journeys they have painstakingly re-iewed every type of accommodation from the bustling tourist hotels to lit-le–known private homes and even tented camps to create a colorful, pinionated guide for the independent traveler. The other half of the inter-ational team, Tuula Sotamaa, Pam Toh and Elizabeth Washburn, spent nonths creating the exquisite maps, line drawings and illustrations that give nis book its special personality. Together with Fielding, they have created ne only in-depth guide to every major safari camp, lodge and homestay in Kenya. In addition, our Quick Reference Safari Guide is a helpful reference o Kenya's national parks, biospheres and nature preserves. This new update rovides complete coverage of Kenya's adventurous and romantic destina-ions and is still the only book that covers each one in depth.

Today, the concept of independent travel has never been bigger. Fielding's olicy of *brutal honesty* and a highly personal point of view has never hanged; it just seems the travel world has caught up with us.

Enjoy your Kenyan safari with Bridget, Susan, Joan and Fielding.

RYP

Robert Young Pelton
Publisher and CEO
Fielding Worldwide, Inc.

DEDICATION

We dedicate this book to the hospitable people of Kenya.

ABOUT THE AUTHORS

Bridget Glenday

Bridget was born and raised in Africa and, with her Harvard professor husband, has also lived in England, the United States and Canada. In addition to being an avid writer, Bridget has a professional background in marketing, consumer research and new product development. Her hobbies include decorative painting and exploring wild, far-flung places. In the past year she has hiked in the Simien Mountains of Ethiopia, climbed the sand dunes of Namibia at sunrise, and bartered in the markets of Rajasthan. She is the only one of the original team still living in Kenya and has gathered the information for the updated book.

Susan Southwick

An American who loves travel, Susan Southwick has lived in Germany, Nepal, Rwanda, Switzerland, Burundi, Niger, and Kenya. With her husband in the U.S. Diplomatic Corps, she has enjoyed many opportunities for travel and cultural exchange around the world. A writer by choice, she has also done professional social work, journalism, and travel industry marketing. She enjoys anthropological studies, community politics, and promoting the arts.

Joan Westley

Joan Westley has lived and traveled extensively in Asia, Africa, and Europe. She has stayed in many of the world's finest hotels. She teaches French and English Literature. A true francophile, she also enjoys classical music, scuba diving and playing tennis.

Fielding Rating Icons

The Fielding Rating Icons are highly personal and awarded to help the besieged traveler choose from among the dizzying array of activities, attractions, hotels, restaurants and sights. The awarding of an icon denotes unusual or exceptional qualities in the relevant category.

RATINGS							
Fielding Award	Author Selection	Money Saver	Expensive	Quality	Warning	Danger	Inexpensive
Spacious	Cramped	Mild Disapproval	Timesaving				

CULTURAL							
Museum/Art	Interesting Architecture	History	Book Reference	Artistically Important	Musically Interesting	Cultural Archeology	Crafts
Theatre	Festivals						

SIGHTS							
Picturesque	Great Scenery	Market	Beaches/Resorts	Cultural	Fortress	Castles	Church

WHERE TO STAY							
Simple	Luxurious	Cottage	Bed & Breakfast	Scenic	Business	Honeymoon	Chateau

TRAVEL TIPS							
Arrival/Departure	By Air	By Water	By Train	By Car	Bus/Local Transit	Barge	River Boat
Calendar	Itinerary	Compass	Kids				

ACTIVITIES

Downhill Skiing	X–country Skiing	Water Sports	Sailing	Scuba Diving	Snorkeling/ Diving	Deep-sea Fishing	Freshwater Fishing
Swimming	Hiking	Walking	Relaxing	Golf	Tennis	Horseback Riding	General Sports
Cycling	Workout	Spa	Camping	Off-Road	Boating	Rafting	Recreational Vehicle

SPECIAL INTEREST

Nightlife	Singles	Romantic	Nude Beaches	Lecture	Spectacular Cuisine	Wine Tasting	Shopping
Cafe Stops	Gardening	Pro Sports	Mystery	Gambling	Wildlife		

TABLE OF CONTENTS

LIST OF MAPS

FIELDING'S
TOP "TOPIS"

We visited more than 230 places. We "tip" our topis to the best Kenyan hotels, lodges, tented camps, ranch/sanctuaries, homestays and grass shacks on the beach. "Phantom" hats have been awarded to places which are not yet fully operational. Three "tipped topis" were the most hats awarded to any one place. Throughout the book, all hotels listed in large print are well worth a visit.

Rating	Accommodation	Page
	Three Hat Accommodations	
▷▷▷	**Blue Safari Club**	*page 357*
▷▷▷	**Borana Lodge**	*page 151*
▷▷▷	**Finch Hattons Safari Camp**	*page 253*
▷▷▷	**Giraffe Manor**	*page 84*
▷▷▷	**Hemingway's**	*page 325*
▷▷▷	**Kiwayu Safari Village**	*page 354*
▷▷▷	**Larsens**	*page 166*
▷▷▷	**Little Governor's Camp**	*page 207*
▷▷▷	**Loldia House**	*page 102*
▷▷▷	**Mfangano Island Camp**	*page 188*
▷▷▷	**Mombasa Serena Beach Hotel**	*page 314*
▷▷▷	**Mundui**	*page 104*
▷▷▷	**Ngare Niti**	*page 149*
▷▷▷	**Ol Donyo Laro**	*page 234*
▷▷▷	**Ol Donyo Wuas**	*page 248*
▷▷▷	**Ol Malo**	*page 177*
▷▷▷	**Palm House**	*page 350*
▷▷▷	**Shela House**	*page 350*
▷▷▷	**Tortillis Camp**	*page 245*
▷▷▷	**Wilderness Trails at Lewa Downs**	*page 147*

Rating	Accommodation	Page
Two & One-Half Hat Accommodations		
⛑⛑½	**Colcheccio Ranch**	*page 178*
⛑⛑½	**Governor's Camp**	*page 204*
⛑⛑½	**Indian Ocean Beach Club**	*page 279*
⛑⛑½	**Indian Ocean Lodge**	*page 333*
⛑⛑½	**Kisimani House**	*page 352*
⛑⛑½	**Mara Intrepids Club**	*page 209*
⛑⛑½	**Ngong House**	*page 87*
⛑⛑½	**Ocean Village Club**	*page 281*
⛑⛑½	**Pemba Channel Inn**	*page 299*
⛑⛑½	**Sekenani Camp**	*page 211*
Two Hat Accommodations		
⛑⛑	**Aberdare Country Club**	*page 129*
⛑⛑	**Galdessa Safari Camp**	*page 261*
⛑⛑	**Grand Regency Hotel**	*page 65*
⛑⛑	**Island Camp**	*page 120*
⛑⛑	**Kiangazi**	*page 106*
⛑⛑	**Kichwa Tembo Camp**	*page 215*
⛑⛑	**Kipangani Bay**	*page 360*
⛑⛑	**Kongoni Valley Game Ranch**	*page 99*
⛑⛑	**Longonot Game Ranch**	*page 107*
⛑⛑	**Mara Safari Club**	*page 217*
⛑⛑	**Mt. Kenya Safari Club**	*page 131*
⛑⛑	**Mpata Safari Club**	*page 226*
⛑⛑	**Nairobi Serena Hotel**	*page 73*
⛑⛑	**The Norfolk Hotel**	*page 70*
⛑⛑	**Peponi Hotel**	*page 346*
⛑⛑	**Rekero**	*page 223*
⛑⛑	**Safari Park Hotel**	*page 81*

Rating	Accommodation	Page
🐾🐾	**Samburu Intrepids Club**	*page 168*
🐾🐾	**Sarova Shaba Lodge**	*page 172*
🐾🐾	**Tana Delta Camp**	*page 342*
🐾🐾	**Takaungu House**	*page 323*
🐾🐾	**The Tamarind Village**	*page 309*
🐾🐾	**Windsor Golf and Country Club**	*page 78*
One & One-Half Hat Accommodations		
🐾½	**The Ark Forest Lodge**	*page 139*
🐾½	**Crater Lake Camp**	*page 97*
🐾½	**Diani House**	*page 292*
🐾½	**Funzi Island Club**	*page 301*
🐾½	**Lerai Tented Camp**	*page 150*
🐾½	**Malu Farm**	*page 115*
🐾½	**Mnarani Club**	*page 320*
🐾½	**Olerai House**	*page 108*
🐾½	**Ol Pejeta Lodge**	*page 152*
🐾½	**Rondo Retreat Center**	*page 193*
🐾½	**Rusinga Island Club**	*page 190*
🐾½	**Siana Springs**	*page 220*
🐾½	**Taita Hills Lodge**	*page 263*
🐾½	**Wingu Kenda**	*page 158*
One Hat Accommodations		
🐾	**Amboseli Serena Safari Lodge**	*page 241*
🐾	**Delamere Camp**	*page 113*
🐾	**Deloraine**	*page 117*
🐾	**Hilton Safari Camp**	*page 267*
🐾	**Holiday Inn Mayfair Court**	*page 75*
🐾	**Jadini Beach Hotel**	*page 283*
🐾	**Kilanguni Lodge**	*page 256*

Rating	Accommodation	Page
👒	**Lagoon Reef Hotel**	*page 284*
👒	**Lake Naivasha Club**	*page 95*
👒	**Macushla House**	*page 88*
👒	**Malindi Beach Club**	*page 334*
👒	**Mara Serena Safari Lodge**	*page 231*
👒	**Naro Moru River Lodge**	*page 134*
👒	**Nyali Beach**	*page 306*
👒	**Olkurruk Mara Lodge**	*page 228*
👒	**Outspan Hotel**	*page 135*
👒	**Salt Lick Safari Lodge**	*page 265*
👒	**Shimba Hills**	*page 303*
👒	**Sweetwaters Tented Camp**	*page 144*
👒	**Whitesands**	*page 311*
One-Half Hat Accommodations		
♭	**Chale Paradise Island**	*page 297*
♭	**Che-Shale**	*page 341*
♭	**Elsamere Conservation Center**	*page 96*
♭	**Fairview Hotel**	*page 75*
♭	**Hotel Intercontinental Mombasa**	*page 317*
♭	**Kaskazi Beach Hotel**	*page 286*
♭	**Keekorok Lodge**	*page 230*
♭	**Kilili Baharini**	*page 335*
♭	**Kingfisher Lodge**	*page 335*
♭	**Lake Baringo Club**	*page 122*
♭	**Leopard Beach Hotel**	*page 287*
♭	**Pinewood Village**	*page 296*
♭	**Tsavo Safari Camp**	*page 259*
♭	**White Elephant Sea Lodge**	*page 336*

FIELDING'S PICKS

Hats, Money Bags, Double Occupancy Rates

The rates quoted here are based on high season double occupancy. Sometimes this will nclude full or half board, breakfast, or no meals depending on what is usual for each specific area.

Kind of accommodation (such as "Hotels" or "Tented Camp" etc.) is indicated in the book by an icon in the outside margin. An asterisk (*) denotes a "small print" hotel.

Where hotel and lodge prices include game drives or fishing, this has been noted. Many private homestay prices include a variety of otherwise pricey extras, e.g. game drives, escorted walks, horse riding, etc.

The following letters are used to note the type of accommodation:

Hotel..H

Hotel (Night Game Viewing Lodge)...H-NGVL

Homestay ....HS

Ranch/Sanctuary ....R/S

Tented Camp ....TC

Grass Shacks/Tents on the Beach ....GS/ToB

Accommodation	Type	Hats	$ Bags	Price	Page
Nairobi					*page 61*
City Center					
Grand Regency Hotel	H	🎩🎩	💰💰	**$159**	*page 65*
Hotel Intercontinental Nairobi	H		💰💰	**$195**	*page 65*
Nairobi Hilton	H		💰💰💰	**$210**	*page 67*
Nairobi Safari Club	H		💰💰	**$113**	*page 68*

Accommodation	Type	Hats	$ Bags	Price	Page
* New Stanley Hotel	H		🪲🪲	$130	page 69
* Six Eighty Hotel	H		🪲	$90	page 70
Beyond City Center					
The Norfolk Hotel	H	☂☂	🪲🪲🪲	$230	page 70
Nairobi Serena Hotel	H	☂☂	🪲🪲🪲	$259	page 73
Holiday Inn Mayfair Court Hotel	H	☂	🪲🪲	$170	page 75
Fairview Hotel	H	♿	🪲	$90	page 75
* Landmark Hotel	H		🪲🪲	$150	page 77
* Boulevard Hotel	H		🪲	$86	page 77
* Panafric Hotel	H		🪲	$85	page 78
City Suburbs					
Windsor Golf and Country Club	H	☂☂	🪲🪲	$185	page 78
Safari Park Hotel	H	☂☂	🪲🪲	$190	page 81
* Utali Hotel	H		🪲	$80	page 83
* The Kentmere Club	H		🪲	$32	page 83
* The Blue Post Hotel	H		🪲	$20	page 84
The Giraffe Manor	R/S	☂☂☂	🪲🪲🪲🪲	$490	page 84
Ngong House	HS	☂☂♿	🪲🪲🪲🪲🪲	$600	page 87
Macushla House	HS	☂	🪲🪲	$120	page 88
L'ol Dacha	HS		🪲🪲🪲	$300	page 89
Rift Valley					page 91
Lake Naivasha					
Lake Naivasha Club	H	☂	🪲🪲	$172	page 95
Elsamere Conservation Center	H	♿	🪲🪲	$116	page 96
* Safariland Club Ltd.	H		🪲🪲	$138	page 97
Crater Lake Camp	TC	☂♿	🪲🪲🪲	$250	page 97
Kongoni Game Valley Ranch	R/S	☂☂	🪲🪲🪲🪲	$320	page 99
Kongoni Game Conservancy	R/S		🪲🪲🪲🪲🪲		page 101
Loldia House	R/S	☂☂☂	🪲🪲🪲🪲🪲	$440	page 102
Mundui	R/S	☂☂☂	🪲🪲🪲🪲🪲	$360	page 104
Kiangazi		☂☂	🪲🪲🪲🪲		page 106
Longonot Game Ranch	R/S	☂☂	🪲🪲🪲	$240	page 107

Accommodation	Type	Hats	$ Bags	Price	Page
Olerai House (Acacia)	HS	🐻🦯	💰💰💰💰	$380	page 108
* Lakeside House	HS		💰💰	$180	page 110
* Morendat House	HS		💰💰💰	$210	page 111
Gilgil					
River House	HS		💰	$65	page 112
Lake Elmenteita					
Lake Elmenteita Lodge	H		💰💰	$140	page 113
Delamere Camp	TC	🐻	💰💰💰	$240	page 113
Malu Farm	HS	🐻🦯	💰💰💰💰	$350	page 115
Lake Nakuru					
Lake Nakuru Lodge	H		💰💰	$160	page 116
Sarova Lion Hill	H		💰💰	$145	page 116
Rongai & Molo					
Deloraine	R/S	🐻	💰💰💰💰	$320	page 117
Juani Farm	HS		💰💰	$180	page 118
Lake Baringo					
Island Camp	TC	🐻🐻	💰💰	$187	page 120
Lake Baringo Club	H	🦯	💰💰	$133	page 122
Lake Bogoria Hotel	H		💰💰		page 124
Kabarnet					
* Kabarnet Hotel	H		💰	$40	page 124
Central Highlands (Mt. Kenya Area)					page 125
Nyeri - Nanyuki & Beyond					
The Aberdare Country Club	H	🐻🐻	💰💰	$165	page 129
Mount Kenya Safari Club	H	🐻🐻	💰💰💰💰	$325	page 131
Naro Moru River Lodge	H	🐻	💰💰	$114	page 134
Outspan Hotel	H	🐻	💰💰	$133	page 135
* Thomson's Falls Inn	H		💰	$20	page 137
The Ark Forest Lodge	H-NGVL	🐻🦯	💰💰💰💰	$385	page 139
Mountain Lodge	H-NGVL		💰💰	$184	page 141
Treetops	H-NGVL		💰💰💰	$209	page 143
Sweetwaters Tented Camp	TC	🐻	💰💰	$195	page 144
Wilderness Trails at Lewa Downs	R/S	🐻🐻🐻	💰💰💰💰💰	$440	page 146

Accommodation	Type	Hats	$ Bags	Price	Page
Ngare Niti	R/S	👀👀👀	🎒🎒🎒🎒	$300	*page 149*
Lerai Tented Camp	TC	👀🦵	🎒🎒🎒🎒	$380	*page 150*
Borana Lodge	R/S	👀👀👀	🎒🎒🎒🎒🎒	$650	*page 151*
Ol Pejeta Lodge	R/S	👀🦵	🎒🎒🎒	$233	*page 152*
Sangare Ranch	R/S		🎒🎒🎒	$260	*page 155*
Aberdare House	HS		🎒🎒🎒🎒🎒		*page 156*
Mokorindo Cottage	R/S		🎒🎒		*page 157*
Wingu Kenda	HS	👀🦵	🎒🎒🎒🎒	$300	*page 158*
* Ken Trout	H		🎒		*page 159*
Meru National Park					
* Meru Mulika Lodge	H		🎒🎒	$120	*page 160*
Patricks Camp Meru			🎒🎒🎒🎒🎒		*page 160*
Kindani Camp	TC		🎒🎒🎒	$250	*page 161*
Embu					
* Izaak Walton Inn	H		🎒	$75	*page 161*
Northern Kenya					*page 163*
Samburu Area					
Samburu National Reserve					
Larsens	TC	👀👀👀	🎒🎒🎒	$228	*page 166*
Samburu Intrepids Club	TC	👀👀	🎒🎒🎒	$201	*page 168*
Samburu Serena Safari Lodge	H		🎒🎒	$199.50	*page 169*
Samburu Lodge	H		🎒🎒	$165	*page 171*
Shaba National Reserve					
Sarova Shaba Lodge	H	👀👀	🎒🎒	$185	*page 172*
Buffalo Springs National Reserve, Introduction					
Buffalo Springs Lodge	H		🎒🎒	$160	*page 174*
Marsabit					
The Marsabit National Park					
* Marsabit Lodge	H		🎒🎒	$120	*page 175*
Matthews Range					
Kitich Camp	TC		🎒🎒🎒🎒🎒	$600	*page 175*
Rumuruti - Wamba - Maralal Area					
Ol Malo	R/S	👀👀👀	🎒🎒🎒🎒	$490	*page 177*

Accommodation	Type	Hats	$ Bags	Price	Page
Colcheccio Ranch	R/S	🕊🕊🕊	👝👝👝👝	**$400**	*page 178*
Maralal					
Maralal Safari Lodge	H		👝👝	**$175**	*page 180*
Maralal - Loyangalani - South Horr					
Desert Rose Lodge	H		👝👝👝	**$330**	*page 182*
Lake Turkana					
Loiyangalani					
The Oasis Club (East Shore)	H		👝👝	**$150**	*page 183*
Ferguson's Gulf					
* Lake Turkana Lodge (West Shore)	H		**Closed for renovations**		*page 184*
Western Kenya					*page 185*
Lake Victoria					
Mfangano Island Camp	H	🕊🕊🕊	👝👝👝👝	**$900** (fishing & flight)	*page 188*
Rusinga Island Club	H	🕊🕊	👝👝👝👝	**$970** (fishing & flight)	*page 190*
Western Highlands					
Barnley's House	HS		👝👝	**$106**	*page 192*
Lokitela Farm	HS		👝👝👝👝	**$490**	*page 192*
Rondo Retreat Center	HS	🕊🕊	👝👝	**$184**	*page 193*
* Imperial Hotel	H		👝	**$46**	*page 194*
* Kakamega Golf Hotel	H		👝	**$75**	*page 195*
* Kericho Tea Hotel	H		👝	**$84**	*page 195*
* Kitale Club	H		👝	**$50**	*page 195*
* Mt. Elgon Lodge	H		👝👝	**$120**	*page 196*
* Sirikwa Hotel	H		👝	**$60**	*page 196*
* Sunset Hotel	H		👝	**$60**	*page 196*
Southern Kenya					*page 197*
Masai Mara National Reserve					
Governors' Family of Camps, all include game drives					
Governors' Camp	TC	🕊🕊🕊	👝👝👝👝	**$410**	*page 204*
Little Governors' Camp	TC	🕊🕊🕊	👝👝👝👝	**$410**	*page 207*
Governors' Paradise Camp	TC		👝👝👝👝	**$410**	*page 208*

Accommodation	Type	Hats	$ Bags	Price	Page
Governors' Private Camp	TC		🎒🎒🎒🎒	**$820** (x2 as 4 must book)	*page 209*
Mara Intrepids Club	TC	👒👒👒	🎒🎒🎒	**$304** (with game drives)	*page 209*
Sekenani Camp	TC	👒👒👒	🎒🎒🎒	**$330** (with game drives)	*page 211*
Kichwa Tembo Camp	TC	👒👒	🎒🎒🎒	**$280** (with game drives)	*page 215*
Mara Safari Club	TC	👒👒	🎒🎒🎒	**$390** (with game drives)	*page 217*
Siana Springs	TC	👒👒	🎒🎒🎒	**$280** (with game drives)	*page 220*
Mara River Camp	TC		🎒🎒	**$175**	*page 221*
Sarova Mara Camp	TC		🎒🎒	**$185**	*page 222*
* Fig Tree Camp	TC		🎒	**$70**	*page 222*
* Oseur Tented Camp	TC		🎒🎒	**$100**	*page 222*
* Talek River Camp	TC		🎒🎒	**$100**	*page 223*
Rekero	HS	👒👒	🎒🎒🎒🎒	**$640** (with game drives, walks)	*page 223*
Bush Tops	HS		🎒🎒🎒🎒🎒	**$400** (with game drives)	*page 225*
Mpata Safari Club	H	👒👒	🎒🎒🎒🎒🎒	**$560** (jacuzzi & game drives)	*page 226*
Olkurruk Mara Lodge	H	👒	🎒🎒🎒	**$230**	*page 228*
Keekorok Lodge	H	👢	🎒🎒	**$193**	*page 230*
Mara Serena Safari Lodge	H	👒	🎒🎒🎒	**$212**	*page 231*
Mara Simba	H		🎒🎒🎒🎒🎒		*page 232*
* Masai Mara Sopa Lodge	H		🎒🎒	**$180**	*page 233*
* Paradise Mara Camp	H		🎒🎒	**$240** (with game drives)	*page 233*

Accommodation	Type	Hats	$ Bags	Price	Page
Nguruman Escarpment					
Ol Donyo Laro	R/S	⪧⪧⪧	🎒🎒🎒🎒	**$1000** (with game drives)	*page 234*
Melepo Hills					
Sirata Suruwa	TC		🎒🎒🎒🎒		*page 238*
Amboseli National Park					
Amboseli Serena Safari Lodge	H	⪧	🎒🎒🎒	**$220**	*page 241*
Ol Tukai Lodge	H		🎒🎒		*page 244*
* Amboseli Lodge	H		🎒🎒🎒	**$210**	*page 244*
* Kilimanjaro Buffalo Lodge	H		🎒🎒🎒	**$200**	*page 244*
* Mt. Kilimanjaro Safari Club	H		🎒🎒	**$193**	*page 245*
Tortilis Camp	TC	⪧⪧⪧	🎒🎒🎒	**$280**	*page 245*
Kimana					
Kilimanjaro Camp	TC		🎒🎒🎒🎒	**$400** (with game drives)	*page 246*
* Kimana Lodge	H		🎒🎒	**$190**	*page 247*
* Kimana Leopard Camp, Ltd.	TC		🎒	**$80**	*page 247*
Chyulu Hills					
Ol Donyo Wuas	R/S	⪧⪧⪧	🎒🎒🎒🎒	**$440** (with game drives, walks)	*page 248*
Tsavo National Park					
Tsavo National Park West					
Finch Hattons Safari Camp	TC	⪧⪧⪧	🎒🎒🎒🎒	**$350**	*page 253*
Ziwani Tented Camp	TC		🎒🎒	**$143**	*page 255*
Kilanguni Lodge	H	⪧	🎒🎒	**$144**	*page 256*
Ngulia Safari Lodge	H		🎒🎒🎒	**$200**	*page 257*
* Hunters Lodge	H		🎒	**$20**	
Tsavo National Park East					
Tsavo Safari Camp	TC	♭	🎒🎒	**$190**	*page 259*
Voi Safari Lodge	H		🎒🎒🎒	**$200**	*page 260*
Baobab House	HS		🎒🎒🎒	**$260**	*page 261*
Nyika Safari Camp	TC		🎒🎒	**$160**	*page 261*

Accommodation	Type	Hats	$ Bags	Price	Page
* Tsavo Inn	H		🛍	$80	page 261
Galdessa Safari Camp	TC	👓👓	🛍🛍🛍🛍		page 261
Tiva River Camp	TC				page 262
Epiya Chapeyu	TC		🛍🛍		page 262
Taita Hills Wildlife Sanctuary					
Taita Hills Lodge	H	👓🦿	🛍🛍🛍	$268	page 263
Salt Lick Safari Lodge	H	👓	🛍🛍🛍	$268	page 265
Hilton Safari Camp	TC	👓	🛍🛍🛍	$268	page 267
Lake Jipe					
* Lake Jipe Safari Lodge	H		🛍🛍	$126	page 268
The Kenyan Coast					page 269
Mombasa					
The Castle Hotel	H		🛍	$75	page 275
New Outrigger Hotel	H		🛍	$65	page 275
Manson Hotel	H		🛍	$80	page 275
* Oceanic Hotel	H		🛍🛍	$120	page 276
* Polana Hotel	H		🛍	$80	page 276
South of Mombasa					
Shelly Beach					
* Shelly Beach Hotel	H		🛍	$29	page 277
Tiwa Beach					
* Minilets	H		🛍		page 277
* Tiwa Villas	H				page 278
* Tiwa Seacastles	H				page 278
* Travellers Beach Hotel Tiwi	H				page 278
Diani Beach					
Indian Ocean Beach Club	H	👓👓🦿	🛍🛍🛍	$231	page 279
Ocean Village Club	H	👓👓🦿	🛍🛍🛍		page 281
Alliance Hotels:					
Jadini Beach Hotel	H	👓	🛍🛍	$168	page 283
Safari Beach	H		🛍🛍	$192	page 283
Africana Sea Lodge	H		🛍🛍	$152	page 284
Lagoon Reef Hotel	H	👓	🛍🛍	$166	page 284

Accommodation	Type	Hats	$ Bags	Price	Page
Kaskazi Beach Hotel	H	🥾	💰💰	$150	page 286
Leopard Beach Hotel	H	🥾	💰💰	$146	page 287
Two Fishes Hotel	H		💰💰	$152	page 288
Diani Reef Grand Hotel	H		💰💰💰	$220	page 288
Diani Sea Lodge	H		💰	$55	page 289
Diani Sea Resort	H		💰	$55	page 289
Leisure Lodge	H		💰💰	$175	page 290
* Golden Beach	H		💰💰	$160	page 291
* Robinson Baobab Club	H		💰💰	$130	page 291
* Southern Palms Beach Resort	H		💰💰	$108	page 291
* Trade Winds Hotel	H		💰	$91	page 291
Diani House	HS	🍽️🥾	💰💰	$130	page 292
Nomad	GS/ToB		💰	$60	page 294
Galu Beach					
Neptune Hotels on Galu Beach:					
Neptune Cottages	H		💰💰	$145	page 295
Neptune Paradise	H		💰💰	$158	page 295
Pinewood Village	HS	🥾	💰💰	$110	page 296
Chale Paradise Island	GS/ToB	🥾	💰💰💰	$200	page 297
Msambweni Beach					
* Club Green Oasis	H		💰💰		page 297
Seascapes Beach Villas	HS		💰	$87	page 297
Funzi - Shimoni - Wasini					
Pemba Channel Inn	H	🍽️🍽️🥾	💰💰	$150	page 299
Shimoni Reef Lodge	H		💰💰	$166	page 301
Sea Adventures, Ltd. (includes fishing)	HS				page 301
Funzi Island Club	GS/ToB	🍽️🥾	💰💰	$190	page 301
Shimba Hills National Reserve (Night Game Viewing)					
Shimba Hills	H-NGVL	🍽️	💰💰	$150	page 303
Sable Valley	HS		💰💰💰💰		page 305
Shimba House	HS		💰💰💰💰💰		page 305

Accommodation	Type	Hats	$ Bags	Price	Page
North of Mombasa to Kilifi					
Nyali Beach & English Point					
Nyali Beach Hotel	H	☂	💰💰💰	$274	page 306
Silver Beach Hotel	H		💰		page 308
Silver Star Hotel	H		💰		page 308
* **Mombasa Beach Hotel**	H		💰💰	$160	page 309
* **Reef Hotel**	H		💰💰	$175	page 309
The Tamarind Village	HS	☂☂	💰💰💰💰	$1000	page 309
Bamburi Beach					
Whitesands	H	☂	💰💰	$145	page 311
Severin Sea Lodge	H		💰💰	$146	page 313
* **Bamburi Beach Hotel**	H		💰	$52	page 313
* **Kenya Beach Hotel**	H		💰	$50	page 313
* **Ocean View Beach Hotel**	H		💰💰	$120	page 313
* **Neptune Beach Hotel**	H		💰💰	$134	page 313
* **Plaza Hotel**	H		💰	$76	page 314
* **Travellers Beach Hotel**	H		💰	$82	page 314
Shanzu Beach					
Mombasa Serena Beach Hotel	H	☂☂☂	💰💰💰	$279	page 314
Hotel Intercontinental Mombasa	H	৬	💰💰	$141	page 317
Oyster Bay Beach Hotel	H		💰💰	$110	page 317
The African Safari Club	H				page 318
Kikambala Beach					
* **Le Soleil Beach Club**	H		💰💰	$150	page 319
* **Club Sun and Sand**	H		💰💰	$116	page 320
* **Thousand Palms**	H		💰	$57	page 320
* **Whispering Palms Hotel**	H		💰	$67	page 320
Mnarani Club	H	☂৬	💰💰		page 320
Kilifi					
Baobab Lodge	H		💰	$91	page 322
Kilifi Bay Resort Hotel & Village	H		💰	$90	page 322
Takaungu House (Phillip & Charlie Mason)	HS	☂☂	💰💰💰	$320	page 323

Accommodation	Type	Hats	$ Bags	Price	Page
African Rainbow Sea Safaris	HS				page 323
Kildini (Michael & Jean Skinner)	HS		👜👜	$110	page 324
Watamu					
Hemingways	H	🕊🕊🕊	👜👜👜	$266	page 325
Turtle Bay Beach Club	H		👜👜	$160	page 329
Ocean Sports	H		👜👜	$120	page 330
Blue Bay Village	H		👜👜	$156	page 331
* Barracuda Inn	H		👜👜	$100	page 332
* Temple Point Village	H		👜👜	$101	page 332
* Mrs. Simpson's	HS		👜	$90	page 332
Malindi and Vicinity					
Indian Ocean Lodge	H	🕊🕊♿	👜👜👜👜	$400	page 333
Malindi Beach Club	H	🕊	👜👜	$146	page 334
Kilili Baharhini	H	♿	👜👜		page 335
Kingfisher Lodge	H	♿	👜👜	$160	page 335
White Elephant Sea Lodge	H	♿	👜👜👜	$200	page 336
The Driftwood Beachclub	H		👜	$67	page 336
Silversands Villas	H		👜👜	$130	page 337
Kivulini Beach Hotel	H		👜👜	$126	page 337
Coconut Village	H		👜👜	$135	page 337
Eden Roc Hotel	H		👜👜	$100	page 338
* African Dream Village	H		👜👜	$140	page 338
* Blue Marlin	H		👜	$56	page 338
* Bougan Village	H		👜		page 338
* Dorado Cottages	H		👜		page 339
* Lawfords Hotel	H		👜	$50	page 339
* Palm Tree Club	H		👜		page 339
* Scorpio Villas	H		👜	$85	page 340
* Stephanie Sea House	H		👜	$70	page 340
* The Tropical Village	H		👜👜	$140	page 340
Malindi to Tana River					
Che-Shale	GS/ToB	♿	👜👜👜		page 341

Accommodation	Type	Hats	$ Bags	Price	Page
Tana Delta Camp	GS/ToB	2	5	$460	page 342

Lamu and North

Lamu Island, Lamu Town

Petley's Inn	H		1	$72	page 345
* Lamu Palace Hotel	H		1	$56	page 345
* Stone House	H		1	$43	page 345
* Yumbe House	H		1	$38	page 345

Lamu Island, Shela

Peponi Hotel	H	2	3	$220	page 346
Kijani House	H		2	$130	page 349
Island Hotel	H		1	$72	page 350

Shela Private Houses

Shela House	HS	3	3	$300	page 350
Palm House	HS	3	4	$300	page 350
Garden House	HS		2	$150	page 352
Beach House	HS		5	$600	page 352
Kisimani House	HS	3	3	$200	page 352
Johari House	HS				page 353

Beach Resorts Near Lamu

Kiwayu Safari Village	GS/ToB	3	4	$320	page 354
Blue Safari Club	GS/ToB	3	5	$900	page 357
Kipangani Bay	GS/ToB	2	4		page 360
Munira Safari Camp	GS/ToB		3		page 361

BEGINNINGS

Although we have lived in Nairobi for several years, we first arrived with conflicting images and expectations of Kenya. Like most people we were drawn by the excitement of wildlife, "Out of Africa" romantic adventure, and warm coral beaches. However, like many first-time visitors, we were also concerned about personal security and health and about how welcome we would feel. We have written about what we have found, and we hope our experience will give you a good perspective for planning your trip to Kenya.

For the tourist, the extraordinary beauty of this country, its friendly people, and its sophisticated tourist industry can provide an experience of a lifetime, a unique and wonderful holiday. It is no surprise that many who visit keep returning, and those of us lucky enough to live here for a while are deeply saddened at the thought of leaving.

Why Kenya?

Living here, we have discovered much about this diverse, modern, yet ancient land. Why come to Kenya? Here's a "short" list:

Magnificent wildlife

See the big five (lion, elephant, rhino, buffalo, leopard) along with graceful giraffe, and herds of zebra and gazelle in their spectacular natural setting—conservation issues take on new meaning.

Amazing landscape

From the snows of Mts. Kenya and Kilimanjaro to the great Rift Valley with its string of unusual lakes; from open savannah with no apparent horizon to mountain ranges with strange inselbergs and mesas; from plantations of coffee, tea, and coconut palms to tropical gardens lush-green and brilliant with flowers and colorful birds.

Beautiful lakes

Lake Victoria, almost an inland sea; lakes ranging from emerald green to flamingo pink; lakes with land and water birds galore…an ornithologist's heaven.

Tropical coastline

Miles of white sandy beaches, waving palms, and coral reefs bright with exotic fish. Big game fishing, windsurfing, snorkeling.

Strong ethnic traditions

Masai and Samburu herdsmen with lion spears, red cloaks, and beadwork; Kisii soapstone carvers; Akamba wood carvers; Swahili coastal villagers with their strong Arabic influence; and more.

Hospitality

You have many choices: highland ranches, some dating back to first European settlements; relaxed and spacious coastal resorts; historic hotels such as the Norfolk, the Aberdare Country Club, and the Mt. Kenya Safari Club. You will love the traditional Kenyan welcome—a big smile and a tropical drink.

Weather

Generally sunny and warm, with occasional showers—practically perfect vacation weather, amazing blue skies with an astonishment of clouds, and right on the Equator.

Food

Tropical fruits, highland vegetables, fresh beef and lamb, freshwater Nile perch and highland trout, every kind of seafood (try the Swahili preparations), wines and spirits from local vineyards, Europe, and South Africa.

Handicrafts, some fine, some useful, some amusing

Wood and soapstone carvings, handwoven fabrics, gemstones (especially tsavorite and tanzanite), ethnic and modern jewelry, leatherwork, embossed chests and mirrors, handwoven carpets, baskets, baskets, baskets.

Pre-history

The Leakey family and others study early man in 5-million-year chunks of time—see the Turkana Boy (5 million years young) in the Nairobi Museum.

There is something about Kenya—perhaps it truly is the birthplace of mankind, and we all feel a returning, that the land is not unknown to us.

It's Not Perfect...

Kenya is a fairly new nation on the modern scene. There will be some aspects of being here that you may not "enjoy" or even find "shocking":

- Bone-jarring potholes in highways and city streets.

- Trucks and buses loaded to bursting with cargo and passengers and belching clots of black smoke.

- Nairobi streetboys begging with hungry looks and a ready curse if their expectations are not met.

- Brash young vendors, pushing their wares on the beach, in the markets, and sometimes on the street.

- Gecko lizards, sometimes on walls and ceilings, with a scary swift slither (in reality a true mosquito-eating friend).

- The slow pace of bureaucracy, especially if you are in a hurry.
- Telephones which only connect after the tenth dialing.

Other things that may "disturb"...

- No working elevators, walkways, or escalators at the international airport...luggage carts that creak and lack paint.
- Old women carrying impossible loads of wood on their backs.
- Men straining to pull handcarts laden like pickup trucks.
- Fruit stands that are little more than shacks, but with jewel-toned fruits in beautiful display.
- Market stalls created by spreading a cloth on the ground.
- Homes in the country handmade of sticks, grass, mud, and dung.
- The occasional metal roof shines as a mark of status.
- Farming with hand implements.
- Brilliant bougainvillea blossoms camouflaging webs of barbed wire.
- Public bathrooms you wish you had never entered...keep some tissues handy.
- Strange smells, not all of them pleasant.

Weathering it all is part of enjoying and learning the difference of a foreign place. It is challenging to see beyond what seems grimy and grim to the real beauty of Kenya and to the real charm of the Kenyan people.

So, no problem, HAKUNA MATATA.

Be ready to enjoy all of Kenya, even the "salt." Take heart—the tourist industry is well-developed and major, dedicated to making visitors from other lands COMFORTABLE.

Why This Book?

We were keen to discover as much of this splendid and varied country as possible. Guides, friends and travel agents were quick with recommendations: go to the game parks, go to the coast, go to the mountains, go to this or that accommodation.

However, we were amazed to find no comprehensive guide to help independent travelers like us decide where to spend weekends and holidays on sometimes limited resources. Since we were spending several years in Nairobi, we decided to visit every corner of Kenya where tourists go and to record our impressions of Kenya and Kenya's best hotels, lodges and homestays.

Quest for the Best

We felt well-qualified for the task ahead. All of us have traveled widely in the world, and as a group have a variety of skills, experiences, and perceptions which were invaluable in creating this book.

Each of us has moved from place to place as part of families connected with different institutions and organizations: the U.S. Department of State, Harvard University's Institute for International Development, U.S. Agency for International Development, the Finnish Foreign Service, or American International Schools.

We traveled around Kenya and gathered firsthand information. Our quest was to discover the best that this country had to offer. In reviewing accommodations, we defined "best" as being places which were special in some way—they might have magnificent views, outstanding buildings, or captivating histories; or they might offer wonderful, memorable experiences. They would all have to meet a certain standard of accommodation.

Such lodgings and the people who run them can be as much a part of the travel adventure as experiencing firsthand the wonder of the Rift Valley or the drama of the Great Wildebeest Migrations.

Armed with hotel brochures, tips from friends, and advice from people experienced in the Kenya travel business, we set off. We travelled by 4-wheel drive, by train, by planes of all sizes, by boats of all sorts, by steam tractor, by balloon, by horseback, by camel.... We stayed in big, bustling tourist hotels, tented camps, mountain lodges and small private homes and ranches.

Everywhere we were charmed by the friendliness and courtesy of the people we met. To do justice to all we had learned on our travels, we describe what we feel is important or unique about a place, giving you sufficient information to decide whether or not it appeals to you. We hope you enjoy reading *Fielding's Guide to Kenya*, and we wish you wonderful adventuring.

Travel Tips

Getting Ready

Most travelers to Kenya come from Europe, North America, or Asia. This involves some serious travel, preparing for international formalities, and being ready for some cultural differences.

When to Come

The main tourist seasons are December–January and July–August, responding to international vacation schedules. The Great Migration of wildebeest and zebra usually reaches Kenya's Masai Mara during July–August. October–January is the best time for a beach holiday, as there is less seaweed.

Residents love the rest of the year as well—fewer tourists, brilliant green of new tropical growth, cooler temperatures, and lower rates everywhere. Temperatures are temperate all year. Day temperatures are typically between 20–30 C. or 65–85 F. The rainy seasons are usually in April–May and November.

AVERAGE MONTHLY TEMPERATURES

CITY		Jan.	Feb.	Mar.	Apr.	May	Jun.	Jul.	Aug.	Sep.	Oct.	Nov.	Dec.
ELDORET (Tropical Plateaux), alt. 3085 m/6840 ft.													
Avg High	°C	25	26	26	24	23	22	21	21	23	24	24	24
	°F	77	79	79	75	73	72	70	70	73	75	75	75
Avg Low	°C	9	9	10	11	10	9	9	9	8	10	10	9
	°F	48	48	50	52	50	48	48	48	46	50	50	48
GARISSA (Northern Desert), alt. 128 m/420 ft.													
Avg High	°C	35	36	36	35	35	34	33	32	33	34	34	359
	°F	95	97	97	95	95	93	91	90	91	93	93	5
Avg Low	°C	22	23	24	24	24	24	23	23	24	24	23	23
	°F	72	73	75	75	75	75	73	73	75	75	73	73
KISUMU (Tropical Plateaux), alt. 1157 m/3795 ft.													
Avg High	°C	30	31	30	29	28	28	28	28	29	31	30	30
	°F	86	88	86	84	82	82	82	82	84	88	86	86
Avg Low	°C	17	17	18	18	17	17	16	16	16	17	17	17
	°F	63	63	64	64	63	63	61	61	61	63	63	63
Rainfall	mm	48	81	140	191	155	84	58	76	64	56	86	102
	in.	1.9	3.2	5.5	7.5	6.1	3.3	2.3	3.0	2.5	2.2	3.4	4.0
LODWAR (Northern Desert), alt. 506 m/1660 ft.													
Avg High	°C	36	36	36	35	35	34	33	33	35	35	35	35
	°F	97	97	97	95	95	93	91	91	95	95	95	95
Avg Low	°C	22	23	24	24	24	24	23	23	24	24	23	23
	°F	72	73	75	75	75	75	73	73	75	75	73	73
MAGADI (Tropical Plateaux), alt. 619 m/2030 ft.													
Avg High	°C	37	37	36	34	33	33	32	33	35	36	35	35
	°F	99	99	97	93	91	91	90	91	95	97	95	95
Avg Low	°C	23	24	24	23	23	22	22	22	23	24	23	23
	°F	73	75	75	73	73	72	72	72	73	75	73	73
MOMBASA (Tropical Coast), alt. 17 m/57 ft.													
Avg High	°C	32	32	32	31	29	29	28	28	29	30	31	31
	°F	90	90	90	88	84	84	82	82	84	86	88	88
Avg Low	°C	23	24	24	24	22	22	21	21	21	22	23	23
	°F	73	75	75	75	72	72	70	70	70	72	73	73
Rainfall	mm	25	18	64	196	320	119	89	64	64	86	97	61
	in.	1.0	0.7	2.5	7.7	12.6	4.7	3.5	2.5	2.5	3.4	3.8	2.4

AVERAGE MONTHLY TEMPERATURES

CITY		Jan.	Feb.	Mar.	Apr.	May	Jun.	Jul.	Aug.	Sep.	Oct.	Nov.	Dec.
MOYALE (Northern Desert), alt. 1113 m/3650 ft.													
Avg High	°C	31	31	30	27	25	24	24	25	26	26	27	29
	°F	88	88	86	81	77	75	75	77	79	79	81	84
Avg Low	°C	18	19	19	20	18	16	15	16	17	17	17	18
	°F	64	66	66	68	64	61	59	61	63	63	63	64
NAIROBI (Highlands and Mountains), alt. 1661 m/5450 ft.													
Avg High	°C	26	27	27	26	24	23	23	23	26	26	25	25
	°F	79	81	81	79	75	73	73	73	79	79	77	77
Avg Low	°C	13	13	14	15	15	13	12	12	13	14	14	14
	°F	55	55	57	59	59	55	54	54	55	57	57	57
Rainfall	mm	38	64	125	211	158	46	15	23	31	53	109	86
	in.	1.5	2.5	4.9	8.3	6.2	1.8	0.6	0.9	1.2	2.1	4.3	3.4
NAKURU (Highlands and Mountains), alt. 1850 m/6070 ft.													
Avg High	°C	29	29	28	27	25	25	24	24	26	26	26	27
	°F	84	84	82	81	77	77	75	75	79	79	79	81
Avg Low	°C	9	9	10	11	11	10	10	10	11	11	11	11
	°F	48	48	50	52	52	50	50	50	52	52	52	52
NANYUKI (Highlands and Mountains), alt. 1945 m/6380 ft.													
Avg High	°C	25	26	25	24	23	23	22	22	23	23	22	23
	°F	77	79	77	75	73	73	72	72	73	73	72	73
Avg Low	°C	7	7	8	10	10	9	8	8	8	9	9	8
	°F	45	45	46	50	50	48	46	46	46	48	48	48
NAROK (Tropical Plateaux), alt. 1890 m/6200 ft.													
Avg High	°C	26	27	26	25	23	22	22	23	24	26	26	26
	°F	79	81	79	77	73	72	72	73	75	79	79	79
Avg Low	°C	8	8	9	11	11	8	8	8	7	8	8	8
	°F	46	46	48	52	52	46	46	46	45	46	46	46
VOI (Tropical Plateaux), alt. 560 m/1837 ft.													
Avg High	°C	31	33	33	31	30	29	28	28	29	31	31	31
	°F	88	91	91	88	86	84	82	82	84	88	88	88
Avg Low	°C	20	20	20	20	20	18	17	17	17	18	20	20
	°F	68	68	68	68	68	64	63	63	63	64	68	68

International Travel

Most people travel to Nairobi by air. It is not possible to fly directly to Nairobi from North America. You must connect with a flight leaving from London, Amsterdam, Paris, Geneva, Rome, or Zurich.

Reputable travel agents or the various airlines flying into Nairobi or a connecting European city can sometimes find bargain fares, but beware of time and refund restrictions. Book in advance to be sure of a seat, especially at peak travel times. Be aware that there will be a $20 departure tax levied when you leave Kenya.

Passport and Visas

Passports should be current and valid for at least six months after your stay in Kenya. Visas are required. Before you travel, you should request your visa from any Kenyan embassy, consulate, or high commission, or from any British embassy in countries where there is no Kenyan embassy. Visas take at least 24 hours to process plus mailing time if you live at a distance. You need to send two passport photos with the application and your passport, along with proof of your ability to leave Kenya such as an air ticket.

Although visitors are usually given a six-month visa, the length of stay granted at the airport may be less. It is important to know what is granted so that you can renew your length of stay if necessary. It is also possible to purchase a visa on arrival at the airport. We do not recommend this.

Embassies in Kenya:

U.S. Embassy

Moi and Haile Selassie Avenues, P.O. Box 30137 or Unit 64100, APO AE 09831, Nairobi, ☎ [254] (2) 334141.

Canadian High Commission

Comcraft House, Haile Selassie Avenue, Box 20481, Nairobi, ☎ [254] (2) 214804.

Contact in the United States:

Embassy of the Republic of Kenya

2249 R Street, N.W., Washington, D.C. 20008, ☎ (202) 387-6101, FAX: (202) 462-3829, E-Mail: KLQY53A☆Prodigy.Com

The Consul General/Kenya Consulate

9150 Wilshire Boulevard, Suite 160, Beverly Hills, CA 90212, ☎ (310) 274-6635, FAX: (310) 859-7010.

The Consul General/Kenya Consulate

424 Madison Avenue, New York, NY 10017-1106, ☎ (212) 486-1300, FAX: (212) 688-0911.

Kenya Tourist Development Corporation

P.O. Box 42013, Nairobi, Kenya, ☎ [254] (2) 229751, FAX: [254] (2) 227615.

Kenya Airways

424 Madison Avenue, New York, NY 10017, ☎ (212) 832-8810, FAX: (212) 688-3720.

Kenya Airways

9150 Wilshire Blvd., Suite 160, Beverly Hills, CA 90212, ☎ (310) 278-9851, FAX: (310) 859-7010.

In Australia:

Kenya High Commission Canberra
P.O. Box 1990, Australia, A.C.T. 2601

In the United Kingdom:

Kenya Tourist Office
25 Brook's News, Mayfair, London LWY ILG, ☎ *(411) 355-3144.*

In Canada:

Kenya High Commission
Gillin Building, Suite 600, 141 Laurier Avenue, West Ottawa, Ontario K1N 6R4, ☎ *(613) 563 1773, FAX: (613) 233 6599.*

Commercial Or Trade Matters

The Commercial Attache/Kenya Embassy
2249 R Street, N.W., Washington D.C. 20008, FAX: (202) 667-8507, E-Mail: KLQY53A@Prodigy.Com

Chief Executive/Export Promotion Council,
P.O. Box 40247, Nairobi, Kenya, ☎ *[254] (2) 228534/5, FAX: [254] (2) 218013*

Investment Enquiries

Executive Chairman/Investment Promotion Centre
P.O. Box 55704, Nairobi, Kenya, ☎ *[254] (2) 229751, FAX: [254] (2) 227615*

The Managing Director/Export Processing Zones
P.O. Box 50563, Nairobi, Kenya, ☎ *[254] (2) 712800, FAX: [254] (2) 713704*

Money

The number of shillings to the U.S. dollar varies often, but follows the Central Bank of Kenya exchange rates which are quoted daily in the local newspapers. U.S. dollars and pounds sterling are easy to exchange as are travelers' checks, which can be replaced if stolen. Kenyan shillings are a soft currency.

Currency converter websites:

http://www.xe.net/currency/
The Universal Currency Converter -Currency converter with information updated daily.

http://www.olsen.ch/cgi-bin/exmenu
Currency Converter - more than 80 foreign exchange rates for any day since Jan. 1, 1990 for more than 80 currencies.

Major Credit Cards

Also accepted by many hotels, travel agencies, car rental companies, airlines, restaurants, and city shops. Cash, especially in lower denominations, is needed in a bargaining situation.

Immunizations

The U.S. Department of State recommends that you carry up-to-date immunization records of the following:

❏ Tetanus boosters

❏ Polio boosters

❏ Typhoid shots

❏ Gamma-globulin shots (against hepatitis A)

❏ Yellow Fever Vaccination*

❏ Cholera Vaccination*

* (Most doctors will provide these even if they feel the shots are unnecessary.)

Free Sources for Health Information

Center for Disease Control
http://www.cdc.gov/travel/travel.html

Travel Health Advisories
http://www.leland.standford.edu/~naked/stms.html

Interpreting Travel Advisories

The U.S. Department of State has issued warnings to travelers based on danger from tourist-related crime. You may also read sensational news stories of unfortunate crimes against tourists. Bear in mind, however, that thousands of tourists visit Kenya with no such unfortunate incidents. Before canceling or postponing a trip to Kenya, check with your travel agents, the airlines, or the Department of State, ☎ *(202) 647-5225*, to get more information about the basis of the warning. You should not disregard such warnings, but sometimes the actual danger is not as serious as it sounds.

Free Travel Safety Information from English Speaking Governments:

United States Travel Advisories (Overseas Security Advisory Council)
http://travel.state.gov/osac.html

Australian Government Travel Advisories
http://www.dfat.gov.au/consular/advice/advices_mnu.html

Canadian Government Travel Advisories
http://dfait-naeci.gc.ca/english/menu.htm

United Kingdom Travel advisories
http://www.fco.gov.uk/reference/travel_advice/frames_index.html
U.S users should check the date of the Travel Advisory, and make use of other services available besides Travel Warnings, i.e.: downloading incident reports, embassy addresses, tourist office addresses, terrorist profiles, and a number of special reports on specific criminal problems.

Luggage

Traveling by air, you are allowed two bags to check and one carry-on bag. Leaving Europe or Kenya, you may be subject to overweight charges if a checked bag weighs more than 20 kilograms or 44 pounds.

Try to plan your packing to allow for the possibility of repacking a smaller bag with clothes for a particular safari. Sometimes there isn't a lot of room for luggage in a small airplane or a safari vehicle.

Clothing

You will need comfortable clothes that are cool, but that can layer up to keep you warm at night or at higher altitudes. Casual is fine for daywear, but you may want some possibilities for more dressy dinners and evenings. Traditional "camouflage" colors are best when near wildlife. More rugged clothing would be necessary for camping, hiking, or riding.

❏ Bring a sweater or a light jacket for early morning game drives.

❏ Lightweight, comfortable walking shoes are sufficient for most safaris.

❏ Pack a bathing suit. Don't forget a hat or your sunglasses.

We advise to pack lightly. It is possible to get clothing washed and ironed.

Optional Equipment

You may also like to bring:

❏ Camera equipment (extra film; video recorders are great for game)

❏ Field binoculars (lightweight)

❏ Snorkel and mask

❏ All-purpose knife, with corkscrew

❏ Flashlight (extra batteries)

❏ Pocket calculator

❏ Alarm clock

❏ Large and small plastic bags (for storage, against dust)

❏ Notebook and pens for safari journal

❏ Reading material

❏ Guides and maps

❏ Sugar substitute (if desired)

❏ Decaf coffee (if desired)

❏ Humor

❏ Patience

Taking Care Of Yourself

First Aid Kit:

Most drugstore items are available and inexpensive in Kenya. Consider including for your safaris:

❏ Sunblock (bring lots)

❏ Lip balm

❏ Moisturizers/lotions (bring plenty: hot sun, low humidity)

❏ Insect repellant

❏ Acetaminophen, aspirin, or ibuprofen for pain or fever

❏ Antimalaria tablets for prophylactic or attack

❏ Antidiarrheal agents

❏ Antibiotics (for lower bowel problems and for broad spectrum use against infections).

❏ Antihistamines for allergic reaction

❏ Antifungal powder

❏ Antiseptic ointment

❏ Alcohol swabs for cleaning wounds or insect bites

❏ Adhesive bandages, gauze dressings, tape

❏ Thermometer

❏ Lens solution for contact lenses

❏ Small packs of tissue (for allergy "noses" or "rest-stop" emergencies)

❏ Disposable towelettes

Hospitals and Doctors:

Major hotels have some kind of medical officer. Nairobi Hospital is considered well-equipped. The Flying Doctors service the more remote areas. You can buy traveler's insurance for medical evacuation from them or from international companies in advance or after your arrival. There are American and European trained doctors and dentists in Nairobi.

Malaria:

A mosquito bite can kill. Take appropriate precautions. Follow updated medical advice on which prophylactic to take, and remember to complete the dose when you get back home. If you do get sick, especially with flulike symptoms of fever, headache, or stomach problems, be sure to tell your doctor you were in a malaria area.

These malarial mosquitoes tend to bite in the evening and at night. You can help protect yourself in the evenings by using mosquito repellant and by covering arms and legs. Most hotels and lodges in malaria areas do their bit to help protect you. They often provide mosquito nets, spray the rooms, and leave a sachet of mosquito repellant by your bed.

Malaria is more prevalent in low-lying areas. The coast, the game parks, and Lake Victoria are the most affected areas.

AIDS:

Come for the animals, come for the sun, come for the panoramas. Kenya has one of the world's highest incidence of AIDS.

Water:

As a rule of thumb, don't drink the tap water. Most hotels/lodges provide a thermos or flask of drinking water in the rooms or tents. You can also buy bottled mineral water—local or imported. Carbonated club soda is an inexpensive alternative.

Food:

Most travelers are impressed by the quantity and diversity of food offered in Kenya. Even when you are deep in the bush and miles from any agricultural or commercial center, you are almost always assured of finding a buffet groaning with appetizing-looking food including many salads. These elaborate "Safari Buffets" usually look better than they taste and become repetitive after several times through the line. It is relatively safe to try most of the food offered by hotels and lodges which cater to international tourists.

Rays:

Beware of the tropical sun. Wear sunblock. Bring a hat, or better, two. You burn faster at high altitudes and near the Equator. Many parts of Kenya meet both of these criteria.

Highs and Lows:

In Kenya, altitudes range from sea level to over 5000 meters. Be alert to the fact that quick altitude changes can be dangerous to your health. Mountain climbers—beware!

Rain or Shine:

Kenya is not all hot, or all dry.

Early morning game drives in an open vehicle can be very cold—come prepared. There is snow on the summits of Mt. Kenya and Mt. Kilimanjaro. Staying in the vicinity of the mountains or on the highlands can be very cold, especially at night.

Kenya's seasons are classified by "rainy" and "dry." The "long rains" usually come in April and May, and the "short rains" in November. The rains are not always neatly confined to the months "allocated."

Exercise:

The word safari means "journey" in Swahili. A "Safari in Kenya" sounds like such an outdoor, healthy activity. It connotes exercise (perhaps strenuous) and possibly hiking boots. A false impression. For most tourists, game-watching safaris in the major game parks mean game drives in vehicles, vast amounts of food in the form of generous buffets, perhaps a siesta, and sitting around the campfire. Hardly great for those abdominal muscles.

Many game lodges are now realizing the popularity of game walks. There is a move to offer more personal interactive experiences with the African bush. Because of park regulations, this is easier for places outside of game park boundaries. Ranches and homestays often specialize in this kind of interaction.

Ironically, it is easier to get more exercise at the coast. There is always swimming, perhaps disco dancing at night, and long walks along the beach. However, sun and humidity, the languid pace, big meals, and good beer also mean that exercise might not feature in your coastal holiday. You can always return to your aerobic classes when you get home.

Security:

Kenya has had more than its share of bad press, particularly in the north and in Nairobi. While theft and violence are real concerns, the tourism industry and the government of Kenya are taking every possible step to ensure your safety.

Travelers should exercise good sense and take some reasonable precautions:

- Don't parade valuable jewelry.
- Don't stroll the streets at night.
- Catch cabs rather than walk in strange areas.
- Don't carry lots of money and important papers.
- Don't take valuables to the beach.
- Don't walk around Nairobi at night.

Culture Shock/Stress:

Although Kenya is one of the wealthier countries in Africa, there is still a great deal of poverty. Visible poverty. Poor mothers with babies beg in the streets, makeshift shacks mushroom next to modern buildings, trash heaps never completely disappear.

Life goes on in public—hairdressers ply their craft under a tree, sewing machines sing on sidewalks, furniture makers display their wares in the sun.

Kenya jars and excites with color and chaos, vibrant life and the unexpected. It can be an exhilarating, eye-opening cultural experience.

If you come from a fast and efficient lifestyle, you may feel frustrated by the slow pace and the inefficiencies. Humor works better than anger. Surely, slowing down and appreciating a different culture is part of what makes a holiday.

Remember one of the most common Swahili expressions: "Hakuna Matata"—no problem.

Vendor Vigilance:

You may be pestered by local souvenir vendors. Bargaining is the order of the day. Bartering is an option—T-shirts and pens are popular. Remember! Use humor and don't be dismayed at persistence.

Photo Ops:

Photograph landscapes, photograph animals, but ask permission before taking photos of people, and be prepared to pay for the privilege in some instances.

Creepy Crawlies:

You will see less of these than you expect but they do exist. You should not walk around at night, or in the bush, without shoes. Hopefully you will be lucky enough to see some brightly colored lizards or perhaps the odd chameleon. (P.S. Most of us who have lived here for years have yet to see a snake.) Don't forget your insect repellant.

Our Furry Friends:

The animals are wild. They are not paid to entertain the guests. Respect them, and keep your distance. The fact that hippos are grazing next to your tent at night does not mean you can pat them. Hippos are very dangerous. So are lions, elephant, buffalo, rhino, crocodiles, monkeys, teddy-bear-like hyrax.... It is just not prudent to pet.

The Big Five are lion, elephant, rhino, leopard and your choice of buffalo or hippo. Remember, each animal is more than an addition to a list. It is fun to see how individuals react with each other, in groups, and with the environment.

Favorites of the Tiny Five: a scarlet nit, an iridescent emerald fly, and the walking stick.

Planning Your Stay in Kenya

Most tourists coming to Kenya for the first time are surprised by the variety of experiences the country has to offer. Not only is there a great range of topography, scenery and wildlife, but there is also an amazing choice of ways in which you can enjoy these attractions. It is worthwhile to decide exactly what you want to do and see, and in what style you want to do it.

Your memories of Kenya could include:

- Eating breakfast under a thorn tree with Mt. Kenya in the distance and a herd of giraffe nearby.

- Lying in a hammock at the beach after a feast of fresh crab.

- Looking up at the moon through a mesh tent after an exhilarating day on your camel safari.

Your memories of Kenya could also include:

- Long, bumpy and dusty rides in a minivan crowded with other tourists.

- Queuing for the third consecutive day for the same buffet lunch.

- Blocking the sound of the disco as you try to go to sleep at your beach hotel.

The Choices Are Yours

Don't feel that the only way you can see Kenya is with a package tour. Kenya's tourist industry is quite sophisticated. There are many experienced travel agents and private tour operators who can tailor a holiday to meet your needs and preferences.

You have many options:

- Vehicle rentals—often come with the service of a driver who is familiar with the country and the roads.

- Flying in small planes—although pricey, can save a lot of time, give you marvelous views of the country, and can often land very close to your destination. Many private homestays have a landing strip and even planes of their own.

- Special interest tours—focus on fishing, photography, bird watching, anthropology, mountain climbing, horseback riding, hiking, and camping. There are even camel safaris.

This Fielding guide can help you plan a holiday tailor-made for you.

Tour Options

These range from roughing it to exclusive up-market tours. You could travel from lodge to lodge in a minivan or be flown in small planes from one private homestay to another. You could enjoy the pampering and service of a deluxe tented safari, or save money with a more basic "participation" camping trip where you do some of the camp work. You could make up your own private group and travel with a professional safari guide, or you could join a bus load of other tourists and have the local driver doubling as your guide. Besides offering standard tours, most tour operators will also custom-tailor tours for clients. Although the descriptions below focus primarily on camping or bush safaris, most operators and agents can also organize beach holidays.

Private Upmarket Safari Guides and Outfitters

Almost all of the tour guides on these safaris have a great deal of experience in Africa and with wildlife. Generally, their safaris are based on personal leadership and charisma. Most have rugged safari vehicles with professional drivers. Some are pilots and own their own planes to fly you from place to place. Many have exclusive rights to pitch their luxury camps in out-of-the-way scenic spots. Some also cater to special interests such as horseback riding, fishing, ornithology or walking.

In previous years some of the guides were "great white hunters" who could thrill you with tales of adventure. Some are more at home in the bush than entertaining people and others are smooth, chatty hosts—nearly all are characters you will enjoy and remember. On many of these safaris you will spend some of the time in tented accommodations and some of it in lodges, hotels, or homestays.

Daily rates are usually per person and vary by the size of the group. They generally include all meals, park fees, game drives, and in some instances drinks. Rates range from $400 to $1000 per day.

PHONING KENYA

International telephone code for Kenya: ☎ *254.*
When calling from outside of Kenya dial 011 + 254 + *city code* + *number.*
When calling in Kenya dial 0 + *city code* + *the number.*
Time difference is plus 13 hours CST.

Allen Safaris

Box 14712, Nairobi, Kenya,
☎ *& FAX: 521538*
London: ☎ *071-9372937.*

Or U.S. contacts:

Anton Allen, *Austin, Texas*
☎ *(512) 858-7045, FAX: (512) 264-2862.*
Joanna Allen, *New York, New York*
☎ *(212) 772-7720, FAX: (212) 772-6223.*

60+ years experience. Exclusive and customized photographic and sight-seeing safaris. Hosted by David Allen or associate. Travel by light aircraft.

Ron Beaton

c/o Bush Homes of East Africa,
Box 56923, Nairobi, Kenya,
☎ *(2) 571647, FAX: (2) 571665.*
Ron hosts guests at his Rekero Farm adjacent to the Masai Mara. Best known for his walking safaris.

Carr-Hartley Safaris

Box 59762, Nairobi, Kenya,
☎ *(2) 882453, FAX: (2) 884542.*

Or U.S. contact:

Mr. John Take or Ms. Sandy Sullivan

Convention Planning Services Inc.
5422 Carrier Drive, Suite 203, Orlando, Florida 32819
☎ *(407) 351-5333, FAX: (407) 351-1784.*

Cheli & Peacock Ltd.

Box 39806, Nairobi, Kenya,
☎ *(154) 22551, FAX: (154) 22553.*
Luxury customized tented safaris

Chrissie Aldrich

Box 82, Nanyuki, Kenya,
☎ *(176) 22053, FAX: (176) 23302.*

Long time guide. Custom and special safaris.

Cottar's Safari Service

Box 44191, Nairobi, Kenya,
☎ *(2) 884508, FAX: (2) 882234.*
E-mail: Cottars@form-net.com
Upmarket 1920's lifestyle safari with white tents, canvas baths, silver and candlelight—romance and elegance in the bush. Bird shooting. Hunting safaris in Tanzania.

U.S. contact:

Jimmy Stockton

Stockton Safaris Inc., Box 1069, Pont Vedra Beach, Florida 32004
☎ *(904) 285-4884, FAX: (904) 285-4893.*

Clive Lee Private Safaris Ltd.

Box 55905, Nairobi, Kenya,
☎ *(2) 882271, FAX: (2) 714628,*

UK contact:

"Fairfield", *St. Mary's Road, Portishead, Avon, England BS20 9QP*
☎ */FAX: (275) 847017.*
Custom and special interest safaris.

Iain MacDonald Safaris

Box 24957, Nairobi, Kenya,
☎ *(2) 882030, FAX: (2) 533529.*
Experienced small company offering flexible safaris: luxury tented, lodge safaris, sporting safaris.

Ker & Downey

Box 41822, Nairobi, Kenya,
☎ *(2) 556466, FAX: (2) 552378.*
Oldest established safari specialists in Africa with a sterling reputation and unsurpassed in their knowledge of the bush and wildlife. Ker and Downey run luxury camping safaris

and a wide range of special interest safaris. Experienced host/guides are shareholders in the company and attract their own clientele. The following guides come highly recommended: Alan Binks, Derek Dames, Peter Davey, Allan Earnshaw, John Fletcher, Nigel Dundas, Dave Richards, James Robertson, Tony Seth-Smith, John Sutton, Bill Winter, Dave Williams, Don Young.

Mark C. Ross

Box 60157, Nairobi, Kenya,
☎ *(2) 338041, FAX: (2) 338072.*
Or U.S. agent:

Table Mountain Travel

14062 Denver West Pkwy, Ste 100, Golden, Colorado 80401, ☎ *(800) 999-1580, FAX: (303) 277-1589.*
American, offers flying safaris. Knowledgeable ornithologist.

Richard Bonham Safaris Ltd.

Box 24133, Nairobi, Kenya,
☎ *(2) 882521, FAX: (2) 882728.*
Or U.S. contact:

Frontiers International Travel

Box 959, Wexford, Pennsylvania 15090, ☎ *(800) 245-1950, FAX: (412) 935-1570.*
Richard has an exclusive lodge in the Chuluyu Hills, Ol Donyo Wuas; leads walking safaris in Tanzania, and is a pilot.

Royal African Safaris

Box 24397, Nairobi, Kenya,
☎ *(2) 567251, FAX: (2) 564945.*
E-mail: Royal.Africasaf@commsol.sprint.com

Or Canadian contact:

84 Pricefield Road, Toronto, Ontario, Canada M4W 1Z9,
☎ *(416) 929-7053, (416) 929-7054.*
E-mail:
103354,2761@CompuServe.com
Extremely experienced upmarket safari company. The owner/guides Jonny Baxendale, Peter Silvester, David Penrose and Robert Carr-Hartley, have firm roots in Kenya and a great love and knowledge of the land, its wildlife and people. They pride themselves on providing a customized and personal "real" safari of the highest standards. Aim to give a relaxing and enjoyable holiday, an "up close" view of Kenya's wildlife, and insight into traditional cultures. Ratio of guides to guests never more than one to three. Never put groups together, believing a safari should be an intimate experience.

Tor Allan Safaris

Box 15114, Nairobi, Kenya,
☎ *(2) 891190, FAX: (2) 890142.*
Tor customizes upmarket tented safaris. Snippets from the *The New York Times*: "Sterling reputation...spares no extravagance...staff cater to every whim...unsurpassed in the knowledge of the bush and wildlife."

Tropical Ice Ltd.

Box 57341, Nairobi, Kenya,
☎ *(2) 740811 FAX: (2) 740826.*
Adventure safari company specializing in mountaineering expeditions. Iain Allan is the experienced guide.

Other Travel Professionals

There are many companies and individuals in Nairobi who offer a wide range of travel services. These can include booking and operating standard itineraries, general accommodation bookings and transport services, and customized adventure safaris. Most Kenyan travel professionals can direct you to experts in special interest safaris.

Abercrombie & Kent International (A&K)

Box 59749 Nairobi, Kenya,
☎ *(2) 334955, FAX: (2) 335442.*

Or U.S. Headquarters:

1420 Kensington Rd., Oakbrook, Illinois 60521, ☎ *(312) 954-2944 or (800) 323-7308.*
A&K offer lodge tours and more exclusive tented safaris. Well-known—been in the business since 1962.

A & K Travel Ltd.

Box 5974, Nairobi, Kenya,
☎ *(2) 449461, FAX: (2) 449463.*
Full service travel agency part of Abercrombie & Kent.

Across Africa Safaris

Box 49420, Nairobi, Kenya,
☎ *(2) 332744, FAX: (2) 332419.*
Variety of tours: road, air, special interest. Mainly mini-bus package safaris.

Archer's Tours & Travels Ltd.

Box 40097, Nairobi, Kenya,
☎ *(2) 223131, FAX: (2) 212656.*
Tailor-made holidays in established upmarket lodges and homestays.

Bateleur Safaris Ltd.

Box 42562, Nairobi, Kenya,
☎ */FAX: (2) 891007.*
Or U.S. contact:

Sporting International Inc.

13201 Northwest Freeway, Suite 880-C, Houston, Texas 77040, ☎ *(800) 231-6352.*
Special interest safaris: walking, ornithology.

Big Five Tours and Safaris Ltd.

Box 10367, Nairobi, Kenya,
☎ *(2) 229803, FAX: (2) 337965.*
From package group tours to private safaris. Bookings and car hire.

Black Wing Safaris

Box 42532, Nairobi, Kenya,
☎ *(2) 891241.*

Advertised as "personalized all inclusive safaris at an affordable price."

Bookings Limited

Box 56707, Nairobi, Kenya,
☎ *(2) 225255, FAX: (2) 216553.*
Well-established tour operator offering variety of excursions and safaris. Car rentals.

Bruce Safaris Ltd.

Box 40662, Nairobi, Kenya,
☎ *(2) 227311, FAX: (2) 223647.*
In the business 40 years. Can customize adventure safaris and book standard itineraries.

Bunson Travel Service

Box 45456, Nairobi, Kenya,
☎ *(2) 221992, FAX: (2) 214120.*
Offers wide range of safari services.

Bushbuck Adventures

Box 67449, Nairobi, Kenya,
☎ *(2) 212975, FAX: (2) 218735.*
Specialize in safaris for the more adventurous—from basic to more luxurious. Special interest safaris. Actively involved in conservation.

Bush Homes of East Africa

Box 56923, Nairobi, Kenya,
☎ *(2) 571647, FAX: (2) 571665.*
Booking and marketing office for upmarket homestays. Can coordinate safaris to homestays and small camps.

East African Ornithological Safaris Ltd.

Box 49019, Nairobi, Kenya,
☎ *(2) 331191, FAX: (2) 330698.*
Established special interest safari operators. Owned and run by Steve and Don Turner. Use only experienced guides. Visit areas of prime ecological interest in East Africa.

Flamingo Tours Ltd.

Box 45070, Nairobi, Kenya,
☎ *(2) 600900, FAX: (2) 502566.*

U.S. address:

Flamingo Tours of East Africa Inc.

520 North Michigan Avenue, Suite 1016, Chicago, Illinois 60611.
Wide range of tours, most by minibus.

Gametrackers

Box 62042, Nairobi, Kenya,
☎ *(2) 338927, FAX: (2) 330903.*
Less expensive and special interest safaris: camel, canoe, foot, mountain bike, mountaineering.

Going Places Ltd.

Box 14776, Nairobi, Kenya,
☎ *(2) 442312, FAX: (2) 446402.*
Full service travel agency including tailor-made safaris. Managing director, Mrs. Glen Rogers is particularly knowledgeable and was invaluable in helping to gather information for this edition.

Just the Ticket

Box 14845, Nairobi, Kenya,
☎ *(2) 741755, FAX: (2) 740087.*
Full-service travel agency.

Kenya Wildlife Trails Ltd.

Box 44687, Nairobi, Kenya,
☎ *(2) 228960, FAX: (2) 214532.*
Tours and car hire.

Jade Sea Journeys Ltd.

Box 39439, Nairobi, Kenya,
☎ *(2) 218336, FAX: (2) 224212.*
Journeys by boat on Lake Turkana and the Omo River.

Let's Go Travel

Box 60342, Nairobi, Kenya, ☎ *(2) 340331/213033, FAX: (2) 336890.*
Several branches in Nairobi, publish updated rate sheets for most hotels and lodges, rent vehicles.

Maggie Von Lekow Travel & Safaris

Box 47219, Nairobi, Kenya,
☎ *(2) 720704, FAX: (2) 720710.*

Muthaiga Travel Ltd.

Box 34464, Nairobi, Kenya,
☎ *(2) 740034, FAX: (2) 750035.*
Full-service travel agency.

Mythos Ltd.

P.O. Box 57683, Nairobi, Kenya,
☎ *(2) 333569, FAX: (2) 216391.*
Booking and marketing office for a few select properties.

Prestige Safaris Ltd.

Box 43987, Nairobi, Kenya,
☎ *(2) 227977, FAX: (2) 333669.*
Wide range of services and tours—standard and customized.

Pollman's Tours and Safari Tours

Box 45895, Nairobi, Kenya,
☎ *(2) 337952, FAX: (2) 337171.*
Range of minibus tours

Rafiki Africa Ltd.

Box 76400, Nairobi, Kenya,
☎ *(2) 561562, FAX: (2) 561562.*
Offers range of safaris in East Africa. Safaris differ in terms of comfort, adventure and price levels.

Rhino Safaris Ltd.

Box 48023, Nairobi, Kenya,
☎ *(2) 332372, FAX: (2) 338427.*
Well-established tour operation offering range of lodge safaris and tours as well as budget camping safaris.

Rickshaw Travels Kenya Ltd.

Box 46536, Nairobi, Kenya,
☎ *(2) 338633, FAX: (2) 210697.*
Full service travel agency.

Safari Camp Services Ltd.

Box 44801, Nairobi, Kenya,
☎ *(2) 228936, FAX: (2) 212160.*
Range of safaris from budget to exclusive.

Safaris Unlimited (Africa) Ltd.

Box 24181, Nairobi, Kenya,
☎ *(2) 891168, FAX: (2) 891113.*
Camping and special interest safaris, especially horseback. In the business for 21 years.

Smart Tours & Travel Ltd.

Box 42830, Nairobi, Kenya,
☎ *(2) 225850, FAX: (2) 216293.*
Classic or special interest safaris.

Somak Travel

Box 48495, Nairobi, Kenya,
☎ *(2) 337333, FAX: (2) 218954.*

United Touring Co. (U.T.C.)

Box 42196, Nairobi, Kenya,
☎ *(2) 331960, FAX: (2) 331422.*

Or U.S. address:

United Touring International

400 Market Street, Suite 260,
Philadelphia, Pennsylvania 19106,
☎ *(800) 223-6486.*
Large operation offering wide range
of safari and package options.

Universal Safari Tours (U.S.T.)

Box 49312, Nairobi, Kenya,
☎ *(2) 221446, FAX: (2) 218686.*
Large tour operator.

Wilderness Trails (K) Ltd./
Bush Homes of East Africa Ltd.

Box 56923, Nairobi, Kenya,
☎ *(2) 506139, FAX: (2) 502739.*
Booking agent for many homestays
and ranches.

U.S. Companies Dealing with Africa

Abercrombie & Kent International (A&K)

(see above)

Bush Homes of East Africa

887 West Marietta Street, N.W., Studio
5-101, Atlanta, Georgia 30345,
☎ *(404) 888-0909, FAX: (404) 888-*
0081.
Exclusive safaris, specializing in
homestay accommodations.

CATS (Custom African Travel Services, Inc.)

30 Shepard Street, Cambridge, Massa-
chusetts 02138, ☎ *(617) 491-1678,*
FAX: (617) 491-1042.
Upmarket, customized safaris, often
with an adventurous or exotic touch.

Safariworld!

425 Madison Ave., New York, New
York 10017, ☎ *(212) 486-0505, (800)*
366-0505, FAX: (212) 486-0783.
Upmarket safaris.

TRAVCO - Travel Corporation of America

P.O. Box 2630, Newport Beach, Cali-
fornia 92658, ☎ *(714) 476-2800 or*
(800) 992-2004, FAX: (714) 476-
2538.
Upmarket safaris, well-established,
cover much of Africa.

Choosing a Safari

- If you have a guide, check on his/her experience and background. Does the guide have any special expertise? Is the guide familiar with the local people and the region you will visit?

- Any of the larger 4-wheel drive vehicles is better than a mini-bus.

- The driver should be experienced.

- Find out what safety measures are planned for your safari.

- A small group costs less than going by yourself. If the group is too large it is cumbersome. Six to eight people in two vehicles is ideal.

Travel Options Within Kenya

Car Rental

Various car rental companies operate in Nairobi, Mombasa and Malindi. A valid driver's license (from country of residence, or an International license) is required. Driver must be between the ages of 25 and 70 and have held a license for a minimum of two years.

Major credit cards are accepted. Car rentals and the price of petrol are high by U.S. standards. Saloon/sedan cars as well as 4-Wheel drive safari vehicles can be rented (ranging from $100 to $460 for a one day all-inclusive rate—daily cost can drop to about half of this if you keep the car for a week). Many routes and circuits require 4-wheel drive, especially in the rains. Driving is on the left side of the road. Parks and reserves are open to private and rented vehicles.

Many travelers prefer to rent a car with a driver. Driving in Kenya is hard work. Having an experienced Kenyan driver who knows the country, the roads, and often a lot about the wildlife, can add to your relaxation if not your privacy. The added expense of a driver is usually very reasonable.

Here is a partial list of car hire agencies. More are listed in the Nairobi Yellow Pages.

Apollo
Box 42391, Nairobi, Kenya,
☎ *(2) 333606/337534,*
FAX: (2) 214026.

Budget
(Abercrombie & Kent), Box 59749,
Nairobi, Kenya, ☎ *(2) 334904,*
FAX: (2) 332033.

Concorde Car Hire
Box 25053, Nairobi, Kenya,
☎ *(2) 448653.*

Let's Go Travel
Box 60342, Nairobi, Kenya,
☎ *(2) 340331/213033,*
FAX: (2) 214713.

The Car Hire Company
Box 56707, Nairobi, Kenya,
☎ *(2) 225255, FAX: (2) 216553.*

Avis
Box 49795, Nairobi, Kenya,
☎ *(2) 336794/334317,*
FAX: (2) 215421.

Central Rent a Car
Box 49439, Nairobi, Kenya,
☎ *(2) 222888, FAX: (2) 339666.*

Hertz - UTC
Box 42196, Nairobi, Kenya,
☎ *(2) 331960/331973,*
FAX: (2) 216871.

Rasuls
Box 18127, Nairobi, Kenya,
☎ *(2) 558234, FAX: (2) 540341.*

Driving

Driving in Kenya is a challenge. Drivers are frequently impatient and incautious. Many vehicles are old, and emission standards unheard of. Most notorious are the Matatus—brightly painted, invariably overloaded minivan taxis who all seem to think they are "king of the road" and totally invincible.

You frequently have to slow down for jolting and often unmarked speedbumps. You may also encounter police checkpoints where you have to wind between lethal metal spikes. Usually only commercial vehicles are made to stop at these checkpoints. Goats in the road, a herd of cattle on the highway or even a real "zebra" crossing may well liven up your trip. Try to make sure you reach your destination before nightfall—driving at night is even worse than in the day and not advisable.

You also have to contend with bad roads. Many tarred roads are in poor repair with potholes and ragged edges. Dirt roads often require four-wheel drive, especially on rocky slopes and during the rainy seasons. Traveling from one place to another generally takes longer than you would expect from the projected mileage. It can also be a lot more uncomfortable and dusty than you bargained for.

There are two ways to deal with these problems. Either you can embark on road travel with a sense of adventure, admire the scenery, ride the bumps, brush off the red dust, and think "this is certainly more fun than rush hour traffic at home!" or—you can fly. We suggest flying for at least part of your safari if you can afford it. Game drives will give you a taste of bumps and dust.

Flying

Jomo Kenyatta Airport in Nairobi, and Moi International Airport in Mombasa are both international airports, but are also used for some in-country flying. Wilson airport is for local and shorter flights.

Kenya Airways

Reservations: ☎ *(2) 210771, Departures/Confirmation:* ☎ *(2) 229291.*
This is the national airline and flies out of Jomo Kenyatta airport in Nairobi. It services Kisumu, Mombasa and Malindi in Kenya. Its reputation for tardiness has improved somewhat. Remember to confirm your booking a day in advance to avoid being bumped.

Wilson Airport is one of the busiest small plane airports in the world. There are regularly scheduled commercial and charter flights and a lot of private planes. Listed below are some of the airlines which operate out of Wilson Airport.

Air Kenya

☎ *(2) 501421/2/3, FAX: 500845. Coast Flight* ☎ *(2) 607750.*

Operates scheduled flights from Nairobi to the Masai Mara, Nyeri, Nanyuki, Samburu, Amboseli and the coast (Mombasa, Malindi, Lamu and Kiwayu). Private charters are also available.

Prestige Air
☎ *(11) 221443 (Mombasa), FAX: (11) 228157 (Mombasa).*
Flies mainly out of Mobasa to the Masai Mara. Some charter flights out of Nairobi.

Eagle Aviation
☎ *(11) 606015, FAX: (11) 606011, Various connections out of Mombasa.*
Scheduled flights to Masai Mara from Wilson Airport and to Mombasa from Kenyatta Airport.

Aircraft Leasing Services ALS
☎ *(2) 504523, FAX: (2) 607185.*
Scheduled flights to the Masai Mara from Wilson Airport.

Africair/Boskovic Air Charters Ltd.
☎ *(2) 501210/501226, FAX: (2) 505964.*
Offers charter flights on a variety of different small planes.

Excel Aviation Ltd.
☎ *(2) 501751, FAX: (2) 501751.*
Offers charter flights.

Tropic Air
☎ *(176) 32890.*
Offers chartered flights out of Nanyuki. Single engine planes.

Ninety-Nines
☎ *(2) 500277.*
Club offers light aircraft for hire with an instructor from the Aeroclub at Wilson Airport.

Classic Aerial Safaris Ltd.
☎ *(176) 22960, FAX: (176) 22494.*
Scenic flights in a nostalgic open cockpit biplane operates from the Nanuki area.

Charter rates are usually based on the size of the airplane and the distance to the destination. There is an airport Tax of 100ksh for all flights within Kenya.

Kenya Railways

The only train trip frequently used by tourists is the overnight sleeper between Nairobi and Mombasa. Although some consider this one of the world's great railway journeys, the equipment is old and the romance is dusty. Since most of the journey is at night, you see little from your train window, but save on a night's accommodation. Train meals are for the adventuresome. The first sitting is cleanest. NBI office hours ☎ *(2) 221211* outside office hours ☎ *(2) 210851*, Mombasa ☎ *(11) 312221.*

Taxis

Many taxis do not have working meters. Make sure you agree on a price before you start. In town, you might bargain your own deal for a half day or day's tour. Some Nairobi taxi companies:

Archer Cabs
☏ *(2) 220289/221935.*

Avenue Car Hire Ltd.
☏ *(2) 221666/336442.*

Kenatco
☏ *(2) 338311/221561/221523.*

London Taxi
☏ *(2) 225123.*

Mini Cabs & Tours
☏ *(2) 226944/220743.*

Accommodation Options

Kenya has an amazing variety of accommodation types. Hotels range from city high-rises to sprawling thatched beach "villages." You can stay in private homes in the middle of a ranch/game sanctuary or in an "Arabian Nights" Swahili-style house in a fishing village. You can stay in tents in the bush or grass shacks on the beach.

Homestays

A homestay gives you the closest relationship with the country. You stay in private homes and very often the owners are your hosts and guides. The homes range from upcountry colonial game ranches and homey farm houses to elegant villas by sea or lake.

Many of our favorite places to stay in Kenya are the private homestays. When we began our research on this book, we had no idea that there were so many homestay options, or that staying at such places would be so wonderful.

Some of the main features of homestays include:

- Being hosted by people who are willing to share their love and knowledge of Kenya with you. Many host families date back to early European settlement days. There are still some Lords and Ladies among them!

- Personalized and individual treatment—you are one of a "select few" rather than part of a "tourist crowd."

- Staying in some very beautiful homes and ranches—some with fascinating histories and many in stunning and unspoiled settings.

- The opportunity to experience Kenya in a very personal and interactive fashion—you might go on a game walk or a horse ride on a ranch, go fishing or sailing with your host at the coast.

- Enjoying food and service which are often superior to most larger establishments.

- Being free to do what you want in your own time. Don't hesitate to say if you just want to relax and enjoy the view.

Tents

Most established tented camps in Kenya have very fancy tents which bear no resemblance to most people's mental image of a "tent." They are not cramped, dark, uncomfortable, or a way of roughing it. Often more luxurious than most hotel rooms, some tents even have bidets and four-poster beds. You can even stay in a tent with a beautiful wooden floor and a big bathtub. On the other hand some tents offer more adventure with bucket showers and no electricity. They all tend to be completely enclosed with a floor attached to the sides—to keep out unwanted reptiles or insects. Mesh windows let in light and air, but canvas blinds can be zipped shut for privacy.

Try sleeping in a tent in Africa—it has a certain magic.... feels like an adventure. You hear the night sounds, and you know you are somewhere special.

Grass Shacks on the Beach

See "Tents:" but substitute thatch and *makuti* (woven palm leaves) for canvas and put the shack on sand.

In the accommodation section, the descriptions can help you get a good idea if you would enjoy a place or not. The choices are yours.

Safari Options—on the Move

All the places described in the accommodation section have fixed sites. There are other safari options which involve moving from one campsite to another. These are typically up-market private accompanied safaris offered by well-known guides and small companies. There are also more modest alternatives which involve a greater degree of "roughing it."

You can travel on foot, by four-wheel drive vehicle, on camels, on horses, by ox wagon, by air...These safaris can be focused on wildlife, bird watching, bird shooting, fishing, photography, mountain climbing, anthropology...Check with your travel agents for details.

Hot Air Balloons

Early morning hot air balloon trips take off from several places in the Masai Mara (including Little Governor's Camp, Mara Serena Lodge, Mara Safari Club, Fig Tree Camp, and Masai Mara Sopa Lodge). Transportation can be arranged to take you from other lodges and camps to the nearest balloon launching site. These trips are extremely popular and very pricey ($300+ per person, including breakfast).

The Masai Mara has become one of the busiest hot air ballooning centers in the world. While out on early morning game drives in the Mara, you are bound to see one or more brightly colored balloons majestically rising at about the same time as the sun. They look so silent and romantic.

When you splurge on this unique adventure, the excitement starts while it is still dark. Loud, bright flames roar as they heat the air filling the colorful skin of the balloon. Up to 12 passengers climb into the basket grinning in fear-tinged anticipation tinged with a little fear. White knuckles grip the basket edge. You lift up, the burners roar loud and close. You float over forests, savannah, river and game—sometimes soaring way up high, sometimes brushing branches of trees, and sometimes just skimming the tops of termite mounds. Herds of animals scatter below you, a bull elephant with a long shadow crosses a field, there are hippo humps in the curve of the river. It is warmer than you expect—you don't feel the wind when you travel at wind speed. It is also noisier than imagined—the burst and flare from the burners punctuate the commentary of the pilot.

You land for a champagne breakfast in the bush—holding tight to the sides and ducking down as the basket tips and is dragged along the ground. The sides are well-padded and passengers inelegantly crawl out to emerge laughing. A full breakfast is cooked over the balloon burners, animals dot the scene, large hawks fly down for tidbits, and there is a sense of camaraderie among the passengers. Champagne glasses clink—a memorable adventure complete with your own souvenir flight certificate.

Walking, Hiking and Trekking

Another way to experience the adventure of the Kenyan bush is to put one foot in front of the other as directed by knowledgeable guides. Usually designed to make the most of Kenya's spectacular scenery and wildlife, these foot safaris give you the feeling of being part of the life of the bush. Very often, the hiking is combined with game drives either after a lunch in camp or when an early morning hike is designed to rendezvous with camp vehicles at a prearranged place.

Depending on the guide or safari company you choose, you can be totally pampered in camp or you can be responsible for a certain amount of camp life, such as putting up your own tent. Typically, as with other kinds of adventure camping in Kenya, a new camp is set up every day, with the supplies and equipment being transported by camp staff in camp vehicles.

The pace for most walking safaris is considered suitable for hikers of average fitness. However, clients are encouraged to ride the camp vehicles for a rest day or to enjoy staying in camp if the camp is to remain in one place for several days. All hikers are encouraged to have adequate medical insurance before coming to Kenya, and most companies require that a waiver form is signed before the beginning of the safari.

Rates range from $38 to more than $1000 per person, depending on what supplies and services are provided, how many people are included in the safari, and how long the safari lasts.

For Walking Safaris Contact

1. Tropical Ice

Box 57341, Nairobi, Kenya, ☎ (2) 740811, FAX: (2) 740826.

These are upmarket safaris ranging from mountain treks to slow walks along the remote Galana River in Tsavo. They are led by expert and renowned naturalists such as Clive Ward, author of *The Mountains of Southern Africa* and photographer for *Snowcaps on the Equator*, and Iain Allan, author of *Guide Book to Mount Kenya and Kilimanjaro* and *Snowcaps on the Equator*. Prices cover everything including park fees, rangers, fresh food, beer, sodas and wine. Alcoholic drinks and tipping are extra.

2. Ron Beaton - Off the Beaton Path

c/o Wilderness Trails (K) Ltd./Bush Homes of East Africa Ltd. Box 56923, Nairobi, Kenya, ☎ (2) 506139, FAX: (2) 502739 REKERO.

Ron Beaton will tailor his adventure safaris to suit. Very often a five-day walking safari will be incorporated into a private homestay at his Rekero Farm at the edge of the Masai Mara. (See accommodation section.)

3. Richard Bonham Safaris Ltd.

Box 24133, Nairobi, Kenya, ☎ (2) 882521, FAX: (2) 882728.

Richard Bonham will organize unusual safaris to suit. Walking safaris are his specialty.

4. Bushbuck Adventures

Box 67449, Nairobi, Kenya, ☎ (2) 212975, FAX: (2) 218735.
Walking in the hills and plains around their "Out of Africa" camp near the Masai Mara. Masai guides. Possible to spend nights away from camp in fly camps.

5. Naturetrek Adventure Safaris Ltd.

Box 70933, Nairobi, Kenya, ☎ (2) 220491, FAX: (2) 337686.
Various set itineraries to choose from. Some safaris combine a micro-bus photographic holiday with walking.

6. Samburu Trails and Trekking Safaris

Bush Homes of East Africa
Box 56923, Nairobi, Kenya, ☎ (2) 571667, FAX: (2) 571665.
Experience and expedition into untamed, untouched, unspoiled Africa with a mobile camp carried on pack animals. Three to five nights camping in the Karisia Hills north of Maralal.

7. Tribal Treks & Wildlife Walks Kentrak Safaris Ltd.

Box 47964, Nairobi, Kenya, ☎ (2) 441704, FAX: (2) 441690.
These safaris seem a little more basic, with more set itineraries to choose among.

8. Bike Treks: Walking & Cycling in Kenya

Box 14237, Nairobi, Kenya, ☎ (2) 446371, FAX: (2) 442439.
These are organized by Nigel Arensen, a third generation Kenyan, who also specializes in cycling safaris. Prices range up to $720 per person for a six-day walk.

9. Hiking & Cycling Kenya Ltd.

Box 39439 Nairobi, Kenya, ☎ (2) 218336/8, FAX: (2) 224212 or
Sobek's International Explorers Society
Box 1089 Angel's Camp California 95222 USA, ☎ 800-777-7939.
These trips seem very basic, often using public transportation to and from safari points.

10. Savage Wilderness Safaris

P.O. Box 44827, Nairobi, Kenya, ☎ (2) 521590, FAX: (2) 501754 or
USA Office
925 31st Avenue, Seattle, Washington 98122, ☎ (206) 323-1220.

Camel Safaris

Several different camel safaris are offered in the drier Northern parts of Kenya. They range from regularly scheduled safaris to trips customized to meet the size and time schedule of your group. Typically only four to 12 clients would be on a camel safari at any one time, usually for about five nights. Camel safaris are suspended during the rainy seasons. Prices tend to vary by group size and duration of the safari.

In most cases, camels are used primarily as pack animals to move camp from one site to the next. You can also ride camels if you like, or you can walk. Camels are rather bad tempered and not especially comfortable to ride—many clients spend more time on foot than on the camels. Typically, you walk through dramatic, unspoiled scenery with your guides. You may encounter wild animals or occasionally come across Samburu herdsmen or small tribal settlements. You don't have to be particularly fit for these safaris. The pace and amount of walking will be geared to the group. You usually reach the new campsite around midday, rest after lunch and take an optional late afternoon game walk. Each night a tented camp is set up in a preselected spot. Dinner is prepared for you, a camp fire is lit, and water is warmed for a bucket shower. The night noises of the bush surround you. Above are brilliantly star-spattered skies.

Simon Evans Ewaso River Camel Safari Bookings Ltd.

Box 56707, Nairobi, Kenya, ☎ *(2) 225255, FAX: (2) 216553.*
Highly recommended. Departs from Colcheccio Ranch, north of Rumuruti. All trips customized. Minimum of five clients. Most safaris are guided by Simon or a relative. Beautiful campsites next to the Ewaso Nyiro River. Good food and thoughtful service. $150 per person per day. Transport from Nairobi and back $640 for a nine pax vehicle. "Our young teenagers had the time of their lives...we saw elephant, kudu and buffalo...airy mesh tents allowed us to watch the full moon from our beds...each campsite was more remarkable than the last...possibly the best thing we've done in Kenya." (quote from long-term Kenya resident).

Kenya Camel Safaris Let's Go Travel

Box 60342, Nairobi, Kenya, ☎ *(2) 340331, FAX: (2) 336890.*
Recommended. Departs every Monday from Nairobi. The group meets in Isiolo town (north of Timau, south of Samburu) and is transported from there to the base camp. These safaris cater from four to 20 people, last for three or five nights, and are usually guided by Malcolm Destro and/or his wife. Campsites are near the Ewaso Nyiro river. When the weather is dry, clients often sleep under mosquito netting rather than in a tent. Cost is $560 per person for a five night safari and $450 per person for a three night safari. Optional transport from Nairobi is $100 per person return.

Geosafaris

Box 24696, Nairobi, Kenya, ☎ *(2) 884258, FAX: (2) 882124.*
E-mail: geosafaris@form-net.com
Known for being more adventurous than other camel safaris. All trips customized—several choices of where to start from: Samburu, Mathews Range, Maralal. Minimum six days. Usually 4–8 clients. Guides Helen Douglas Defreshne, Emma or Yoav Chen. Approximate price per person, per day $204.

Yare Safaris Co. Ltd.

Box 63006, Nairobi, Kenya, ☎ *(2) 214099, FAX: (2) 213445.*
Weekly departure on Saturdays from Nairobi to Maralal for five night camel safari. Typically 2–6 clients. Campsites are moved by Land Rover and set up near the Ewaso Nyiro river. Clients have a Samburu guide and ride camels or walk. Total cost (including transport) $300 per person. Bring your own sleeping bag... Mixed reviews.

BEGINNINGS

Donkey Safaris

Samburu Trails Trekking Safaris
  Box 40, Maralal, Kenya or

Bush Homes of East Africa Ltd.
  Box 56923, Nairobi, Kenya,
  ☎ *(2) 571667, FAX: (2) 571665.*

Although donkeys carry all the supplies and gear, these are essentially walking safaris for the fit, the adventurous and lovers of wild and remote places of beauty. The trails wind and climb through magnificent landscapes in the northern region of Kenya—around Losiolo (near Maralal). Clients are likely to see wild animals and many species of birds. These safaris typically include at least four nights camping under the stars in comfortable but unpretentious style—there are camp beds, safari showers, and meals cooked over the campfire. Hosted by Peter Faull and his wife.

Horseback Safaris

Experienced horseback riders can enjoy the unique experience of exploring some spectacular wild savannah and bush on even terms with the wild animals. You begin your ride from a base camp or ranch house to follow game trails cross-country on horseback. There is no sign of modern roads or even telephone poles, just space and freedom for the four-to-six-hour ride to the saddle safari camp, usually set near a shady waterhole.

The rides begin in the early morning, which is also the best time for viewing wildlife. There are stops for drinks and lunch. You arrive at the day's camp in time for tea and hot showers, with everything all set up and waiting for you. The *syces* or grooms attend to the horses as well as provide additional protection at night. You can relax or take a walk around camp before sundown and later enjoy your meal around the traditional campfire.

Saddle safaris usually use specially designed English trekking saddles (there are no Western saddles) and Anglo-Arab Somali ponies. The camp moves daily by truck along bush roads that the main group avoids. Some saddle safaris combine horseback and four-wheel drive photographic segments, some are "no frills" with riders taking care of some of their own camp needs, some include a "rest" at a house on the beach. There are several different itineraries to choose from, and some trips are offered on a guaranteed departure basis with the price changing depending on the numbers of riders who actually go on the trip.

As a rider you must have your own accident and medical insurance before arriving in Kenya. Only riders confident at all paces are accepted. You must have suitable riding attire including warm clothing and a waterproof jacket, coat, or poncho in case of rain.

For those horsemen who wish to ride as a relaxing form of exercise or to add an extra dimension to their stay at a ranch, lodge, or hotel, there are a number of places offering guests opportunity. There are some where the trail ponies are even suitable for beginners. See accommodation section for details.

For a horseback safari in Kenya contact the following:

Safaris Unlimited (Africa) Ltd.
P.O. Box 24181, Nairobi, Kenya, ☎ *(2) 891168/890435, FAX: (2) 891113/882723*
or
FITS Equestrian
685 Latin Road, Solvang, California 93463 USA, ☎ *(805) 688-9494, FAX: (805) 688-2943.*
Organized by Tony Church, this was the first saddle safari company in Kenya. Prices for a full safari range from $804 to $4630 depending on number of days and numbers of riders on safari. Prices cover ground transfers only, and bottled drinks are supplied on a Pay Bar basis. There are no safaris scheduled for the April-May rainy season.

2. Offbeat Safaris Ltd.
P.O. Box 56923, Nairobi, Kenya, ☎ *(2) 506139, FAX: (2) 502739 or*
Equitour **Worldwide Riding Holidays**
Bitterroot Ranch, Box 807, Dubois, Wyoming 82513 USA, ☎ *(800) 545-0019, FAX: (307) 455-2354.*
Directed in Kenya by Tristan Voorspuy, who was trained by Tony Church.

3. Richard Bonham Safaris Ltd.
P.O. Box 24133, Nairobi, Kenya, ☎ *(2) 882521, FAX: (2) 882728.*
Richard Bonham is known for arranging unusual safaris. He will work with riders to create riding safaris suitable to their skills. He knows many areas of Kenya well, including the Chyulu Hills.

Cycling Safaris

This is the newest form of adventure safari in Kenya. It follows the idea of meeting experiences in the wild as a participant. Most of the organized trips use a combination of cycling, walking, boating and traveling by vehicle to camps that follow a set itinerary with you.

Some companies pamper you and do all the camp work, some ask you to participate in camp chores. Again, prices vary depending on numbers of cyclists and number of days required for the safari. They range from $360 per person for three days to $720 per person for six days. If you do not bring your own, a mountain bike is provided.

For further information contact:

1. Bike Treks: Walking & Cycling in Kenya
P.O. Box 14237, Nairobi, Kenya, ☎ *(2) 446371, FAX: (2) 442439.*
These are organized by Nigal Arensen, a third generation Kenyan, who specializes in cycling safaris.

2. Hiking & Cycling Kenya Ltd.
P.O. Box 39439, Nairobi, Kenya, ☎ *(2) 218336/8, FAX: (2) 224212 or*

Sobek's International Explorers Society

P.O. Box 1089, Angel's Camp, California 95222 USA, ☎ *(800) 777-7939.*

These trips seem very basic, often using public transportation to and from safari points.

3. Gametrackers

P.O. Box 62042, Nairobi, ☎ *(2) 338927, FAX: (2) 330903.*

White Water Rafting

Depending on water levels, White Water Adventures can give you rafting trips ranging from 40 to 400 miles, from one day to several weeks, and all a a level of luxury designed to suit you. Rafts are put in on the Tana or the Athi River. You can see plenty of bird life and wildlife along the shore. Class III to V rapids are interspersed with calmer water.

For longer trips, you camp along the river. Rafting trips can be combined with caving in the Chyulu Hills or game drives in Tsavo or Amboseli National Parks. You are required to sign a release and assumption of risk before making the trip.

Savage Wilderness Safaris Ltd.

P.O. Box 44827, Nairobi, Kenya, ☎ *(2) 521590.*

USA Office

925 31st Avenue, Seattle, Washington 98122 USA, ☎ *(206) 323-1220.*

Bird Shooting Safaris

According to Mr. Charles W. Waring, III, of Charleston, South Carolina, bird shooting is good in Kenya, especially on safari with Joe Cheffings of Bateleur Safaris Limited, who has organized personal safaris for more than 25 years.

One of Kenya's best professional hunters, Joe also offers photographic safaris throughout Kenya, though he specializes in bird shooting. He makes certain you are far, far away from other tourists. His favorite haunt is located in arid acacia woodlands over 100 miles south of Nairobi and roughly 40 miles north of the Tanzanian border.

The private camp is set up in the traditional East African style with a shower tent, a toilet tent, mess tent, and sleeping tents with camp beds. There are lots of friendly staff to look after laundry and the day to day running of the camp. All meals, beer, and soft drinks are included, and the food in camp is delicious.

The day begins early with tea or coffee delivered to your tent. You can have breakfast before you go out or after you come back; it is up to you to set the schedule. After you arrive at the waterhole, expect flocks of sandgrouse and doves. They come by the hundreds. The limits are generous: 20 per person per day for sandgrouse, 25 for doves, and 15 for a mixed bag of ground birds. Not only can you expect very challenging shooting, you may also see magnificent Mt. Kilimanjaro!

The rest of the day will include lunch back in camp and naps to avoid mid-day equatorial heat. Perhaps you might request a game drive at nearby Amboseli National Park. Afternoon ground bird shooting includes guinea fowl, spurfowl, and francolin. Sundowners in the cool of the evening and safari stories by the warm campfire are the traditional finish to an exciting day.

Walking around camp you can be sure of seeing plains game and perhaps a rare lesser kudu. You can hear lion roaring at night. You will be amazed at the quantity and brightness of stars in the East African sky. With Bateleur Safaris, you will experience the beauty of one of the last pieces of "old Africa."

Prices: $350 per person per day (exact amount depends on the number of clients) plus 10% more per shooter per day plus cartridges and spirits at cost.

For the most current information about guns and licenses, contact Joe or Sporting International direct.

Joe Cheffings, Bateleur Safaris Ltd.

Box 42562, Nairobi, ☎/FAX: (2) 891007.
or his agent:

Sporting International Inc.

13201 Northwest Freeway, Suite 880-C, Houston, Texas 77040, ☎ (800) 231-6352.

Bird Shooting Safaris are also offered by the following:

Guy Grant of El Karama Ranch

c/o Let's Go Travel, P.O. Box 60342, Nairobi, ☎ (2) 340331, FAX: (2) 336890.

Richard Bonham Safaris Ltd.

P.O. Box 24133, Nairobi, ☎ (2) 882521, FAX: (2) 882728.

Fishing In Kenya

Mr. Charles W. Waring, III, of Charleston, South Carolina, reports that fishing in Kenya is as good as the finest anywhere, depending on what you are after and the time of the year. While Kenya is best known for big game fishing, you can also fish for trout, bass, nile perch and tiger fish.

Big Game Fishing

From Ernest Hemingway to European royalty, all have found the challenge of landing a big marlin, sailfish, shark, or yellowfin tuna to be worth the trip. Chartering a boat is not inexpensive, but it is very reasonable in terms of international standards ($500–$650 per day and $350–$465 per half day) includes everything for up to four fishermen except tips).

The main centers for big game fishing are Lamu, Malindi, Watamu, Mombasa, and the Pemba Channel Area (Msambeweni, Funzi Island, and Shimoni). While many hotels can arrange big game fishing, many serious fishermen place high value on the Pemba Channel Inn (formerly the Pemba Channel Fishing Club). Hemingways in Watamu is one of the best fishing hotels. Both Hemingways and its middle grade neighbor hotel, Ocean Sports, sponsor fishing tournament weekends as well as chartering fishing boats.

All of the coast hotels are well-known, and booking should be made as far as a year in advance for peak high season fishing in February–March. Some captains are highly recommended and can be booked privately. Mr. Andrew Wright, captain of the Snowgoose, is one of these. He can be reached through **Baharini Ventures**, *P.O. Box 124, Malindi, Kenya (FAX: (2) 31650 or ☎ (2) 20879)*.

The more adventurous fisherman can hire outfitters such as Mike Carr-Hartley of **Carr-Hartley Safaris**, *P.O. Box 59762, Nairobi, Kenya (☎ (2) 882453/882810 FAX. (2) 884542)* or the Paul family of **Kingfisher Safaris**, *P.O. Box 29, Malindi, Kenya (☎ (2) 21168)*. The most productive sailfishing is at the remote northernmost tip of the Kenyan Coast, and the outfitter sets up a private camp very close to where you will be fishing.

You should decide what fish you would like to try for before you go out to avoid disappointment. If you stay close to shore you are likely to get bonito, dorado (dolphin), yellowfin, sailfish, or kingfish. If you want big marlin, say so. Your captain will take you far out to concentrate on spots known to hold the big ones. You risk finding nothing, but you may get the chance to have the fight of your life with one of the giants of the sea.

Many captains will use light tackle at your request, which can add tremendous sport to bringing in a good fighter, even one which may not be that big. Remember, you have chartered the boat and have the right to add your direction to the trip. A "tagged release" policy is encouraged for willing fishermen. You will receive a certificate verifying your catch.

Trout

If trout are your prey and you enjoy beautiful mountain scenery, you will love the Aberdare Mountains. Since there are few tourists in the area, it is peaceful and quiet. Although the fish are not large, they are plentiful, despite the bait fishing of temporary residents.

A map of the area is a good investment regardless of how far you wish to go off the beaten track, but an easy trip for beginners is the Fisherman's Camp in the Aberdare National Park. Check with the Kenya Wildlife Service (KWS) about road conditions and book one of the bandas at the camp through them. KWS can also help you to obtain a fishing license. You should always fish with a companion in the Aberdares as wild animals (including lion) and slippery paths and rocks can be dangerous. It is also a good idea to take two reliable four-wheel drive vehicles on the trip.

The Chania River is very near the camp and holds significant numbers of trout. Above the bridge is a very narrow stretch of water, but you can pull out many trout in a very short period of time. (You won't have much space to cast, but if you practice on the wide stretch below the bridge, you'll be ready.)

Below the bridge are some lovely pools full of trout, and if you continue to hike along the river, you will find some very large pools with larger fish. Roll casting is best here due to overhanging branches. Depending on whether fishing conditions are dry or wet, the best flies to use are the Adams Irresistible, Kenya Bug, Mrs. Simpson, and Royal Coachman. **Kenya Trout and Salmon Flies Limited** (☎ *(2) 569790)* of Nairobi is a good place to buy your flies. With three or four days advance ordering, they can tie a few dozen for you for an extremely reasonable price.

Another good place for the beginner is the Aberdare Country Club. The Club stocks the stretch of the river running along the boundary of the Club's property, and the friendly staff at reception will gladly direct you to the best fishing spots. If you walk for about two kilometers upstream, you will find a very large pool that looks like a fisherman's dream. It is. If you fish this pool, you will very likely have your own fish for breakfast!

Larger Trout

For the experienced fisherman, the more remote streams in the Aberdares hold what you would expect: larger fish. Verify your route with a warden before going, but the largest fish caught in the Aberdares are often a result of long hikes through beautiful terrain. The bamboo line is mainly below the boundary of the park and has some very difficult-to-reach streams, but the trout there are the largest in all of the Aberdares.

The streams on Mt. Kenya are also worthwhile. If you are very fit, a seven-hour hike to Lake Alice will produce five- and six-pound rainbows. This requires camping for the night at 12,000 feet. Bring a warm sleeping bag!

It is easy to find the Sirimon River on the northwestern side of Mt. Kenya. About 15 kilometers past Nanyuki, a sign on the right points to the Sirimon Gate. The unmarked road on the left leads to the river. After turning off the main road, take the first right to an open area below the road (only 10 minutes from the highway). Park. Walk upstream. You will find many pools with overhanging branches to test your patience and skill.

The Cherangani Hills are known to hold the biggest brown trout in all of Kenya, but it is a long drive from Nairobi. Nearby bandas may be booked in Nairobi, and the proprietor will gladly give directions to fishing spots.

Many dams in the highlands also hold fish, but the best ones are on private property, so getting written permission is a must. The Kericho Area is very accessible to the beginner, with the streams and dams controlled by the **Kericho Sotik Fishing Association**, *P.O. Box 281, Kericho, Kenya.*

For a day trip from Nairobi, try the stream on top of the Rift Valley escarpment on the road to Lake Naivasha. After you go under the overpass (about 40 minutes from Nairobi), take your first right. Turn right again and follow the road to a village. Ask for directions to the river. For a small tip, you can hire a guide who knows exactly where the good pools are. You should always bring a guard to stay with your car while you are fishing.

Trout fishing in Kenya is always changing. Some places are better at different times of the year. Mr. John Lyal of **Bookings Limited in Nairobi** (☎ *(2) 220365/225255)* is a reliable contact. As a fisherman himself, he can advise on where to go for any type of fishing in Kenya. He can make bookings for lodges and hotels at the coast and elsewhere, and he is the agent for Mr. Mike Carr-Hartley, one of Kenya's best fishermen and outfitters.

Nile Perch

If you are after nile perch, you can go to Lake Turkana or to Lake Victoria. Going to Lake Victoria is the easier trip, and there are several luxurious fishing lodges on various islands, where fish over 100 pounds are brought in regularly.

Lake Turkana has tiger fish in addition to perch, but a rough two-day drive or a chartered flight are the only ways of reaching the lake. You can try fly fishing for perch, but Mike Carr-Hartley is probably the only one who can guarantee your success in this most challenging venture. The lodges around the lake and on Central Island are very spartan, and a private tented safari is the better way to go, though pricey.

Bass

Bass fishing is not exceptional in Kenya, but if you are visiting Lake Naivasha, why not try it? Some fish are more than five pounds, and some boats have brought in as many as 50 fish.

Four hours from Nairobi, Mr. Clive Aggett has a ranch near Rumuruti with dams holding bass and rainbow trout. You can book a cottage on his largest dam. Commercial duck shooting could be combined with fishing. Ask for details if this appeals. Write him at P.O. Box #2, Rumuruti.

Across Kenya, there are many small ponds, dams and streams which may be worth trying. Mr. Waring has visited and proven all the places listed above. However, any fisherman knows catching a fish is never a sure bet. No matter what the catch, however, fishing in Kenya always takes you to beautiful settings which never fail to lure anglers back to Kenya.

Classical Aerial Safaris

The ultimate in romance and nostalgia! You don a leather flying jacket, long white scarf, soft leather helmet and goggles and climb into a cheeky red open cockpit biplane. You are up and away—with the wind in your face, Mt. Kenya in front and music from *Out of Africa* in your ears. Pinch yourself, it is real.

Classic Aerial Safaris is the culmination of a lifelong dream for Andrew Garratt who is the owner and the pilot. The three-seater plane is a modern replica of a 1935 Waco biplane. The pilot sits at the back with two passengers side-by-side in the front cockpit.

Andrew's base is at Mawingu Airstrip adjacent to Mt. Kenya Safari Club near Nanyuki. A second biplane operates from Lewa Downs near Isiolo. Trips are priced by flying time. An hour's flight is $300 per person sharing—you can opt for shorter, less expensive flights. There is also a choice of special aerial safaris: a dawn flight over the Aberdare Mountains into the Rift Valley with breakfast at Lake Elmentaita, or a flight to Lewa Downs including a game drive and lunch.

On demand, the biplane operates from other Lonrho Hotels in the Mt. Kenya area as well as from private homestays in the region. A superb way to appreciate the magnificent and varied scenery—pure romance and adventure!

Quotes from the Passengers Book:

> *"My soul was filled to overflowing"*
> *"The highlight of our trip. It brought tears to my eyes."*
> *"I always imagined that heaven would be higher."*

Contact:

Classic Aerial Safaris Ltd.

Box 35, Nanyuki, Kenya, (176) 22960, FAX: (176) 22494.
E-mail: agaratt@form-net.com

Smoothing Your Way

A potpourri of safari tips:

- If you want a double bed, ask for it when booking, make sure it is noted on your voucher, and ask for it again when checking in! Sometimes they are available.

- Ask for a description of special activities. Maybe there is a game walk or a snorkeling trip that is not mentioned at check-in.

- Overseas telephone calls are very expensive—plan ahead.

- Game park fees: often an extra. Be prepared.

- Decaffeinated coffee & sugar substitutes are not readily available. Bring your own.

- Bush stops: Easier in a skirt. Carry tissue or T.P.

- Washcloths: Bring your own. There will be towels.

- Cucumber slices: Cucumber slices are great naturally pH-balanced skin wipes, very cooling on all exposed skin and soothing to tired eyes as well. Cucumber slices are also very thirst quenching! Don't forget your pocketknife.

- Bottled water: Carry some.

- Beer: Try different brands. They are good and inexpensive.

- Baridi sana: What to say if you want your drinks cold.

- Bargains: Fresh flowers including roses and orchids; massages and manicures, sodas, most handicrafts, cashews and macadamia nuts, coffee and tea.

- Expensive items: Gasoline (petrol), wine, photography, boutique fashions.

- Frustrations: Telephones that don't work, power failures, water shortages, time spent waiting, bad roads, manic traffic (including roundabouts).

- Essential: Sunblock, insect repellent, a hat.

- Electricity: Don't count on it everywhere you go. Some lodges and camps don't have it or don't have it 24 hours a day.

- Solar heated showers: Best taken at the end of a sunny day. The water won't be hot the next morning.

- Laundry services: Remember many hotels, lodges, and camps have these.

- Morning game drives need windbreakers; some evenings need warm wraps.

- Bathrooms go under these aliases: W.C., choo, loo, long-drop, cloakroom, restroom.

How to Use the Accommodation Sections

These sections have been divided geographically. Each chapter deals with a different part of the country. The map below defines the areas covered in the different chapters.

Chapter	Page
Nairobi	61
The Rift Valley	91
The Central Highlands, Mt. Kenya Area	125
Northern Kenya	163
Western Kenya	185
Southern Kenya	197
The Coast	269

Each chapter has a brief introduction to the area. After each introduction we discuss the hotels, lodges, homestays, tented camps, ranches and grass shacks in that area. These have been grouped according to the symbols that follow below.

Hotel/Lodge

Tented Camp

Grass Shacks/Tents on the Beach

Homestay

Ranch/Sanctuary

Our favorites appear first in each group, and we have devoted more detail to these places. In smaller print is a brief description of other places we visited (or know of) in the area. Where we have no clear preferences, we have alphabetized our listings.

We make no claims to have a comprehensive list of all tourist accommodations, and we are well aware that new places are opening all the time, while others are closing. Since there is a frequent turnover of chefs and even managers, food and service change. So, except where there is an established and reliable history of good food or service, we have focused our attention on the more enduring aspects of a place—location, design, history, ambiance.

Hats Off

We have marked our favorite places with traditional safari hats (topis). "Three Hats" is our highest rating. This means that all three of us agreed that this place was special and stood out from the rest. Our hat awards are personal and were often influenced by ambiance, location, and activities. The "best" in our view was not necessarily a function of facilities or amenities. Sometimes it was the lack of them that made a place special. Our hats have no particular relationship to any Kenyan or international star system. The hats and our descriptions tell you how it feels to be in a place rather than how it measures up to any set criteria. "Phantom" hats have been awarded to places which were not yet operational when we visited.(See "Top Topis" list at end of the book.)

Money Bags Required

Prices in Kenya tend to vary according to season and market conditions. There are frequent promotional specials, package rates, and often discounts for residents, families, diplomats, conferences, and tour groups. Because of extremes in variation, we have not included specific tariffs for each listing. Instead, we have classified hotels by the number of "moneybags" it would require to stay there based on double occupancy, high season rates.

💰 = $100 Per Double	
💰💰💰💰💰	Over $400
💰💰💰💰	$300–$399
💰💰💰	$200–$299
💰💰	$100–$199
💰	Under $100

Most tariffs in Kenya are now quoted in American dollars (used above) or British pounds sterling.

Except for city and coastal hotels, most rates include full-board. Some tariffs also include additional extras such as watersports, game drives, horse riding etc. which could add substantially to the basic price if purchased separately. It is to your advantage to check out all options and activities being offered by a hotel since they are not always advertised.

In Kenya, a voucher system is frequently used for confirmation and advance payment of bookings. You often need to show this voucher for entry into the property. If you pay for any extras, be sure they are listed on the voucher. Although you may request certain rooms, you have no real guarantee of getting them. Your chances improve if you contact the hotel directly

Trends and Changes

- **Conservation** and **eco-tourism** are big issues and more hotels, lodges and homestays are "doing their bit." Places situated away from urban areas are recycling waste, using solar energy etc. Several of the camps and homestays are involving themselves in protection of game and in active measures to increase the wildlife in their areas. Hooray!

- The appeal of **hosted homestays and small exclusive lodges** continues to grow and there is an increasing number to choose from. The best are exceptional. Some are overpriced.

- Several of the **newer accommodation** options have not yet been personally visited by the authors. The **lack of any hat ratings** on these places simply signifies the absence of a personal evaluation.

- The popularity of **walking** in the bush and a desire for a closer **interaction with the environment** is being recognized. More places are offering game, bush or bird walks.

- There is a trend to include **more** in the tariff—e.g. mineral water in the rooms, laundry services, free local drinks, etc. Linked to this is the increase of hotels on the coast operating as a club and offering an **all-inclusive package**—where meals, drinks, activities etc. are included in the price.

- **Tsavo East**, which had been largely closed in the 1980s due to poaching problems, has now opened up and several camps have been established.

- There are more **ways to appreciate** and enjoy this marvelous country than ever before. Camel safaris, ballooning, donkey trekking, aerial safaris, horseriding safaris, scuba diving, deep-sea fishing, etc., are increasingly popular. Enjoy.

- The rise and fall of **security issues** continues to plague Kenya. The severity and location of the concerns keep changing. These are generally very localized events and often appear to be worse in the foreign press. It is also a matter of astonishment to those in Kenya that distant disasters such as Rwanda and ebola in Zaire should affect tourism here. Our security advice on page 25 remains the same.

Web Directory

Search Engines

http://webcrawler.com/	**Web Crawler**
http://www.excite.com	**Excite**
http://www.yahoo.com/	**Yahoo**
http://lycos.cs.cmu.edu/lycos-form.html	**Lycos**

Before You Go

http://www.embassy.org
Various foreign embassies

http://www.stolaf.edu/network/travel-advisories.html
U.S. State Dept. Travel Advisories

http://www.cdc.gov/cdc.html
Center for Disease Control

http://gnn.com/cgi-bin/gnn/currency
Current foreign currency rates

http://www.embpage.org
Embassies in the U.S. and around the world.

http://travel.state.gov/travel_warnings.html
U.S. State Department's travel warnings and advisories.

http://www.taponline.com/tap/travel/xenon.html
Currency converter for over 50 different currencies.

http://www.usatoday.com/weather/wfront.htm
Weather forecasts

Kenya Web Sites

http://www.cityn.net/countries/kenya
Good starting point for web info on Kenya

http://www.odci.gov/cia/publications/nsolo/factbook/ke.htm
1996 World Factbook: Kenya

http://www.sas.upenn.edu/African_Studies/Country_Specific/Kenya.html
Kenya African Studies at UPenn

http://www.travlang.com/languages/english/english.html
English for Travellers

http://www.sil.org/ethnologue/countries/Keny.html
Languages of Kenya - Ethnologue Database

http://www.cis.yale.edu/swahili/
The Kamusi Project: Internet Living Swahili Dictionary

http://www.kenyaweb.com/
KenyaWeb

http://www.hotelstravel.com/kenya.html
Hotels and Travel on the Net - Kenya

http://www.africaonline.co.ke/AfricaOnline/eastafrican.html
East African Interactive AfricaOnline

http://www.africaonline.co.ke/AfricaOnline/karengata.html
Karengata Chronicle- AfricaOnline

http://www.africaonline.co.ke/AfricaOnline/nation.html
The Nation Interactive - Kenya's Online Newspaper - AfricaOnline

http://www.leftbank.com/CosWeb/pictures/kenya.html
Cos Photos - Kenya

http://www.chem.surrey.ac.uk/~chp1mk/
Weird World View - Unofficial Kenya Home Page

http://www.lawrence.edu/~bradleyc/kenya.html
Western Kenya and Maragoli- Lawrence University

http://www.gorp.com/gorp/location/africa/kenya/parkindx.htm
Kenya National Parks and Reserves

http://www.interknowledge.com/kenya/index.html
An Introduction to Kenya - interKnowledge Corp.

http://www.bwanazulia.com/kenya/
Bwana Zulia's Kenya Travel Guide

http://www.travelchannel.com/spot/kenya/welcome.htm
City Profile: Kenya - The Travel Channel

http://www.cdc.gov/travel/eafrica.htm
East Africa Traveler's Health Information - U.S. CDC

http://travel.state.gov/kenya.html
Travel Advisory: Kenya - U.S. State Department

News Sources

http://www.africaonline.co.ke/AfricaOnline/nation.html
The Daily Nation

http://www.africaonline.co.ke/AfricaOnline/eastafrican.html
The East African

Language Converters

http://www.travlang.com/languages
Foreign language for travelers. Translate or look up basic words and phrases in most major languages.

Other Travel Info Sources

Recommended sources for travel information from Robert Young Pelton, Fielding's The World's Most Dangerous Places.

www.fieldingtravel.com
Fielding's DangerFinder™

http://www.fco.gov.uk/reference/travel_advice/frames_index.html
United Kingdom Travel advisories

http://dfait-naeci.gc.ca/english/menu.htm
Canada Travel Advisories

http://travel.state.gov/osac.html
United States Travel Advisories (Overseas Security Advisory Council)

http://www.dfat.gov.au/consular/advice/advices_mnu.html
Australia Travel Advisories

http://www.cdc.gov/travel/travel.html
Center for Disease Control

http://www.leland.standford.edu/~naked/stms.html
Travel Health Advisories

http://www.isn.eth2.ch/
International Relations and Security Network

For a fee travelers can get information from Kroll Associates (www.krollassociates.com), Pinkerton's and Jane's. Also currency conversion, visa information, on-line ticketing, embassy addresses are all available on line. Use Excite search to locate.

Web Addresses for Tour and Safari Packages

The following websites can help you explore some travel options online. In most cases you can e-mail the travel providers with your specific questions or requirements. Fielding does not endorse, nor do we have any affiliation with, any of the sites or listings provided in this book. Note: All website addresses begin with http:// followed by the address below:

www.accesstravel.com
www.adnet.bc.ca
www.africaonline.co.ke
www.aquarius-tvl.com/kenya.html
www.africaparkeast.com/prod04.htm
www.atevo.com
www.blackworld.com
www.bvt-usa.com/africa/kenya1.html
www.cyberpages.com
www.deepriver.com
diogenes.baylor.edu
www.dolphin.ca
www.footventure.co.uk
www.globalcon.org/untpdc/incubator/africahp/ken/kesp.htm
www.lhw.com/nanyuki/mountkenyasafariclub.html
www.inficad.com
www.interconti.com
www.jambokenya.com
www.kenyatours.com/itinerary.html
www.kenyaweb.holowww.com
www.kilimanjaro.com
www.knightline.com/letsgotr/ksi.htm
www.learningvacations.com/safari3.htm
www.nobhilltravel.com/ba-kenya.htm
www.onsafari.com
ophelia.fullcoll.edu/fc/alumni/fcalumha.htm
ourworld.rst.de
www2.premiertours.com
www.safaris.com
www.smartworld.com
www.travelvantage.com
www.travelon.com
vagabondtravel.com
www.vei.com
www.vrenpo.com/~sakimura/j/travel/volken.html
www.wildlife-safari.com

NAIROBI

Nairobi is the largest city in East Africa. It began as a shantytown depot of the East African Railroad in 1899. In a little over 90 years it has become one of the major cities of modern Africa and a headquarters of the United Nations. It is a vibrant and growing city—a mosaic of many races and cultures.

Most of the many tourists to Kenya only spend about one or two nights in Nairobi. From a variety of sightseeing options, we recommend:

The Nairobi National Game Park

(11,300 hectares). The Park is not far from the city center, but gives you a real bush experience. You'll see the most game except elephant. This is possibly your best chance of seeing rhino. Stay in your vehicle. See page 388 for more information on the park.

AFEW Giraffe Center

In Langata. See giraffe eye to eye and feed them by hand—long, sticky, blue tongues and giant eyelashes. Fun for children and adults. Tea room, gift shop and nature trails. Operated by African Fund for Endangered Wildlife.

Karen Blixen Museum

Pleasant house and gardens. Worth a visit if you read the book. The nearby Karen Blixen Coffee Garden, gallery and gift shop echo themes of the museum.

Ostrich Farm

In Langata. Feed ostriches and stand on their eggs. Display and sale of various crafts—see craftsmen at work.

Bomas of Kenya

Tribal dancing in an amphitheater and displays of traditional Kenyan homesteads (boma). Many tour groups and heavy-duty souvenir selling.

National Museum

There is much to see, famous for Leakey prehistoric discoveries and tribal artifacts.

Tourist time in Nairobi is also often spent shopping—searching out Kenyan mementoes and gifts to take home. There are soapstone carvings, wonderful ethnic jewelry, many wooden carvings, colorful cloth *kanga* and *kikoi*. Most hotels have souvenir shops. African Heritage shops (downtown and on the airport road) have a broad selection and good displays. If you are more adventurous, try the block of small blue duka across the road from the Nairobi City Market Building. Leave behind your valuables, but take your humor, patience and bargaining skills and have fun. Downtown Nairobi is full of souvenir shops. Farther out in the suburbs are Utamaduni (an up

NAIROBI

market craft center) and Kazuri Beads (original ceramics) in Karen, and th
Craft Market and Undugu (co-op store) in the Westlands area.

Where to Stay

Hotels in the Nairobi area are either in the city center, just beyond th
center, or in the city suburbs. Price is not necessarily linked to location
Many of these hotels could be anywhere in the world and most are accept
able rather than exceptional. To phone Nairobi from outside Kenya dial *01*
plus the country code *254* before the number.

City Center Hotels

Tend to be high-rises on city streets—lots of shops, activity and noise. They are
handy for those conducting business in the city and good for tourists who want to
be in the "hub" of Nairobi. To phone Nairobi dial the country code 254 and the
city code 02 before the hotel number.

Beyond City Center Hotels

Tend to have gardens, are usually low-rise and have less traffic noise. Some are a
short walk or an inexpensive taxi ride into town.

City Suburb Hotels

Tend to have a more defined character and extensive grounds. Most are 15 or more
minutes from downtown and farther from the airport.

City Center Hotels

As this book goes to press, there appears to be a "race for renovation
among the leading city hotels. None too soon. A great many of the room
looked tired and tawdry. Fabrics, overwhelmingly in browns and green
seem to be wearily serving overtime. To make matters worse, the large new
suburban hotels are wooing away tourist trade, and a brand new high-rise
hotel has just opened in the city center. In addition, international tourism
has been affected by world recession. Many downtown hotels have not kep
pace with the business demands of today. Huge function/conference room
are not enough: business centers with fax machines and modern electronic
are needed.

So...it's "time to renovate." We heard of proposed state-of-the-art tele
phone/communication systems. We saw beautiful and elegant interior deco
in "sample" guest rooms. We learned of applications for casino licenses
plans for lobby face-lifts, and the introduction of business services. After ren
ovations, there could be some very attractive hotel options in the city center
Since no city center hotels currently qualify as "best" hotels, we have simpl
listed them alphabetically.

Grand Regency Hotel

Grand Regency Hotel, Box 40511, Nairobi
☎ *(2) 211199, FAX: (2) 217120*

This new and fancy 300-room hotel combines executive sophistication with modern comfort. Located in Nairobi's newest upmarket business area, this whitewash and solar glass high-rise overlooks Uhuru Park.

The hotel center is a soaring multi-story atrium. A gleaming glass mosaic suggests ethnic bead work as it rises in swirls of color to rooftop skylights many floors above. Local marble and granite are softened by hanging plants. Brass and mirrors multiply light and space. Glass elevators to room levels give panoramic views of the atrium bar, restaurant and piano lounge below. (Shades of Hyatt Regencys!)

A very large outdoor terrace has a roofed pool, glass windshields and views of the park and Nairobi skyline. The hotel boasts the largest ballroom/conference room in Kenya. Shimmering with the cut glass of ceiling chandeliers, it can accommodate 1500 guests.

Nairobi has waited and wondered about this hotel. Ownership changed hands while it was being constructed, and its opening kept being delayed. When it finally did open with advertising heralding its modernity and luxury, it got unplanned front-page media attention as well when ownership changed once again—this time seized by the Central Bank of Kenya.

Accommodations

Rooms are on open levels around the atrium. Each has a sitting area including a desk. Rooms are carpeted, have mahogany furniture and large windows. All have TV, video, telephone and minibar. Bathrooms are well-equipped with bath/shower, bidets, hairdryers, guest robes and a telephone. There are 40 suites and one Presidential Suite.

Other Facilities

À la carte restaurant, 24-hour coffee shop, health center, Reuters business center, parking for 180, customer service counter, private Summit Club with restaurant and rooftop lounge, shopping arcade, casino, airport shuttle.

Hotel Inter-Continental Nairobi

Hotel Inter-Continental, Box 30353, Nairobi
☎ *(2) 335550, FAX: (2) 214617*

The Hotel Inter-Continental Nairobi is part of the international chain and is located in downtown Nairobi, bordering on the Uhuru Highway and convenient to the Kenyatta Conference Center. This large seven-story hotel with 440 rooms has a wide range of services and facilities.

The spacious lobby has a bustling international air. There are tourists in khaki shorts clutching binoculars, African businessmen in pinstriped suits, European aircrews, and even a Japanese courtesy desk. Phones are ringing, luggage is being stacked, and the doorman is trying to untangle a traffic jam.

There are four restaurants. The Chateau Bar and Restaurant on the top floor with windows right around, is popular for its views over Nairobi and dancing in the evenings. On the ground level are the Pool Terrace Restaurant, which overlooks the pool, the small and elegant Le Mistral restaurant, and a coffee shop.

Two heated pools (one for children) are in a huge patio area with many loungers and chairs around umbrella tables. Food and drinks can be served outside, and landscaping and planters add color.

The guest rooms are off claustrophobic passageways which seem to stretch on and on. Rooms have recently been refurbished. We saw a sample. Some have pleasant views across a park and towards the Parliament Buildings.

In a city with major parking problems, the Inter-Continental has constructed a multistory car park. This is a particular boon when the hotel has large functions in the evening.

Accommodations

All rooms have air conditioning, TV with in-house videos, phones and minibar stocked on request. There are a handful of suites including a very large executive suite which can include three bedrooms.

Other Facilities

Bank, shopping arcade, travel agencies, large function and conference rooms, business center and services, pool, beauty salon, health spa, casino, airport shuttle service.

Nairobi Hilton

Nairobi Hilton, Box 30624, Nairobi
☎ *(2) 334000, FAX: (2) 339462*

The distinctive circular tower of the Nairobi Hilton is a landmark in downtown Nairobi. It can accommodate more than 600 business travelers and tourists. Its ground floor covers a small city block, with a row of shops, offices and restaurants lining all sides. A massive makonde wood sculpture seems to teem with life at the main entrance to the hotel, echoing the sidewalk crowds and frontage street flooded with "London" taxis, tourist group mini-buses, and other vehicles of all descriptions. Through the main doors of the hotel, the reception area is full of activity and the impression of people on the move. However, thick carpets, cool granite friezes high on the walls, and high ceilings reaching up two floors or more have a calming effect.

Most of the rooms are located in the cylindrical tower and have at least one curved wall with big picture windows, many with panoramic views of Nairobi. Rooms were refurbished in 1996, and a new Executive Floor was set aside for business travelers.

The Hilton has extensive meeting and conference rooms, including a very large and newly redecorated ballroom. Most of these are on the mezzanine level which can be reached from the lobby via the grand curving stairway. The Hilton's Residents' Lounge is wonderful—reminiscent of an Edwardian living room. There are comfortable groupings of sofas and wingback chairs; polished wood bookcases, desks, and overhead beams; and accents of brass in lamps and at the bar. The lighting is good, but not harsh, and the fireplace is warming. It is truly inviting, a home away from home.

The Hilton has a wide range of restaurants and bars. You can choose from an informal pizzeria, pool terrace snack bar, English-style pub, and the Mara Restaurant, which is open all day. For more elegant dining, the Amboseli Grill is open for lunch and for dinner, when there is also dancing.

Accommodations

Standard rooms have either twin beds or a queen-sized bed. Suites have sitting and dining areas and one or two bedrooms, and there are six parlor rooms with space for a sitting area. There are also 24 more spacious rooms with French doors opening onto the pool terrace. All rooms have en suite modern bathrooms with plenty of hot water from the Hilton's own wells. Guest rooms also have air conditioning, direct-dial telephone, radio, electronic safe, mini-bar stocked on request, hair dryer, and color television.

Executive Floor room facilities include complimentary beverages and refreshments served all day, newspapers and magazines, fax and photocopying services, large screen TV and video tape player, club lounge, private check-in and check-out, complimentary airport shuttle.

Other Facilities

Business Center, health club with gym and heated swimming pool, doctor/dentist, packaging service, airport shuttle, travel agency, airlines office, parking, boutiques, beauty and barber shop, drugstore, newsstand, photo shop, and East African Wildlife Office and Shop.

Nairobi Safari Club

The Nairobi Safari Club, Box 43564, Nairobi
☎ *(2) 330621, FAX: (2) 331201*

The Nairobi Safari Club is an all-suite hotel managed by Pullman International with the promise of comfort and privacy for every guest. The hotel is a striking white circular tower rippling with vertical rows of bay windows and balconies. It is located on University Way across from the University. The entry is elegant with broad white marble steps and facade, a dramatic cascade of tropical plants and a handsome brass plaque announcing The Nairobi Safari Club.

A doorman in caped livery greets you with pomp and smiles. The circular reception area is somewhat dark with wood paneling. You are almost overwhelmed by the thick carpets, chandeliers, brass friezes of African bush themes, leather armchairs and striking arrangements of tropical flowers. A circular fountain with sheets of falling water is a dramatic focal point.

The hotel is run as a social club, with hotel guests having temporary memberships. In the center of the hotel, the Kirinyaga Lounge gives residents a private club lounge and reading room furnished with more leather armchairs and cut-glass mirrors, lamps and barware. Down the hall, the Kirinyaga Restaurant serves an à la carte menu in a room heavy with mirrors, linen, crystal and silver. Both rooms are somewhat dark and stuffy with no windows, but certainly recall the more formal traditions of London clubs.

In contrast, the Brasserie and Safari Bar bring in the light with floor to ceiling windows. The Brasserie is open for snacks and meals, and the Safari Bar serves snacks and drinks on two airy levels overhung with ferns.

There are 146 suites in the hotel including four luxurious penthouse suites with plenty of space for entertaining and very beautifully furnished. Other suite sizes vary, and some are very small. Furnishings in all but the penthouse suites are somewhat tired. However, suites have comfortable and separate sitting areas which could be desirable for those of you that wish to have a longer stay.

Accommodations

All suites have sleeping, sitting, and eating areas or rooms. There are three telephones, TV, mini-bar, 24-hour room service, and en suite bathrooms, some with bidet.

Other Facilities

Outdoor swimming pool with sun terrace and snackbar, conference facilities, health center with exercise room, airport shuttle, parking, boutique, gift and sundry shop.

New Stanley Hotel
Sarova Hotels Ltd., Box 30680, Nairobi
☎ *(2) 333248, FAX: (2) 211472*

Located on the corner of Kimathi Street and Kenyatta Avenue, the New Stanley Hotel has been a central landmark of Nairobi since 1906. It was first opened to cater to the needs of Kenya's fledgling railroad staff. Today it can accommodate more than 400.

Over the years, young travelers have made a tradition of visiting the hotel's famous sidewalk Thorn Tree Cafe. The young Ernest Hemingway and other famous travelers liked to talk and people watch there. The cafe today does not live up to the romance of its history. However messages, which sometimes wait months for pickup, are still fastened to the trunk of the cafe's live thorn tree spreading its branches above.

Compared to the size of the hotel, the New Stanley's lobby seems small, dark, and crowded with guests coming and going. There are dark leather furnishings and wood paneling. However, the place feels lively, and the rather dim corridor beyond reception beckons with glass shop fronts displaying fine jewelry and gifts.

On the first floor, the Safari Bar overlooks the colorful crowds of Kenyatta Avenue through floor to ceiling glass walls. You feel you are suspended in air. The Tate Room, the hotel's main restaurant, serves an à la carte menu and is open for lunch and dinner. The grand ballroom has been recently redecorated.

There is a wide range of room sizes in the hotel. A much needed refurbishment of rooms is underway.

High on the fifth floor of the hotel with views over Nairobi is a strikingly tiled swimming pool, large enough for recreation and laps.

Six Eighty Hotel
Six Eighty Hotel, Box 43436, Nairobi
☎ *(2) 332680, Telex: 22513*

This hotel, built in 1972, has 340 rooms on 10 floors. Now, it needs a facelift. The hotel is rather unwelcoming and unexciting, with tired linoleum floors and carpeting. Guests may use the pool at the Boulevard Hotel, as there is none at the "Six-Eighty."

Beyond City Center Hotels

The Norfolk Hotel
Lonrho Hotels Kenya Ltd., Box 58581, Nairobi
☎ *(2) 216940, FAX: (2) 216796*

The Norfolk Hotel's international reputation for hospitality and excellence began with its opening on Christmas Day in 1904. It soon became a gathering place for new arrivals, men and women of affairs in business, in land development, and in government. Big Game Hunters with safari clients such as Theodore Roosevelt, aristocrats eager to experience the new Kenya, authors, adventurers and actors, all came to the Norfolk with its promise of stone-built coolness, quiet tile roofs, good food and baths. It was an island of civilized comfort in the early wild and dusty days of country and capital. Now it is among "The Leading Hotels of the World."

The Norfolk has evolved into an unusual collection of half-timbered turrets, terraces, wings and walks. These are loosely grouped around an interior grassy courtyard which has rambling gardens, aviaries and a display of vintage rickshaw, oxcart and cars. On arrival at the cobblestone entry, you are greeted by a beaming doorman in top hat and livery. Passing through the high-arched gateway, you are reminded of horse and buggy days. To one side is the Lord Delamere Terrace and Bar where people gather to meet friends or take time out from safari or business schedules. This popular spot to enjoy a quick meal is always a lively swirl of activity. It is open on one side to a street busy with traffic and London-style taxi cabs.

The small lobby is low-ceilinged, dark with wood paneling, and sometimes crowded with baggage. Although the Norfolk can accommodate approximately 270 guests, there is a sense of intimacy, and reception staffers make an effort to learn your name.

The Norfolk is possibly most remarkable for its history. The name conjures images of romance, adventure and camaraderie of a bygone era. In its heyday, many guests were regulars and knew each other well. They came for long stays with leisure to drink and dine in style, to plan safaris, business deals or swindles. Today, however, most international tourists come to this famous hostelry for one-night stays. They can have good service and pleasant surroundings, but the leisurely magic of those early days is a memory.

Accommodation wings have been added, rebuilt or refurnished, and many rooms have now become typical superior hotel rooms. The exceptions are in the 1937 Wing and the Cottage Wing. These rooms have charm and character—they overlook the courtyard and, more than the other rooms, they allow you to savor the historic, homey atmosphere of this gallant old hotel. The recently added Mugumo wing offers superior rooms, some with split-level accommodation.

The excellence of Norfolk cuisine has figured in the hotel's reputation since it first opened its kitchens with a French chef from the Waldorf Astoria Hotel of New York. One of the best places to eat in Nairobi today is the **Ibis Grill**, a cozy little à la carte restaurant. Diners can enjoy world-class cuisine created by Norfolk Head Chef Eamon Mullan, winner of many international awards. Emphasis is placed on local ingredients, and main courses are served under shiny silver salvers. Many tables are drawn up to comfortable banquettes and are set to perfection with heavy linen and silver. Ibis tapestries on the walls bring the restaurant's namesake to life. Visible through a wall of tall Palladian windows, other tables are set on the cool courtyard terrace shaded by broad vine leaves on the overhead trellis. Locals and guests can enjoy a quiet lunch or dine by candlelight and piano music during the dinner hours.

The **Lord Delamere Restaurant** serves breakfast, lunch and dinner. The outdoor **Lord Delamere Terrace** serves a varied menu. There is also a poolside terrace and bar near the pool which is reached down one of the hotel's access alleys.

The Norfolk continues to play an active role in the community by hosting various events in a series of function rooms. Occasionally there are even Music Hall or dramatic productions featuring imported and local talent.

Safari Journal
Thursday – late

The Ibis pianist swooped into his dreamy version of
"Somewhere My Love", the candles gave the room a soft glow,
there was a muted buzz of conversation . . .
He helped me with my wrap. It was hard to leave.
The head waiter presented me with a perfect pink carnation
and a box of Ibis Grill truffles.

Accommodations

Most accommodations are grouped in wings around the central courtyard. The four 1937 Wing studio suites have a garden entrance, spacious bedrooms, high ceilings, a separate dressing room and, best of all, a private little veranda overlooking the central courtyard. The Cottage Wing is all homey luxury: each cottage has a private garden veranda, living room with sofa and easy chairs, and either one or two bedrooms.

After renovations, there are several wings of the "typical modern hotel room" with two beds, two armchairs, luggage bureau unit, and modern ensuite bathroom. Some of these rooms are also considered mini-suites when space permits a larger sitting area. Some of the newly renovated rooms are upstairs over the main public rooms and overlook a noisy street; others are in wings built behind the main courtyard and at some distance from the heart of the hotel. Air conditioning, mini-bars and satellite TV have been added to all rooms. *Our Favorites*: 1937 and Cottage Wings.

Other Facilities

Travel desk, gift shops, beauty salon, pool, health club with gym and sauna, hair dresser, secure parking lot.

Off-Notes

There is no comfortable lounge for hotel guests that is not a restaurant or bar.

Nairobi Serena Hotel
Serena Lodges & Reservations, Box 48690, Nairobi
☎ *(2) 711077, FAX: (2) 718103*

The Nairobi Serena is a beautiful garden hotel just a 10-minute walk from the city center. The hotel's clean white silhouette rises at the edge of Nairobi's extensive Central Park. Surrounded by its own tropical garden, the hotel's rather stark lines are softened by cascades of plants and flowers growing on terrace areas and individual balconies. From the gardens, terraces, swimming pool, and many of the rooms, there is a striking view of modern Nairobi's distinctive skyline, especially beautiful at night.

The Serena can accommodate more than 300 guests in 197 luxurious double rooms. It has been accepted as a "Leading Hotel of the World." You are met by a liveried doorman wearing white gloves and fresh carnation boutonniere. The Serena's beautifully appointed lobby is rich with colorful tile borders on walls and floors. Carved cedar paneling and brass accent pieces glow under skylights set off by a profusion of indoor tropical plants. A raised lounge area is inviting with velvet Swahili-style sofas. From there, you can look through wall-sized windows to the garden beyond.

Throughout the hotel there is an abundance of natural light from windows and skylights. Many plants create the welcome effect of bringing the garden indoors, and you often hear the running water that is part of the landscaping. This enhances and unifies Serena decorative themes which have been drawn from all over Africa.

The Mandhari is one of Nairobi's finest à la carte restaurants. The elegance of the food, fine linens and silver is perfectly complemented by the inspired use of Kisii stone from western Kenya. Square columns are faced in hand-polished stone tiles and framed in cedar. The skylight overhead is edged in hanging plants. Appropriately, since *mandhari* means landscape in Swahili, one whole wall is hung with a unique Kisii stone mural carved into an African landscape. On the other side of the restaurant, the windows and dining terrace overlook the Serena's panoramic view of Nairobi.

The popular and more informal Cafe Maghreb is North African in style with arched recesses displaying pieces of brass or copper, and colorful tapestry screens separating tables. The Bambara Lounge has wood carvings and designs from West Africa.

The Kisima Bar is decorated to reflect the importance of water themes in Swahili coastal life. "Kisima" means watering hole in Swahili. There are low divans and stools, Swahili implements and murals on the walls. The elaborate health and fitness center, one of Nairobi's best, is named "Maisha," which means life in Swahili. Both the fitness center and the sparkling outdoor swimming pool are decorated in Arabic style tiles.

Accommodations

Rooms at the Serena are fairly uniform luxurious doubles. Although the rooms are not spacious, each has a wall-size picture window with garden or city view. The furniture is the typical two bed, two chair, baggage and bureau combination, but has been crafted and carved from African wood in African designs. African fabrics brighten beds and windows.

Modern en suite bathrooms have both bathtubs and showers. Each room has a stocked mini-bar, direct-dial telephone, electronic private safe, radio and TV.

There is an additional suite more elaborately furnished with separate sitting and dining area, bedroom, kitchen and bath. Thirty junior suites can be created on demand by opening connecting doors between double rooms and furnishing one as a sitting room.

Other Facilities

Business center, conference rooms, boutique, gift shop, hairdresser, book shop.

Holiday Inn Mayfair Court Hotel

The Mayfair Court Hotel, P.O. Box 66807, Nairobi
☎ *(2) 740920, FAX: (2) 748823*
e-mail: mayfair@users.africaonline.co.ke

Near the entrance of the busy Westlands suburb, the newly refurbished Holiday Inn Mayfair Court hotel bustles with activity and captures the charm and crisp service of an English country inn.

The hotel has a quaint charm and the lobby and reception glow with brass figures, wood paneling and Kenyan marble underfoot. Light flows into the hotel through the louver windows which allow views of the gardens. In the courtyard tall bay windows light the paneled stairway leading to the second floor, and flowing plants accent the deep window ledges.

The hotel has 171 rooms and is built in several wings rambling under mature trees. The central garden areas are traversed by pathways. The newly landscaped gardens feature fish ponds, fountains and two swimming pools. Breakfast and dinner are served in the Oasis Restaurant. The popular Mischief Bar and Grill has an extensive snack menu, and is open from 11 a.m. to midnight. Room service is also available.

Accommodations
Rooms are spacious with en suite bath and shower. Each room has a telephone, satellite TV and tea and coffee-making facilities.

Other Facilities
Health club with sauna, hair salon, safari boutique, casino, business center, courtesy shuttle bus to the city center and three conference centers for up to 450 delegates.

Fairview Hotel

Fairview Hotel, Box 40842, Nairobi
☎ *(2) 723211, FAX: (2) 721320*

The Fairview bills itself as "the country hotel in town." This family owned hotel, which has been operating since the 1930s, offers good value to guests. The hotel is a huge rambling old stone house with two garden cottages on two hectares of grounds. There are big trees, wide lawns, flower beds, and the sound of birds. Although it is just over a kilometer from the city center, the hotel feels like a calm oasis after the hustle and bustle of downtown Nairobi. It has a sense of history and individuality.

The Fairview attracts a wide range of clientele, from international consultants to up-country Kenyan residents. Many guests stay several days. Large tour groups are unlikely to be there. The atmosphere is friendly and relaxed—continuing the image of a traditional English country hotel.

New additions and some upgrading were completed recently to give the hotel entrance an elegant appearance with gleaming stone floors, curved stairway and skylight. There is a rather clubby lounge with a central fireplace and a small, hideaway bar with character and attractive decor. The sunny and spacious dining room has lovely big Palladian windows and opens out onto the garden. At the front of the hotel is a newly built outdoor dining terrace which serves à la carte meals. The main dining room serves both set/buffet and à la carte meals and is a popular lunch spot for Nairobi businessmen. A traditional African lunch buffet is served two days a week with the food attractively presented in ethnic clay pots.

There is a large bright room which can be booked for conferences or receptions. There is no swimming pool or health spa. Guests have free access to the pool at the nearby Panafric hotel. The Fairview has its own generator and borehole to ride out the vagaries of Nairobi's water and power supplies.

The hotel can house almost 200 guests in a wide variety of rooms ranging from singles to family units. As the executive assistant informed us proudly, "This hotel is not standardized anywhere." Each of the rooms has an individual character.

The tariff at the Fairview includes bed and breakfast. There is quite a variation in rates to match the range of room types and sizes. The Fairview is known for being good value for the money.

Accommodations

In general, the decor is rather old-fashioned and functional. Some rooms have nice oriental-style rugs and unusual chandeliers. Although the rooms do not feel updated, they do have an appearance of being well kept and maintained. In general, they are bright, clean, spacious, and comfortable. Most of the rooms have bathrooms en suite—some with tub and shower and others with shower only. There are televisions (including a video channel), telephones and radios.

Most accommodations are in the main house where two rooms have balconies and several have lovely restful views over the gardens. You could also choose to stay in one of the garden cottages or "annexes," where the room variations are even more extreme. In Annex #1 there is a large family unit with bay window, 1950's decor and a children's room. In Annex #2, which is a historical building with corrugated iron roof and a big veranda, there are six rooms with shared bathrooms and no TV. Just across a small road from the hotel are the Fairview Flats—a rectangular concrete-looking building without the charm of the main hotel or cottages. The upper floors are leased out for long term lets but the ground floor is used as part of the hotel with spacious family units leading out to a large lawn.

Please Note

Deposit required, no credit cards accepted, no air conditioning, no pool on grounds (free access to pool at neighboring hotel), 24-hour room service, mosquito nets, park.

The Landmark Hotel
Block Hotels, Box 40075, Nairobi
☎ *(2) 540780, FAX: (2) 545948*

This is the Nairobi-based Block Hotel and is located in the suburb of Westlands, only a few minutes drive from downtown. It is a fairly middle-of-the-road tourist and business hotel. It has recently been refurbished, given a new name (it was previously the Jacaranda Hotel) and a large, attractive new restaurant has been added. There is a swimming pool set in quiet attractive gardens and facilities for mid-sized conferences. Westlands has many shops and a selection of restaurants. There is a hotel shuttle bus to downtown Nairobi.

Boulevard Hotel
Hotel Boulevard, Box 42831, Nairobi
☎ *(2) 227567, FAX: (2) 334071*

Located right at the foot of Museum Hill, this no-frills hotel is only a 10-minute walk to the city center. It has 70 small guest rooms on three floors, each with en-suite bathroom and private balcony. Public areas are furnished in a functional '50s style. There are conference facilities. The hotel gardens overlook the Nairobi River on one side, and rooms with garden view are less noisy than those on the street side. The Boulevard has a pool and a tennis court.

Panafric Hotel
Sarova Hotels Ltd., Box 30680
☎ *(2) 333248, FAX: (2) 211472*

The Panafric Hotel can accommodate approximately 350 guests. You drive through an Agip Gasoline Station to reach the entrance of this modern concrete structure. Set on a rise near Nairobi's Central Park, the hotel has an oblique view of the city skyline, which is just a few minutes away by car. In addition to single and double rooms, the hotel has six suites and 42 service apartments suitable for longer stays. There are comprehensive conference facilities. The outdoor pool is larger than most in-city hotels.

The decor is very plain and tired. The public rooms tend to be dark and need re-furbishing. However, the Panafric has recently been sold to the Sarova Hotel Chain. Complete renovations are planned throughout to appeal to business travelers and tourists.

City Suburb Hotels

Windsor Golf and Country Club
Box 45587, Nairobi
☎ *(2) 862300, FAX: (2) 802322*

The Windsor Golf and Country Club is a larger-than-life Victorian extravaganza built in the Nairobi suburbs. There is nothing to prepare you for the overpowering impact of this hotel. It seems to be in the middle of nowhere. You drive past some suburban houses and through coffee fields and then....

The imposing main building follows the Grand Victorian style. It is built of stone and crowned by ochre tiled peaks and cupolas. The soaring entrance concourse has Victorian street lamps and shop fronts. There are dramatically high windows, miles of curtaining, wide stairways—everything is on a grand scale. The hotel was designed to recall the early days of Kenya's aristocratic British pioneers, to compare with the elegance and service of the Savoy Hotel or Claridges in London, and to create a setting for world-class golf to rival the renown of Gleneagles in Scotland. With all of its "nouveau" splendor, there is also a chic resemblance to Hollywood's Rodeo Drive.

The decor is reminiscent of a grand English country hotel. There is a huge copper fireplace in the vast ballroom. There are countless armchairs and sofas in richly woven fabrics. You see lots of etched glass, polished brass, wood and leather. Ornate draperies billow around towering small-paned windows and there are many cozy drawing rooms and bars set at different levels. Throughout the hotel, original works of art have been hung to compliment the decor.

Most of the public rooms and the expansive open-air terrace below command wonderful wide views over the golf course with its forests and ponds. The sky seems to stretch forever, and there are hills and mountains in the far distance. The separate accommodation buildings and cottages stride out to each side of the main complex, lining the first and last holes—a frame for this beautiful, world-class golf course.

The club has been designed and equipped in grand style, and there is a whole directory of services and facilities. They have tried to include everything including a shopping arcade, a full-service health and beauty spa, a huge baronial banquet hall, conference and business facilities, a variety of clublike lounges, several bars and restaurants, a state-of-the-art kitchen gleaming with all the latest imported equipment, and sophisticated up-to-date electronic audio and visual systems. There are also special "Butler Service" stations spaced to conveniently service bedrooms. It all seems so ambitious and rather incongruous in its setting. However, the hotel is still too new to gauge its ambiance and operation. When it has mellowed a bit, has a smooth operation, and the huge rooms are filled with animated guests, this might become a very special place. Effort and expense have certainly been expended to create something of quality and stature.

Quotes from Visitors:

> "The golf course is magnificent. It ranks with the best."
>
> "It's like a grand Victorian Railway Station with some Tudor thrown in."

Accommodations

The hotel can accommodate 230 guests in a choice of rooms, studio suites or cottages. The accommodation has been arranged in a series of separate buildings which stand along the edge of the golf course to each side of the main hotel. The buildings look rather grand with their large red tiled roofs and high chimneys. They all offer woodland or golf course views.

Rooms are furnished to resemble an English country-style hotel or inn. All have a full bathroom ensuite and a seating area. They are well-equipped with direct dial telephone, hairdryer and electronic digital safe. Guests have the convenience of parking near individual rooms.

The "Windsor Butler Service" on each floor is designed to help guests with everything from laundry to hiring cars, from getting newspapers to reserving golf tee times.There are 15 cottages. A central living room with fireplace is flanked on each side by a double room with full bath. There is an outdoor terrace. *Our Favorites*: Cottages overlooking the first fairway.

The 20 studio suites are situated on the top floor of each guest wing. They feature fireplaces, a sitting area with sofa and chairs, cathedral ceilings with exposed beams and a separate dressing area.

The 80 standard rooms, called superior doubles, are on the bottom two floors of the guest wings. They have one double or two larger-than-twin beds. Rooms on the bottom floor also have garden access doors.

Recreation

18-hole golf course (putting green, golf tuition, golf driving range), heated swimming pool, tennis courts, squash courts, bowling green, croquet lawn, jogging trails through forest, fishing for Tilapia and Black Bass in three lakes on the grounds, bird and nature walks with ornithologist, beauty and health spa with aerobics and exercise machines.

Other Offerings

Shopping (wide selection of shops including fashion, gifts, African arts and crafts, sports equipment); excursions (local trips and major safaris can be arranged); car hire, Nairobi shuttle every two hours, doctor.

Safari Park Hotel

Safari Park Hotel, Box 45038, Nairobi
☎ *(2) 802493, FAX: (2) 802477*

The Safari Park Hotel is an exciting 25-hectare hotel and convention complex that feels like a resort. About 15 minutes from downtown, it has dramatic architecture and a complete range of facilities spread out in beautifully landscaped grounds.

There is a relaxed holiday atmosphere, and the hotel feels like a theme park version of "larger-than-life exotic Africa." You are greeted at the entrance by imposing Masai morans in red shuka and beads. The thatched roof of reception soars above you. Inside is a life-sized sculpture of an elephant, exotic Lamu-style furniture from the coast, and a sign to the Hemingway bar upstairs: a potpourri of African images.

At the Safari Park Hotel you can be as sporty or as decadent as you like—play squash or have a massage, go shopping or gambling, lie by the pool or read on your private balcony. Also, there are a whole host of restaurants, specializing in various cuisines and offering different atmospheres and price ranges.

The many restaurants and facilities of this complex are scattered around the grounds. You are never far from lovely gardens and the sounds of birds. In the center of the grounds is an amazing swimming pool, reputed to be the largest in Africa. The pool has a rock water-slide and islands; it meanders through tropical gardens and is crossed by footbridges. A second, more traditional pool is set off to one side and there are floodlit tennis courts and a squash court. A brand new fitness center has saunas, jacuzzi, gymnasium and beauty parlor. There is a posh gambling casino. With your winnings, you might choose to browse through the shops and boutiques which sell a selection of curios and clothing.

NAIROBI

The Safari Park Hotel is a popular place for conferences and exhibitions. The large, up-to-date Jambo Conference Center has recently been completed. This can accommodate up to 1000 people and is fully equipped with audio visual and communications equipment. Multilingual translation facilities and secretarial services are also offered. There are separate subcommittee rooms and a business lounge equipped with fax facilities. The hotel prides itself on its ability to organize and cater for various events and conferences.

A wide variety of international cuisine is represented in the restaurants including Korean, Japanese, Chinese, African, Italian, French, and Indian. Some of the restaurants are small and intimate with very elegant decor, while others are larger and more relaxed. You can have a classy, French gourmet meal, or opt for a quick bite at the Cafe Kigwa which is open until 4 a.m. You might like to sample some game meat while watching African dancing or select vegetarian dishes at the Indian Mamta Restaurant. There is a pizzeria and a British pub with live music. During the day you can be served drinks and snacks around the pool. The main Le Bougainvillea restaurant spills out onto a wide stone patio where chairs and tables are set up under an enormous spreading tree.

At the moment, the Safari Park Hotel can accommodate 400 guests. However, there are plans for almost doubling this capacity. There is a choice of rooms, suites and cottages. The rooms are in two-story, thatched buildings which are spread out among lawns and trees. The Safari Park Hotel seems constantly to be expanding and updating. There is a sense of quality and attention to detail. Experts have been employed in the hotel's design and landscaping. It shows.

Accommodations

Each room has a private veranda or balcony with a garden view. The well-equipped rooms are bright and spacious with big windows, Lamu furniture and four-poster beds. The ensuite bathrooms have marble, gold fittings and hairdryers. There are a variety of suites with special extras such as oriental carpets and two balconies.

Special Offerings

Pool, tennis, squash, complete health spa, casino, free shuttle bus to town, shops and boutiques, conference and business facilities.

Utalii Hotel

Utalii Hotel, Box 31067, Nairobi
☎ *(2) 802540*

This pleasant modern hotel eight kilometers from the city center acts as a practical training unit for students at Utalii College. Students work with the hotel's professional staff to learn the hotel industry. With all those students learning to help you, the service and food are great. Utalii is good value for money.

The three-story hotel has 43 double rooms and seven suites with kitchenettes. All have been recently redecorated and have ensuite bathrooms, large windows, and balconies. Rooms on the highway side of the hotel have air conditioning to block out the noise, but we prefer the rooms on the garden/pool side.

Although the Utalii Hotel is tastefully decorated, it has no real African character—the hotel could be anywhere. However, the gardens around the pool and pool bar are very inviting, and the pool is one-half Olympic size. There are two tennis courts and guests can golf at the Muthaiga Golf Course.

Other Facilities

Free shuttle to city center, conference rooms, boutique, TV, direct-dial telephone, room service, mini-refrigerator, English breakfast included.

The Kentmere Club

The Kentmere Club, Box 39508, Nairobi
☎ *(154) 41053*

The grounds and country setting are the best features of the Kentmere Club. This small hotel nestles on the side of a hill in the Tigoni Highlands about 20 kilometers from Nairobi. There are colorful gardens all around and lush green tea in the distance.

The club is like an English country inn. There is a large dining room with Tudor beams and red tablecloths. The club bar is wood paneled. Lunches are served on the veranda and in the garden—if you can afford the wait.

There are 16 double rooms in several garden cottages. Each room has its own bathroom, fireplace and veranda. The beds and decor are both tired.

Guests at the Kentmere Club are welcome at the nearby Limuru Country Club for golf, tennis and swimming.

The Blue Post Hotel

*The Blue Post Hotel, Box
42, Thika*
☎ *(151) 22241*

Just off the Thika Road (A2) approximately 40 kilometers from Nairobi, the Blue Post Hotel still attracts a mixed cross-section of Kenyan residents. The hotel was built in 1906 on a promontory where the Chania and Thika Rivers meet to form the Thika and Chania Falls. Early settlers stopped there for tea and talk and to see the falls from the hotel's garden. Today the falls are quite wide, but rather muddy with more than a whiff of industry.

The hotel has seen better days. It still has expansive grounds with outdoor eating areas, viewpoints for the falls, and an outdoor market where local crafts are made and sold. There are large conference facilities. Except for the Blue Post Hotel and the Del Monte Company, Thika has little appeal for the tourist.

The Giraffe Manor

The Giraffe Manor, Box 15004, Langata, Nairobi
☎ *(2) 891078*

Staying at the exclusive Giraffe Manor is a unique and special experience. This mellow old stone house has an appealing history which is kept alive today. It was home to Daisy, the famous Rothschild giraffe. Today her grandchildren eat the flowers in the manor's extensive gardens. It's hard to believe Nairobi is only minutes away.

The manor house was built in 1932 in Langata, part of the Karen suburban area of Nairobi. It became the home of Jock Leslie-Melville and his wife Betty in 1974. They founded the African Fund for Endangered Wildlife (AFEW) and moved five babies of the endangered Rothschild giraffe to this property. They were successful at raising these giraffe, who have since grown and had their own offspring. Now, your hosts at the Giraffe Manor are Betty's son, Rick Anderson, and his wife Bryony—an energetic and charming couple who bring a great deal of professionalism to this role. Rick is active in continuing and expanding AFEW. Thanks to him and AFEW, there are still giraffe on the grounds of the manor today. You are quite likely to have a giraffe peer in at you through the front door or amble up to be hand-fed.

Giraffe Manor is only a short drive from downtown Nairobi. However, when you turn into the gates and bump along the dirt road winding through bush and riverine forest, you feel that you are far away from civilization. Warthogs run by, and there are giraffe among the trees. Your first, full frontal view of the manor is particularly impressive. It is an imposing double-story stone building with gables, tall chimneys, and red tiled roof. The house is set on large open grounds with mature trees and gardens reduced to those flowers which the giraffe will not eat. Off to one side you can see the distinctive knuckle-shaped peaks of the Ngong Hills.

NAIROBI

Safari Journal

August

BLAST! None of us remembered a camera and this scene should be recorded. Framed in silhouette against the bright light outdoors was an enormous giraffe, her legs splayed and her long neck and head peering in through the high arch of the front door. Joan giggled as the gooey, long, blue tongue curled around the food pellets she held out in her hand.

The high-arched front door leads to a grand entrance hall with a fireplace and a wide stairway. There is a generous living room arranged with chairs and sofas. With its old rugs, bowls of flowers, books, family photos, and piano, the room feels old-fashioned and lived-in. Through an archway is a long sun-room bright with big arched windows looking towards the Ngong Hills. Decorated with ferns and floral fabrics, this room is cheerfully elegant. It is here that breakfast and lunch are served. The main dining room is formally paneled in wood with a huge table and chairs covered in rich fabrics. At Giraffe Manor, a great deal of emphasis is placed on elegant, gourmet dining. In fact, when there are no guests staying at the manor, it is possible to arrange for a group of 10–12 to be served sumptuous meals in this grand setting. For larger groups a marque can be set up in the grounds—a perfect place for a special event.

You are paying for exclusivity when you stay at Giraffe Manor. There are seldom more than eight guests at a time, and they are usually all from one party. However, there are expansion plans to accommodate a few more guests without sacrificing the manor's personal or exclusive atmosphere.

This is meant to be a home, not a hotel. The bedrooms vary considerably in size and grandeur. Four bedrooms have bathrooms en suite. A smaller room off the master bedroom has a shower and would be suitable for children traveling with their parents. The master bedroom has a fireplace and a huge bed. The walls are covered in bright striped fabrics. In the black and white tiled bathroom, water spouts into the bath from a lion's head. Another room has some of Karen Blixen's original furniture. The smaller rooms are rather ordinary. The upstairs is not as impressive as the lower floor.

As Rick says, the "whole point of this place is to relax." Guests are free to wander in the extensive grounds, feed and photograph the giraffe and warthogs, or go on a nature walk in the adjoining forest. There are more than 170 species of birds, and you might also see bushbuck or dik-dik. You are encouraged to make yourself completely at home in the manor—settle down and read a book, admire the view, help yourself to a drink.

Right next door, and in view of the manor is the popular and successful AFEW Giraffe Center. Here visitors can come to feed the giraffe, take the Nature Walk, and learn more about wildlife and conservation.

The manor has been visited by a host of famous people—Margaret Mead, Bobby Kennedy, Brooke Shields, Hal Prince, Mick Jagger and Johnny Carson, just to name a few.

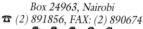

Ngong House

Box 24963, Nairobi
☎ *(2) 891856, FAX: (2) 890674*

Ngong House will make you want to extend your stay in Nairobi. It is luxurious, romantic, and fun and gives the impression that you are way out in the African bush, even though you are barely 20 minutes from downtown Nairobi.

Guests stay in wooden treehouses facing the distinctive knuckle-shaped Ngong Hills. But what treehouses! These are double-storied fantastic creations with superb attention to detail and every comfort imaginable. There are stained-glass windows, a fully stocked bar, brass showerheads, comfy couches, kilims and saddle bags, lovingly hand-made furniture and lamps. The cupboard doors have been fashioned from old Arab dhows, and the basins in the bathrooms look like old-fashioned painted bowls. Big windows make the most of the view, and a small kitchen allows Ngong House staff to serve you meals in the privacy of your own treehouse if you prefer. You can sit out on your veranda watching the sun set over the Ngong Hills or marvel at the variety of birds visiting your bird-feeder.

The four thatched treehouses are well-spaced and hidden from each other by natural bush. You enter by climbing up wooden steps and through a big "trapdoor." One of the treehouses is lower and requires less climbing (it is also the only one with a bath as well as a shower). The treehouses are named for the four points on the compass and each has a different decorative theme. For example, "East" has furniture from Bali including a huge four-poster bed with carved headboard, and "North" is decorated in blues and wrought iron to simulate "cold."

Guests have use of the expansive (10 acre) grounds, including the pleasant swimming pool and adjoining bar and change room. Breakfasts and lunches can be taken out on the shady lawns. Dinner is served in an open-sided thatched rondavel with fireplace. Hand-blown glass and delicate silver graced the table and we dined extravagantly on tilapia, zebra and a sinful dessert. All were elegantly presented in mouthwatering sauces and accompanied by good South African wines.

Paul Verleysen, a Belgian who has decided to make Africa his home, is the creative force behind Ngong House. He lives in the main house on the property and, together with his son, Chrestof, will act as manager and host. They bring flair and energy to the task.

Quotes from the beautiful hand-made guest book:

> *"It's a world of harmony and tranquility. I love these treehouses nestled on the hill. Such a wonderful idea."*

"We were so lucky not only to have the beginning but also the end of a wonderful journey through Kenya here at the Ngong House. Just enjoying the warm hospitality, the excellent cooking, the amazing surroundings, the unforgettable sunset..."

At night, guests arrive to a campfire and safari chairs under a huge fever tree—what an introduction to Kenya! The Giraffe Center is only a 10 minute walk away and a four-wheel drive vehicle is available for travel further afield. Trips to the Nairobi National Parks, museums, local markets, shops and galleries can be arranged. When you stay at Ngong House, all meals, alcohol (excluding champagne) and transport to and from the airport etc. are included in the price. On special request, the main house is also available. Dinners and lunches can be arranged for groups.

Macushla House

Box 42510, Nairobi

☎ (2) 891987, FAX: (2) 891971

Macushla House is a charming private homestay in the suburb of Langata. It is twenty minutes drive from downtown Nairobi and close to many of the best sightseeing attractions in the area.

The house has been recently built in a newish suburb very close to the AFEW Giraffe Center, and faces out over indigenous forest. The house is delightful, with high beamed ceilings and a wonderful feeling of space. It has been lovingly and tastefully furnished by Carrie Henkel who is the owner/manager. There are kilims on gleaming wood floors, comfortable sofas, artistic flower arrangements and interesting and eclectic art work.

There are two lounges each with a fireplace. They open out to a terrace and the attractive swimming pool which is dominated by a whimsical stained-glass sculpture of a dragon. Loungers with bright yellow cushions and umbrellas with tables and chairs are arrayed on the stone paving around the pool.

Between the lounges are the communal dining room and bar, both painted in a rich ochre and attractively furnished. The food is simple, fresh and home cooked. There is also an extensive snack menu at lunch and guests can eat inside or by the pool. Items such as savory stuffed pancakes, fish kebabs and Italian pasta caught my eye. Prices looked very reasonable. Macushla House is becoming a popular place for Nairobi residents to dine. Reservations are required for evening meals. Small cocktail functions can be organized.

There are two bedroom wings each with two spacious doubles and a smaller single bedroom. All have private bathrooms. Everywhere there is nice attention to detail. There is a small private study—ideal for consultants to set up a computer. Guests can se the phone and fax in the office and arrangements can be made for secretarial ser-ices. Transport and restaurant reservations can also be arranged.

rom the Visitors Book:

> *"Macushla is wonderful for peace and tranquility. We enjoyed the personal fondue."*

> *"A haven to come back to between safaris. The kids love the pool."*

Macushla means "my beloved" in Gaelic and certainly a lot of love and care has gone into the creation of Macushla House.

L'ol Dacha

Bush Homes of East Africa, Box 56923, Nairobi
☎ *(2) 571647, FAX: (2) 571665*

L'ol Dacha offers an alternative option for a Nairobi stopover. At the opposite xtreme from a city hotel, L'ol Dacha is small, simple and basic and commands a marvelous view from its position at the edge of the Rift Valley.

L'ol Dacha is off the Magadi road, 10 kilometers along a dirt road which passes motley buildings and small plots. The site is superb—quiet, peaceful and looking out over vast vistas. Guests can go for walks, cool off in the splash pool or just soak in the peace and the scenery.

Guests stay in simple stone cottages with bathrooms en suite. All is ultra casual and revolves around your desires. Caro and David White will personally host your isit. There are various trips on offer including a drive to the prehistoric site at Olor-gasailie or further on to the soda lake at Magadi.

NAIROBI

THE RIFT VALLEY

The Rift Valley is the greatest valley in the world, a continental fault system which stretches from the Dead Sea all the way to Mozambique. In Kenya, the valley forms a great rift through the middle of the country beginning from Turkana in the north to Lake Magadi in the south. In between are a series of other lakes: Baringo, Bogoria, Nakuru, Elmenteita, and Naivasha. Only two of these lakes (Naivasha and Baringo) are fresh water lakes. The others are shallow soda lakes.

Dozens of volcanoes erupted in and around the Rift Valley. Most of them are now extinct, but have left their mark on the landscape in the form of half-submerged islands, giant calderas, and the distinctive cone shapes which dot the landscape. The Rift Valley evokes a sense of immense mystery and the power of time.

Most visitors to Kenya first see the Rift Valley when travelling on the Nairobi-Naivasha road. This first view is almost always a stunning surprise. After driving through cool conifer forests suddenly you are at the edge of the Rift. The land drops way down to the dry and dusty plains below, and the distinctive volcanic shape of Mt. Longonot dominates the scene. Forty-eight kilometers across rises the dark blue escarpment of the other side of the valley. At the viewpoints, persistent souvenir salesmen force you back to reality.

The Masai have been in the Rift Valley for centuries. Today, the most popular tourist areas in the Rift Valley are around Lakes Naivasha, Nakuru and Baringo. All of these lakes have several accommodation options and are linked by relatively good tarmac roads. The lakes are known for their exceptional birdlife, especially the pink flocks of flamingos which feed in the soda lakes. National Parks have been established around Lakes Nakuru and Bogoria.

Lake Naivasha Area

Lake Naivasha, 83 kilometers from Nairobi, is the highest of the Rift lakes. Surprisingly, Lake Naivasha (1888 meters) is at a higher altitude than Nairobi (1670 meters). This beautiful freshwater lake has large floating islands of papyrus, a mysteriously fluctuating water level, a healthy hippo population and wonderful and diverse birdlife (340 species). Its shores are lined with yellow-barked fever trees and horticultural farms and vineyards. There is a yacht club on Crescent Island for sailing and windsurfing. Fishing is popular and there are even fresh water crayfish in the lake. There are a whole host of places to stay around the lake, ranging from bustling hotels to catered home stays.

Naivasha's proximity to Nairobi makes it ideal for a weekend (or longer) getaway. There is much to see and do in the area:

Crescent Island

This small island in Lake Naivasha is the outer rim of a submerged volcano. There is a private game sanctuary on the island, and it is safe to walk among wild animals (no big cats or elephant).

Hell's Gate National Park

Entrance Fee. The geological formation of this park is particularly impressive with soaring red cliffs, isolated volcanic plugs, spreading grasslands dotted with game, and a deep gorge where visitors can walk. There is a geothermal project at the far end of the park. See page 387 for more information on the park.

Elsamere Conservation Center

This former home of Joy Adamson of *Born Free* fame is now a residential conservation center. It is open to visitors for afternoon teas (3–6 p.m.). Entrance Fee.

RIFT VALLEY

KERIO VALLEY ~ KAMNAROK N.R.
Lake Kamnarok
LODWAR B4
LORUK
Lake Baringo Club
Lake Baringo Saruni
Island Camp
Kabarnet Hotel
KABARNET
MARIGAT
MARALAL
Lake Bogoria Hotel
C51
LAKE BOGORIA N.R.
Lake Bogoria Hot Springs
MARALAL
R.IMURUTI
C78
NYAHURURU
C76
B5
ELDORET A104
B5
KERICHO
MOLO
Tsuni Farm
Menengai Crater
NAKURU
LAKE NAKURU N.P.
Lion Hill Camp
C78
Lake Nakuru
Lake Nakuru Lodge
Delamere Camp
Lake Elmenteita Lodge
Lake Elmenteita
River House
GILGIL
Malu Farm
NAIVASHA
A104
Lake Naivasha
HELL'S GATE N.P.
LONGONOT N.P.
B3 MASAI
B3
LIMURU
A104
NAIROBI

Crater Lake Sanctuary

A vivid green lake has formed in the caldera of an extinct volcano. This is a peaceful and remote spot with lovely views. Entrance Fee.

Mount Longonot

This extinct volcano (2776 m/9105 ft.) has a path to the top and around the rim. There are magnificent views. Security is an issue. See page 387 for more information on the national park.

Elmenteita Weavers

Attractive and colorful handwoven items (kikoi, cushion covers, shawls etc.) as well as other locally produced handicrafts. Located next to the Lake Naivasha Club.

Bee's Herb Garden

It is possible to visit this herb garden with advance arrangements.

La Belle Inn

This popular and relaxed restaurant in Naivasha town serves surprisingly good food at reasonable prices. The long outdoor veranda overlooks a street busy with trucks

Lake Naivasha Club

Block Hotels, Box 40075, Nairobi
☎ *(2) 540780, FAX: (2) 545948*

This beautiful old hotel was Kenya's international air terminal just after World War II. The flying boats of British Overseas Airways landed there as they followed the Nile south and on to South Africa. Today, only glimpses of Lake Naivasha are visible through tall acacia trees at water's edge.

The hotel is centered on an elegant old house with wood floors, French doors and a long covered veranda leading to the lawns. Several wings and clusters of rooms and cottages are set in 12 hectares of cool lawns, shaded by spreading fever trees and accented by colorful gardens. Rustic wooden chairs and benches invite the traveler to relax and listen to birds and watch the grazing waterbuck. Meandering walkways lead down to a wooden gazebo built over the water, perfect for watching birds, water-life, or sunsets.

The hotel is a popular overnight transit point and is often busy with international tour groups. It provides an easy weekend getaway from Nairobi. It is also a convenient base for exploring the many attractions in the Naivasha area.

The public rooms are elegant and relaxed. The comfortable residents' lounge has a magnificent fireplace and large bay windows. The bar area is inviting with its mural of Lake Naivasha and color-washed walls with floral stencils. Located at one end of the commodious veranda, the dining room is light and bright, with a panoramic view of the grounds. On holidays and weekends lunch buffets are served on the lawns. Day visitors are required to pay a hefty club membership fee to enter the grounds.

The Lake Naivasha Club is the most convenient place on the lake for exploring Crescent Island. There is a jetty and several boats. You can be ferried to the island where you can wander freely among wild animals, or you can go on longer lake trips to enjoy the birdlife and spot hippos.

Accommodations

The hotel has 51 rooms in separate one-story wings and garden cottages. Each room has a private entrance and a small veranda with a view of the grounds. There is variation in room sizes and decor, but all have been attractively furnished, many in an English country style, some with Lamu-style beds. All have clean and pleasant bathrooms (many with bathtubs only). Each room is available for at least double occupancy. Most have two twin beds, a few have a double bed. There are mosquito nets.

An extravagant and private Lake View Cottage sits at the edge of the lake. This delightful cottage is reached by a raised wooden walkway and has a wraparound porch with panoramic views of the lake. There are two bedrooms and a spacious central living room. The decor is rustic: wooden furniture, throw rugs, and baskets of dried flowers. *Our Favorites:* Rooms 17 and 23 (for size, Lamu-style furniture and bathrooms with both tub and shower); The Lake View Cottage.

Special Offerings

Swimming pool and children's wading pool, conference/function room, souvenir and sundry shop, massage, boats and fishing rods for hire, hotel ferry service to Crescent Island, environmentalist-guided boat trip, Lake Cruiser with bar, bird walks led by an ornithologist, indoor board games, videos (wildlife and classics), excursions to local attractions. Sundowner cruises, children's activity area.

Off Notes:

The hotel can be crowded with tour groups coming and going.

Update:

We hear the hotel is looking a little worn.

Elsamere Conservation Center

Elsamere, Box 1497, Naivasha
☎ *(311) 30079*

Elsamere was once the home of Joy Adamson of *Born Free* fame. Several pleasant and bright cottages have been built on the grounds near the main house for guests. As this is a residential conservation center, guests are required to be members of the conservation society, and the rates have been kept very reasonable.

The conservation center is beautifully situated under huge old trees on a grassy slope at the edge of Lake Naivasha. There are lovely views through the trees and across the water. In the main house there is a Joy Adamson memorial room and a separate video room with an extensive library of conservation and wildlife videos. Communal meals are taken in the main house at long tables. You might find yourself sitting next to someone doing research on the lake or the nearby Hell's Gate National Reserve. There are areas for relaxing and reading, a wide veranda, and lots of conservation magazines and materials.

It is particularly relaxing and pleasant sitting out on the lawn, listening to the birds, and watching the resident troupe of black and white Colobus monkeys cavorting in the grounds. There are nature trails along the edge of the lake and on higher ground across the road, where you can see many wildflowers and get good views of the lake. It is possible to rent boats to explore this end of the lake.

Elsamere can handle 15–18 guests in three cottages. Each cottage has a veranda and faces towards the lake. The rooms are bright and attractive and have en suite bathrooms. Our Favorites: #6 and #8 for space and view. Guests may also stay in the main house in the Joy Adamson bedroom.

In addition to overnight guests, Elsamere attracts day visitors who may come for lunch or a traditional tea on the lawn. They are invited to watch the film *The Joy Adamson Story* and to visit the memorial room. Lunches should be booked in advance. There is a gift shop. No pool.

Safariland Club, Ltd.

Safariland Club Ltd., Box 72, Naivasha
☎ *(311) 20241, Telex: 39051 Safarclub*

Safariland is the only other large hotel on the shores of Lake Naivasha. It has a fine setting overlooking the lake. A wide range of rooms and cottages are scattered over the spacious grounds. Most cry out for maintenance and decor. Hotel staff spoke of renovations and expansions to come, including a golf course and health spa. At the moment there is a pool, an unkempt tennis court, an aviary, horses for riding, boats for hire and conference facilities. Safariland Club can accommodate 114, and there is a campground next door.

Crater Lake Camp

Mythos Ltd., Box 57683, Nairobi
☎ *(2) 333569, FAX: (2) 216391*

Crater Lake Camp offers luxury accommodations on the tree-lined shores of this unusual jade green volcanic lake. The walls of the crater encircle the camp and the lake, giving an enclosed sense of privacy and isolation. To reach the camp you walk down attractively built rustic steps—a great many of them.

Built under giant fever trees and facing the lake are eight attractively furnished tents and two wooden bandas. The accommodations are romantic and private. You climb stairs up to your spacious "tent" which is on a raised wooden platform, has a thatched roof and a nice stone bathroom. From the rocking chairs on your veranda and from your bed you look out towards the peaceful lake and the steep crater walls beyond. There are some particularly nice touches such as the use of carved acacia and chunks of obsidian in the construction. Colorful bed covers, decoratively painted clay pots and unusual roofs (thatch lined with hessian) all add to the charm of the place. There are dressing gowns in the bathroom and mineral water by the bed.

The pleasant bar and dining area are fronted by a large open-sided veranda which looks out over the lake. There are chunky wooden chairs with big cushions and day beds for resting out on the lawn. Guests can take a walk along the edge of the lake and there is a wooden jetty with steps into the lake for those bent on a swim. The bird life is incredible—hosts of waders are in the shallows and swifts skim the water. At certain times of year pink flamingos add a surreal touch to the vivid green of the lake. Black and white colobus monkeys cavort in the trees and wake you in the morning with their strange calls echoing over the water.

The camp's owner, Yvonne Lury, is known for her cooking and enjoys chatting with her guests. It is possible to take escorted walks on the plains of the historical Ndabibi Estate—home to a variety of game including giraffe, eland and cheetah. Lady Delamere and her two husbands are buried on a panoramic outcrop on the estate. An early morning walk (for the surefooted) around the rim of the crater offers

ovely views over the plains and escarpments beyond and down into the peaceful cra-
er below. Night game drives are also offered.

Crater Lake Camp is a wonderfully tranquil and romantic spot—a perfect place to
low down and recharge.

Accommodation:

Eight tents, some with double and some with twin beds. The two bandas each have
two beds and two bunk beds—handy for families but a little darker than the tents. En
suite bathrooms with showers and plenty of hot water. *Best Bet:* #3 has the best view.

ff Notes:

The many steps make this unsuitable for the aged or infirm.

Kongoni Game Valley Ranch

Kongoni Game Valley Ranch, Box 15026, Nairobi
☎ *(2) 890184, FAX: (2) 890096*

You become one of the "privileged few" when you stay at the Kongoni Game Val-
ey Ranch. The elegance of the Brighetti ranch house and its dramatic setting make
his a very special place.

The Kongoni Game Valley Ranch has been home to the Bruno Brighetti Family
or the last 25 years. The ranch house is on a hilltop overlooking Lake Naivasha and
he surrounding volcanic peaks. The romance of the place begins in 1901 with a
rench Marquis who built this home in Africa for his new American bride. They lived

there happily until the early 1940s. They are both buried in a secluded part of the garden where the view they loved is absolutely breathtaking.

When you come to Kongoni Game Valley Ranch, you come as Gianna's personal guests. She welcomes you to her home with grace, warmth and enthusiasm. She takes pleasure in the fact that she herself has personally decorated every room. There is an eclectic mix which creates a harmonious and interesting effect. You want to browse slowly through her home looking at everything: Lamu furniture from the coast, Oriental rugs, impala trophies, brass pots filled with dried grasses, books piled on low tables, and shell collections. Watch for the Kongoni motif—the distinctive outline of this rather peculiar looking antelope—which is repeated here and there on firescreens, ashtrays and glassware.

The long, low stone house, with its ochre-tiled roof stands in a wide expanse of mowed lawns and tended gardens. It all feels very established and well-cared for—there is an aura of quality. The house is built around a central courtyard. The communal living and dining rooms overlook the lake and open out to a wide veranda furnished with commodious wicker furniture and cushions. Guests are encouraged to relax in this restful spot and enjoy the magnificent view.

Below, shining beyond its fringe of acacia trees is the lake framed by extinct volcanoes and the soaring sides of the Rift Valley. A forest of primeval euphorbia contrasts with the clipped lawns and English style flower beds of the garden.

Meals at Kongoni are memorable: intimate tables, garden flowers, views from the sunroom at breakfast, cozy candlelight inside at night. The food is wonderful. You can smell the bread baking; pizza arrives fresh from the oven. The emphasis is on gourmet Italian cooking, and the pasta and ice cream are homemade. Gianna jokes that the "Big Five" at Kongoni Valley Ranch are parmesan cheese, olive oil, capers, risotto, and pasta—mouth-watering.

Guests can take a walk at the lake shore or go boating. You are likely to see a wide variety of birds and perhaps a wide-open toothy yawn from a hippo. You may decide simply to sit on the veranda in cushioned comfort and absorb the beauty and peace.

Quotes

"In this beauty we have to be silent."—Gianna leading early morning game walk.

Accommodations

Kongoni can accommodate up to 26 guests. Every guest room has been furnished by Gianna. The many personal touches remind you that you are in a private home...a squash racquet in a cupboard, a family photograph on the wall. The bedrooms each have a different atmosphere, a unique "theme"; all are attractive and comfortable. Each room has a rather charming and old-fashioned bathroom, many with turn-of-the-century European fixtures, including bidet. Most rooms open onto the central courtyard, but some are in separate cottages or have private outside entrances. Some have fireplaces, and one even has an en suite sauna.

Kongoni Valley Ranch has recently opened another house very near the lake with beautiful water views. Though separate, this house is still on ranch property and can accommodate a private party of up to seven guests in one single and three double bedrooms. It is fully catered and can enjoy all the activities and facilities of the ranch.

Kongoni Game Conservancy

La Pieve Ltd., Box 209, Naivasha
☎ *(311) 20792, FAX: (311) 30353*

A small lodge and tented camp is being built on land previously belonging to Kongoni Game Valley Ranch and now owned by the Zwager family. The primary focus is on conservation, and the plan is to introduce a variety of endangered species to the wildlife already on the Conservancy. New additions include six white rhino, striped hyena, Besia oryx and Grevy's zebra. There is reputed to be 5500 head of game on this 18,000 acre property including cheetah and 20 leopard. No lion or elephant.

The country here is magnificent. It stretches from the shores of Lake Naivasha, where you can see hippo and a multitude of birds, up to the high open plateaus with herds of plains game and vistas of range after range of mountain peaks and volcanic remains. The network of roads is being extended and improved, and waterholes for the animals are being landscaped. There are electric fences and many rangers to help protect the wildlife.

The conservancy is being managed by Marcus Russell. He and Annabelle also care for a range of orphaned animals with the objective of reintroducing as many as possible to the wild. When we visited there were cheetah, baby buffalo, kongoni, zebra, warthog, a baby aardvark and an adorable and friendly clawless otter. Most were interacting very well with each other, with us, and with the camp dogs.

For added privacy and exclusivity, the small tented camp and the lodge are being built in different places. Each will cater for only eight guests at a time, guaranteeing a very personal experience.

The tented camp, called Nyati (Buffalo) Camp is closer to the lake and has been built in thornbush country. Tents are rustic with separate long drop toilets and safari showers. The lodge, to be called Chui (leopard) Lodge, is being constructed of stone and thatch under a stand of giant candelabra with beautiful views of hills and valleys.

Guests can go on game drives, enjoy meals out in the bush and go out on Lake Naivasha in a boat. It sounds like Kongoni Game Conservancy may well qualify for a Hat rating when it is properly up and running. Check it out.

Loldia House

Musiara Ltd. (Governor's Camps) Box 48217, Nairobi
☎ *(2) 331871, FAX: (2) 726427*
e-mail: govscamp@africaonline.co.ke

This old-fashioned stone house with views across Lake Naivasha has a supremely peaceful setting sheltered by giant wild fig trees and surrounded by lawns and flowering shrubs. Loldia House is on the cattle ranch of Rick and Bette Hopcraft and was built in the 1940's by Rick's grandfather with the help of Italian prisoners of war.

Today Loldia House is open to guests and run by Musiara Ltd. (Governor's Camps)—perfect hosting, wonderful food, and attention to every comfort. One of the senior members of the Musiara team is your host. The attentive resident manager, Peter Njoroge, who was described in *Country Living* as "probably the world's best butler," makes sure you are extremely well-cared for throughout your stay.

Loldia House is built of rough-hewn lava rock around a central grass courtyard in the up-country Kenyan style. There is a wide, welcoming veranda along the lake side of the house. From its shady coolness you have wonderful views across the long sweep of the lawn and the shimmering lake with Mt. Longonot rising dramatically beyond. Comfortable chairs are set out on the lawn under trees and a croquet set beckons.

Inside the house, there is an aura of earlier days. The paneled sitting room is cozy and rather dark with comfortable sofas and chairs, a fireplace and a grand piano. A large abstract mural adds interest to the dining room.

In the main house there are two double bedrooms with en suite bathrooms and two singles. The master bedroom is spacious and has views of the lake. Enjoy the old-fashioned claw-foot bathtub. There are two more double rooms in a small guest cot

age near the main house. The cottage is surrounded by flowers and also has good
views of the lake. The rooms have been attractively decorated and are cool and pleasant with high ceilings and lovely old windows. Together, the house and cottage can
accommodate up to 10 guests.

In addition, guests have the choice of staying in a luxurious but rustic cottage
built high on a cliff, near the home of Rick and Bette Hopcraft and a short drive up
the hill behind Loldia House. Up to six guests can stay here and have the option of
complete privacy—they can even take their meals here if they wish. This large rondavel is beautifully and imaginatively built of local stone and timber. The sitting
room has a high vaulted papyrus ceiling, a large fireplace and opens out onto a
veranda which has dramatic views of the lake. There are two large bedrooms downstairs, each with en suite bathroom and one loft bedroom upstairs with no loo, but a
simply marvelous view.

Loldia never feels crowded, and activities and meal schedules can be arranged to
suit the guests. The meals we sampled were delicious and beautifully presented and
served.

There are a variety of activities to choose from, both on the ranch or further afield.
A very knowledgeable ornithologist/botanist can take you on walks and will accompany you on boat rides on the lake. Loldia owns two motorized boats—a canoe with
a shade canopy and a colorfully painted sailboat.

> *"Being out on the water is supremely peaceful and beautiful. Wonderfully shaped hills and extinct volcanoes ring the lake and there is an amazing variety of bird life. A goliath heron stands motionless, coots busy about, and a flock of pelicans lift themselves heavily into formation. The water heaves and a hippo snout comes into view, then another, and a third. The lake changes color and mood with every shift in the light and the weather. At times it is a blue mirror reflecting puffy clouds, at others it is mud-colored and wind-whipped. Mt. Longonot can transform from floating mauve mirage in the heat of the day to sharply etched reality, every crevice accentuated in the clear evening light." (Safari Journal)*

A Loldia vehicle, complete with gourmet picnic, can take you on day trips to Hell's Gate near Naivasha, Lake Nakuru National Park, the forested Aberdares or Lake Bogoria. If you are feeling particularly athletic you might opt to climb Mt. Longonot. You could choose to ride Loldia's horses or go on escorted game walks. There are still wild animals on the ranch—buffalo, antelope, ostriches—and hippos regularly graze on the lawns at night. Perhaps you'd like to do a spot of fishing, or end a perfect day with sundowners on the lake.

There is an airstrip suitable for a twin-engine plane.

Mundui

Bush Homes of East Africa Ltd., Box 56923, Nairobi
☎ *(2) 571647, FAX: (2) 571665*

Past the southern end of Lake Naivasha, on the adjoining small lake, lies the elegant and beautiful Mundui Estate. The long dirt road leading to the house is ablaze with bougainvillea. The main house and grand two-story cottage are fronted by wide lawns partly shaded by trees with enormous spread. There is bright color in the shrubs and gardens which reach to the shimmering lake. Coming upon this scene for the first time leaves you silent or running for a camera. Mundui offers the best shore view of Lake Naivasha waters we've found.

This is the home of Sarah and Andrew Cole, the Earl and Countess Enniskillen. (Yes, dig into your "Out of Africa"—the Cole family has played quite a role in Kenya's history.) Sarah greets with a welcoming smile—you are at ease. An immensely artistic and capable woman, she is the main force behind the beauty of Mundui and its relaxed perfection. She has created rooms with taste and flair, adding the artistic decorative paint effects herself. Hats and books abound, pale cream colors predominate. There are wonderful wooden floors, colorful handmade quilts, and an impressive collection of elephant statuary in various sizes and colors.

Guests stay in the "Cottage" adjacent to the main house. This lovely double story building with its rather flat and formal facade was originally built by an Austrian as a hunting lodge for his friends. On the upper floor are two bedrooms and one bathroom, with a second bathroom downstairs. Below, an enormous living room is light and airy with high ceiling and huge fireplace. Guests have the whole cottage exclusively to themselves. The Coles do not combine different parties of guests.

"This is a home and they are houseguests," says Sarah, "but they can spend as much or as little time with us as they wish."

There is a private, enclosed swimming pool set between the houses. Early morning tea is served in bed or outside so you can enjoy the birds. Breakfast is on the veranda, perhaps after an early morning walk in the private Mundui game sanctuary. Mundui has 1200 acres of mainly open, rolling grasslands dotted with thorn trees. Plains game is plentiful, and 254 species of birds have been identified here. Views are spectacular all around—extinct volcanos, the Rift Escarpment and the lake. You can putter about in a quiet boat, siesta before enjoying an English tea with scones, or arrange for something more active like a trip to Hell's Gate Game Reserve, Elsamere, or Lake Nakuru National Park. You might end the day with drinks under a full moon, a three-course dinner with wine, and neighbors invited for good conversation and to add more local color to the table. (A 900 meter private airstrip is a boon to fly-in guests) Exclusivity, elegance, and beauty at a price.

THE RIFT VALLEY

Kiangazi

Kiangazi, Box 719, Naivasha
☎ *(311) 21052, FAX:(311) 21059*

Kiangazi means a "hot dry season." However, when you drive through the gates of Kiangazi you leave hot and dry behind and come upon thick green lawns, brilliant flowerbeds, and the cooling sound of water falling over rocks into the sculptured swimming pool. Cesare and Daphne Bellingeri carefully chose this spot on which to build their spacious stone house. It was hard work flattening the area for a house, but well worth it for the soul-satisfying views and the fact that wild animals pass right next to the house as they come down to the lake.

Following the old settler style, the Bellingeris' house is built around an open grassy courtyard. A huge living room with fireplace to match opens onto a wonderfully wide veranda. The view takes in the zebra and kongoni grazing by the waterhole below, the silver of the acacia-lined lake, and beyond, a cluster of volcanic cones and the mountains of the Rift Valley rising blue and purple on the horizon.

Kiangazi accommodates only a handful of guests who stay in a separate guest cottage to the side of the main house. There are two rooms for doubles and one single. All are en suite with attractive bathrooms using natural materials. A veranda stretches in front of the cottage and is edged by colorful rock gardens—playground of jewel-bright birds.

Kiangazi is a homestay in the best sense of the word. Daphne and Cesare are around to make you feel at home and help plan your day. At night you join them and other guests for drinks and conversation around the fire and then for dinner in the dining room. You feel like privileged guests in this lovely and relaxed setting. During the day, however, you can be as private as you choose. A separate table was set for us on the veranda for breakfast and for lunch. Meals were tasty and well-prepared.

When we arrived from Nairobi in the heat of the day, we headed directly for the pool in its garden setting, and stretched out on comfortable loungers. A tray with fresh juice, cold beers, and tasty snacks "magically" appeared at pool side.

You can walk in the hills behind Kiangazi or cross the road to enjoy the bird and animal life along the lakeshore. On one of our walks a tame young kongoni and his zebra buddy (both orphans raised by Daphne) skittered and played along beside us. In the late afternoon we went alone to the edge of the lake. Seven giraffes ambled by, hippos snorted in the shallow water and waterbuck, gazelle and kongoni grazed at the edge of the lake. Water birds waded along the shore and a flock of flamingos flew low overhead in the last light.

Special Offerings:

At an extra charge the following can be arranged: game drives to Hells Gate (with picnic breakfast or lunch) or Crater Lake Sanctuary. Night game drives, boat rides to see birds and hippos, and visits to Elmenteita Weavers or Elsamere Conservation Center. Full day excursions can be arranged to Eburru Mountains and Forest, Lake Nakuru, Aberdare National Park, Mt. Longonot and Crescent Island.

Longonot Ranch House

Safaris Unlimited (Africa) Ltd., Box 24181, Nairobi
☎ *(2) 891168, FAX: (2) 891113*

Longonot Game Ranch is on the slopes of Mt. Longonot near Lake Naivasha in the Rift Valley. This private ranch of 32,000 hectares is home to a wide variety of wild animals. The traditional ranch house, with its long verandas and central courtyard, sits on the top of an open hill. There are views all around and a sense of wonderful space and distance. On one side rises the dormant volcano, Longonot, and on the other, you look into the distance towards shimmering Lake Naivasha.

As you drive away from the lake and up the long dusty road to the ranch house, you leave cultivation and civilization behind. There are gazelle at the side of the road, and the grass is bleached and dry. The ranch house is dramatically sited on top of a rise. There are a few trees around the house, and a wide open lawn leads to a natural sunken rock garden filled with cactus and aloes. Beyond, the veld continues—waving yellow grass and thorn trees. It is peaceful and isolated, a place to take a deep breath and feel on top of the world.

Quotes

"This place is heaven for landscape junkies."
"I saw two cheetah on the dirt road."

The ranch house is at 2134 meters above sea level. It is currently owned by Tony Church and was originally built by Martha Gellhorn, one of Ernest Hemingway's wives.

The ranch can cater to a maximum of twelve people. It is very personalized, relaxed and casual. Guests stay either in the main ranch house (four double bedrooms) or in the separate cottage (two double bedrooms). The rooms are attractively decorated in country floral prints, and each has a bathroom en suite. The living/dining room is friendly with a large stone fireplace and comfortable chairs. Most of your time, however, will be spent outdoors—walking, riding horses, or eating out on the veranda or the lawns.

Horseback riding is one of the main attractions of Longonot Ranch. There are stables and plenty of mounts. You ride over hills and down onto plains, practically touching giraffes and herds of antelope. The scenery is stunning—you have views of

THE RIFT VALLEY

Hell's Gate Gorge, Lake Naivasha and mountains in the distance. Side trips to Hell's Gate or around the lake can be arranged. You set the pace and choose the activities.

You can head off walking in any direction enjoying the amazing space, the views and the wildlife all around. Crest a ridge and you may see herds of Zebra, Kongoni and Grant's gazelle. Eland and Giraffe are plentiful. There is a small hide not far from the ranch house where you can watch animal visitors to a small waterhole below.

For an especially memorable evening you can arrange for a bush sundowner followed by a night game drive. In the late afternoon light you walk or ride to the sundowner spot at the edge of a lava flow. The crevices of Mt. Longonot are clearly etched and the game seems spotlit. A campfire awaits you with safari chairs in a circle, drinks and snacks. As the sun sets you can watch the stars appear and listen for the eerie calls of hyena. Drive back to Longonot Ranch House with a bright spotlight to catch the eyes of the animals you pass—a spring hare bounces along, a jackal passes, gazelle stare.

Although this is a private Ranch house, it is not someone's permanent home. You will be hosted by your tour operator or, if you are traveling independently, by the ranch manager. The ranch feels as though it belongs to you and your group.

Off note:
    Avoid the bedroom next to the kitchen if you want to sleep in!

Olerai House

Oria Douglas-Hamilton, Box 54667, Nairobi
☎ *(2) 334868*

This charming, flower-covered farmhouse is the former home of Oria and Ian Douglas-Hamilton (renowned elephant conservationists). In its wide expanse of emerald lawn, the house is partly shaded by the enormous acacia trees for which it is named. Olerai is the Masai name for the Naivasha Acacia Tree. Although the house is quite a distance from Lake Naivasha and the water obscured by reeds, the setting is bucolic, timeless, and peaceful. There is a wonderful sense of space and green. The distinctive volcanic shape of Mt. Longonot, purple and blue with distance, adds a certain African drama.

This is a place to unwind, rest, read and enjoy your companions. The house, which easily sleeps up to ten people, is ideal for a large family or a group of friends. The living/dining room is spacious and comfortable, with a cozy fireplace, casual cushioned seating areas and a big round dining table. There are homey touches of fresh flowers, magazines on tables, a drinks table set up in the evening.

Quotes

> *"We wanted to create true Kenyan hospitality—it's like coming to a homestead…"* Oria Douglas-Hamilton.
>
> *"My family would love it here. What a perfect weekend break from Nairobi."*

Four separate double bedrooms are arranged around a central garden courtyard. Two of these rooms are on split levels with charming upstairs lofts and extra beds. All four have bathrooms. The Douglas-Hamiltons plan to add a couple more cottage bedrooms in the garden. Since this was a family home, it retains its feeling of comfort and individual character. There are dramatic murals in some of the bathrooms, and there is something whimsical about the loft bedrooms with their mosquito netted beds and casement windows. You feel as though you have come to a weekend getaway cottage—casual and informal.

Olerai House offers complete privacy. There is no "host" hovering or joining you for meals. However, very capable and unobtrusive staff make sure you are completely comfortable. The meals are memorable and are served when and where you want them—lovely to eat outdoors under those giant trees. There are wonderful fresh soups, tempting pastas, roast lamb and decadent desserts. Not the place for a diet weekend!

If you feel the need to work off some of this lazing about and eating, you can go on walks. There is someone to guide you in the surrounding hills, and you can go for a bird walk near the lake. You come back to a fire and tea and more irresistible food.

The Douglas-Hamiltons now live in Sirocco House which was built in the early 1930s by Oria's parents. This unique art deco house is only a short walk from Olerai House. It is possible to make arrangements to visit Sirocco House for tea or sundowners.

You can buy soda and beer, but remember to bring your own wine and spirits.

When you leave Olerai House you can stock up on fresh farm produce.

Safari Journal

Wednesday ~ lunch

Feeling warm and lethargic and at peace with the world.
I can hear bees buzzing and cows mooing. Everything looks
green and slightly hazy. and there is such a "telephoto" expansiveness
in the distance. i "zoom" back to the foreground ~ a long table
spread with a patterned cloth. a vase of bright flowers.
platters of food and glasses of red wine catching the sun.
And friends ~ women in floppy straw hats ~ we should be
part of a Fellini movie set

Special Offerings

For an additional charge you can have farm walks with breakfast, tea or cocktails at Sirocco House, walks in Crater Lake Sanctuary with picnic or cocktails, ox-wagon ride and lunch, picnic lunch at Hell's Gate National Park, Mt. Kenya morning or evening flights.

Off Notes

Being near a lake and on a farm, insect life abounds. No lake view or access.

Lakeside House

Lakeside House, Box 1262, Naivasha
☎ *(311) 20908*

Lakeside House is a small home near the turnoff onto Moi South Lake Road. The grounds and gardens are not very grand, but you can look toward the papyrus at the edge of Lake Naivasha from the veranda. June Shaw is the hostess: she treats her guests like family. Hospitality seems part of the decor in the dining room and in the blue and chintz sitting room.

Guests sleep in one double room in the main farmhouse and in a nearby cottage. The cottage rooms have en suite shower bathrooms. The rooms are very small and rather crowded with furnishings. There are some homey touches such as books, magazines and instant coffee/tea trays.

June and her family can help guests locate boats and horses to rent and plan day excursions in the area. June says you can walk to Crescent Island through the adjoining property.

Morendat House

Morendat House, Box 299, Naivasha
☎ *(311) 20041*

Just off the main Nakuru Road, this gracious old Lake Naivasha house of white-washed stone is the home of Giulia Bisleti. It has a convenient position between Lake Naivasha and Lake Nakuru. She wants her guests to feel that Morendat House is their own home base in Kenya.

The huge garden is fragrant with orange trees; the veranda is cool with over-hanging plants; the living room is spacious with elegant arches. She has furnished her home with many polished antiques, and objets d'art. A central stone fireplace gleams with copper pots and utensils. Her decor is eclectic with an enriched country elegance.

There are two double bedrooms in the house, both graciously furnished, both with private bathroom including bidet. A third double bedroom is in a private cottage at the side of a pleasant swimming pool.

All meals are included, but guests are asked to bring their own wines and spirits. Because of the antique glass and a serious commitment of quiet relaxation, younger children are not invited. Although the property extends to the shore of Lake Naivasha, there are no views of the lake from the house.

Gilgil

There is not much of interest for the tourist in this small town between Naivasha and Nakuru.

River House

Bunson Travel Service Ltd., Box 45456, Nairobi
☎ *(2) 221992, FAX: (2) 723599*

This private country house in Gilgil belongs to the Barratts. River House is best known for its cuisine—Nann Barratt is a trained cordon bleu chef.

River House is surrounded by well-tended lawns and flower beds. Indigenous forest edges a stream which runs through this 20 hectares property and there are shady paths for pleasant walks. The vegetable gardens are amazing—ordered rows of healthy produce just waiting to be transformed into the most memorable of dishes.

Guests stay right in the house. There are two double bedrooms each with private bathroom. The living room has a huge fireplace which is lit on cool nights. Pictures by a talented family member grace the walls and dog baskets line the wide passage. There are oriental rugs, family antiques, frills, and memorabilia. You are treated as a family guest. Nann is a warm and friendly person who loves to talk and make you welcome.

Golf and tennis are available nearby. River House can be used as a base to explore the Rift Valley lakes or the Aberdares. You can also arrange to go to River House for lunch if you are en route to somewhere else.

Lake Elmenteita

Most of this shallow soda lake is on private land—part of the Delamere Estate's Soysambu property. There is game in the bush around the lake, and flamingos and pelicans congregate along the shores.

Lake Elmenteita Lodge

Lake Elmenteita Lodge, Box 70559, Nairobi
☎ *(2) 224998, FAX: (2) 230962*

Lake Elmenteita Lodge has been created around the original home of the English settler Galbraith Cole. Built in 1916, this typical colonial home is of red brick with an internal courtyard, paneled walls and a shady veranda. Now the main building houses a rather functional sitting and dining room, a bar and a small conference room.

Guest cottages have been built in the garden behind the house. A large terrace with swimming pool looks towards Lake Elmenteita. The lake is home to lesser flamingos and is a stop for migrating birds. Guests can go on guided bird watching walks and ox wagon safaris. There is horse riding within the reserve.

Accommodation:
33 bedrooms each with private bathroom.

Off Notes:
Cottages behind the main house have no view. Furnishings and atmosphere do not reflect the history of the original home.

Delamere Camp

Savannah Camps & Lodges, Box 48019, Nairobi
☎ *(2) 331191, FAX: (2) 330698*

Just one hour by road from Nairobi, Delamere Camp has one of the most beautiful sites in Kenya. A small tented camp, it is located within the Soysambu Wildlife Sanctuary on the shore of Lake Elmenteita, deep in Kenya's Great Rift Valley. The lake is often pink with thousands of lesser and greater flamingos, and the near and far skyline is mysterious and beautifully primeval with the weathered remains of broken volcanic peaks. The surrounding forest and bush are very green; they tend to soften the harshness of the volcanic rock and ash that are part of this setting.

Because the sanctuary is located within the vast estates of the current Lord Delamere (Hugh, the Fifth Baron), the camp feels very private, separate from outside life. It is a birder's paradise: besides flamingos, there are also great white pelicans and scores of other water and land birds. You can go on game or botanical drives in the camp's open-air four-wheel-drive vehicles. Camp guides or naturalists will help you to spot and identify game. They will also identify plants and trees and show how they are used by the local people (the sap from an aloelike plant seemed to heal my cut finger in just a few hours!). Guides can lead you on walks and take you for night game drives in search of bush baby, aardvark and zorilla. You may also have a close-up view of elusive game and birdlife from several camp game blinds nearby.

On a cliff rising above the lake, natural stone benches and tables create the perfect place for grand views of the lake and the volcanoes—especially spectacular at sunrise or sunset. This high view point is perfect for sundowners with hot brochettes of gazelle cooked over an open fire. You could also arrange to have brunch or a picnic there.

The camp's 16 tents and main lodge are spread out on a shallow hillside sloping down to the lake. The main lodge is a rather utilitarian concrete and wood structure with one side open to view the lake. Small tables are arranged in the dining area at one end; a small bar is at the other. Rush sofas and chairs form a lounge area around a central fireplace, which smokes a bit as it tries to fight off the chill night breezes. When you check in, be prepared to sign a waiver releasing the camp from any liability for theft or injury.

Accommodations

The individual tents are raised on large concrete pads with very large concrete shower bathrooms attached to the rear of the tent. The tents are spacious with plenty of room for two—good twin beds, wardrobes, desks, shelves. Windows are large with zip covers over screens. Tents are sprayed at night, but there are no mosquito nets. Floors are unpainted concrete: the effect is utilitarian but comfortable. Safari chairs furnish the outdoor cement porch. Hammocks have been rigged in shady spots (Bliss...zzz). *Best views*: tents # 6, 8, 10, 12, 14, 16. Tent #16 is a suite. Seven kilometers away is a treehouse which sleeps four in bunk beds—there is a bathroom, but no electricity. There is a small waterhole below, an open deck on the roof, and a battery-powered spotlight for night game viewing—a private adventure. Best of all is the bush breakfast the following morning.

Other Facilities

Souvenir and sundry shop, safe at reception.

Malu Farm

Archer's Tours and Travel Ltd. Box 40097, Nairobi
☎ *(2) 223131, FAX: (2) 212656*

Malu is a 1700 acre farm and fishing camp in the heart of the Kenyan Highlands. It lies at the base of the Kinangop Escarpment, sixty miles from Nairobi. This is lovely and varied countryside with wide-open vistas south towards Lake Naivasha, fern-edged bubbling streams, thick indigenous forests and the meandering Malewa river known for good fishing.

Guests stay in self-contained cottages (2) each with two en suite bedrooms, a spacious living/dining room with fireplace, a small kitchen and a veranda facing the open view. The cottages have been attractively furnished with antiques and oriental rugs. Malu staff can prepare your meals to serve in your private cottage. We dined deliciously on trout we'd caught only hours before.

Guests also have the choice of staying in a high wooden Tree House at the edge of the river. This rustic tree house is built at some distance from the rest of the camp and can accommodate two people. It has a flush toilet and shower, but no electricity. The bird life in the surrounding forest is superb, there are black and white colobus and red-backed sykes monkeys, and it's only steps to cast a line into the river.

A dramatic main lodge building has been erected in a grassy meadow with views towards the forested hills behind. Built out of natural materials, it is circular and has a high thatched roof and roll down canvas walls.

On Malu Farm, guests can take walks, fish for rainbow trout, ride horses or mountain bikes, or simply relax in this isolated wilderness.

Free transport to and from Nairobi is included in the rate —driving up to Malu Farm from the Naivasha-Nakuru road is a tough haul and requires a 4-wheel drive vehicle. Fly-fishing equipment is not included in the rate.

Optional Excursions:
4-wheel drive safari to Lord Delamere's wildlife sanctuary, boat excursion on Naivasha Lake, trips to Hell's Gate National Park, Mt. Longonot, and Lake Nakuru.

THE RIFT VALLEY

Nakuru

Nakuru is the capital of the Rift Valley Province and is the fourth largest town in Kenya. It is noisy, dusty and chaotic. Tourists go to this area for the Lake Nakuru National Park which is best known for its flamingos. There are also large flocks of pelicans. The parkland surrounding the lake has acacia and euphorbia forests as well as areas of grassland and rocky cliffs. It is home to many animals including waterbuck, leopards, and Rothschild giraffe. Surrounded by an electric fence, the park is also a sanctuary for black rhinos brought here from other areas. Outside the park, on the other side of the town, rises Menengai, a huge extinct volcano. Hardly recognizable as such from below, the view when you reach the top is breathtaking. You can drive to a lookout point and gaze down over an expanse of black lava and bush in the massive caldera.

Lake Nakuru Lodge

Lake Nakuru Lodge, Box 70559, Nairobi
☎ *(2) 224998, Telex: 22658*

High on a hilltop in the southeast corner of Lake Nakuru National Park, this small lodge enjoys a particularly commanding view of the lake. Although the lodge has room for 120 guests, it can fill up fast with tour groups. A new all-suite deluxe wing is very private and has sweeping views from individual verandas. Older standard rooms in small bandas may be disappointing. Your first impression of the lodge is color—rampant bougainvillea lines all the stone pathways, and the many resident birds flit iridescent feathers.

From reception (cool drinks, a natural decor of rough wood and stone), you walk down more garden pathways with guest bandas on each side. The heart of the lodge is the dining area, view terrace, and swimming pool. The view is wonderful—you look down the hill and across a good bit of the park to the lake with its fluffy edging of pink flamingos. Frequently, other park animals are also on view. They often come right up to the low rock wall at the edge of the lawn.

Accommodations

Standard rooms in little peaked-roof bandas with en suite bathrooms are sparsely furnished for double occupancy. Beds are hard, bathrooms have seen better days, but work. Rooms are sprayed, beds have mosquito nets. Standards of cleanliness are not high. *Our Favorites*: New deluxe wing suites.

Sarova Lion Hill

Sarova Lion Hill, Box 30680, Nairobi
☎ *(2) 333248, FAX: (2) 211472*

Sarova Lion Hill is in Lake Nakuru National Park. Its location on a small plateau gives views of the lake. You can sit outside on the terrace of the rustic Rift Valley Bar to enjoy the gardens or the lake view—there is even a telescope for up-close viewing. From the Flamingo Restaurant patio, which overlooks the swimming pool, you also have views of the lake and the hills beyond.

Accommodations

In contrast to the surroundings, the lodge buildings are disappointingly stark and functional. The lodge can accommodate up to 150 guests in two-room units scattered on the hillside near the main lodge. Each room has en suite bathroom and private veranda, some with panoramic views of the lake. The rooms are not outstanding. There are six nonsmoking rooms and a surprisingly elegant honeymoon suite with two bedrooms. There are two new luxury suites. Each has a private lounge with fireplace, desk and a mini-bar. *Best Choice for View of the Lake*: #60–65 on the hilltop.

Special Offerings

The lodge has a sauna, boutique, conference center for 80 and dancers to entertain the guests at night.

Off Notes

You are likely to share your safari buffet with noisy tour groups.

Rongai and Molo

Traveling northwest of Nakuru you pass Rongai before climbing the western escarpment of the Rift Valley to Molo. Approximately 2500 meters high, the garden-green town of Molo has highland meadows and flocks of sheep. Molo lamb is known throughout Kenya for its fine quality.

Deloraine

Bush Homes of East Africa Ltd., Box 56923, Nairobi
☎ *(2) 571647, FAX: (2) 571665*

Deloraine is a grand colonial home built in 1920 by a prominent settler, Lord Francis Scott. Until her death in 1992, Pamela Scott, a well-known livestock breeder lived in the house. Today, Deloraine is the home of Tristan and Lucinda Voorspuy, who are best known for their riding safaris, and who have opened their home to small safari groups. Both are accomplished riders and polo players, and Lucinda is a pleasant and accommodating hostess.

Situated at 6000 ft. on the western side of the Rift Valley at Rongai, Deloraine is in the middle of a 5000 acre commercial farm. The imposing double-story stone building has a shaded veranda running the full length of the upper story and tall stone archways leading from the lower veranda to steps which descend to broad lawns and lovely gardens. There is a croquet lawn and a tennis court.

On the farm are about 40 horses—some of which are used on the riding safaris. There are also polo ponies which Deloraine guests can ride if they want to explore the farm or the surrounding hillsides.

The Voorspuys have been slowly redecorating the interior of Deloraine. The house has charm and some lovely features. It exudes a sense of the faded grandeur of Colonial Kenya—a shabby chic. The ground floor is the best feature of the house, with spacious living and dining rooms. The living room has high timbered ceilings, a large fireplace, comfortable chairs and sofas and many prints hanging on cheerful yellow walls. There are three double bedrooms with bathrooms in the main house, and three more in the garden cottage.

The Voorspuys' first love and primary interest is in the private riding safaris which they operate under their company name "Offbeat Safaris," although they will host nonriding guests at Deloraine. Day trips to Lake Nakuru National Park or Lake Bogoria are an optional extra.

Juani Farm

Box 1375, Nakuru
☎ *(363) 21279*

"Juani" means a place in the sun, and Juani Farm enjoys sunshine most days of the year. Situated near Molo, this is the home of Dennis and Jane Leete. It is a typical settler, rambling old farmhouse with an ambience of colonial times. When you stay at Juani, you are the guests of the Leetes' and enjoy their beautiful surroundings.

One of the most memorable features of Juani is the magnificent garden. A breathtaking series of English flowerbeds, profuse with blooms, curve through thick green lawns. Beyond is the base of the Rift Valley with the opposite escarpment rising sheer on the horizon. During the day, meals are served outdoors in this lovely garden setting.

The farmhouse is rather charming. Several rooms have been added on over the years and outdoor passageways link some of the rooms. There are three guest bedrooms, each with fireplace and a private bathroom. These spacious rooms are cozy with collected knickknacks, bowls of wonderfully arranged flowers, and thoughtful touches such as drinking water and hand lotions. In the evening you join your hosts around the fire in their large and comfortable living room. An English-style home-cooked dinner is elegantly served.

Jane and Dennis are old "Kenya hands" and one of Dennis' hobbies is early Colonial history. Guests are sure to enjoy hearing stories of pioneer days, gold prospecting and the mau mau campaign. Dennis is also a keen fly-fisherman and rugby fan.

Juani Farm is very self-sufficient. "We make our own water and our own light." Water is heated by wood fires, and the generator goes off before midnight.

Juani is a convenient location for exploring Lake Nakuru, and it is an easy drive to Lakes Bogoria and Baringo. It is conveniently placed for those traveling to and from Uganda.

Lake Baringo

Lake Baringo is a freshwater lake. It is particularly well known for its amazing variety of birds (448 species) and is a popular destination for birders.

As is true with all the Rift Valley lakes, Baringo has its own unique character. Surrounded by harsh dry countryside, the lake has an isolated peacefulness. The water is heavily silted with soil. It is an unusual muddy-brown color which takes on dramatic tones depending on the light and weather. There are several rocky islands, and mountain ranges are visible in many directions. There is a sense of incredible space and a stark wild, beauty.

The lake is home to many hippos and crocodiles. The local tribesmen, the Njemps, fish there. You can often see them paddling in their small precarious-looking canoes made from branches of the Ambatch tree. They reckon the Baringo crocodiles are not dangerous.

It is usually extremely hot in this area. Go well prepared with hat and sun-block and take swimwear. This is a malaria area.

Most visitors to Baringo combine their stay with a trip to the neighboring Lake Bogoria National Reserve. This side trip is well worth it. Bogoria is best known for its impressive hot springs and its flamingos. This long narrow lake is beautiful—unspoiled, dominated by high steep hills and, when inhabited by thousands of flamingos, ringed with an amazing pink border. You might also be fortunate enough to see a herd of the Greater Kudu here.

THE RIFT VALLEY

Island Camp

Let's Go Travel, Box 60342, Nairobi
☎ *(2) 340331, FAX: (2) 336890*
e-mail: Letsgo.Travel@commsol.sprint.com

There is something unique and special about Island Camp—a sense of adventure and timeless Africa.

The adventure starts when you have to leave the civilized tarmac road at the Baringo Club Hotel. You then follow an unlikely and rocky track winding up to a headland parking spot. Here you leave your vehicle in the care of a Camp askari. Grab your bag, hang on to your hat, and hop aboard a motorized canoe for the 20 minute boat ride to the island.

The lake looks like mud, an unrelenting brown. The boat passes hippo—humps in the water or perhaps a pink yawning mouth and small eyes. There are several islands; your destination is Ol Kokwe, which means "place of rocks." You can see for great distances, and all around tower magnificent high hills and extinct volcanoes—ridge after ridge in dark, smoky tones of blue, purple, and grey, like an Oriental water-color. In the middle of all this water it feels dry. And hot. You'll be pleased you brought a hat.

From the Visitor's book:

> *"Superb Africa"*
> *"Slowed down to a stop. A wonderful place to be at peace."*

When you land you are greeted by shade and a welcome drink. Because the camp is built on a hill, to reach the various tents and communal places, you walk and climb along winding stone paths. There are spreading trees, exotic vegetation, bright lizards and scores of different birds. You feel the whole camp is in harmony with its setting—walls are made of round yellow and tan stones, roofs are high thatch and the tents a faded green.

There is a lot of climbing along paths and up steps. At the highest point of the camp is the swimming pool. We vote this the best positioned pool in Kenya and, in this extremely hot place, one of the most necessary. From this high vantage point, you have views across the lake to the mountains beyond. You can marvel for hours at the play of light and the movement of weather over the land and water. There is great drama about this place—an awesomeness which reminds you of man's insignificance.

Around the pool there are comfortable loungers under creeper-covered trellises. There is a large open-sided thatched lounge and bar at this level—you don't have to move for a cold drink in the heat of the day. Afternoon tea is also served here, and the place is small and intimate enough for guests to strike up conversations.

If the spirit takes you, you can be more active. The camp is at the end of quite a big island, and you can take lengthy walks—to see birds, to visit the local Njemps Village, or to hike to the hot springs at the far end of the island. Island Camp is a paradise for bird-watchers—their enthusiasm is contagious.

Popular and well worth doing are the boat trips to the marshes and up the mouth of the Molo River. These are offered morning and evening and are accompanied by a guide to help identify the birds. You will see flocks of spectacular birds, and up the river, crocodiles suddenly slither out of the reeds to sink invisibly into the brown water.

Those who like water sports will also find plenty to do. There is waterskiing and windsurfing. Plans are afoot to expand watersports at Island Camp.

The dining locations at the camp are more memorable than the meals served. When you sit in the main thatched dining area, you are at the height of tree tops. Unhindered by walls or glass, you can enjoy the breezes and look down across the lake. Sometimes, on fine evenings, barbecue dinners are served alfresco around the

THE RIFT VALLEY

pool area. With candlelight, the stars above, and the haunting notes of a Njemps reed pipe being played under a tree, there is a feeling of magic, of timelessness.

You come to Island Camp for its unique and unusual beauty, not for fancy accommodation. The tents are perfectly adequate, but are not of the same standard as luxurious tents found in some tented camps. The best thing about Island Camp tents is their position. Most have spectacular views over the lake and a nice sense of privacy. It is difficult to believe there are as many as 23 tents scattered around the camp property. Some are on the side of a steep rocky hill, some are tucked under trees, others perched on a rocky outcrop.

Accommodations

The tents have thatched shelters to help keep them cool and provide a shady veranda where you can sit on safari chairs and admire your view. Behind each tent is a solidly built functional bathroom with a flush toilet and solar heated shower. To get there you must unzip your tent and open the bathroom door. *Best bets:* #15 has a double bed, a great view, and is very private. Tents # 1 & 2 are private and have a good view.

Special Offerings

Boat trips, bird walks, walk to hot springs, waterskiing, windsurfing, pool, sundowners on neighboring island, traditional Njemps dances. Residents (on special rates) pay extra for boat ferry to island.

Off Notes

Not easy for people who would have difficulty climbing. Some people may not enjoy the host of insects and reptiles living on the island.

Lake Baringo Club

Block Hotels, Box 40075, Nairobi
☎ *(2) 540780, FAX: (2) 545948*

The Lake Baringo Club is most memorable for its beautiful gardens. After driving through the parched and rocky countryside, the club feels like an oasis of green and color. Spread along the shore of Lake Baringo, it faces lovely grounds and the lake.

In the wide lawns stand big exotic trees ablaze with flowers. A profusion of brilliant bougainvillea cascades over trellises and walls. Sturdy wooden tables with groupings of chairs are scattered around the lawns and under trees. It is all so still and hot and bright. Nothing moves except a big monitor lizard and the air busy with the sounds of birds.

The birds! They are the main attraction of this area. Some 448 species are found on and around the lake. The Baringo Club, with its resident ornithologist, is well organized to make the most of this natural attraction. Bird walks are led around the hotel grounds and on the nearby rocky cliffs. There are boat trips on the lake and to the marshy mouth of the Molo River—marvelous for water birds. Each evening a slide show on birds is presented.

Birds are not the only wildlife. There are lots of hippos in the lake. During the day you can see parts of hippos sticking out of the muddy water—backs, twirly ears, a yawning mouth. In the evening and at night, however, you might see the whole beast—grazing on the hotel lawns. You can ask for a "hippo call"—to be called when there are hippos outside. The big signs in the grounds which read "Wild Animals Are Dangerous" are there for a very good reason. Hippos are extraordinarily ornery and account for many deaths in Africa. Don't venture close.

Baringo Club has a relaxed and friendly air. The buildings are low and unobtrusive, and have been designed to take advantage of the view. With bedrooms on each side of the main building, it all looks a bit like a glorified motel covered in bougainvillea.

There is a small but pleasant swimming pool edged with stone paving. In the intense heat of this area, the pool is a real blessing.

Although the club is right on the shores of Lake Baringo, you are not conscious of being on the lake in the same way as when you stay on Ol Kokwe Island. The lovely garden, with its mature trees, obscures the wide stark vistas across the lake and hides the drama of the mountains beyond. When you stay at the club, the strange beauty and isolation of the area seems tamed and softened. Make sure you walk out to the jetty to appreciate the distances. Better yet, go on a boat trip—add some adventure.

Accommodations

There are a total of 52 bedrooms, most of which are in the "new wing." The rooms here are simple and functional with linoleum floors and high ceilings. Most have twin beds which can both be enclosed by a huge mosquito net. Each has a small bathroom with shower. There are ceiling fans and a private veranda facing the lake. The old wing is on the other side of the main building, near the swimming pool. Rooms in this wing are less uniform. The bathrooms tend to be bigger and some have bathtubs. These rooms are somewhat darker and more enclosed with lower ceilings and deeper verandas.

Special Offerings

Bird walks, boat trips, pool, games room, camel rides in the grounds, visits to the local Njemps fishing village, trips to Lake Bogoria. You can hire horses and go for escorted rides. In the campground next to the club is a shop selling colorful hand printed cotton items made by a local company called "Dry Season."

Designated as a "club," this hotel charges an entrance fee to casual visitors.

Lake Bogoria Hotel

African Tours and Hotels Ltd., Box 30471, Nairobi
☎ *(2) 336858, FAX: (2) 218109*

This is the closest hotel to Lake Bogoria with its bubbling hot springs and thousands of flamingos. It is about 20 kilometers from the hotel to the lake. The hotel can accommodate 90 people. There are standard rooms in blocks, and pleasant and spacious cottages, some with living areas. There are two swimming pools one of which is filled with natural warm spa water. The authors have not visited this hotel.

Kabarnet

The small town of Kabarnet has a spectacular setting on top of the Kamasia Massif with views in one direction down over the Rift Valley towards Lakes Baringo and Bogoria, and in the other direction down into the plunging Kerio Valley.

Kabarnet is the home town of President Arap Moi. An unusually good road winds up to Kabarnet from Marigat.

Kabarnet Hotel

African Tours & Hotels, Box 30471, Nairobi
☎ *(2) 336858, FAX: (2) 218109*

This is the main hotel in Kabarnet. It is fairly new, modern in design, and is operated by African Tours and Hotels Ltd. The only striking aspect of the Kabarnet hotel is the dramatic view over the Kerio Valley. The hotel has 30 rooms, a conference center, and a swimming pool.

CENTRAL HIGHLANDS (MT. KENYA AREA)

The Central Highlands of Kenya are an amazing geography of contrasts. The deep green of cultivated farmland gives way to the purple-gray scrub grass of high ranches where cattle, sheep and plains game graze. Mountain ranges are covered in forests with hidden trout streams. These highland streams flow to swift moving rivers that suddenly burst out and down into dramatic falls of water. Other mountains stand stark and dry, broken and weathered into moonscapes and mesas. Climbing a small rise can yield a panoramic vista of plains and plateaus rising to range after range of distant mountains. In the center, Mt. Kenya dominates.

With a base diameter of more than 150 kilometers and a height 5189 meters, Mt. Kenya is among the world's largest free-standing volcanic mountains. The equator crosses its northern slopes at 3350 meters with the mountain's twin snowcapped peaks, Batian and Nelion, brushing the sky some 17 kilometers south. Mt. Kenya has many moods—wisping clouds can cloak the peaks in mystery. Thunder and lighting can rage. Falling rain can obscure and hide even the lower slopes with curtains of water. Glinting sunshine can illuminate the peaks.

Traveling in the Central Highlands

At the equator, slight variations of altitude create enormous changes in both climate and landscape. This means that the traveler can enjoy diverse experiences and surroundings without having to cover great distances. In just a short drive you can pass from the cool, misty forest of the Aberdares to the dry Laikipia Plateau with its miles of open ranch land. When you drive around the western side of the mountain you are on a long straight road through dry, flat scrub lands. The road around the eastern side however, curves and dips in a roller-coaster course through green farms, red cliffs and rushing waterfalls.

The great variation in the scenery is also reflected in the many choices available to the traveler. There is a great range in the types of places where you can stay, as well as in the kinds of activities and experiences you can enjoy. In terms of accommodations, there are night game viewing lodges deep in indigenous forests, elegant colonial country-club type hotels, and huge private ranches where you can ride and walk among wild animals. There are even sanctuaries and national reserves where you can stay in tents or bandas and go on game drives. You could also plan climbing or fishing trips.

There are three **national parks** in this region:

The Aberdare National Park

The volcanic massif of the Aberdare Mountains is part of the eastern side of the Rift Valley. With steep hillsides and thick forests, these mountains have not been tamed into farmland. Leopard, buffalo, and elephant inhabit the forests, and on the high misty moorlands are lions and antelope. There are streams and waterfalls, magnificent views, and lots of rain. It is frequently cold and misty. Four-wheel drives are essential. The park is often closed during the wet season. See page 380 for additional information on the park.

Mt. Kenya National Park

Mt. Kenya (5189 m/17020 ft.) is the second highest mountain in Africa. Although it is right on the equator, its peaks are snow-covered all year. There are four main routes to climb the mountain and a few basic cabins and mountain huts. You are likely to see wild animals and an amazing range of unusual vegetation. The peaks of the mountain are more often than not obscured by clouds. Your best chance of seeing them is in the early morning or just before sunset. See page 387 for additional information on the park.

Meru National Park

Situated east of Mt. Kenya and over the high Nyambene Hills, this is one of the least visited national parks in Kenya. With its many streams, and higher than average rainfall, the park is luxuriant and bushy. There is long grass, a swamp and riverine for-

CENTRAL HIGHLANDS

ests. Tall distinctive doum palms add an exotic touch and contorted termite creations dot the grasslands. It is more difficult to spot animals here than in the wide open panoramas of some of the other parks. But, as a bonus, you are unlikely to see other vehicles when you are out on a game drive. It was in this area that the lioness, Elsa, heroine of *Born Free*, was released back into the wild. The park is home to many of the species found in northern Kenya—reticulated giraffe, Grevy's zebra, and gerenuk. There are also elephant, lion and cheetah, and more than 300 species of birds. Options for tourist accommodations are limited. See page 385 for additional information on the park.

The extremely fertile soil in the Central Highlands Area has resulted in extensive cultivation, especially to the south and the east of Mt. Kenya. Here you will see small farms on almost every available piece of land, and fields carved out on the sides of incredibly steep slopes. There are a number of major towns in the Central Highlands.

Nyeri is the administrative headquarters of Kenya's Central Province. One of the largest towns in the Central Highlands, it has a lively market and architectural reminders of colonial days. It is in a very lush and intensely cultivated area. Nyeri is where many of Kenya's most renowned athletes first trained.

Nanyuki is just north of the Equator. It is a social and market center for the ranch lands of the Laikipia Plateau and the lower slopes of Mt. Kenya. North of Nanyuki, at Timau, there is a trout farm, Kentrout—good for a lunch stop under the trees and possible to stay overnight. Soon after Timau, the road drops down towards the semi-arid northern deserts which seem to stretch on without end to Lake Turkana.

Nyahururu is best known for Thomson's Falls which are formed by the Ewaso Narok River and plunge 72 meters to the dense forest below. It is one of the highest towns in Kenya.

Meru town is both an agricultural center and the beginning of any visit to the Meru National Park. Dense forests surround the town, and the high altitude means that it is often misty.

Embu is the provincial headquarters of Eastern Province and is located amongst hills on the southeastern slopes of Mt. Kenya.

None of these towns is a major tourist attraction. Most of the accommodations described for this region are in the countryside, not the towns.

Nyeri – Nanyuki – Beyond

The Aberdare Country Club
Lonrho Hotels Kenya Ltd., Box 58581, Nairobi
☎ *(2) 216940, FAX: (2) 216796*

Most people only see the Aberdare Country Club because it is the departure base for the Ark, a night game viewing lodge. The minivans disgorge their international, camera toting cargo before lunch. After lunch, the dark green Ark buses roll out, heading for the Aberdare Forest. The crowds come back next morning, looking weary and disheveled, to be herded back into minivans and on to the next stop.

For those who have the time to stay, however, the Aberdare Country Club can be a supremely quiet and relaxing getaway. The main house, a romantic stone building with red tiled roof, was built in 1937 by the Lyon family from England. They named the house "Steep" because of its position on the side of a hill, commanding sweeping views in all directions.

The Lyons were part of the notorious "Happy Valley Set." Apparently some pretty wild parties were thrown at "Steep" during World War II—difficult to imagine debauchery in this rather staid, British house with its mullioned windows, dark wood paneling and heavy drapes. Today the windows are larger, but the lounge and bar are still dark with maroon carpeting, leather couches and big stone fireplaces, reminiscent of an old British club.

The beauty of the place is best enjoyed sitting out at tables scattered on shaded lawns in front of the house. From here you can see forever out over grassy banks which extend down the hill—tempting children to run or roll. Vivid bougainvillea brighten the scene, and the swimming pool is partly visible through flowering shrubs. The open-sided Karuru Bar next to the pool overlooks two tennis courts. On a clear day you can see Mt. Kenya. There is a nine-hole golf course—rather steep and often host to families of baboons.

Guests stay in grey stone cottages, most of which are nestled among wonderful gardens on the hill behind the main building. They have high pitched shingle roofs, fireplaces, big picture windows and private outdoor sitting areas. There is a feeling of peace and privacy, and the fireplace is welcome on the many cool and misty evenings up in these highlands.

The dining room occupies a large part of the main house. There are yards of dark wood paneling and big windows frame lovely views. Lunch and breakfast are self-serve safari buffets. Children under 12 are encouraged to eat early. Adult dining is candlelit with a set menu. We had excellent smoked trout and baked ham. Special dining arrangements such as barbecues or bush banquets can be made for safari groups or conferences.

Beyond the stables is a game sanctuary where guests can take a walk or ride the club horses. There are no lion, elephant or buffalo in this 1100 acre sanctuary, but you are likely to see giraffe, zebra, impala and eland at close range. You can go on night game drives in the sanctuary. It is also possible to go on game drives to the "Salient" (in the Aberdare forest) and to "Solio Ranch," a private ranch which is home to both black and white rhino.

Accommodations

There are accommodations for about 100. Guests stay either in the original "Nursery Wing" or in cottages. The Nursery Wing is a separate building with five rooms. The cottages each contain two double rooms (one with a double bed and one with twin beds). Each room has a fireplace and en suite bathroom. If you want connecting rooms, you can book the whole cottage. For a view of Mt. Kenya choose Rooms #28 or #29. Golfers might prefer the cottages down the hill and close to the golf course.

Special Offerings

Conference facilities for 50, club membership available, nine-hole golf course, pool (unheated), tennis courts, horse riding, game sanctuary (1300 acres), game drives, trout fishing, superior gift shop.

Off Notes

Lunchtime can be busy and loud with the Ark crowd. Cottages are more impressive from the outside than inside.

Mount Kenya Safari Club

Lonrho Hotels Kenya Ltd., Box 58581, Nairobi
☎ *(2) 216940, FAX: (2) 216796*

The Mount Kenya Safari Club, with its blend of romance, history and scenery, has become a Kenyan tradition. Built right at the equator, on a ridge facing Mt. Kenya, the site is truly magnificent—well worth a visit, just for the view alone. The grand main building gleams white against the green sweep of surrounding lawns, and there are dramatic views of the foothill forests rising to the peaks of Mt. Kenya.

The original building was designed as a dream home by Rhoda Prudhomme for her husband, Gabriel. As a wealthy New York matron of 50, Rhoda fell in love with the young French aviator who took her big game hunting on her safari in Kenya. She gave up all to marry and live with him in Njoro among the Happy Valley Set of the 1930s. The land had been owned by a Mrs. Wheeler who agreed to sell it to them as "only lovers should live there." The Prudhommes called the house they built *Mawingo*, Swahili for the clouds cloaking the slopes of Mt. Kenya.

The house, with its many guest rooms, became an inn in 1948 when it was purchased by Abraham Block. In 1959 William Holden and two friends rested there during a shooting safari. They fell in love with the place, bought it, and turned it into one of the most unusual and exclusive clubs in the world, the Mt. Kenya Safari Club. Sir Winston Churchill was a founding member, as were Lord Louis Mountbatten, Robert Ruark, U.S. President Lyndon Johnson, Conrad Hilton, Bob Hope, Bing Crosby and more. During the last 30 years, the Club's guest book has been signed by many of the rich and famous of the world. It is now a "Leading Hotel of the World."

The sense of history remains strong in the main building and the original "William Holden Cottages." There is an odd mix of colonial Kenya and the glitz and glamour of the Hollywood set. In the Trophy Lounge are big leather seats, and the walls sport antlers and mounted heads—the room oozes "hunting" and "gentlemen." In the nearby Mountain View Lounge zebra skins vie for wall space with glossy photos of film stars. It is not hard to imagine these rooms peopled with film stars and celebrities of earlier days.

Today, the Mount Kenya Safari Club is a large and complex organization. The grounds of over a hundred acres contain a wide and diverse range of accommodations. A whole host of sporting options are available, and there are conference facilities, shops and galleries. Hotel vehicles are even necessary to transport you from your cottage or villa to the main hotel! The fame and popularity of the club has meant expanding the accommodations and services to cope with the influx of tourists who visit.

The hotel maintains a tradition of upscale elegance. There is a dress code for dinner, there is live music for dinner dancing, and children must eat separately. The manicured gardens encourage sedate strolls. There is a sense of formality harking back to an earlier era, a hint of snobbery and pretension. The Mount Kenya Safari Club operates as both a club and a hotel. Although anyone can stay here, there are also paid-up club members who get special attention.

It is the setting of the Mt. Kenya Safari Club which is so special, so memorable. The view is spectacular. You look across sweeping lawns, past the idyllic swimming pool to the dark evergreens of the foothill forests, and further up to the clouds and peaks of Mt. Kenya. Moving back and forth across the lawns is an amazing parade of enormous birds: marabous, peacocks, and cranes.

There is a varied selection of things to do here. You can browse through the excellent art gallery, ride horses through the forests, laze by the pool, have a massage, play a round of golf, visit the boutiques, shop for books or curios, wander through the aviary…the list goes on and on.

The accommodations at the Mt. Kenya Safari Club cover a wide range of styles, locations and prices. You can have quite a different experience here depending on which room you get. For example you can be social and feel steeped in history if you stay in one of the rooms or suites in the main building. On the other hand, if you want a more private experience, you can opt for one of the lavishly appointed newer cottages tucked down by the river. You can be in a rather functional room with small windows, or you can luxuriate in front of a massive stone fireplace in a grand cottage with stunning views of the mountain. The options are wide, varied and confusing. Perhaps our "Accommodations" section will help you make your selection.

Quotes:

> *"This is my favorite place for a romantic getaway."*

Accommodations

The club has room for more than 250 guests. There are various types of accommodations.

Standard rooms: These are in the main building and the new wing annex. All have fireplaces and many have good views of the mountain and grounds. Rooms #62–65 have the best views.

Main building studios and suites: These rooms are older and have more character. Some have good views. *Our Favorites*: Presidential Suite, Royal Suite #34/35 and studios #44 and #46.

Garden Suites: These give a sense of privacy, but not much view. Curtains separate the bedroom from the living area. Some suites connect and are good for families.

Riverside Cottages: These modern, spacious cottages are tucked down by the river. They have cathedral ceilings, fireplaces, nice verandas, double beds and sunken bathtubs. They are private, but far from the main building. Each cottage has two studios, with a suite in the middle. *Our Favorites*: For the view—Suites #104 and #107, and Studios #103 and #108. For privacy near the river and trees #97 and #99.

William Holden Cottages: These older cottages are our favorite accommodations at the Mt. Kenya Safari Club. They are luxurious and private, and some have magnificent views. In each cottage there is a central living room with a large stone fireplace. Leading off this are two bedrooms each with a private bathroom. *Our Favorites*: for view #3 and #4.

Luxury Villas: There are three large villas; each has a kitchen, large living room, dining room, and jacuzzi. They are far from the main building, near the river and a pond.

Special Facilities

Nine-hole golf course, heated swimming pool, horseback riding on trails, tennis, bowling green, table tennis, museum of African art, tribal dances, fashion boutique, curio and gift shops, club souvenir shop, conference facilities, health and beauty treatments, doctor, transportation in grounds, gas pump.

Off Notes

Busy with tour groups and buses...Calling and waiting for transport from your cottage to the main building is tedious.... Children are to be seen and not heard.... You need to pack a tie and jacket.

Naro Moru River Lodge
Alliance Hotels, Box 49839, Nairobi
☎ *(2) 337501, FAX: (2) 219212*

Sixteen kilometers south of the equator on the rather flat and dry western side of Mt. Kenya is the Naro Moru River Lodge. This rustic "mountain" style lodge is set among trees along the banks of a rushing stream. The lodge serves as the most popular base for climbing Mount Kenya and offers a wide variety of accommodations.

Tree shaded lawns and the sound of the snow-fed stream create your first impression of Naro Moru—tranquility and refreshing coolness. The place seems well established—colorful gardens flourish, birds are all around, jasmine scents the air, and the wooden chairs and tables seem to be growing under the trees. The entire lodge is informal, comfortable and relaxed.

The original lodge, a two-story dark timber building, houses the main dining room and the Pt. Lenana Bar and Lounge. This spacious lounge is bedecked with mementos of successful ascents to the top of the mountain.

Rooms meander among terraced rock gardens that follow natural contours above the river. Beyond are larger self-service cottages and further on are bunk houses and a campsite. There are accommodations to suit every pocket and style.

On the rise above the lodge, an inviting swimming pool commands an impressive view of Mt. Kenya. A bright, contemporary restaurant with adjoining bar and lounge overlooks the pool and serves lunch, tea, snacks and sundowners.

There is a sense of sportiness and outdoor activity at Naro Moru. Many visitors come to climb the mountain, others come for bird-watching or trout fishing. There are many choices: tennis, squash, swimming, darts, and table tennis. A peaceful forest path winds along the riverbank.

The lodge specializes in safaris to Mt. Kenya and offers a wide range of options from one day hikes to week long treks. Guides, porters and equipment can be hired, and the lodge operates Met Station Cabins and Mackinders Camp on the mountain. Book in advance.

Quotes:

> *"It's great value for the money—there's so much to do here."*

Accommodations

There are a wide range of accommodations—from deluxe rooms to a campsite. Most rooms have private decks overlooking trees and the river. *Our favorites* are the deluxe rooms, which have cathedral ceilings, blond wood-paneling, a fireplace and generous balconies. They are decorated in attractive local fabrics and have large modern bathrooms with a bathtub and separate shower. From deluxe rooms #24 and #25 you might see Mt. Kenya in the morning.

Special Facilities

Mountain trekking safaris, hire of climbing and camping equipment, transport hire to Mt. Kenya, heated swimming pool, tennis (two new courts), squash, fishing (river stocked with trout), horseback riding, bird walks, sauna, indoor games, conference facilities (up to 40 participants), video room and laundry service.

Off Notes

Main lodge rather tired and dowdy. Poor maintenance in older sections.

Outspan Hotel

Block Hotels, Box 47557, Nairobi
☎ *(2) 335807, FAX: (2) 340541*

The Outspan Hotel has a history of up-country colonial elegance. It was built in 1927 facing Mt. Kenya with the Aberdare Mountains rising behind and the Chania River tumbling below. The site was chosen by Sherbrooke Walker and his wife, Lady Bettie.

Walker had been Lord Baden-Powell's private secretary and first Boy Scout Commissioner. His travels took him to the West Indies, Eastern Europe and America, but it was his dream to build in Kenya. When the railroad was built to Lake Victoria, he and his wife wanted to construct a "proper hotel." It was to be a haven of convenience and luxury (first flush loos) for the up-country area opened for ranching and farming.

Outspan was named to suggest how early travelers prepared to rest at journey's end by unyoking or "outspanning" weary oxen from oxcarts.

The hotel stands solid, comfortable and elegant in well-tended rolling lawns accented by travelers' palms. Lush tropical gardens are laid out English style to frame distant views of Mt. Kenya. The hotel building itself has a certain graciousness that is now rather tired. The lively, elegant crowds of yesteryear have faded into the past.

It is the lovely setting, established gardens and feeling of history which still make Outspan worth a visit today. When you sit on the veranda facing Mt. Kenya, you enjoy the bright flowers, the garden scents and the birds. You might also be treated to a performance by the elegant peacock who loves to shiver his tailfeathers in display.

Breakfast and lunch buffets are served on this open veranda with chippendale chairs and white linen. The set-menu dinner is in the baronial dining hall. Our dinner was unusually good and nicely presented. This room has a well-worn elegance—mellow wood in the moldings, parquet floors and cathedral roof beams. Candlelight makes each table an intimate little island.

The main lounge, sherry bar and snooker room have paneling, fireplaces, brass fittings and overstuffed chairs and sofas in soft pastels and chintz. There are full-length windows and glass doors, many of which open to the garden.

The hotel acts as the reception point for visitors to Treetops, the original night game viewing lodge. In fact most visitors to Outspan are on their way to Treetops and only stay for lunch. Except for the Treetops crowd, the hotel has a very quiet almost abandoned air.

Lord Baden-Powell, the founder of International Scouting, loved Outspan and its beautiful location. With the consent of his friends, the Walkers, he chose to live here during the last years of his life. "Paxtu," the two hotel rooms of his "cottage," have been set aside as a small museum of scouting.

Accommodations

Outspan can accommodate approximately 65 guests. The hotel's 37 rooms are spacious and airy, most with fireplaces and easy chairs, many with garden access, some with views of Mt. Kenya. Large connecting rooms, suites and garden cottages provide plenty of space for small groups or families. Unfortunately, many rooms are shabby and sparsely furnished. This is a particular shame because the beautifully proportioned rooms have such potential. *Our Favorites*: Suites & Cottages. Room #24 & 26, which are light and airy and have a large sitting area, fireplace, enclosed terrace, French doors opening onto garden lawns. Room #62, which is quite large, with access to the more private garden of the Baden-Powell Scout Museum.

Safari Journal — Saturday morning

We got up at dawn to see Mt. Kenya and to go for a walk before breakfast. The gardens were beautiful in the morning light. Sunbirds and turacos were as brilliant as the flowers. Everything seemed scented with sunshine. We were glad to find early breakfast in progress on the terrace. From our table, the top of Mount Kenya was still showing through the mist. We had to smile at the dishevelled appearance of the Treetops people. One lady was heard to say that she wished she had spent the night in comfort here at Outspan!

Special Offerings

Bird and nature walks, river walk, Mt. Kenya hikes, Kikuyu dance group, golf, tennis, squash, billiards, table tennis, darts, trout fishing, video room, card room, pool, souvenir shop, conference facilities, and a visit to a nearby coffee plantation.

Staff Notes

Room decor is not up to the elegance of the original construction or dimension.

Thomson's Falls Lodge

Thomson's Falls Lodge, Box 38, Nyahururu
☎ *(365) 22006, 22319*

In 1883 at the age of 25, Joseph Thomson made a journey commissioned by the Royal Geographical Society in London. It took him through the uncharted land that later became Kenya. He traveled through a mountain range he named Aberdare after the president of the Royal Geographical Society, and his name stuck in the case of Thomson's gazelle. He was the first to chart the falls of the Nyahururu River—now Thomson's Falls, near the present day town of Nyahururu in the Aberdare Mountains.

In 1930, a rambling brick lodge was built with garden views of the falls. Today the lodge is old, ramshackle and greatly in need of renovations. Unfortunately, the view of the falls is almost completely blocked by the many souvenir dukas lining the cliff.

Night Game Viewing Lodges

Night Game Viewing Lodges are an alternative way to see wild animals. Instead of going in search of animals, you stay in one place and hope that the animals will come to you. There is a special excitement and magic about this late night game vigil. If you are lucky you will observe animals from close quarters and for long periods to appreciate more of their behavior and interaction.

We have visited five night game viewing lodges in Kenya. Three of them (The Ark, Treetops and Mountain Lodge) are in the Mt. Kenya Area, and the others are described in later chapters. Shimba Hills is near the South coast, and Salt Lick Lodge is in the Taita Hills Game Sanctuary.

Of the three night game viewing lodges in the Mt. Kenya area, the Ark probably offers the best chance of seeing the most game. Remember, it is always a matter of chance and luck—there are nights when you might see one lone buffalo, and other times when elephant, rhino, buffalo and lion may all be "on stage" at once. Treetops, despite its famous history, is suffering the encroachment of man, and is no longer deep in the forest. Both the Ark and Treetops have rather spartan accommodations: small cabin style rooms, many with shared bathrooms. Of the three, Mountain Lodge is certainly the most comfortable, with its private bathrooms and larger bedrooms.

The Ark Forest Lodge

Lonrho Hotels Kenya Ltd., Box 58581, Nairobi
☎ *(2) 216940, FAX: (2) 219212*

The Ark gives you a night passage into the secret wildlife world of the Aberdare forest. Visitors from all over the globe begin their Ark experience from the Aberdare Country Club. After check-in and a leisurely lunch admiring the Club's sweeping views, you board the Ark buses for the 30-minute drive into the Aberdare Forest. The first view of the Ark is across a valley—its high curving roof dramatic and in the forest.

A raised wooden walkway is the "gangplank" to the Ark. The forest spreads out on each side as you leave the everyday world to embark on your adventure.

Next comes a "mandatory" briefing on rules, facilities, and schedules: don't frighten the animals with loud voices or flash bulbs; a buzzer in your room will wake you if something new or exciting is spotted during the night, breakfast is, etc. Finally you are allowed to find your room—not much to see there—and head to the end of the building which overlooks the waterhole and natural salt lick.

The game and the public viewing areas make the Ark special. You see animals from three different levels and can choose to be indoors or out. The ground level photo hide, with no glass in the windows, is brisk and exciting. A herd of elephant might be just feet away—you can hear and smell and see everything. Or you can sit in warmth and comfort with a cup of tea and look at the animals through big windows.

Safari Journal
Monday night

I squeezed my sister's arm ~ we exchanged silent smiles of
amazed delight. Below us an incredible scene is unfolding:
There was some charging and trumpeting from the elephant trying
to assert dominance over the best area of the salt lick. The two rhino
kicked up a bit of dust but have now settled down. A large
lion family rests in a semi-circle on the grass .... the young lions
are playing what we have christened "sniff-the-rhino's-bum game".
They take turns sneaking up close behind the young rhino.
The rhino suddenly turns and charges, sending the little lion
racing back to the grassy area. Soon, another lion tries the
same thing. Extraordinary to witness this interaction of the
animals ~ had never imagined them playing together this way.
My children will be green with envy ~ they saw nothing
like this on our previous visit.

The light rain is cold, but my shivers are partly from
excitement. We could go in and warm up by the fire,
but we stay out here on the open deck, getting wetter,
glued to the amazing scene flood-lit below. This memory
will stay with us forever.

The main lounge has an impressive stone fireplace—a cheery warmth at this alti
tude. The mounted rhino head is a relic of a fatal fight with an elephant in front o
the Ark. A log book records sightings of animals, and a naturalist is on hand to
answer questions. Tea and cakes are served in the afternoon. With the late hour
kept, the bar does brisk business.

The dining room has long communal tables. It does not overlook the waterhole. On a very active night, dinner may be quite an interrupted affair as guests rush out to see which new animal has made an appearance.

An expectant hush pervades the Ark. Conversations are whispered, and binoculars and video cameras abound. It can be very cold and damp standing outside trying to glimpse a leopard at midnight—so come well prepared with protective clothing. There is an early wake-up call—often a good time to catch a clear glimpse of snow-capped Mt. Kenya towering above the forest. After breakfast, it's time to return, rather bleary-eyed, to the Aberdare Country Club.

Accommodations

The cabinlike rooms are small, functional and rather dark with wood paneling and relatively small windows. All rooms have en suite bathrooms with a shower. There are 46 doubles, six singles and eight triples. Each room has a buzzer to wake you (you can turn it off). To see what exciting animal prompted the buzz, you have to join the rush to the front viewing rooms.

Special Offerings

Photo hide, outside viewing terrace, bar, souvenir and sundry shop.

Reminders

No children under seven are allowed except on "Children's Night"—call for dates. Only small bags are permitted. Bring protective clothing (it can be cold and wet); cameras and binoculars (great video opportunities and good results with the strong night lights); warm and comfortable night wear (you are likely to spring out of bed and rush down the passage to see the game—your lacy negligee is hardly ideal).

Off Notes

You cannot see game from your room.... Regimentation.... A noisy crowd can disturb the animals.

Mountain Lodge

African Tours and Hotels Ltd., Box 30471, Nairobi
☎ *(2) 336858, FAX: (2) 218109*

Mountain Lodge is located in indigenous forest 7200 feet up in the foothills of the Mt. Kenya National Reserve. You are likely to see elephant and buffalo along the scenic road which leads to the lodge. Unlike the Ark and Treetops, you can drive yourself to Mountain Lodge, and can arrive and depart when you choose. The lodge caters primarily to international tour groups.

The lodge, a four-story timber boxlike structure, was built in 1970. It overlooks a natural waterhole and salt lick surrounded by dense forest. On a clear day you can see the jagged peaks of Mt. Kenya's summit through the trees. A boardwalk leads through dense forest from the parking area to the lodge. The lodge is rustic and natural. Walls are covered with yellow reeds, and there are timber columns and dim lighting. The atmosphere is casual, the service, friendly and attentive.

Each of the bedrooms faces directly over the waterhole. This is what makes Mountain Lodge appealing. You can view the game in the comfort and privacy of your own room—no need for a midnight dash to a public area in order to see the animals. Each room has a private bathroom and either an open balcony or a large picture window.

Game most frequently seen include: buffalo, elephant, rhino, forest hogs, suni, red duiker, spotted hyena, genet cat, and if you are lucky, a leopard or the big male lion who makes his appearance every now and then. Since the lodge was deliberately located beside a route animals travel between Mt. Kenya and the lowlands, it is not uncommon to see very large herds of animals. At night the waterhole area is lit by floodlights.

There are three public areas for watching game. The top floor is an open-sided roofed viewing area without seating, there is a viewing balcony which leads off from the bar, and a very small subterranean photo hide with open grill windows.

Animal sightings are kept in a log book near the bar, and binoculars can be borrowed. There is a "game porter" who will supposedly wake you up during the night if animals you have specified appear. At 6:30 a.m. tea or coffee will be brought to your door.

The dining room is bright, cheerful and functional. Windows along both sides look out over the forest. Each table seats six with a window at one end. Trout (fresh from nearby trout farms) and turkey are specialties of the lodge.

Accommodations

The lodge has 42 bedrooms on three floors. There are three VIP rooms and 39 standard double rooms. Ground floor rooms are better for close up game viewing. VIP rooms have a comfortable sitting area, small fridge, phone, and bathtub with shower. Standard rooms have showers only, and most have one double bed and one single bed. Some rooms have narrow open balconies with a cushioned bench. The others have a large picture window with comfortable chairs for game viewing.

Special Offerings

Slide shows of animals, gift and sundry shop, telephone operator for long distance calls on the solar powered telephone.

Off Notes

There is poor soundproofing between rooms and floors, and the smell of mildew is pervasive.... Public rooms are not very inviting—there is no cozy fire.

Note

Children under eight are not allowed to stay at Mountain Lodge.

Treetops

Block Hotels, Box 40075, Nairobi
☎ *(2) 540780, FAX: (2) 545948*

After leaving the colonial comfort of the Outspan Hotel, Treetops is a spartan contrast. Located just inside the gates to the Aberdare National Park, Treetops overlooks waterholes and a salt lick. You know you've left comfort behind as you trudge up the dirt path behind an armed escort.

Treetops rises straight and stark on stilts. It is solely dedicated to game viewing. The possibility of seeing wild animals up close has drawn thousands over the last 60 years to create the Treetops tradition. Unfortunately, today's visitors are often disappointed since the forest has been denuded by elephants and buffalo, and game is less plentiful.

However, there are some unique aspects to the Treetops experience: there is a sense of history (it was here that Elizabeth II became Queen overnight); and living tree trunks branch naturally through rooms and corridors. The lounge is friendly, with big picture windows and warm wood, and there is a roof deck with open viewing in all directions.

The narrow, dark paneled dining room features long communal tables and bench eating. The linen is crisp and white, the menu elaborate, the food disappointing. The tiny guest rooms, dark narrow passages and twisting stairways can contribute to a feeling of claustrophobia.

Treetops has recently been treated to an entire refurbishment. The dining and lounge areas have been expanded, wall-to-wall carpeting installed and a new floor added with nine larger sized "superior" rooms.

Accommodations

The 48 guest rooms, called "nests," are tiny bed closets with dark wood paneling, small windows and no bathrooms. Small communal shower bathrooms are down the hall or sometimes downstairs. Since Treetops "sells beds, not rooms," you may meet a new roommate. Rooms A and B, just as small, with shower, and a double bed are called suites. In 1983 the Queen slept in "Suite A." *Our Favorite*: A room back at Outspan. Or Buckingham Palace.

Sweetwaters Tented Camp
Lonrho Hotels Kenya Ltd., Box 58581, Nairobi
☎ *(2) 216940, FAX: (2) 216796*

Sweetwaters is a luxury tented camp. Like Ol Pejeta Lodge, it is on the game ranch previously belonging to Adnan Kashoggi.

This Lonrho operated camp has 30 well-appointed double tents all facing toward a waterhole, with Mt. Kenya dramatic in the background. The tents are arranged in two rows on a huge expanse of cropped lawn. The back row tents are built up on platforms to see over the front row. Only a matter of meters in front of the lower tents is a deep ditch hiding an electric fence. This means that when you sit on your private canvas-covered veranda, or even lie in bed with the flaps open, you can see nimals just a few meters away without any visual sense of something separating hem from you. You are completely safe, but you are so close to that big elephant ating branches or the giraffe splayed long-legged to drink. Add a red sunset and a lear view of Mt. Kenya, and you know what makes Sweetwaters special.

The main building includes reception, a lounge and the dining area. The attractive ounge with big windows and a fireplace is cleanly decorated with white fabric on lark Lamu-style furniture. The dining area is part of the old gate house which existed on this site. Unfortunately, it feels rather enclosed and does not take advantage of he view. For better vistas there is a thatched treehouse viewing area. There, from a haded vantage point, you can look down at the animals gathered round the water ole. Sweetwaters also has a pretty swimming pool which is unheated and requires trength of purpose.

Safari Journal

Saturday Sundown :

We've invited the Irish nurse to join us for a sherry on our veranda. The blood red glow in the sky is fading fast — so sudden, these equatorial sunsets. We are almost right on the equator and yet there is snow on Mt. Kenya and a chill in the evening air. There are two big elephant just over by the waterhole. They are so close we can hear their ears flap. The nurse had arrived the night before from Saudi Arabia where she is a sister in a major hospital. A needed break before burn-out, she said. Where would be a nice quiet place to get away from it all, she'd asked. And been directed to Sweetwaters. She took a sip and sighed in contentment.

You can take game drives in the 22,000-acre sanctuary and are bound to see eticulated giraffe, plenty of plains game, and hopefully elephant. In certain areas of he sanctuary you will also drive past small local villages and herders. Quite often you vill see domestic cattle and goats side by side with wild plains game. You are not ikely to meet many other tourists on the roads—another plus for Sweetwaters.

Rhinos are being brought into the area. In an enclosed sanctuary is Morani, the friendly Rhino who previously lived in an orphanage and is now quite happy to be petted and photographed up close. Camel walks, horseback riding, and night game drives can be arranged from Sweetwaters. There is a Chimp Sanctuary and boat trip on the river.

Sweetwaters is very relaxed and low key. You will not see the volume or variety of game of the Masai Mara, nor will you see the dramatic mesas of Samburu, but it i not a bad drive from Nairobi, and the road is tarmac until the turnoff. Sweetwater is a pleasant relaxing stop for a night or two.

Accommodations

We have a preference for the "front row" tents at ground level. Tent #7 has a particularly good view. Tent #1 has a four-poster Lamu-style double bed.

Please Note

It can be cold at night (hope they are still placing hot water bottles in the beds)... The long dirt road from the turnoff suggests 4-wheel advisability especially during the rains.

Lewa Downs Wildlife Conservancy

Lewa Downs is now incorporated as an operating Conservation area—the Lewa Wild life Conservancy. Within this 240sq. kilometer expanse of stunning landscape and vibran wildlife population, travelers have a choice of three different visits:

1. Lewa Conservancy Centre for day visits

2. Wilderness Trails at Lewa Downs

3. Lerai Tented Camp

Lewa Conservancy Centre
Bookings Ltd. Box 56707, Nairobi
☎ *(2) 225255, FAX: (2) 216553*

Day visitors can come to the Conservancy Centre for lunch and enjoy the small museum with its displays of the rhino story based on Anna Mertz's conservation work with black rhino. Groups can organize ahead for wildlife lectures and for guided game drives.

There is an open-air dining area attractively created out of natural materials. The Center is built near the edge of a swamp, and guests are frequently treated to close views of the various wildlife which come to this area.

Wilderness Trails at Lewa Downs

Bush Homes of East Africa, Box 56923, Nairobi
☎ *(2) 571647, FAX: (2) 571665*

Lewa Downs is possibly the best known and most successful ranch/homestay in Kenya. A magical combination of thoughtful hospitality, unforgettable scenery, and abundant wildlife makes Lewa Downs deserving of this renown.

Located near Isiolo in the foothills of Mt. Kenya, Lewa Downs is a 45,000 acre cattle and game ranch, and has been home to the Craig family for three generations. The Craigs or their team welcome you almost as family-come-home. The atmosphere is understated, relaxed and easygoing. Those at Lewa Downs have a thorough knowledge and deep understanding of this land and its animals, and are eager to share this with their guests. They will take you horseback riding among the giraffe; drive you to ridge-tops with views in all directions; and to stop in a field full of pre-historic stone artifacts.

To reach Lewa Downs, you leave the tarmac between Timau and Isiolo. A dusty ranch road winds through rolling hills with wildlife and candelabra cactus. Finally you reach the main house which is built strongly of cut Kenyan lava-stone and softened by a thatched roof and clouds of white and fuchsia bougainvillea. There are three quaint guest cottages constructed of thatch and volcanic rock. Each rustic cottage has two guest rooms sharing a common rondavel-style living room with fireplace and huge veranda.

A new outdoor sitting area is canterlevered over the gorge and has views down to the river below. Meals are served in the outdoor dining terrace reached by a natural stone stairway through rock gardens. Three open stone arches frame views down a steep gorge and up to the volcanic rock on the next hill. The food is memorable— fresh from the ranch and home-cooked. Sometimes there is wonderful bread, baked into loaves shaped like elephants and other animals. Conversation at the communal table is lively, and you have the opportunity of getting to know the other guests. Lanterns light the way for dinner, which is accented by wine and candlelight. Sometimes the Craigs take guests for breakfast in the bush or for sundowners at a viewpoint.

Most activities at Lewa Downs center on experiencing the wildlife and scenery. The ranch horses are well trained and sedate—even novice riders can enjoy the proximity to wild animals which riding allows. You can practically touch giraffe! There is still a great deal of wildlife at Lewa Downs because the Craig clan is very conservation minded. They have helped to establish and protect the Ngare Sergoit Rhino Sanctuary and the property, which is now incorporated as the Lewa Wildlife Conservancy.

Guests go on game drives in customized four-wheel drive vehicles with open roof hatches and seats covered in cavas or sheepskin. There are field guides, binoculars and always a very knowledgeable driver/guide. Amazing how these vehicles tackle steep rocky hillsides with such gusto! It is wonderful to be out in these high hills. You may come close to elephant families, rhino and zebra. There are "tail-up" wart hog, herds of impala, and buffalo. All around are spellbinding views of ridge after ridge stretching to blue distant mountains.

Night game drives are a specialty at Lewa. A guide sits on the roof with a hand-held searchlight to spot the elusive animals of the night. Brilliant stars and perhaps a flood of moonlight add to the excitement.

Lewa Downs is part of the area of Kenya where traces of some of the earliest humans have been found. You are free to search for their carved stones, hand-worked tools, and other artifacts. It is thrilling to hold something made by another human being thousands of years ago. It feels right to replace such items gently, for another to find.

Quotes:

"...A delightful experience in everything. The rides with patient horses, the excellent cuisine, the comfortable rooms, the views, the air, the company..."

"...Lewa Downs is magical! The Craigs shared their paradise with all of us..."

"...Great to return from a sunset ride and find a roaring fire, a bowl of hot popcorn, and a well-stocked bar waiting for us in our own living room!"

Accommodations

There are six simple guest rooms with rustic decor. Booking two guest rooms gives you your own private cottage complete with veranda, living room and fireplace. Each room has a no-frills bathroom with shower and flush toilet.

Special Offerings

Children might enjoy a visit to the Craig's farmyard and vegetable gardens. You can visit the ranch spinning and weaving project and make orders for rugs, etc. You can also go on guided game walks at your own pace and inclination. A craft shop and a new, good-sized swimming pool are located near the main house. There is an airstrip on the ranch and Lewa Downs is now a request stop on the Air Kenya daily scheduled flight between Nanuki and Samburu.

Off Note

A lunchtime tour group may crowd your private experience.

Ngare Niti

Wilderness Trails (K) Ltd., Box 56923, Nairobi
☎ *(2) 506139, FAX: (2) 502739*

In a separate location, Ngare Niti is a dream house designed by Will Craig. Here you have all the space and grandeur of Lewa Downs scenery plus the luxury of your own private and beautiful house. This gem is a two-story oversized cottage—an ingenious English country creation using local African materials: lava rock, timber and thatch.

You arrive at the house after a drive across Lewa Downs Ranch. The road leads up a long but gentle slope through acacia savannah. A green oasis suddenly confronts you as you swing into the circular drive and see Ngare Niti. Flowers and climbing vines on the stone and thatch exterior give an intimacy to the entrance. However, when you pass through the house to the wide veranda and terrace, the scale dramatically changes. You feel you can see at a glance all the sky, land and mountains of northern Kenya.

The generous living room has a cathedral ceiling, a sculpted wood mantelpiece over the fireplace, and leather-cushioned chairs. It suggests cozy conversations with friends. Meals are taken in the dining room around a table for ten fashioned from a single piece of wood. From the entrance a wide rustic staircase sweeps to the upper floor. Here the spacious master bedroom has views in both directions with French doors leading to an outdoor balcony. There are papyrus-fronted cupboards, animal pictures, safari chairs and hand-woven carpets. A large bathroom and a child's bedroom also share this floor.

Arching over the entire house is the thatched roof. Inside, the grasses are intricately woven to create a remarkable ceiling resembling a grand version of a Kenyan basket.

There are two separate double accommodations in cottages next to the main house. Although the cottage rooms are not as impressive as the master bedroom, they are engagingly decorated with simple fabrics making the cottages cozy and comfortable.

Lerai Tented Camp

Savannah Camps & Lodges. Box 48019, Nairobi
☎ (2) 331191, FAX: (2) 330698

Lerai Tented Camp is situated within the Ngare Sergoi Rhino Sanctuary on Lewa Downs. The sanctuary was set up in 1983 by the conservationist and author, Anna Mertz, to protect some of the few black rhino remaining in Kenya. Today it is home to some twenty black and sixteen white rhino who now have free range in 240 sq kilometers of protected habitat known as the Lewa Downs Conservancy.

There are 12 spacious guest tents at Lerai Tented Camp. The tents are spaced well apart to provide privacy, and are built on raised platforms and sheltered by beautifully thatched papyrus. The tents have been comfortably furnished with handwoven rugs on the floor and attractive covers on the twin beds. There is safari style furniture including a writing table and luggage rack. The en suite bathrooms have flush toilets and showers.

The main lodge building has been created from a small wooden cottage which was part of the original rhino sanctuary. There is a dining room and lounge with a stone fireplace and plate glass windows overlooking a waterhole. The waterhole is floodlit at night and you may see rhino, elephant and other wildlife coming to drink.

When you stay at Lerai Tented Camp you are able to take bird and game walks with an experienced guide and go on both day and night game drives. The Camp's open sided 4-wheel drive safari vehicles give you wonderful all-round game viewing. The Conservancy is home to a wide variety of plains game including Grevy's Zebra, Reticulated Giraffe and Gerenuk. On a night game drive you are sure to enjoy seeing bushbabies jumping between branches and the funny hopping Spring Hare. You may be lucky and see a genet cat or even an aardvark, zorilla or leopard.

Guests may visit the swamp to try and spot the shy Sitatunga—a semi-aquatic antelope. There is also the option of horseback riding, which is a wonderful way to enjoy the wide open spaces and marvelous scenery of the area while getting close to wildlife. Sundowners with a view complete a perfect day.

Borana Lodge

Tandala Limited, Box 24397, Nairobi
☎ *(2) 567251, FAX: (2) 564945*
e-mail: Royal.Africasaf@commsol.sprint.com

Six luxurious suites in rustic cottages—a ridge top in the bush—staying at Borana Lodge is wonderful and relaxing. It is a wilderness immersion combined with surprising extravagance, elegance, privacy and homey comfort.

From its spectacular site on Borana Ranch (35,000 private acres), the lodge commands dramatic views of the high bush and mountain ranges of Mt. Kenya and the Laikipia Plateau.

Curving contours of hill and rock determine the unique shape of each structure. There are steep pathways, terraced rock gardens and lawns, and surprising lily ponds. A beautiful stone swimming pool is set right at the edge of the escarpment with views of distant mountains and a nearby waterhole below.

Walls are natural stone; plaited thatch forms tall rounded rooflines; and boulders are unusual points of interest in bathrooms, bedrooms, gardens and main lodge. Local cedar has been polished to frame floor-to-ceiling windows and to create unusual fireplace mantels. It is also used in ranch-made bedsteads and huge lounge chairs with leather cushions.

Each cottage has its own niche on the hill, with private view terrace and spacious rooms. Some cottages are high on the slope, some are lower, one has two levels, and one has two suites with shared terrace. Even bathrooms have huge windows. And privacy is assured, so many bathtubs are turned to enjoy the view. Beds are large and comfortable. Some are four-posters with canopies. Even the twin beds seem large enough for two. Each cottage has a sitting area with fireplace.

Due to sloping terrain and surrounding vistas, the central lodge is built on two levels at the very edge of the cliff. Since this high spot can be very windy, glass is used for protection, even on the open terrace.

Enormous windows curve to frame the panorama and fill the living room with light and space. A huge fireplace juts out from one wall and is open on three sides. The adjacent drawing room with its own big fireplace is perfect for pre-dinner drinks. The stuffed sofas and chairs are huge, and the atmosphere is cozy.

A staircase climbs to the dining room with its dramatic rosewood slab table. The crackling fire and candlelight give the feeling of a hospitable country manor, where every effort is being made to see to your comfort. By day, the dining room is bright with a whole wall of glass doors open to terraced lawns and gardens of indigenous plants.

Because it is small, Borana can cater to the individual desires of guests. From Laikipia, many activities are possible. You can make day or night game drives in an open Land Rover with high seating on two levels—not even a windscreen between you and the animals. Besides the ranch cattle, you can see elephant, lion, buffalo, and various plains game including the elusive Greater Kudu.

You can also go on guided game walks, ride horses, or swim, and a tennis court is planned. You take camel safaris or an extravagant flying excursion to Mt. Kenya or to Lake Turkana for fishing. Borana is receiving rave reviews. A must!

Ol Pejeta Lodge

Going Places, Box 14776, Nairobi
☎ *(2) 442312, FAX: (2) 446402*

Ol Pejeta was a private game ranch belonging to millionaire Adnan Kashoggi. The ranch in the dry savannah country on the west side of Mt. Kenya was used for game hunting—especially for buffalo. A 23,000-acre rhino sanctuary has been created within the 110,000-acre ranch. The luxurious ranch house "Ol Pejeta" has kept some of the original furnishings and operates as an exclusive self-catering establishment.

The main ranch house is light and airy, with a relaxed indoor-outdoor feel. There are wide verandas with comfortable cushioned chairs, cool courtyards ablaze with bright bougainvillea, and enormous picture windows framing views of Mt. Kenya. Everything is outsized, extra large: you feel like a child sinking into the giant-sized chairs and couches, the fireplace is huge, and the beds in the suites are the biggest we've ever seen.

You are clearly in Africa. The conservation-minded might balk at the impressive testament to earlier hunting safaris. Buffalo horns and heads of antelope, cheetah and leopard literally line the veranda and dining room walls. Gold-mounted ivory tusks stand guard over the bath, stuffed rhino feet act as doorstops; there are lion-skin rugs with bared teeth intact—all seem quite in harmony with this slightly unreal place.

To savor Ol Pejeta in proper style, we strongly recommend staying in Mr. or Mrs. Kashoggi's suites. Pretend you are one of the rich and famous for a day as you get lost in the enormous bed, luxuriate in the family size bath, pad the expanse of your carpeted suite. Mrs. Kashoggi's suite is upstairs. You can look out a window as you lie in the bath. The headboard is an impossible creation of towering blue and white clouds. Mr. Kashoggi's suite, larger and more masculine with impressive woodwork, is on the ground floor with big sliding doors leading to a shaded veranda. Ol Pejeta is a popular place for weddings.

Beyond the veranda, a swimming pool with a rock waterfall is surrounded by emerald lawns and imaginatively colorful gardens busy with birds. The outsized lounge chairs are made of soft interwoven leather. The outdoor whirlpool in the shade is an original jacuzzi. You can play croquet on the front lawn or try your hand at badminton. For the more energetic there are horses to ride and two tennis courts.

Safari Journal — The morning after.

We were lying in the vast wood-encased bath in Mr. Kashoggi's suite, luxuriating in the imported Forest Pine Oil and holding onto the handles so we wouldn't slip under the water — our feet couldn't reach the end and my husband is six feet tall. Two candles flickered among flowers at each end of the bath — candles for romance and atmosphere, but also in anticipation of the generator being switched off at midnight! From the bath, which is raised and surrounded on three sides by mirrors, we looked past two enormous elephant tusks that are mounted on the floor and frame the bath, then over the head of the lion skin on the floor and then across the 100 foot length of the suite.

I wonder what strange sights this bathtub has seen . . .

Past the green lawns and tropical flower gardens you can see the dry bush country with its scattering of thorn trees. There is a water-hole to attract the animals, and the massive bulk of Mt. Kenya is a purple-blue backdrop. You can go on game drives; visit the tame rhino, morani; or the chimp sanctuary at nearby Sweetwaters.

Quotes:

"Ours is a seven-roll bed. I could roll over seven times before I fell out the other side. It was so big, I couldn't find her in the night—so much for romance!" Guest

Accommodations

Ol Pejeta can accommodate 12 adults and six children sharing. There are six deluxe suites—four in the main house, and two in Buffalo Cottage. Check current regulations regarding children. *Our Favorites:* Mr. and Mrs. Kashoggi Suites.

Special Offerings

Barbecue meals, swimming pool, two tennis courts, croquet, badminton, horse riding among wild animals, game drives, night game drives, game/bird walks, sauna, jacuzzi. Catering can be arranged.

ff Notes

Maintenance is needed on some facilities. The original furniture is looking a little tired

Sangare Ranch

Savanah Camps & Lodges, Box 48019, Nairobi
☎ *(2) 229009, FAX: (2) 330698*

Just getting to Sangare is quite an adventure. It involves a gate (which you open with a key collected at the entrance to the Aberdare County Club), steep and winding roads, marvelous and varied views, and preferably a four-wheel drive. Sangare is situated on the Prettejohn's ranch. You first come to their delightful ranch house with its long veranda and colorful creepers. After a welcome, you will be guided to Sangare.

Sangare offers peace and privacy for a very small group. Staying here is a little like up-market camping in a remote spot with all the work done for you. Meals are provided, and camp fires are set. There is no electricity, but there is water. An experienced game person (with a gun) can accompany you on your game walks or horse rides. There is abundant game in the area, especially elephant, and a variety of buck...leopards, but no lion.

Sangare is designed to be very simple and basic. Three separate small buildings are set on the banks of a modest man-made dam. One building is the mess room—small and cozy with a fireplace. This room opens onto an outdoor veranda which faces the dam. A second compact structure houses the kitchen—no electricity, and wire-mesh for windows. Meals are prepared here, and everything is "homemade" using dairy products and vegetables from the farm. The third building, set at some distance from the mess room, is a basic banda which contains two rather spartan but pleasant bedrooms. The walls are lined with papyrus and the low windows face towards Mt. Kenya. Each bedroom has an adjoining bathroom with proper toilet and hot water.

Basically, you can decide how to spend your time. You could fish for trout, watch birds and game from the veranda, arrange to have picnics in the bush, go on a night game drive...Your "hosts," the Prettejohns, can pick you up from the Nanyuki airport, drive you into the Aberdare Salient National Park and Solio Game Ranch, or even arrange overnight horse riding safaris. All is very personalized.

There is radio contact with the Prettejohn ranch house.

Aberdare House

Bush Homes of East Africa Ltd., Box 56923, Nairobi
☎ *(2) 571647, FAX: (2) 571665*

Aberdare House opened to guests in December 1996. The house, owned by Patrick Pape (who has been a safari guide for 17 years), is situated between Mt. Kenya and the Aberdare Range and is within easy reach of two unique and undisturbed wildlife areas.

Aberdare House is a red brick and shingle roofed home situated on a 50 acre property. The house faces over lawns which drop down to a river. Across the river you can see the thick indigenous forest of the Mt. Kenya Forest Reserve. There are colobus monkeys in the garden and sometimes elephant and other game come to the river. There are walks along the river.

Guests stay in a double bedroom in the main house or in a separate cottage also with a double bedroom and an annex which would make it ideal for families.

When you stay at Aberdare House you can go on game drives in the Aberdare National Park and in Solio Game Sanctuary. The Aberdare National Park is situated on a high range of mountains. As you gain altitude, the vegetation changes from rain forests to bamboo to open moorlands. There are trout streams and spectacular water falls. On game drives you will look for elephant, lion, leopard and buffalo. This area is also home to the rare bongo and the tiny suni antelope.

From Aberdare House you can also take game drives in the privately owned Solio Game Reserve with it's high rolling plains and bountiful marsh. This 18,000 acre reserve has over 120 black and white rhino and is home to most of the plains game and their predators.

Getting There:

By Plane: daily scheduled flight to Nanyuki from Wilson Airport, Nairobi and then road transfer. By road: Two and a half hours drive from Nairobi.

Mokorindo Cottage

*Mokorindo Cottage, c/o Clive Aggett,
Kifuku Est., Box 2, Rumuruti*

Mokorindo Cottage is a quiet retreat in a rural setting. This two bedroom cottage is on the edge of a freshwater dam in the middle of a working cattle ranch of several thousand acres.

The cottage is fully equipped complete with a cook and food. It has a spacious sitting and dining room with a fireplace. There are two light and airy bedrooms, each with a private bathroom. Windows frame views of green lawns extending to the sparkling waters of the lake-like dam. A Mokorindo tree, from which the cottage gets its name, stands all alone by the water. The cottage is covered with golden shower vines, and bougainvillea climbs along the pillars of the lovely veranda.

There is abundant bird life surrounding the dam. You will see cormorants, Egyptian geese and sacred Ibis. There is ground bird and limited duck shooting. You can fish from the banks of the dam or go out in the fiberglass dinghy which is for guests. There is good largemouth bass fishing. The staff will prepare your freshly caught supper.

There are no wild animals on the ranch, so walking is perfectly safe. There are even walking sticks on a rack in the cottage!

Situated in the wide open spaces of the dry thorn tree country known as Laikipia the beauty and seclusion of this farm with its 200 species of birds make this a very special place.

Wingu Kenda

Wingu Kenda, Box 321, Nanyuki
☎ *(176) 22829, FAX: (176) 32020*

Donna Hurt, ex-wife of the actor John Hurt, is opening her home to paying guests. This luxurious villa, close to the well-known Mt. Kenya Safari Club, has beautifully landscaped gardens with a magnificent view towards the peaks of Mt. Kenya. The house is called *Wingu Kenda* (Cloud Nine in Swahili)—an appropriate name for a dream house in this idyllic setting.

When you stay at Wingu Kenda you are Donna's guests, sharing her home. She has a relaxed American way and is very enthusiastic about this new venture.

Says Donna, "I love people. It'll be great fun. I always have visitors here...friends I love entertaining people."

The house is one of a series of homes built along one rather incongruously suburban road near the gates of the Mount Kenya Safari Club. The houses are grand and tend to have owners who are rich, famous and interested in wildlife conservation.

Wingu Kenda is a rather modern ranch design and is built at the top of a ridge. It is long and rambling and is beautifully constructed and finished. There are big windows nicely encased in wood, wonderful tall stone chimneys, a huge veranda with grand wood posts supporting the high roof. The house is very well setup and equipped for guests. There are three guest bedrooms each with small bar fridge, modern bathroom and sliding glass doors leading out to a veranda.

When you stay at Wingu Kenda there are many attractive activities. On the five acre property are a lovely pool, a sauna, a tennis court and horses to ride. You can take walks or go riding in the forests, and golfing is also very convenient. For those who prefer indoor activities, or for evening entertainment, there is a room for playing pool, a separate and comfortable video room with an awesome video library and John Hurt on the walls.

The house is friendly, relaxed and full of personal memorabilia. There are jewel-colored Tiffany style lamps, wonderful custom wooden furniture by Nairobi-based Marc Van Rampelberg, a gruesomely humorous flying monster by Jim Henson of *Muppets* fame, loads of photos, books, magazines and music. Settle yourself into the comfortable couch by the fire and feel right at home. Smokers will feel especially at ease here.

Activities and meal times are arranged to suit the guests. We sampled a delicious dinner around Donna's glorious large dining table. Breakfast and lunch are usually eaten on the veranda with Mt. Kenya dominant across the valley and a riot of color tumbling over walls and down steps in the terraced garden.

Animal lovers will enjoy staying at Wingu Kenda. In addition to the horses and the huge warthog who is usually confined in the paddocks, there are a host of dogs (mainly large rottweilers) and a bushpig called BP who likes the company of humans. Bushbabies play in a large outdoor cage close to the front entrance.

Staying with Donna is a rather unique experience in Kenya. Most other homestays are hosted by long-time Kenya residents who have a lifetime's knowledge of the bush, the animals, and the country, and tend to offer a rather colonial exX″tence. In contrast, Wingu Kenda feels more like a Hollywood view of Kenya. There is every luxury, comfort, and modern convenience in a relaxed American ambiance. It provides a far more exclusive and personal experience than its busy and touristy neighbor, the Mt. Kenya Safari Club, which, like Wingu Kenda, also has beauty, style and more than a touch of Hollywood.

Ken Trout
Box 14, Timau
☎ *(2) 228391*

Best known for its wonderful trout lunches, which now attract groups of tourists, Ken Trout also offers simple accommodation for overnight stays. There are three cottages and two suites.

Meru — Embu

Meru Mulika Lodge

Msafiri Inns, Box 42013, Nairobi
☎ *(2) 330820, FAX: (2) 227815*

This lodge looks directly over the Mulika swamp which attracts many animals. There are accommodations for 130 guests in a series of thatched bandas and a double-story complex. The main living and dining areas and all the guest rooms have lovely wide open views across the swamp with its scattering of doum palms. In the distance are the high ridges of the Nyambene Hills.

The lodge has pleasant gardens, many exotic trees and a small swimming pool. Guest rooms are threadbare and in need of refurbishing. There are mosquito nets and en suite bathrooms with shower or bathtub. Each room has a private veranda. The lodge is seldom busy and has a rather deserted air. At press time the lodge was closed for renovations. Call for the reopening date.

Patricks Camp Meru

Bush Homes of East Africa Ltd., Box 56923, Nairobi
☎ *(2) 571647, FAX: (2) 571665*

A seasonal tented camp opened in Meru National Park in December 1996. Patrick Pape, who has been a safari guide for 17 years, selected this wild and little visited park to establish a safari camp which he has based on the old hunting camps evident at the turn of the century. There are only six twin tents, each with a safari shower and a private long-drop loo.

According to Patrick Pape, "The camp offers every luxury to the modern day traveler, whilst still retaining the ambiance of a bygone age. The experienced crews, including cordon bleu chefs, are highly skilled in every aspect of client care."

Guests can go on game drives in the park which has been largely untouched by modern tourism. The vegetation is very varied and the animals are quite shy. There is a great abundance of birdlife and the many streams support crocodiles and hippos.

We have not visited this new camp. It is encouraging to know that there is now the option of this style of tented camp in Meru and that nature lovers will have a chance to explore this unspoiled area.

Getting there:

By Plane: private charter from Nairobi or Nanyuki to Meru National Park airstrip transfers included.

Kindani Camp

Langwenda Safaris Ltd., Box 56118, Nairobi
☎ *(2) 445797, FAX: (2) 443267*

Kindani is a small camp which has recently opened in a secluded spot in the seldom visited Meru National Park. The camp caters to a maximum of only 12 people. Instead of tents, guests stay in simple thatched rondavels.

This very basic camp is built on the banks of the narrow Kindani River and is surrounded by riverine forest. The appeal of Kindani Camp is its remote and natural setting. You know you are deep in the African bush, miles from any other tourists. There is a relaxed peacefulness here, rather than any scenic grandeur or excitement.

The managers want to maintain this unspoiled, rustic atmosphere. Roofs are thatched in raffia leaves, there are open-air showers, and there is no electricity. The concept is to provide a natural, bush experience while also catering to basic creature comforts—hot water, flush toilets and comfortable rondavels.

There are five spacious rondavels, each with three beds, mosquito nets, and a wash basin. Close to each rondavel is a toilet in a separate little stone outhouse, and an open-air shower within a shoulder-high circular wall. The rondavels do not have verandas—guests gather in the main open-sided mess with its prime position on the river bank. Typically, only one group of guests are at Kindani at a time.

A mud-colored swimming pool has been built along the side of the river and is filled with river water. Besides relaxing at camp, guests can go on game drives. You are unlikely to see other vehicles. Four-wheel drives are essential—there are many streams to ford, and the earth roads are slippery after rain. There are two Land Cruisers at Kindani for game viewing. The bush is being cleared for a landing strip close to the camp.

Izaak Walton Inn

Msafiri Inns, Box 42013, Nairobi
☎ *(2) 229751, FAX: (2) 227815*

This small inn has 42 very basic double bedrooms each with private bath. It is set in eight and a half acres of lovely gardens and lawns, two kilometers from Embu town on the Nairobi–Meru Road. The inn was originally a farmhouse and is named after the famous English angler because there is good fishing in the mountain streams nearby. The hotel has a bar, lounge, dining room and conference/function rooms for up to 300. It is a convenient stop for tea.

CENTRAL HIGHLANDS
(MT. KENYA AREA)

NORTHERN KENYA

Northern Kenya is a vast expanse of scrub desert extending north from the foothills of Mt. Kenya to the emerald waters of Lake Turkana. It is also a magnificent wilderness with dramatic rock formations, towering mesas, and surprising green slashes of riverine forest to break the rolling flow of endless sun-scorched plains. This area begins at Isiolo where the tarmac ends: the paved road goes from Nairobi to Nanyuki at the foot of Mt. Kenya. From there it climbs through the mountain ranch lands of Timau, then across the northern shoulders of Mt. Kenya to plunge 900 meters in the 40-kilometer descent to the desert and Isiolo, where the unpaved highway north begins.

Unlike the more-traveled Samburu Area, the rest of northern Kenya is seldom included on safari itineraries. The distances are great, the roads are rug-

NORTHERN KENYA

Kubi Fora

SIBILOI N.P.

Lake Turkana

Lake Turkana Fishing

Loiyangalani

CENTRAL ISLAND N.P.

LODWAR

A1 KITALE

Oasis Lodge

SOUTH ISLAND N.P.

LOYANGALANI

C83

C81

MARSABIT N.P.

MOYALE A2

MARSABIT

Marsabit Lodge

Desert Rose

SOUTH HORR

BARAGOI

Matthews Range

Kitich Camp

0   30 Km

N

MARALAL N.S.

MARALAL

Maralal Safari Lodge

C78

WAMBA

C79

ARCHER'S POST

Lake Baringo

Gallmann Memorial Foundation

Ol Malo

Colcheccio

SAMBURU N.R.

BUFFALO SPRINGS N.R.

SHABA N.R.

ISIOLO

B4

D

C51 ELEMENT

NAKURU

NYAHURURU

RUMURUTI

A2

NANYUKI ↔ MERU

ged, and there are fewer places to stay. Traveling in this area requires a major time commitment and serious preparation. The stunning scenery is worth the effort.

Samburu Area

About 65 kilometers beyond Isiolo on the eroded dirt surface of the northern highway to Marsabit are the Samburu, Buffalo Springs, and Shaba National Reserves. As these reserves are essentially one area, you can make game drives in all three no matter where you stay. However, each has separate park fees.

Samburu National Reserve

The Samburu National Reserve extends for an area of 105 square kilometers north of the meandering Ewaso Ngiro or "Brown" River. It is part of a lava plain that includes a varied landscape of red dirt, thorn scrub, broken volcanic rock, dried river beds, steep hills, and rocky outcroppings, some large enough to be called mesas. Following the river curves, a riverine forest of doum palms, acacia, and tamarind is a magical contrast of cool green. It is attractive to the region's wildlife and visitors alike. There are elephant, hippos, crocodiles, and leopards, as well as plains game, other small mammals and birdlife. The region is home to the rare Grevy zebra with large furry ears, gerenuk antelope standing on hind legs to feed, Somali ostriches with their distinctive blue legs, and the shy *oryx beisa*. Most of these can be seen near the tourist lodges and camps that have been built close to the river. See page 398 for additional information on the reserve.

Larsens

Block Hotels, Box 47557, Nairobi
☎ *(2) 335807, FAX: (2) 340541*

Larsens is a small, luxurious, tented camp set in lush lawns at the edge of the muddy river. Everything is green canvas: tents, reception, bar, dining-room. However, the grounds give a sense of permanence and order: clipped and watered lawns stretch between the tents and down to the river; well-kept paths meander among the tall trees; and spacious tents sit on raised wooden decks.

Larsens was named in honor of Eric Larsen, a pioneer of camping safaris and founder of the United Touring Company. The present Larsens was rebuilt in 1988 by the camp staff. The first was washed away during severe floods only months after its initial construction. Those difficult days forged a strong bond among the staff. Together they provide efficient, personal, and friendly service. On arrival, you are greeted with a cold drink under the trees while the manager briefs you on meal times, hot water times, game-drives.

Staying at Larsens is a relaxing and private experience. With only 17 tents, there are no crowds, and children under 10 years are not allowed. There is a feeling of peace and tranquillity—the main sounds are birdsong and the flowing of the river.

Guest Quotes:

> "We've come here many times. It's our favorite place in Samburu...and the food is really first class."

> "We were just sitting on our deck looking towards the bend in the river when two elephant came through the trees and waded right across to the other side."

This is camping in high style, a casual colonial elegance. Toweling gowns are in your tent, the safari chairs have maroon leather seats, and complimentary sherry is served from a decanter at dinner. Brass mugs gleam above the bar, Eric Larsen's old cabin trunks and pith helmet add authenticity, and there are stacks of games and wildlife books. At night you can sit companionably around the campfire listening to the sounds of the night bush, gazing at the Milky Way. In the heat of the day you can relax on your private deck looking towards the river—monkeys play in the trees around you, and you might see animals drinking on the opposite banks.

The mess tent, open on three sides, faces the river. Larsens takes pride in its high quality cuisine. Dinner is served by candlelight. Tables are set with silver and Larsens' china. The food is good and elegantly presented. Breakfast and a barbecue lunch are buffet style, dinner a set-menu with choice of entree. Lunches are packed on request; dinner can be served in your tent.

Safari Journal

The candles flicker, casting shadows on the green canvas of the mess tent. There are only seven tables and the feeling is intimate. I love the contrasts: open sided mess tent and worn safari khaki next to the charming elegance of candles, crystal, and unobtrusive service. Feels as though I've stepped back into an earlier and more gracious time.

Accommodations

The 17 tents, arranged in a row, all face the river and are each named for a bird. The tents have campaign-style furnishings and pleasant en suite bathrooms. Hurricane lamps are hung on each private deck at nightfall. There is generator-produced electricity in the early mornings and evenings for hot showers.

Standard tents have twin beds. There are four tent suites each with one double plus one twin bed. *Best Views*: Hornbills, Bateleurs, Curlews, and Swifts.

Special Offerings

Transportation to swimming pool at Samburu Lodge, game drives.

 ### Samburu Intrepids Club

Prestige Hotels Ltd., Box 74888, Nairobi
☎ *(2) 338084, FAX: (2) 213387*

The Samburu Intrepids Club is like a fantasy tree house with decks built around trees, wooden walkways leading from one area to another and high thatched roofs towering above. The space is breathtaking.

The main lodge stretches above sandy river banks. Shaded by thatch and trees, this soaring lodge is open to the air and river views. The decor is casual, and high quality—smooth leather and wood. You have a sense of harmony with your surroundings. The river flows muddily past, birds are everywhere, and you are likely to see monkeys and lizards. Across the river you may see Samburu tribesmen and their herds.

Safari Journal — Monday

I've never seen anything like the space in this lodge.
The long vaulted corridor, the high log beams reach up... and up...
The thatched roof seems to brush the treetops. Everywhere
the light is touched with cool green as it filters gently
through the trees. How different this is from the pounding sun
of the desert surrounding us.

Beneath trees, high on the river banks are 25 luxury tents. They are furnished in African mahogany and have wooden decks with reclining chairs. There are four-poster beds, overhead fans, and double sinks. Luxuriant vegetation has been trained into lovely gardens near the tents.

Breakfast and lunch are served buffet style outside on wooden decks. Dinner is in the large dining area, open sided, roofed by thatch and lit by hanging gourds. There is an attractive swimming pool, and lounge chairs are placed under a creeper covered trellis.

Accommodations

There are 25 luxury tents, most with twin beds, five with double beds. *Our Favorites*—Best river views #2,#3 & #5. Best double bed tent, #10. The VIP Tent with living room, very special.

Special Offerings

Game drives, camel safaris, nature and bird walks, pool, souvenir and sundry shop, airstrip transfers, river rafting, bush breakfasts, sundowners.

Off Notes

Big game is rather sparse at this end of the Samburu National Reserve.

Samburu Serena Safari Lodge

Serena Central Reservations, Box 48690, Nairobi
☎ *(2) 711077, FAX: (2) 718103*

The Samburu Serena Safari Lodge is located across the river outside the Samburu National Reserve. The lodge is built mostly of natural stone and is surrounded by tall trees and lush established gardens. After driving the dusty roads and trails of the area, walking into reception with its rock garden and pool full of lily-pads gives you the feeling of stepping into another world. The shade is cooling, and there is the suggestion of age and permanence in the rock, the river, and the trees.

Symbols, implements and weapons of the Samburu people are used extensively in the lodge decor to bring guests closer to the life of this land and its people. There are murals on walls and on roofbeams of the dining area. Friendly staff will explain the symbols and subjects, and it is moving to learn that Samburu villagers provided drawings for the decorating artist to enlarge.

The dining area opens out to the terrace lounge overlooking the river. Below is the swimming pool, with several grassy game viewing areas descending down to the sandy river bank beyond. The whole area is a pleasant melding of shady old trees, mellow rock and flowers, sparkling water and sunshine. There are comfortable armchairs at the lounge level, deck chairs and loungers around the pool, and safari chairs scattered for game watching convenience along the lower terraces.

It is easy to watch wildlife from this lodge. You might see an elephant family stroll very close by on the other side of the river wall. You share the excitement with fellow guests when leopards are baited into floodlit view across the river. Crocodiles come up the bank practically at your feet to find their meat, and marabous and wild cats watch carefully for a chance to grab some too.

The lodge is popular with international tour groups and can accommodate up to 132 guests. Cottages have private verandas, most with river view; colorful bougainvillea climbs each high-thatched roof. The rooms are simply furnished and have clean whitewashed walls and bathrooms with shower. Bright local fabrics and natural matting have been used with imagination to create a pleasing decor. The pathways of natural stone are lined with plants and flowers, and on the walk to the main lodge you may spot game along the river or encounter monkeys.

All meals are served buffet style in the open-sided dining room with complimentary champagne at breakfast. A Samburu tribesman protects the tables and buffet from monkeys and birds: they know he is dangerous to them as tourists are not! Kenyan folksingers perform during the dinner hour.

Quotes:

"We just came from London yesterday. This place is beautiful, very exotic and African. We love being right among the animals."

"I liked learning that a Samburu warrior brushes his hair against things and people he loves. That's why the man's hair on the mural touches the hut...it's his home."

Accommodations

There are two standard bedrooms per guest cottage, and all have private bathrooms with shower, ceiling fans, and small verandas. Most have twin beds; some have double beds. There are also six luxury family suites. *Our Favorites*: Standard Rooms #42, 43, 50 & 51 and Luxury Suites #14 & 17 with great river views from balconies.

Special Offerings

Game drives, wildlife lectures, bird walks, swimming pool, camel riding, boutique.

Samburu Lodge
Block Hotels, Box 40075, Nairobi
☎ *(2) 540780, FAX: (2) 545948*

At this large established game lodge, you are greeted by a Samburu tribesman. The lodge is bustling with tour groups. It has a beautiful setting right on the river banks, with the popular Crocodile Bar almost overhanging the water. The dining room is open on the river side with long tables, long lines and the usual safari buffets. The main lodge is polished stonework with high thatched roof.

Rooms for visitors are spread up and down the river in various sizes of cottages and bandas, with a confusing mixture of decor styles. A swimming pool is a welcome relief in the heat of the day. At night Samburu dancers perform, and there is leopard and crocodile baiting. There are daily bird walks, wildlife video shows, and outdoor barbecues twice a week. Four-wheel drive vehicles are available for game drives, and wildlife is usually plentiful in this prime area of the Samburu National Reserve.

Accommodations

All rooms have en suite bathrooms. Some are quite a distance from the main lodge. Some have verandas. *Best River Views*: #60–63 (river deck), #32–33 (standard banda), and #5 & 6 (luxury cottages).

Other Offerings

Gas station, shop for souvenirs and sundries. There is a swimming pool, gas station, and a shop for gifts and sundries.

The Shaba National Reserve

The Shaba National Reserve is south of the Ewaso Ngiro River, but across the Marsabit road from the Samburu National Reserve. It is 145 square kilometers of pristine wilderness full of more dramatic contrasts. There are intimidating flows of volcanic rock and ash; there are 32 kilometers of riverine forest; grasslands are idyllic with herds of wildlife and well-watered by four springs; and there is even a swamp. The towering Shaba Massif rises elegant and aloof above all, sheltering the wildlife of this desert Eden. The vistas are superb, but the rough tracks can be very difficult, especially after rains. The author, Joy Adamson, camped and was murdered in Shaba while working to return a young leopard to the wild. See page 399 for additional information on the reserve.

Sarova Shaba Lodge

Sarova Hotels Ltd., Box 30680, Nairobi
☎ *(2) 333248, FAX: (2) 211472*

Sarova Shaba Lodge is a fantasy oasis of green luxury in the dry scrub and rocky hills of the Shaba Reserve. The bone jolting road leads through black lava flows and stunted trees surreal under their coating of white dust. Then you arrive.

The contrast is staggering. Clear water seems to be flowing everywhere—under little bridges, forming streams in the stone paving, widening into fish-filled pools, and finally cascading into the muddy waters of the Ewaso Ngiro River. The foliage is lush and green; the swimming pool, sparkling aqua; and the architecture, fantastic and fun—soaring thatch, dining area raised high in the trees—a whimsical blend of Africa, Polynesia, and the East. Small wonder the word "paradise" is mentioned so often in the visitors' book.

Sarova Shaba is near the *Born Free* camp site of Joy and George Adamson and close to natural springs which provide all of that wonderful flowing water. Local materials have been ingeniously used in the construction and furnishing of the lodge—rush chairs, stone floors, bold and colorful curtains. The overall effect is natural and bright.

The imaginative swimming pool deserves special mention. No geometry here; instead, the pool is shaped in a series of blue coves bordered by natural rock gardens and flowers. There is a romantic island with a thatched shelter and bentwood chairs—in one cove water cascades down high natural rock walls while you rest on an underwater ledge. You feel as though you are swimming in a private lagoon.

The dining area is built high on timber stilts and shaded by a series of peaked thatch roofs. It overlooks the river and the pool. Doum palms grow triumphantly through the roof. You can hear the relaxing sounds of birds and the rushing of the spring water below. All combine to create an atmosphere of natural tranquillity. Disney eat your heart out!

Safari Journal
afternoon —

The others went on a game drive. I played Esther Williams in the deserted pool. There were palms overhead and bright birds. The water was "postcard blue" ~ it seemed to flow away without end ~ as though it disappeared over a waterfall....

From your shaded table you can look across the river to the dusty white dryness of the reserve beyond. In the distance, dramatic sheer-faced mesas rise out of the heat. Samburu tribesmen in red herd goats on the opposite river bank.

Eighty-four guest rooms have been built in separate two-story units. Each room overlooks the river, with the upper levels looking beyond to the more distant rocks and crags of the desert.

Stone paths lead between palms and cactus and over streams to the rooms. Some are quite a hike. Rocks accent fantastic sculptured gardens of desert plants, especially dramatic under floodlights at night.

Accommodations

The rooms are colorful, and many natural products have been used with imagination. Although there is no air conditioning, there are ceiling fans and cross breezes. The bathrooms have marble counters and a proper bathtub.

There are standard rooms as well as larger junior suites. A separate fantasy cottage is set in a pond with lilies. A fabulous honeymoon splurge—king-size bed, sunken jacuzzi and bidet... *Best views*: Standard room #84, Suites #5 and #76.

Special Offerings

Conference/banqueting facilities (capacity for 170 theater-style in the "Doum Palm Room"—a beautiful and imaginative setting), pool, crocodile feeding, game drives, bird walks, evening entertainment, petrol station, souvenir and sundry shop.

Buffalo Springs National Reserve

The Buffalo Springs National Reserve makes up approximately 80 square kilometers south of the Samburu National Reserve across the Ewaso Ngiro River. Naturally much of the terrain is similar, but this reserve also includes a stretch of grassy lowland plains and the wonderfully clear Buffalo Springs. See page 394 for additional information on the reserve.

 Buffalo Springs Lodge
African Tours & Hotels, Ltd., Box 30471, Nairobi
☎ *(2) 336858, FAX: (2) 218109*

This is the only lodge in the Buffalo Springs Reserve. Most of the original 40 tents have been converted to concrete bandas with makuti roofs. Bandas are small and tired, but adequate. The main lodge is cool and open to the view at one end. There is a small, poorly maintained swimming pool. Guests can walk down to game viewing areas near the springs. Although the lodge is beautifully sited with incredible vistas and the clear pools of the Buffalo Springs, the lodge does not do justice to its setting.

Marsabit

To reach Marsabit you continue on the corrugated northern highway (A2) past Samburu. You drive through endless flat desert country; then you begin to climb towards Marsabit, a surprising cool, green and hilly oasis rising high above the dry heat of the desert lands. Marsabit means "place of cold," and the temperature can plummet at night. Marsabit is colorful with local Rendille people in their bright reds, beads and earrings. The Marsabit National Park has dense forests, crater lakes, many birds and a variety of wildlife, including elephant and greater kudu.

Marsabit Lodge
Msafiri Inns, Box 42013, Nairobi
☎ *(2) 330820, FAX: (2) 227815*

The lodge has a magnificent location two kilometers within the Marsabit National Park. It is in dire need of refurbishing. The rooms are very basic. Each room has a large picture window overlooking a water hole.

Matthews Range

Kitich Camp
Mythos Ltd., Box 57683, Nairobi
☎ *(2) 333569, FAX: (2) 216391*

Kitich is a small tented camp situated in the remote Matthews Range north of Wamba. The best thing about Kitich Camp is its marvelous valley setting on the banks of the Ngeng River. Surrounded by dense vegetation and beautiful high hills, it is a peaceful, green refuge in the flat semi-desert of Kenya's northern districts—a welcome relief after a long, hot drive.

You go to Kitich Camp for its remoteness, its natural beauty, and the walking.

The new owners,Giulio and Joce Bertolli live at Kitich and have tried to create a pleasant and homey atmosphere. They have spent the last year refurbishing all the tents and public areas using local materials, arts and crafts. A central open-sided din-

ing and bar area is flanked by six tents well spread out along one side of the river. Th
tent interiors have been upgraded and all linen etc. has been brought in from Italy
The bathrooms have also been renovated, but still remain with long drop toilets and
safari showers. Joce takes care of the food, and places an emphasis on good cooking
and individual service.

Kitich is ideal for keen walkers. You can hike up to high rocks for a good view
walk to the deep natural swimming pool in the river and try your skill at swinging
into the pool from a rope. You will be accompanied on your walks by Samburu
guides armed with spears. This valley, which is a forest reserve, is home to many wild
animals including buffalo and elephant. It is a haven for birds and butterflies and ha
some exotic vegetation such as prehistoric cycad palms. Each evening a leopard i
baited across the river from camp.

Getting there: Driving: Kitich Camp is about 480 kilometers from Nairobi
through Isiolo and then Wamba. It can also be a stop on a safari from Samburu to
Baringo. Flying: It is possible to fly to Wamba or to the rough strip somewhat close
to camp. Transfers can be arranged from either Wamba or Samburu.

Kitich closes in April because of the rains.

Rumuruti — Wamba — Maralal Area

Several small, privately hosted places are opening up in northern Kenya
They will appeal to the well-heeled traveler with a yen for exclusivity and a
desire for a more unique "hands-on" experience of Kenya. There are two
places of note south of the Wamba-Maralal road. They are built at the edge
of the same high escarpment, and are only a 30-minute drive from each oth
er. This is high country—too high for malarial mosquitoes.

Getting there: Driving: About five hours drive from Nairobi (through Nyahururu and Rumuruti) or a little longer if you go through Nanyuki. Flying: Both ranches have good landing strips for small planes.

Ol Malo

Bush Homes of East Africa Ltd., Box 56923, Nairobi
☎ *(2) 571647, FAX: (2) 571665*

Ol Malo is a dream come true for Colin and Rocky Francombe who, after many years of ranching in Kenya, purchased this magnificent 5000 acre piece of land for their home. They offer a very personal and exclusive "homestay" experience for up to six guests. They are warm, friendly hosts with a great deal of energy and a love and knowledge of the African bush. For those guests privileged enough to stay at Ol Malo, the memory will remain—and a longing to return.

There are few superlatives which could do Ol Malo justice. The setting is out of this world and the accommodations are indescribably beautiful. On the edge of a steep escarpment, the rock and wood buildings of Ol Malo seem to grow out of the land. Literally everything faces the vast and sweeping view. Immediately below is open bush land punctuated by dramatic rocky outcrops. The land rolls down towards the Ewaso Nyiro River, and, way beyond, range after range of hills and mountains reach for the horizon. Mt. Kenya rises above them all with its distant snow-capped peak catching the light. You are treated to this incredible view wherever you are— lying in bed, in the bath, in the shower, even on the loo...

There are three spacious and romantic guest cottages with the shapes of rooms determined by rocks and the curve of ancient olive wood which has been used as wall beams. Huge picture windows are framed by rough edged stone, and beautifully thatched roofs keep rooms cool. There is sturdy organic-looking furniture, lamps made out of gnarled hunks of wood, handwoven floor mats.... all perfectly in keeping. Touches of comfort are everywhere—bath oil, bottles of mineral water, books and magazines. Each cottage has a sitting area, a large bathroom and a private terrace.

There is a communal living area, part of which is open sided and the other cozy with fireplace and big windows. There are comfortable chairs, masses of books on Africa, a beautiful old grandfather clock, Francombe family photos and, of course, the view. The separate dining room also has a big fireplace, high thatch and the view. The Francombes dine with their guests and dinner conversation is lively with bush adventure stories and tales from the international guests.

Buildings are connected by stone paths which wind through rock gardens with exotic aloes and natural rock bird baths. Here and there are cool green lawns between the rocks—such a surprise and contrast in this wild setting. An outdoor stone terrace serves as a bar in the evening. You sit in camp chairs around an open fire with the stars above and the sounds of elephant below.

A thatched entryway leads to the ingenious swimming pool area. The free-form pool is built right to the edge of the escarpment for a swim-up view. There is a shaded seating area for tea and snacks and seats created out of the natural rocks for sunning. Patches of green lawn add to the exotic. In the golden light of late afternoon I lay in the water marveling at the aerobatics of an eagle riding the thermals while just below me at the waterhole a herd of 40 elephant —several of them very small babies—were vying for water.

It would be heavenly just to spend days relaxing around Ol Malo, but there is all of that African bush below to explore. Colin is an expert and experienced guide who will take you on bush walks. The Francombes are keen conservationists and, in the years they have been at Ol Malo have managed to attract an increasing number of wild animals to their protected piece of land. On one game outing I saw big herds of elephant, giraffe, buffalo, various species of gazelle, a huge hippo sunning itself on the banks of the river, dozens of Kudu and countless species of birds. Ol Malo means "place of the greater kudu" and this area is known for its concentration of these animals, rarely found in other parts of Kenya.

When you are out on a guided game walk or camel ride, you may be treated to breakfast or a picnic lunch in the bush. Escaping the heat of the mid-day sun we settled in the shade of an enormous wild Fig tree on the banks of the river. Two camels trundled down the rocky slope bearing lunch, ice cold drinks and comfortable mats for an afternoon nap.

The rave reviews filling the guest book echoed my reluctance to leave:

> *"We've gone heaven, why do we have to leave?"*
> *"Puts most 5-star hotels to shame. Your hospitality and remarkable facility are tops! We can't wait to return."*
> *"Sumptuous elegance within natural simplicity."*

Colcheccio Ranch

Mythos Ltd., Box 57683, Nairobi
☎ *(2) 333569, FAX: (2) 216391*

Colcheccio is a 26,000 hectare ranch belonging to Count Carletto Ancilotto. This enormous ranch is home to cattle and sheep and to a wide variety of wild animals including elephant, buffalo, giraffe, lion, leopard, kudu, zebras and other plains game. The lodge is built on the edge of a high escarpment with breathtaking views ver plains to distant hills and ridges dominated by Mt. Kenya. These are views which inspire silence and humility.

There are seven attractive bandas which are built right on the edge of the escarpment. The bandas are bright and airy with parquet floors, makuti thatched roofs, and dried papyrus walls. The en suite bathrooms have bidets and are lined in cedar. Best of all, each banda has a huge wooden veranda cantilevered out over the edge of the ridge to make the most of that vast and amazing view.

The lounge and dining area are in a large and rather functional looking building with a high papyrus thatch roof and cement floor. This was a part of the original lodge, and is also right at the edge of the escarpment—again with that grand view. It has a large living room with fireplace and comfy chairs, and big glass doors opening on to a huge wooden veranda where you can look out forever. There is also a smaller room and library. The big dining area is completely open along the view side. Here you can sit on worn leather safari chairs and again appreciate the magnificent views. Far below is a water hole; green grass at the side of a cliff signals a spring; huge rocks standing at the bend of a dry river bed invite exploration. Pan the view with binoculars—there are greater kudu camouflaged amongst the grey thorn bushes, a klipspringer bounces past, and above big birds glide on the thermals—Africa doing its thing—and you are the lucky spectator.

You can get out and be part of it too. There are horses for experienced riders, 4-wheel-drive safari vehicles for day or night game drives and game walks with armed guides. You might walk to a big rock for a picnic breakfast, hike to Crocodile Jaws where the river suddenly disappears to appear 37 meters later in a huge whirlpool, enjoy a sundowner in the bush— the possibilities sound endless. Remember, you are walking where there are wild animals and will be required to sign an indemnity form.

Back on the home front is a good-sized swimming pool and a cement tennis court. Colcheccio's Italian cuisine combines farm fresh produce and high quality imported ingredients. There is a private airstrip on the ranch.

Maralal

Maralal is a Samburu center on cool forested highlands. The "Crossroads of the North," it lies between Lake Baringo and the Samburu National Reserve, and about half-way to Lake Turkana from Nairobi. Maralal boasts a colorful Samburu market, and the Maralal Game Sanctuary lies just outside of town. You can visit "Kenyatta House," where Jomo Kenyatta was last detained before becoming Kenya's first president. Maralal is home of the Maralal International Camel Derby, an annual charity event. Near Maralal is one of the most breathtaking scenes in all of Kenya—the Losiolo Escarpment. You stand at the edge of a colossal amphitheater for this end-of-the-world view. You can see forever, and the land drops dramatically down to the Suguta Valley below.

Maralal Safari Lodge

Maralal Safari Lodge, Box 45155, Nairobi
☎ *(2) 211124, FAX: (2) 214261*

Maralal Safari Lodge is "where the animals come to you." Both the dining room and veranda have views over the water hole and salt lick, and wildlife is less than nine meters from where you eat. Eland, impala, zebra, buffalo, and plenty of warthogs, monkeys and baboons mingle together at close range. Scores of interesting birds are attracted by numerous bird feeders and the water hole. Animals are free to wander in the grounds and guests must look both ways before returning to their cottages. Animals have the right of way!

The lodge is within the Maralal Game Sanctuary. Samburu game rangers lead you on game or bird walks in the cedar forests and hills. A leopard blind is near the lodge, there are camel rides, and arrangements can be made to visit a Samburu village.

The lodge can accommodate up to 54 people in 12 cottages which are built like Swiss chalets of local cedar and stone. Each room has a comfortable sitting area around a fireplace. French doors open on to the sanctuary with a view of the lovely hills beyond. The rooms have cathedral ceilings and a loft for a third bed. There are en suite bathrooms. Gardens and exotic plants add to the charm of this small, personal lodge. New owners have improved the facilities, built a swimming pool and pool bar, added a small conference room and upgraded the cuisine.

Activities:

Guided bird walks and forest plant expeditions, donkey safaris, picnics at World's End or the Petrified Forest.

Getting there

The lodge has an airstrip or you can drive from Nairobi via Nyahururu and Rumuruti.

Maralal – Loiyangalani

This is the last long leg on the way to Loiyangalani on the east side of Lake Turkana. Scenery changes from the high forests of Maralal to barren, hot and dusty plains. There are oases of mountains and ravines from Baragoi to South Horr. Then it is a long rough ride over dark lava plains. Where is the lake?

Desert Rose Lodge

Desert Rose Ltd. Box 44801, Nairobi
☎ *(2) 228936, FAX: (2) 212160*

A new luxury lodge is located in the hills between Baragoi and South Horr. This is the first lodge built north of Maralal in the last 20 years.

The lodge was built on the site of an old hunters' camp where there are lots of acacia trees and a huge rock about 7.6 meters high. There are views up towards the top of mountains and a stream running below.

An enormous rock is the focal point of the lodge and is used as a wall in the dining room. A-frame buildings are constructed of cedar and local brick. There are four double rooms with full bathrooms en suite. A natural pool has water flowing down rocks. There is a permanent water supply, and the lodge will have solar power.

Activities from this lodge are mainly walking—enjoying the vistas, the birds and the vegetation. There is a thick cedar forest, caves, natural springs, rock pools in rivers and abundant bird life. However, not much game is left in this forest reserve. The site is at 1372 meters and is quite exposed. It gets chilly in the evenings, and a big open fireplace is located between the lounge and dining room. A bar and veranda area overlooks the pool and the view.

Emma Chen and her husband Yoav, have been the inspiration and driving force behind this venture. As a child, Emma fell in love with these hills. Now, with a lot of hard work, she and Yoav have turned a dream into reality.

Emma and a partner have been operating Desert Rose Limited Camel Safaris in Northern Kenya for some time. Camel safaris originate from here. Guests have the option of combining a stay at the lodge with a camel safari. There is an airstrip nearby for easier access.

Lake Turkana

Lake Turkana stretches for 288 kilometers up to the northern Kenyan border. It is surrounded by semi-desert and volcanic rock. The heat is intense and can rise to 60° Centigrade. The lake has been called the Jade Sea because of its unusual blue-green color. Strong winds blow, and the lake can become very rough. There are more Nile crocodiles in this lake than anywhere else in the world.

Lake Turkana, formerly Lake Rudolf, has now been named for one of the tribes who live on its shores. It was in this area that Richard Leakey uncovered the three-million-year-old fossils of "Homo Erectus." This prehistoric site is now known as the "Cradle of Mankind." At Koobi Fora there is a museum, and you can see excavation sites.

Loiyangalani

This small settlement on the southeastern shore of Lake Turkana focuses on the Oasis Club.

The Oasis Club

GeoSafaris, Box 24696, Nairobi
☎ *(2) 884258, FAX: (2) 886445*
e-mail: geosafaris@formnet.com

A trip to the Oasis Club can be an awesome experience. The desert looks like a desolate moonscape: there is a certain grandeur in the surreal shapes, and monochromatic colors contrast vividly with the jade of the lake. The Oasis Club brings relief. This cool haven, set back from the lake, is nourished by waters from a natural spring. The spring also fills two swimming pools, and there are forests of doum palms and lush green foliage.

There are 24 very basic concrete cottages—no frills and no fans. Each has its own small veranda and bathroom. The dining room and bar have far more character. They are stone and thatch structures open to distant views of Lake Turkana. Local materials have been used in the colorful, natural decor.

Visitors' Quotes:
"Here you can shake off the shackles of civilization."
"This place is for the traveler, not the tourist."
"The pool is like a warm bathtub—you get cool when you come out!"

The hotel sells the only cold beer for hundreds of kilometers! Food combines tasty German fare with the nightly "Nile" perch from the lake. The owners will help you plan your activities. From the club you can go sport fishing, take a boat to South Island, gape at mounds of crocodiles, go bird watching, prospect for semi-precious stones and crystals, or take a trip to the nearby oasis used in the filming of "Mountains of the Moon." You can also visit the El Molo tribe which has existed unchanged for centuries in this difficult terrain. You could also take an expedition to Koobi Fora (within easy reach by air, but a long haul by car).

Ferguson's Gulf

The other place to stay on Lake Turkana is Ferguson's Gulf on the western side of the lake. To reach this side of the lake, you would take the tarmac road from Kitale. The trip is easier, the views are less spectacular.

Lake Turkana Lodge

Lake Turkana Lodge Reservations, Box 74609, Nairobi
☎ *(2) 760226, FAX: (2) 760546*

This lodge has definitely seen better days. There are rather primitive cabins with verandas facing the lake, a shaded swimming pool, and access to the lake shore. The area is popular with bird watchers and fishermen, and you can often see hippos in the lake. Trips can be taken to Central Island with its crater lakes and to Koobi Fora on the eastern shore. It was closed for renovations at press time. Call or fax them for reopening dates.

WESTERN KENYA

Western Kenya is the most densely populated part of Kenya. It is comprised of the fertile **Western Highlands** and of Kenya's slice of **Lake Victoria**. The Western Highlands extend from Kisii and Kericho in the south to the fertile farming areas of Eldoret and Kitale, which are farther north towards Mt. Elgon. The regional capital, Kisumu, is on the shore of Lake Victoria and is the third largest center in Kenya. The weather is usually hot and humid and has a lively market.

Western Kenya is not on the usual tourist circuit and, for this reason, does not have as many tourist hotels as you find in the game parks or on the coast. Areas of interest to visitors in the **Western Highlands** include:

Tea Estates

Concentrated primarily around the Kericho area, the tea fields undulate into the distance—smooth and uniform in the distinctive light-green "table" of tea bushes.

Kakamega National Forest Reserve

Surrounded by extensive agriculture is this finger of equatorial forest. This tropical jungle, dark, dense and moist, is home to a multitude of birds and butterflies. There are also many reptiles and small mammals. Because this is a unique habitat in Kenya, many species found here are not seen anywhere else in the country. The forest is paradise for birders. There are guides and several nature trails. See page 395 for additional information on the reserve.

Saiwa Swamp National Park

This is a small and seldom visited park. The main attraction is the rare sitatunga deer, a semiaquatic antelope with splayed hooves. There are wooden walkways and raised viewing blinds, many birds and monkeys. See page 391 for additional information on the park.

Mt. Elgon National Park

Mt. Elgon is an extinct volcano which straddles the Kenya-Uganda border. With summit just over 4200 meters above sea level, Mt. Elgon offers plenty of opportunity for walks and hikes. It is well-known for Kitum Cave where elephants mine the salty rock and thousands of bats make their home. See page 386 for additional information on the park.

Cherangani Hills

These high and forested mountains have dramatic scenery and offer wonderful opportunities for walking and trekking.

The towns of Western Kenya hold little of interest for the tourist although there are small but worthwhile museums in Kisumu and Kitale. Most of the accommodations in this region are not in themselves sufficient to prompt a special visit. They are simply mentioned here because they are places to stay if you do want to visit the attractions of the area. The outstanding exceptions are Mfangano Island Camp and Rusinga Island Camp, which are both worthy of special trips.

Lake Victoria

Lake Victoria has an area of almost 70,000 sq. km. The second largest fresh water lake in the world, romantic Lake Victoria featured in early explorers' search for the source of the Nile. Three countries—Kenya, Uganda and Tanzania—border on the lake. Lake Victoria is not a part of the Rift Valley and is a relatively shallow lake. Its shores are host to the bilharzia parasite—don't swim!

Flying Safaris to Lake Victoria

A novel experience is being offered from the Masai Mara—a flying safari to an island in Lake Victoria and a chance to catch giant Nile perch. You fly out of the Mara in the early morning in a single-engined plane. About 45 minutes later, after flying over forests, farms and villages, you pass the hills surrounding Lake Victoria and come to land on either Mfangano Island or Rusinga Island.

WESTERN KENYA

WESTERN KENYA

Mfangano Island Camp

Governors' Camp - Musiara Ltd., Box 48217, Nairobi
☎ *(2) 331871, FAX: (2) 726427*
e-mail: govscamp@africaonline.co.ke

Mfangano Island Camp is a private paradise in the vastness of Lake Victoria. Simply getting there is an adventure. At dawn you squeeze aboard the tiny single-engine "GOV" plane at Musiara Strip in the Masai Mara—then fly west over the escarpment, above the cultivated green checkerboard of the Kisii area, past mountains and over water to land on Mfangano Island. Here you are met and taken aboard one of the camp's motorboats to speed around the island past coves and Luo fishing villages to the secluded bay which shelters Mfangano Island Camp.

Enchantment at first sight. Terra-cotta cottages sit in natural gardens on emerald lawns or appear partly hidden on rocky banks under giant fig trees. A jetty extends from green grass and circular stone steps. The shore is interesting with jutting dark rocks, driftwood, and colorful canoes. Behind it all rise steep forested hills with massive boulders for summits, protecting this magical place from the rest of the world—from time and worry.

The buildings are constructed in the local Luo tribe style, with reddish clay walls and thatched roofs lined with banana leaves. They all have spectacular views over water and are open to the lake breezes. Just steps up from the jetty is the airy lounge with comfortable low rush chairs. The dining area, built higher on the rocky hillside, also has open sides and looks down across the lake. The six spacious cottages, each ightly different in shape and design, have many windows with net, not glass for covering. You are always a part of the environment—feeling the breeze, listening to the aves lap sealike on the shore, or delighting in the evocative call of fish eagles.

The style of service at Mfangano is very personal, friendly and accommodating. ou are made to feel part of a privileged family—one of the managers might join you r dinner; you decide your own agenda for the day, and always there are unobtrusive aff members around to make your stay supremely comfortable. The atmosphere is laxing and laid-back.

om the Visitors Book:

> *"Absolutely beautiful, a rare treat—an island lost in time. Charming decor and delightful fishing."*
>
> *"Robinson Crusoe doesn't have a patch on this. Bloody Fantastic."*
>
> *"I'm not leaving! I'm not! I'm not!"*

An artist's hand has clearly been at work in the layout and decor of the camp. Two ottages sit in gentle lawns close to the water while others are between natural rock rmations reached by winding stone paths. The interiors are interesting and delight-l. Kenyan art and handicraft items have been used in imaginative ways to achieve a armonious effect. You are drawn to wander around your cottage examining musical struments on walls, Kisii carvings on tables, quaint pottery holders for the fresh owers. It is as personal as someone's home.

It is amazing that there can be such a variety of good food served in this remote ot: soups and pasta; roasts and fish; plenty of salads, and a decadent array of des-rts. The fish cakes at breakfast are a specialty, and the coffee is excellent.

Meals are served in the open-sided dining room with views over the lake. There e linens painted in natural colors, fresh flowers, a breeze and the sound of waves reaking.

Mfangano Island Camp emphasizes enjoyment of the lake. There are powerboats well as motorized canoes for fishing and lake exploration, and a traditional dhow fers a tranquil and timeless alternative.

The professionally manned powerboats can take a maximum of four clients to fish r the giant Nile perch. The exhilaration of speeding across water to different islands d from one bay to the next is nicely contrasted with the slow and expectant trolling r perch in the quiet waters. How exciting to catch a big one (some are over 45 g.)—but even if the fish aren't biting, being out in the boat is rewarding enough on s own. Giant fig trees line the shores, villagers do their washing on the banks, fish gles swoop for the fish you throw them, and otters may be playing in the water. here are colorful canoes, romantic fishing dhows and mountain peaks in the dis-nce. The boatman may point out the sacred forest where sacrifices are made when in is needed.

In the quiet of the evening you can choose to fish for tilapia. The bright canoe cks gently near the reeds, the wine is chilled and the clouds tinted in sunset colors.

You can also choose to take a day trip from the Mara to Mfangano Island. Fly an[d] boat in for breakfast, go fishing for perch, and fly back to Governors' after lunch.

Special Offerings

Boat rides, fishing, bird walks, visits to local fishing villages, small lake beach a[t] camp, hikes on the island—caves.

Off Notes

We had to leave.

Safari Journal ~ Thursday finale!

Joan shrieks as the thunder cracks overhead. Lightening must have struck the top of the hill. We are feasting on an elegant dinner in the open sided dining room and looking out over the lake. The storm is awesome and beautiful. Jagged forks of lightening streak across the sky, silvering the lake, and silhouetting a magnificent, gnarled old fig-tree. The jetty and the boats are brilliantly lit for an instant and then we start counting slowly ~ waiting for the thunder. How many miles away is the storm now? I feel so small in this vastness and power. I smile into my wine.

Rusinga Island Club

African Explorations Ltd., Box 24513, Nairobi
☎ *(2) 447224, FAX: (2) 447268*

Most guests fly into Rusinga Island Club from the Masai Mara. You arrive right a[t] the doorstep of the camp. Climb out of the plane, walk through a hedge, under a[n] enormous fig tree, and you are there. Not that there is very much there—and this [is] part of its charm.

A wide stretch of lush lawn grows to the water's edge with just a few huge tree[s,] a wonderful open-sided thatched lounge, three rustic cottages, and a small souveni[r] op. That's all. Oh yes, and the most important features—a jetty, fishing boats, a anding fish scale, and that immense lake just waiting.

Most visitors only come for half a day—do some fishing, eat a single meal and then y back to the Mara. You can also choose to spend the night in this serene and peace-l spot. The papyrus-thatched rondavels (offering accommodation for a total of ten ːople) are simple, attractive, and comfortable. There are en suite bathrooms, elec-icity, and a separate screened sitting area. It is wonderfully relaxing to dine and chat nder the impressive high thatch roof watching the light fade from the sky and the ke.

The fishing for Nile perch from Rusinga is reputed to be especially good, and it is ɔt uncommon for fish over 45 kg. to be caught. There are twin-engined shaded ɔats with up-to-date tackle. In-depth guidance is provided by the expert fishermen ho accompany you. Windsurfing and other watersports are also available.

Rusinga Island Club seems to be home to about a million birds, and along the ιore you are likely to see otters and giant monitor lizards. It is an easy walk to the mous but otherwise unremarkable site of the Mary Leaky Proconsul Man discov-ɾy. Guests might also arrange to go to Ruma Park on the Mainland. This game sanc-ιary is a good place to see roan antelope.

Western Highlands

These highlands are very fertile and densely populated. They form the ag-icultural heartland of Kenya. Most of the towns in this region are small, ag-icultural centers with little to attract the tourist. The hotels in these towns ɛnerally service business travelers and conferences, and are not usually of he same standard as the better known "tourist" hotels in other parts of the ountry. Instead of staying in these "city" hotels, the traveler might find ιore of interest in alternate forms of accommodation such as hosted home-ːays.

Barnley's House

Mrs. Barnley, Box 332, Kitale
No telephone

Jane Barnley's hosted homestay is approximately one kilometer off the main road from Kitale to Lodwar, near the Saiwa Swamp. Jane is a warm hostess and an excellent cook—two reasons to stay in her small, cozy home. She and her daughter, Julia, serve delicious English style meals such as steak and kidney pie and steamed ginger pudding with hard sauce. Vegetarians are given special priority.

Her old settler's house is surrounded by a lovely English garden and is also home to the Barnley's six dogs. There are two comfortable guest bedrooms with twin beds, family bureaus, armoires and a fireplace in each. The small living room, filled with books and magazines, invites guests to relax and read by the fire after tea. A generator provides electricity.

Mrs. Barnley has a gift for making people feel welcome. She and Julia eat with guests and are full of helpful advice about what to see in the area. They can arrange for an extremely knowledgeable guide to take you to the swamp for bird watching. Barnley's box lunches are the best in Kenya! With advance notice, you can also stop at Barnley's for a mouth-watering meal. Campers may use the property and there are three fully furnished tents. Barnley's bird guides may be hired for other safaris.

The Kitale area is a good base for exploring Mt. Elgon and the Cherangani Hills. It makes a convenient stop en route to the western side of Lake Turkana.

Lokitela Farm

Bush Homes of East Africa, Box 56923, Nairobi
☎ *(2) 571647, FAX: (2) 571665*

Here you are guests of Tony and Adrianne Mills on their 350-hectare farm. There are three unassuming guest rooms each with a bathroom. Although there is a private guests' lounge, you join the Mills on their spacious veranda or around the large fireplace in their living room. Meals are taken with the Mills and you are made to feel very much part of the family. As Tony says, "It is our home, not a hotel—there is no late night room-service or masseuse."

The up-country farmhouse looks over a pretty garden with large Nandi Flame trees. Beyond you can see fields of maize—the principal crop on the farm. Mt. Elgon dominates the horizon. You are very aware of being on a farm and can see around the farmyard, admire the dairy cattle, or wonder at the maize "as high as an elephant's eye." The house is hung with farming trophies; early farm noises greet the day; and the food at table is wonderfully farm fresh. Best marmalade we've had!

Staying at Lokitela farm provides insight into the Mills' lifestyle. As one visitor wrote in the guest book, "...a part of Kenya and a way of life that few visitors will experience." This is a place where there is no phone; the generator is switched off at night; the furniture has seen better days; and the bath water is brown. But predinner drinks are offered by the fire; early morning tea can be served in bed; and the hospitality is warm and welcoming.

Lokitela has many well-loved animals. The cats get saucers of milk at teatime; the parrot greets you; and there is a tribe of well-trained dogs. Visiting children can help milk the cows. Paths have been mowed in the riverine forest for riding, walking and bird watching. About 350 species of birds have been recorded on the farm. This, combined with the proximity of the Kakamega Forest and Mt. Elgon, makes this a particularly attractive place for ornithologists. The Mills can arrange to take guests to areas of interest in their 4-wheel drive—complete with viewing hatches.

Activities:

Day visits to Mt. Elgon National Park, Saiwa Swamp, Cherangani Hills and West Pokot—overnight stays at Cherangani Hide.

Rondo Retreat Center

Box 2135, Kakamega
☎ *(331) 30268*

If you want to explore the Kakamega Forest, this is the best place to stay. The center is a nonprofit religious retreat operated by the Trinity Fellowship Project and has only recently been opened to tourists. It is set in beautiful gardens in the middle of the Kakamega forest. There are enormous trees and myriad birds. It is extraordinarily peaceful.

This delightful place has an interesting history. The main house was built in the 1920s by a sawmiller for his wife. She apparently asked for her home to be at the base of the "biggest tree in the forest." The giant Elgon Olive still stands in the gardens. This place has also served as an orphanage and a youth center, and it was the setting for the film *The Kitchen Toto*.

Today, the retreat can accommodate up to 24 people. Guests can choose to stay in the main house, or in self-contained log cottages in the gardens. The cottages have been decorated with flair, and have sitting rooms and kitchens. Guests gather to eat in a beautiful dining hall where good food is served. After dinner guests retire to coffee by the fire.

You can take walks in the garden and set off on paths into the forest. This is " place to be still," to reflect and to relax. You take off shoes before entering the main building. No alcohol is served, and guests are requested not to smoke indoors. Tea is served on the verandah or in your cottage. There is no telephone, but electricity is provided by a generator.

Guides can be arranged for bird-watching and forest walks. Several exotic species of birds found in the Kakamega forest are not seen anywhere else in Kenya. There are a host of butterflies, and monkeys cavort in the trees. The Rondo Retreat Center is 23 km. from Kakamega town and a 4-wheel drive vehicle is needed when it rains.

Imperial Hotel

Imperial Hotel, Box 1866, Kisumu
☎ *(2) 41485*

This is a newer hotel in Kisumu and has a small swimming pool. We did not visit this hotel.

Kakamega Golf Hotel

Msafiri Inns, Box 42013, Nairobi
☎ *(2) 330820, FAX: (2) 227815*

For want of other options, this is where most travelers to Kakamega stay. It is often busy with conferences and birders. This three-story hotel is adequate and rather ordinary. It has a pleasant garden and a golf course. Hotel residents become temporary members of the adjacent sports club.

Kericho Tea Hotel

African Tours and Hotels Ltd., Box 30471, Nairobi
☎ *(2) 336858, FAX: (2) 218109*

Situated in the rolling spring-green tea estates of Kericho is the historic Kericho Tea Hotel, built in the 1950s by the Brooke Bond company. Sadly, it is past its prime—an example of faded colonialism.

The double-story building itself is gracious and charming, conjuring images of an earlier grandeur. There are large public rooms with impressive wood floors, giant fireplaces and plenty of windows. Now, however, the smell of floor polish pervades; huge and inappropriate posters of beach scenes decorate walls; and the place has a scrubbed, but threadbare appearance. Accommodations in the main building range from single rooms to two bright and spacious suites which flank the outdoor dining terrace and have views over the gardens. There are also four sturdy stone cottages with fireplaces. Each cottage has two rooms. Conference facilities are available.

Outdoors, the overwhelming impression is of greens and reds: the red tiled roofs, the spacious green lawns with red cannas and Nandi Flame trees, and beyond, the incredible green of tea bushes. There is a nicely sited and playable tarmac tennis court and a disappointing swimming pool surrounded by stained cement walls. Birds twitter; the pace is slow and peaceful. You can almost feel all that green growing around you.

Kitale Club

Kitale Club Box 30 Kitale
☎ *(2) 20036*

This is one of the oldest full service clubs in Kenya. There are lovely views of Mt. Elgon. The Club is known for its golf course and also has a swimming pool and sauna. There is a restaurant and a bar which is popular with residents in the area.

Besides the old cottages, there are also new ones which are more comfortable and have fireplaces. Rooms have recently been refurnished.

The room tariff includes a low daily membership fee which allows guests to use the sporting facilities.

Mt. Elgon Lodge

Msafiri Inns, Box 42013, Nairobi
☎ *(2) 330820, FAX: (2) 227815*

This very run-down lodge has seen better days. It was once a home with beautiful grounds at the foot of Mt. Elgon. Today you need much imagination to recall its past splendor. The lovely shell is all that remains. The rooms are tatty and cry for renovation. The suite over the front is spacious and full of character. But the decor...(sigh). The restaurant, we hear, does not always have a ready supply of food or even water. Today the impressive grounds and gardens are the best thing going for this lodge. This gracious old building deserves to have past glories restored.

Sirikwa Hotel

African Tours and Hotels Ltd., Box 30471, Nairobi
☎ *(2) 336858, FAX: (2) 218109*

This is the main hotel in Eldoret. Eldoret is seldom on the tourist route. This highrise town hotel has 105 rooms, conference facilities and a large outdoor pool. The rooms are threadbare and the food disappointing.

Sunset Hotel

African Tours and Hotels Ltd., Box 30471, Nairobi
☎ *(2) 336858, FAX: (2) 218109*

If you find yourself in Kisumu, we hear that this hotel has the best view. From your room, you are likely to see the sunset and Lake Victoria. There is also a swimming pool. We did not visit, and cannot comment on the upkeep or ambiance.

SOUTHERN KENYA

South of Nairobi, along the southern border of Kenya, lies some of the most amazing and majestic land in the world. It includes Mt. Kilimanjaro, Africa's most famous mountain, the southern end of the Rift Valley, and three major wildlife reserves: Tsavo National Park; Amboseli National Park, and the Masai Mara National Reserve, which is part of the world-renowned Serengeti ecosystem.

Masai Mara National Reserve

The reserve is 1510 square kilometers of incredible wide open vistas and verdant riverine forests following the looping bends of the Mara and Talek Rivers. It is bounded on the south by the Tanzanian border and is the Kenyan extension of the Serengeti National Park in Tanzania. Ranging in height from 1500 to 2170 meters, the Mara also has some spectacular outcrops and ridgetops. The never-ending views across the grasslands are wonderful, and from Mara ridges and escarpments you see

197

range after range of distant mountains. Looking down on the grasslands marked by thickets and clumps of trees, the land seems spotted or dappled, which is *mara* in Maa, the Masai language.

The quantity and variety of wildlife in the Masai Mara is unequalled in Kenya. This is partly due to increased human usage of the grasslands around the reserve. Beginning in 1949, these human pressures gradually encouraged the animals to find their way into the Mara. Another reason for this movement of animals was the natural increase of elephants in the scrub thickets to the south. By about 1950, when elephant herds became large enough, they opened up the woodlands along the Tanzanian border. Grazing animals were lured there by the new elephant-created grasslands. Predators followed. The result: millions of animals protected and drawing tourists, especially during the great Wildebeest Migration.

Between the Masai Mara and Amboseli lies the southern end of the **Rift Valley** with a moonscape beauty of lava rock, arid undulating plains, and the frothy pink of **Lake Magadi** and its Tanzanian cousin, Lake Natron. Both are rich soda lakes and home to interesting birdlife, including flamingo. Lake Magadi is second in world production of *sodium sesqui carbonate*, or trona. From the lake, it is possible to cross the Rift. However, it takes a four-wheel drive to mount the extremely rough dirt tracks of the **Nguruman Escarpment**, which forms the Rift's western wall. Since maps are sketchy and the bush tracks are often very faint, it is wise to include an experienced guide in your safari group. Through the changing bush and forests, it is possible to reach fantastic viewpoints with the Loita Hills, then the Masai Mara, beyond. See page 397 for additional information on the reserve.

Amboseli National Park

The park became Kenya's first game sanctuary in 1948, when 3260 square kilometers were set aside as a national reserve. Besides being a renowned refuge for wildlife, especially elephant, Amboseli also has perfect views of Mt. Kilimanjaro. At 5895 meters, Kilimanjaro is Africa's highest mountain, its perfect caldera crowned with one-fifth of all the ice in Africa. Although it often seems suspended between low-lying clouds and the deep blue sky, it is actually the highest free-standing mountain in the world. Thanks to movie makers and visitors from around the world, the picture of this magnificent mountain with animals grazing under thorn trees below has become a well-known symbol for Africa.

In 1973, an area of 392 square kilometers of the original reserve was declared a national park. Today, like the Masai Mara, Amboseli's grasslands are in danger of abuse by too many minibuses, though recent regulation may help. The park includes grassy savanna, the seasonal Lake Amboseli, three primordial green swamps and various viewpoints. In the dry season, the dry lake bed and erosion can make parts of the park very dusty. The remains of trees torn by elephant herds make some corners of the park resemble moonscapes or galleries of fantastic driftwood art. See page 381 for additional information on the park.

SOUTHERN KENYA

Chyulu Hills National Park

This park is a young volcanic ridge to the east of Amboseli that extends east and west for 80 kilometers. This park is seldom visited, and the dirt tracks are very rough and require a four-wheel drive. During the rainy season the tracks may be washed away. The 471 square kilometers of this park include beautiful valleys and peaks with views in all directions. From the northern slopes, it is often possible to see Mt. Kilimanjaro in the distance. Rains turn the hills into a soft, rolling green and give rise to underground rivers. See page 381 for additional information on the park.

Mzima Springs

In the adjoining Tsavo National Park West, these waters join other subterranean rivers from Kilimanjaro to create an amazing oasis in the dry scrubland of Tsavo. These springs are a paradise for hippo, fish, and birdlife. A system of ranger-patrolled paths and an underwater viewing room make this a rewarding stop for tourists.

Tsavo National Park

The park covers more than 20,800 square kilometers and includes some of Kenya's most rugged volcanic terrain. Generally very rough, rocky, and wild, Tsavo West includes some of the Chyulu Hills, the Ngulia mountains rising to 1830 meters, and various isolated granite monuments to break up the semiarid plains and bush. This sort of landscape continues into Tsavo East, though much of the eastern sector of the park is flat and empty desert.

To the southwest and surrounded on three sides by Tsavo are the Taita Hills. Rising steeply with spectacular gorges, waterfalls and forests, this striking hill system provides a dramatic backdrop for the Taita Hills Wildlife Sanctuary.

Beyond Taita to the south, the railroad marks the way to Kenya's southernmost town, Taveta. A real outpost since the railroad linked it to Voi in 1924, Taveta is between **Lake Chala**, a crater lake to the north on the Tanzanian border, and **Lake Jipe** to the southwest, a haven for bird lovers. See page 392 for additional information on the park.

Masai Mara National Reserve

The Masai Mara is the most popular game reserve in Kenya. It is an extension of the Serengeti Plains in Tanzania, and offers the best game viewing in

MASAI MARA AREA

Kenya. On these wide open rolling grasslands you can often see an incredible variety of different animals at one time. Perhaps a cheetah mother sits on a termite mound with her punky-looking cubs, while beyond, gazelle, antelope and zebra placidly graze. Giraffe might peer curiously through the trees, while elephant pass on silent feet and vultures circle above. Every year millions of wildebeest migrate north from the Serengeti to the green grass of the Mara. This exciting spectacle usually occurs sometime between July and August.

Even when animals are not highlighting the scene, the views by themselves are worth the trip. Imagine bright oblique rays of evening light slanting under blue-black storm clouds. The rich golden expanses of waving grass are brilliant in this light, and the solitary flat-topped acacia tree is dramatically spotlighted on the crest of a hill. Beyond rise the steep smoky blues of the Oloololo Escarpment—such distances, such breathing space. At sunup you may be hanging on to the open overhead hatch as your Land Cruiser plunges down a rocky track to ford a rushing stream. Your hands feel frozen solid, and the steep climb on the other side looks impossible. You loosen your knee joints, tighten your grip and grin inanely—what fun!

The abundance of game and easy game viewing has led to an explosion of lodges and tented camps in and around the reserve. At the time of writing, there are at least 20 places to stay—more than double the number that existed six years ago. As a visitor you have many attractive choices. You can choose to stay in a luxury tent with no electricity, where animals are free to wander into camp, or you might opt for the opposite extreme—the solid walls of a lodge with a swimming pool.

Some of the camps and lodges are within the reserve itself, others are outside. To enter the reserve you must pay a park fee. Places outside of the reserve do not have to adhere to park rules and can offer game walks as well as night game drives. Animals, however, are not confined to the reserve and are also found in good numbers outside. You are also likely to see human habitation, especially Masai with their herds, when you stay outside the reserve.

Visits to a Masai *manyatta* can be arranged from many of the camps or lodges. Another popular "excursion" is a romantic hot-air balloon trip where you view animals from above and then touch down for an extravagant breakfast in the bush. Pricey but memorable. Another day or overnight jaunt offered from the Mara is a flying trip to an island camp on Lake Victoria where you fish for giant Nile perch (see Western Kenya).

You are likely to go on at least one or two game drives a day when you stay in the Mara. Early morning and evening drives are the most popular—they can also be very cool, so remember to pack some warm layers along with your hats, suntan lotion, binoculars and malaria medication.

The growth in places to stay in and around the Mara also means that there are more visitors and more minibuses. Although you are still guaranteed to see a lot of game, there are times and places in the reserve when vehicles jostle for position around an animal (usually a cat), and the sounds of video cameras and revving engines destroy the peace. Many visitors have their hearts set on seeing "the Big Five." After spotting lion, the minibuses rush off in search of elephant. (It is rare to see rhino here.) Remember that there are great rewards in switching off the engine—just watching and listening to the everyday life of this marvelous part of Africa.

Travelers to the Mara arrive by plane (there are several small landing strips) or by vehicle. The trip from Nairobi is long, bumpy and spectacular

Those driving by minibus tend to concentrate in the southeastern part of the reserve. The camps farther from Nairobi attract more flying customers and tend to be better equipped with their own game watching vehicles. During the rainy seasons the roads become very difficult, especially where there is black cotton soil, notorious for trapping vehicles.

Governors' Family of Camps

The Governors' Family of Camps provides luxury and comfort while retaining the authentic flavor of safari camping. There is still excitement—wild animals in camp, only canvas overhead—and yet you can have a hot shower and iced drinks. The high quality of food and service seem amazing in this rough, bush setting miles from civilization.

Most visitors to the Governors' Camps fly to the Governors' Musiara Airstrip just minutes from the various camps. There are four of these camps all sited among the trees along the banks of the Mara River, which loops back and forth in this western section of the Masai Mara Game Reserve. Each of these camps has its own unique character. They include:

Governors' Camp
Largest and best known.

Little Governors'
Our favorite camp in the Mara and the smallest of the Governors' permanent camps. Its site around a small marsh is reached by crossing the Mara River by boat.

Paradise Camp
Designed to look more like a rough safari camp.

Private Camp
Gives your group the feeling of being on a traditional mobile safari with a camp set up for you alone.

All of the camps give you bush camping without fences. Animals are free to wander very close and even into camp, though armed Masai guards patrol day and night to assure your safety.

Governors' emphasize high quality food and friendly attentive service. Food is generally superior with a tempting array of salads, entrees, breads, and desserts. At Private Camp, you can work with the Governors' Executive Chef to plan your own menus.

Each tent has a covered outdoor veranda with two safari chairs and a small table. Simple tent furnishings include twin beds, a wardrobe rack, a desk/dressing table and safari chairs. None of the camps uses electricity to light the tents. Candles, matches, lanterns and flashlights are provided. Screened windows let in light and air during the day and are covered at night.

All the tents at each camp have private tented bathrooms with a flush toilet and hot showers. The more rustic rely on traditional safari showers, while at the other extreme, Governors' and Little Governors' even have bidets.

Game drives in open-topped green Land Rovers are included in the tariff. Driver/guides will design the game drives to suit individual preferences and are willing to share their extensive knowledge of the birds and animals. Guides can take guided game walks in a conservation area adjacent to the reserve.

Little Governors' Camp is home to **Mara Balloon Safaris**. You can splurge on this unique adventure to float over the Mara at sunrise watching for game below. After landing you are served the traditional champagne breakfast in the bush.

You can also arrange to fly for a day trip to the Mfangano Island Camp in Lake Victoria, or better yet, stay overnight in one of the camp cottages. (See Mfangano Island Camp for details.)

Governors' Camp

Governors' Camps - Musiara, Ltd., Box 48217, Nairobi
☎ *(2) 331871, FAX: (2) 726427*
e-mail: govscamp@africaonline.co.ke

This was the first tented camp to be established in the Masai Mara National Reserve. "Main" Governors', as it is sometimes called, first opened in 1972 on the site of Teddy Roosevelt's Mara camp. It is now one of the best known camps in the Mara, and especially popular with American clients.

Although Governors' is also one of the largest camps, you never see more than a few tents at a time. Amazingly enough, as many as 38 green tents are sited along the high banks of the looping Mara River. Tall old trees, clipped green lawns, and the quiet river give everything a feeling of tranquillity. You can watch and listen to birds, you may even see larger animals which sometimes wander into camp. It is quite possible to wake up to the sound of hippos feeding on grass outside your tent.

Safari Journal
Thursday ~ deep night

Gracious dining ... fine linens. We were lingering over coffee in the candlelit dining tent. Suddenly the quiet of the night was broken by the dramatic arrival of Maasai warriors. First we heard the spine~tingling resonance of their many-voiced chant. Then they were among us, flickering shadows, flowing and twisting and turning just as their river flows and twists and turns. Their movements were strong and fluid, accented by the deep red of their shukas. Mesmerized by the sound and movement, we followed them to the campfire. We were lucky: the trance-like dancing, which is also warrior-training, flowed on ~ finishing with the astonishing and traditional high jumping ~ a test of spirit and strength .... then they were gone, but some of their conjured spirit remains....

Quotes:

> *American businessman sitting in front of his tent, drink in hand,*
> *"This is really hard to take, isn't it?"*

The reception area is built of natural stone and features a small museum showing mounted photographs and bronze sculpture of wildlife.

The tented bar/lounge, open on three sides, is especially inviting with its bar buil
of logs. Nearby, there is a cleared area overlooking the river where breakfast and
lunch buffets are served when the weather is fine.

Fine à la carte dinners are served by candlelight in the dining tent, which seem
intimate and private, though it can seat 100. The meal ends with the arrival of loca
Masai musicians or dancers who then draw you outside to the traditional camp fire.

Accommodations

Each tent is sited on a cement foundation with a private bathroom. There are hot
showers, flush toilets, wash basins, and even bidets. *Our Favorites:* For best view o
river—#19, 22, 23. For privacy—#12, 12a, 14. *Note:* #25–30 are noisy, public and
near parking. #1–3 are set back with no river view.

Special Offerings

Game drives, balloon safaris, fishing on Lake Victoria, museum, superior souvenir
boutique, doctor, airstrip. *Please Note:* There is no swimming pool.

Off Notes

A larger camp means more people and more noise.

Little Governors' Camp

Governors' Camps - Musiara, Ltd., Box 48217, Nairobi
☎ *(2) 331871, FAX: (2) 726427*
e-mail: govscamp@africaonline.co.ke

This is our favorite place in the Mara—getting there is half the fun. First, you cross the Mara River in a little boat pulled along a fixed rope by the boatman. Then you climb steep steps cut into the bank and walk down a shady forest path. Suddenly you step out into an open glade: Seventeen tents curve around the edge of a marsh, looking toward the plains and high escarpment of the Mara. In a word, spectacular!

There is something about this camp that is very friendly, yet private. Guests seem to enjoy mingling with the staff and with each other, and because of the smallness of the camp, you really feel special.

Little Governors', with its open views and no fences, makes it possible to be very close to wildlife. When we visited, a family of giraffe browsed just beyond the last tent, some waterbuck wandered through the marsh, and the elephant, affectionately known as "Winston," made one of his regular visits to camp.

When we visited, the food seemed particularly good, especially the "sinful" desserts. Breakfast and lunch are served buffet-style outside under tall trees with views over the marsh and towards distant ridges. Candlelit dinners are served in the cozy dining tent. In this setting it feels natural to combine the elegance of silver, crystal and linen with canvas, safari chairs, and lanterns. After dining, guests like to sit quietly around the campfire enjoying liqueurs, stories and stars.

From the Visitors' Book:
> *"We came as guests and were looked after like the Royal Family."*

Accommodations
All the tents look out across the marsh. Each tent has an adjoining tented bathroom with flush toilets, bidets and running water. There is no electricity. *Our Favorites:* Spectacular view of escarpment, slightly more private, #1 and 2. Game viewing at tent flap, but quite a hike from camp center, #17.

Balloon Safari Launching
Book a ride with champagne breakfast. Or bring your camera to the launch area. The whole take-off rigmarole is tremendously exciting, and the rainbow-hued balloons are a treat to see. Other Offerings: Same as for "Main" Governors' Camp.

Off Notes
The steps down to the boat and up to the camp across the river are steep, not easy for an out-of-condition middle-aged on-holiday camper...You can hear balloons inflating for early morning flights.

SOUTHERN KENYA

Safari Journal
Friday, high noon ~

"Hey, there's an elephant in the dining area!"
The shout drew me with the other disbelieving new arrivals.
Sure enough, there was an elephant right in camp, reaching under
the screening cloth with his trunk to sample things set out for the
lunch buffet. We all wanted to get near this wonderful, huge beast.
Then i was practically bowled over by a youthful camp manager
hurrying toward the dining area and looking harassed.

"Stay back, just stay back, everyone," he whisper-shouted
in his best quiet—but-projecting voice. "It's only Winston.
He doesn't bother the tents, but you have to remember not
to get in his way. After all, he is wild." Winston didn't look wild
to me, but he certainly looked big. The young manager looked resigned
as Winston ate a potted plant, then stripped a small tree for dessert.
i was sorry when the elephant made his ponderous way
down the path out of camp with an honor guard of camp watchmen...

Governors' Paradise Camp

Governors' Camps - Musiara, Ltd., Box 48217, Nairobi
☎ *(2) 331871, FAX: (2) 726427*
e-mail: govscamp@africaonline.co.ke

💰💰💰💰💰

Governors' Paradise Camp is located in the same general area as Main Governors and Little Governors', but you are just that much closer to real bush camping. Each year after the long rains, this traditional old-style safari camp reappears. Governors canvas tents are pitched directly on the ground in the uncleared bush along another twisting loop of the Mara River.

The 20 tents give you most of the same comforts of the other Governors' camp including tented bathroom with a flush toilet. However, water for washing and bath ing is hand carried to the tents, and hot water is supplied on request for the overhead gravity showers. Again, there is no electricity.

The service and food that have become traditional at the other Governors' camps are brought to Paradise in an unobtrusive way.

You feel very close to nature.

Governors' Private Camp

Governors' Camps - Musiara, Ltd., Box 48217, Nairobi
☎ (2) 331871, FAX: (2) 726427
e-mail: govscamp@africaonline.co.ke

Governors' Private Camp can be booked as your own private safari camp in the cool green Mara River forest. You can include from four to 16 people in your safari party. It must be reserved for a minimum of three nights.

The comfort of the Governors' tents, with behind-the-scenes service, gives you all of the luxurious attention of a mobile safari without the very high costs. Again, there are flush toilets and showers, but no electricity. You can plan your own camp schedule and choose your menus with the executive chef. Bar orders, except for French champagne, are included. The lounge/mess tent can be used for parties or meetings. The camp hosts know the surrounding area and wildlife and will be happy to help you plan your activities.

Mara Intrepids Club

Prestige Hotels Ltd., Box 74888, Nairobi
☎ (2) 338084, FAX: (2) 213387

Mara Intrepids Club is a luxury tented camp in the Masai Mara National Reserve. With the Talek River on the South joining a small tributary of the Mara River to the West, the camp is set apart as an oasis of comfort and privacy under spreading trees.

The 27 tents are scattered among the trees and along the riverbanks in secluded groups of three or four. In camp you walk along flagstone pathways winding through the riverine forest. There are birds and monkeys in the trees, eager to share early morning tea on your veranda. You have the romantic feeling of being on your own private safari in the African bush. In fact, some tent clusters include a club tent equipped with bar, fridge and dining table. You and your party can plan a personal barbecue and campfire with the help of the Intrepids staff.

The tents are fun! They are rustic and natural with handcrafted safari furniture of wood and leather, but they are far from basic. There are canopied beds, hand-woven rugs, full-length mirrors, electrified lanterns sitting on barrel tables and several zip-and-screened windows. Each has a private veranda and en suite bathroom with zip-down door and separate shower. The flashlight and big black umbrella are nice touches. There is even a fascinating safari box with folding mirror and hidden compartments—Finch-Hatton, where are you?

In keeping with the traditional safari experience, breakfast and lunch are served buffet-style in an outdoor dining area. The tall trees above are alive with the sounds of more birds and monkeys. Dinner is served more formally in the open-sided dining tent.

The lookout tower near the airstrip is set up as a sundowner bar in the late afternoon, providing a good place to relax after game drives and to watch for game at sunset. A rustic swimming pool surrounded by interesting rocks offers cool relief and a lazy place to rest in the heat of the day.

There is a rustic bar with comfy leather chairs near the river. Wildlife videos are shown in the adjoining alcove. Every night, leopard bait is hung out across the river to entice this beautiful and secretive animal into floodlit view. Enjoy this exciting spectacle in comfort from the bar, or get an even closer view from the wooden deck extending out over the river.

Quotes:

> *"This camp is like an island. Did you see the bridge we drove over? Just two parallel strips of metal track...we were "intrepid" for sure..."*

Nearby, a wooden suspension footbridge spans the river. The wobbly crossing adds a charming sense of adventure to any Intrepids game drives which set off from the opposite bank. Vehicles are a well-used fleet of green Land Rovers. They have wide open top and sides and are tough and cheerful. Mara Intrepids' unique location means that you rarely see a vehicle from somewhere else. Once you leave camp you are immediately among the wildlife, and the scenery in this part of the Mara is superb—varied and memorable.

Accommodations

Most tents are twin-bedded and some have double beds. *Our Favorites*: You can hear the sound of falling water from Kiboko Cluster, and Mamba Cluster offers a nice view of the river. Chui Cluster, across the river, has more open views.

Special Dining

You can have private meals in your club tent. A barbecue can be cooked and served just for you, and you can end the evening relaxing around an open camp fire near your tents. It feels as though you are on a private fully-catered camping safari—"doing" Africa in style.

Special Offerings

Arrangements for sunrise balloon safaris, airstrip, observation tower, swimming pool, souvenir/sundry shop, bush breakfasts, sundowners and game walks with resident naturalists.

Off-Notes

Private barbecues in the cluster club tent can put a damper on your enjoyment if it is given by another party sharing the cluster and your tent is not invited. All that transpires is audible, and well-meaning staff may have "borrowed" your veranda's safari chairs to furnish the other party's camp fire area.

Sekenani Camp

Chartered Expeditions Kenya Ltd.
and Utalii Tours and Safaris Ltd. Box 61542, Nairobi
☎ *(2) 333285, FAX: (2) 228875*

The Sekenani Camp Visitors' Book is crammed with flattering superlatives and promises to return. Easy to see why. This small gem of a tented camp offers luxury, comfort and personal attention wonderfully mixed with the adventure and excitement of being in the untamed African bush.

Sekenani Camp is just outside the National Reserve (six kilometers from the Sekenani Gate). It has a most unusual setting. From the dense vegetation and deep shade of a stream bed, you climb up to a dry grassy ridge. Here, 15 tents have been thoughtfully sited so that each has a view and is far enough from its neighbor to insure privacy. From your deck you might look down over a marshy stream which attracts game, or up to the hills and plains beyond.

The tents are surrounded by natural vegetation and blend harmoniously with the scenery. The tents at Sekenani are amazing. They get our vote for being among the most luxurious in Kenya. Raised high off the ground on wooden platforms, the tents are extra large with many generous screened "windows." When you walk into the tent, you are struck by its bright airiness and most especially by the bathtub which is centered in the bathroom. Not what you expect under canvas. Nothing bashful or apologetic—a big, elegant bathtub with brass taps and individual gas water heaters.

Other quality touches are the fine wooden toilet seats, beautiful hand-carved and painted chests with locks and handsome polished wood floors. The bedspreads and floor rugs are white, contributing to the light and spacious feel of the tent. A counterpoint to this "sophistication" is the absence of electricity. At nightfall, hurricane lamps glow in the tents. The dining area is built on another rise and faces a wide expanse of natural veld with hills beyond. To reach it from the tents you cross over a small ravine on a wooden bridge.

The dining/meeting space is a log and canvas structure with high peaked roof and completely open at both ends to let in air, light and distances. Extending beyond the covered dining area is a large stone terrace—a perfect place to sit and look for game or chat companionably around a log fire at night, listening for animal sounds and admiring the bright stars above.

Safari Journal ~ 6:30 a.m.

The sun is beginning to rise. I can see pink and gold tingeing the sky, and there is a steaming cup of tea beside me. I am lying in my bathtub ~ quite fantastical in a tent! From here I can see out a window to the hills beyond, and the early morning bird chorus sounds loud and cheerful through the canvas walls. Beside me is the "toothbrush stick" our Maasai guide cut for me on the bush walk yesterday. I arrived back at camp scrubbing at my teeth and with the leaves of another plant under my arms ~ absorbing and aromatic, and used by the Maasai as deodorant when they are on long journeys. It is especially rewarding to be out in this wonderful countryside and not always have to view everything from behind glass in the "safety" of a vehicle.

From the Visitors' Book:

> "This is the ultimate in roughing it in elegance!"
>
> "Three weeks in Africa—this place was the best—good food and the warmest nicest staff. Fabulous. We will be back."

A small attractive building of natural stone looks down over a marshy pond. It houses a small shop with quality craft items and a large covered deck where you can relax while enjoying the many birds and with luck perhaps larger animal visitors.

The small size of this camp allows for great flexibility and privacy. Meal times and bush walks are arranged to suit. A tempting variety of special activities are offered at an extra charge. These range from private dinner parties or sundowners in the bush to game walks with an experienced Masai guide who will also tell you tribal uses of the plants you pass. Remember to ask about these activities if you are not briefed on them.

Quotes:

"A lion took a zebra just nearby. It was 1:30 p.m. so we said 'hold lunch' and took a vehicle to look for the lion." Asst. Manager.

"How exciting walking with the Masai guide—his spear and his knowledge of the wild were our only protection." Guest.

Accommodations

All tents have views and privacy. #4 and 6 have double beds. *Our Favorite*: #6 for open view and double bed.

Special Offerings

Game drives, bush banquets, game walks, talks about Masai culture, airport transfers.

Off Notes

The nearest gate into the Reserve is six kilometers away. However, you are likely to see game from the camp itself.

Kichwa Tembo Camp

Conservation Corporation Africa, Box 74957, Nairobi
☎ *(2) 750298, FAX: (2) 746826*
e-mail: conscorp@users.africaonline.co.ke

Kichwa Tembo is a large and well-maintained tented camp just outside the National Reserve to the northwest. Popular with its predominantly American clientele for its setting and high standards, Kichwa Tembo has an aura of permanence and quality. Although guests sleep in tents, the camp has the trappings and comforts of a first-class permanent lodge. There are notice boards in the lobby, a large gift shop, laundry service and carefully tended and fenced grounds. Most of the camp faces broad, parklike lawns with dramatic circular cactus gardens. Beyond, there are wide open vistas of Mara savanna.

One of the Mara's largest tented camps with 45 well-appointed tents, Kichwa Tembo also has six rondavels to cater to those who prefer to sleep behind walls. The tents are set fairly close together, but they all have private views from their verandas. Many face the long sweeping Mara view while others look over more secluded forested areas alive with birds and monkeys. The tents are spacious with many screened "windows" and a large bathroom with a stone floor. *Kichwa Tembo* means elephant head in Swahili, and the elephant theme is reflected in the rugs and bedspreads.

You approach the camp on a shaded dirt road through a dense stretch of indigenous forest, home to an interesting variety of monkeys. The circular lobby with its high thatched roof and red polished floor is cool and dark, a marked contrast with the view which greets you out the other side—golden space stretching forever.

The long dining room and circular lounge have wide openings between stone pillars and also face this marvelous vista. Afternoon tea and sandwiches are served in the lounge with its heavy wooden chairs, low tables, and yellow lights in hanging baskets. The roof is lovely—thatch lined with pale golden papyrus which contrasts with dramatic black supporting beams.

Safari Journal
dawn . . .

I lean against a tree to watch the sun rise over the vast plain. There is dew on the grass. Zebra and impala catch the early light ~ bright focal points in all that space. . . . The view in front of me is wild and timeless, and yet just behind are tended flower gardens, comfortable chairs, and a swimming pool ~ the hand of man. Early morning tea is being delivered to tents. An impala spronks ~ leaping up and down, white tail showing ~ an expression of joy or a warning? The day begins . . . .

There is a secluded swimming pool, its unusual shape edged by big boulders and gardens of cacti and palms. On the lawns surrounding the pool are chairs and comfortable loungers. It is quite luxurious to swim in the heat of the day, then lie in comfort with a cool drink and watch for wild animals which might be only a stone's throw away.

Most guests fly to the Kichwa Tembo airstrip just five minutes from the camp. There are package rates which include game drives, (the camp operates 26 Land Cruisers). You can go on a nature walk or visit a Masai manyatta. Picnic lunches are available, and there are binoculars for hire. Masai dancers perform most evenings, and it is possible to organize bush breakfasts or banquets—even a "black-tie" dinner which is served under the stars with crystal glasses etc. (P.S. you don't really need a tie).

From the Visitors' Book:

"The service, the game, and the tents were top notch. If all camps were like this, there wouldn't be any hotels."

Accommodations

There are 45 tents and six cottages. *Our Favorites*: Tents H5-H14 for sweeping views, FE A and B for privacy, and D 1–12A if you can't get the others.

Other Offerings

Game drives, balloon safaris by arrangement, nature walks, Masai manyatta visits, swimming pool, games available at reception, registered Clinical Officer.

Off Notes

There are lots of tents close together... A popular camp means lots of people, and canvas is not very soundproof... That marvelous wide view also includes game drive vehicles and the occasional plane landing in the distance.

Mara Safari Club

Lonrho Hotels Kenya Ltd., Box 58581, Nairobi
☎ *(2) 216940, FAX: (2) 216796*

If you love hippos, the Mara Safari Club is the place for you! Set along the looping Mara River at the northeastern part of the Mara, this luxury tented lodge combines the romance of tented accommodations with all the security and comforts of a grand lodge. From the effusive hostess who greets you in her stylish African dress, to the pool which is heated, the Mara Safari Club aims to please in every way.

SOUTHERN KENYA

The spacious lodge, built of dark wood logs with high peaked ceilings, is sited on the edge of the Mara River. The open-plan, multi-level design follows the curve of the river. Although the lodge includes reception, dining room, bar, fireplace, lounge and gift shop, its unusual and asymmetric shape helps to mask its size.

A wooden deck curves along the outside of the lodge over the banks of the river. Here are two pleasant and shaded seating areas with nice views of the river and the resident hippos.

The hippos are a highlight of staying at the Mara Safari Club. You can see and hear them in the river—often from the deck of your tent. There is something humorous and special about lying in a tent at night listening to hippo wuffles and snorts! The high, steep banks of the river and electric fences ensure that they do not wander into camp.

Each of the 45 tents is near the edge of the river bank. The tents are raised on high wooden decks, and the natural growth between them gives a sense of privacy. Stone pathways and green lawns lead from the lodge to the tent sites. The natural and rustic mix pleasantly with the established and well-tended.

Near the lodge is an attractive, heated pool with lounge chairs and stone paving partly shaded by tall trees. There is an outdoor bar and grill. Safari chairs and tables are sometimes set up near the pool for alfresco eating at lunch—very pleasant with the sounds of birds and the river below. (We wished we could have eaten all our meals outside.) Breakfast and dinner are served in the main dining room which is split into two levels with dark wood walls and matching furniture.

Safari Journal
midnight

Suddenly I was wide awake. Hippo Noises . . .
Worse than your snoring.
Wish you were here!

After the evening game drive, a fire is lit in the lounge where tea is served. In the evenings a slide-show/lecture by the resident naturalist alternates nightly with Masai dancing.

Since it is outside of the Masai Mara National Reserve, the Mara Safari Club is able to arrange for morning walks, sundowner cocktails, or bush banquets. On your game drives you are also likely to see stately Masai herders in their vivid red *shuka*.

Up to three game drives a day are included in the tariff. The Mara Safari Club has a fleet of 16 Land Cruisers modified for game viewing: seats covered in green canvas, field guide books, binoculars, a cooler filled with drinks, and well-padded, open roof for game viewing.

Most guests fly in to the all-weather strip close by.

Quotes:

> "This place is rustic but classy, elegant but informal. It's relaxed and friendly with a nice atmosphere."

> "The main building reminded me of a ski lodge—big and dark."

Accommodations

The tents are luxurious, fun and well-equipped. Four-poster beds are bedecked with a striped canopy and mosquito net, and colorful carpets are on the floors. There are thick toweling bathrobes, and the shower and sink in the en suite bathroom are both encased in wood. The electricity is on all night—great for readers. *Best Tent*: #12 has a king-sized bed and sunken bathtub as well as a superb view of the river and the surrounding hills.

Other Offerings

Balloon safaris, bush banquets, sundowner cocktails, B.B.Q. dinners, visit to Masai village, souvenir shop, airstrip, fishing on Lake Victoria (see Rusinga Island Camp), "Off the Beaten Track Walking Safaris" (see Rekero Farm), visit to "Wanga" Rhino

Sanctuary with white rhino roaming freely on private grounds. Off Notes: The interior of the lodge is rather dark.

Siana Springs

Conservation Corporation Africa, Box 74957, Nairobi
☎ *(2) 750298, FAX: (2) 746826*
e-mail: conscorp@users.africaonline.co.ke

Siana Springs is a tranquil tented camp outside of the National Reserve. On the site of the old, well-known Cottars' Camp, Siana Springs is the closest Mara camp to Nairobi and is popular with people driving from the capital. Although it is some distance from the busy Sekenani Gate, you are likely to encounter game close to camp without necessarily driving into the reserve.

Being outside the reserve allows Siana Springs to offer a variety of walking and dining experiences in the bush. You can go on bird or game walks with Peter Blackwell, the camp naturalist. You might pass elephant on foot, or enjoy sundowners from a high rock looking down at game in the plains. After dark you can go on night game drives.

The 20-hectare Siana Springs property ranges from flat grassy spaces with random thorn trees, to areas of lush dense growth around water from natural springs. It is these springs which give the camp its name and which attract animals to the area. The veld grass has been cut between the tents, but there has been no attempt at manicured lawns or planted gardens—the natural bush has been retained. Around the camp stretch wide panoramas of the Masai Mara—golden distances, green acacia and rocky hills.

There are 38 tents which have been arranged in three separate groupings: Acacia, Bamboo and Palm. Each of these groups has its own butler who will bring drinks, clean shoes and so forth. The tent furnishings are large, solid and heavy—chunky beds and tables custom-made from pale logs of Blue Gum. Electric fans provide coolness. The bathrooms are impressive, with super-large shower heads and a separate, private toilet. Each tent has a veranda, and some command wonderful wide-open views of the Mara while others have a more intimate view of nearby trees and bush. The tents are well spread out over the extensive grounds—some are a long walk from the main buildings. An electric fence provides security. *Best Views:* Tents #10 and 8.

The casual dining area, from the Cottars' Camp days, is built in dark wood and is open on one side. Siana Springs has a rustic, bush flavor. There is extensive use of canvas and stone. Canvas-covered doors bring the feeling of camping to the public areas, and there are electric hurricane lamps. The overall image is of solid, no-nonsense camping in comfort and style. Every night the traditional camp fire is lit.

Quotes:

> *"This showerhead is big enough for two."*
> *"Our evening walk took us close to a herd of elephant."*

Special Offerings

Game walks and drives, bird walks, slide shows, swimming pool.

Off Notes

Quite a hike to some tents... If you want to go into the game park, the Sekenani Gate can be quite congested and slow.

Mara River Camp

Savannah Camps & Lodges Box 48019, Nairobi
☎ *(2) 331191, FAX: (2) 330698*

This midsized, friendly and informal tented camp is outside the Reserve (20 minutes from the Musiara Gate in the northeast of the Mara). It is one of the oldest lodges in the area and has a lovely position on the banks of Mara River looking up at the escarpment. There are green lawns and safari chairs, big shady trees busy with birds and hippos in the river. The dining area is largely outdoors under trees and has pleasant views across the river. You welcome to take bird walks with the resident ornithologist, and game drives are available.

There are 26 basic but cheerfully decorated tents. All have en suite bathrooms. Some have good river views, while other tents are set back from the river and rather close together. In the evening a camp fire is lit and guests are sometimes treated to performances by the staff band. There is electricity, no fences and no pool. Four Toyota Land Cruises with driver/guides are available for game drives.

SOUTHERN KENYA

Sarova Mara Camp

Sarova Hotels, Ltd., Box 30680, Nairobi
☎ *(2) 333248, FAX: (2) 211472*

Sarova Mara Camp is a large, established tented lodge inside the Reserve. The entrance is impressive—exotic gardens and a high thatched lobby with ethnic decor. The lodge buildings are attractive and airy, a big dining area includes an outdoor terrace with wide-angle views, and there is a well-used free-form swimming pool with pool-side bar and barbecue/buffet area.

Seventy-five tents are scattered through sizeable grounds. Many paths wind through lawns and gardens, and there are wooden walkways over wide lily ponds. Some tents are quite a hike from the main lodge. Outlooks from the tents differ— some have wide open vistas of the Mara while others feel more like being in a tended garden.

The tents are substantial, with a concrete addition for private bathrooms—secure and neighborly rather than adventurous. Sarova Mara Camp is basically a big, touristy lodge that offers a small taste of the romance of camping in tents.

Fig Tree Camp

Mada Holdings, Box 40683, Nairobi
☎ *(2) 221439, FAX: (2) 332170*

This is a larger camp with 30 basic tents and 30 wood cabins. It is just outside the reserve near the Talek Gate, and is reached by crossing the Talek River on a covered wooden footbridge. The atmosphere is relaxed and casual. The accommodations are basic, and tents and cabins are crowded close together in a rather hodgepodge arrangement. Some have a river view.

There is a pool, video room, outdoor barbecue area, and a large souvenir/sundries shop. Many activities are available at extra charge: game drives, game walks, moonlight bush dinners. Fig Tree Camp is a base for balloon safaris and is the closest lodge to many informal campsites along the river. There is 24-hour electricity; no fences.

Oseur Tented Camp

Oseur Tented Camp, Box 8114, Nairobi
☎ *(2) 556503, FAX: (2) 545833*

This new camp is eight kilometers outside the Reserve (through the Olemutiak Gate). A total of 32 tents is planned. To promote privacy, the camp is divided into three self-contained manyatta, each with its own dining tent and bar. The tents are basic and unpretentious, and are well-spaced in the bush. An electric fence is in place, and a pool is planned. Game walks are offered in the surrounding hills, and the camp is close to Masai *manyatta* which can be visited on foot. There is an airstrip and a nearby petrol station.

When we visited, the camp was not yet completed. There were unpleasant odors and evidence of rushed and cost-cutting construction.

Talek River Camp

Prestige Hotels Ltd., Box 74888, Nairobi
☎ *(2) 338084, FAX: (2) 217278*

This small rustic tented camp is inside the reserve. Eight compact tents and a small mess tent are set in natural bush along an oxbow in the Talek River. There are no fences and no electricity, but there are flush toilets and running water. Game drives are offered. Talek River Camp is a less expensive alternative to its sister camp Mara Intrepids, which is two kilometers away. Talek shares an airstrip with Mara Intrepids.

Rekero

Bush Homes of East Africa Ltd., Box 56923, Nairobi
☎ *(2) 571647, FAX: (2) 571665*

Rekero Farm is the home of the Beaten family. It is built in the Masai Mara Conservation Area adjacent to the reserve, a vast expanse of game country where you are unlikely to encounter other tourists. From here, the Beatons run an exclusive and up-market house-hosting and foot safari operation.

The guests we spoke with were exuberant in their praise. They were sophisticated international travelers who were thrilled by the authenticity of their experience at Rekero—the privilege of being all alone in the middle of the bush with such a knowledgeable and experienced host and guide.

Said Ron during our visit, "I give clients an experience which existed fifteen years ago—in the last four days we haven't seen anyone else." Ron, whose father was the first warden of Nairobi National Park, is a veteran "white hunter" and is permitted to carry a gun when he takes his clients walking in the Mara.

A guest commented, "You feel completely safe and confident because you are with a professional, it's part of the enjoyment."

Wildlife viewing is done in the Mara Reserve as well as the conservation area where you can get a close-up view of Africa—perhaps stalking an elephant on foot or marveling at a crab spider's web in the morning dew. The waterhole, which is only a stone's throw from the bungalows, attracts elephant and buffalo and is sometimes visited by lions and leopards.

Rekero caters for eight guests in simple thatched bungalows with en suite bathrooms, and has a fully furnished double tent with attached bathroom, giving a total capacity of ten guests.

"We are not offering Hilton Hotel accommodations," warned Ron. "This is not five star amenities."

One of his charmed guests piped up, "There's nothing wrong with it. We've had hot showers all the time, and the food couldn't be better!"

Mobile tented camps are set up seasonally in good wildlife areas of the Masai Mara and can cater from four to 12 guests. Itineraries are tailored to each group's requirements.

Guests' Comments:

"This is the best, and we toast it."

"Last night, when we camped out, they cooked the food in a tin trunk, and it tasted fabulous."

Activities:

Night game drives. Balloon safaris and Lake Victoria fishing day visits can be arranged.

Closed:

April and May.

Bush Tops

Cottar's Safari Service, Box 44191, Nairobi
☎ *(2) 884508, FAX: (2) 882234*
e-mail: Cottars@form-net.com

Established in 1987 as a private home by Glen and Pat Cottar, Bushtops is situated in a private valley four kms from the main entrance to the Masai Mara Game Reserve. The house is built on the side of a hill and overlooks a natural salt lick which is often visited by animals.

The building and furnishings are functional rather than elegant. Bygone pioneer days are reflected in the photographs and memorabilia stretching back many decades. The Cottars were among the early settlers of the area.

There are four double rooms and one single bedroom, all with en suite bathrooms with hot showers and flush toilets. Bushtops has recently been upgraded and there are four poster beds with mosquito nets and duvets.

Peter and Louise Behr are the hosts at Bushtops and Peter is an experienced guide. There is a sitting room with fireplace, an upstairs game viewing room looking out over sweeping views and a dining room where personalized three-course dinners are served. It is all very low-key, relaxing and peaceful—no tourist buses, no schedules to keep. At night guests can sit outside with drinks around an open fire and enjoy the stars above and the sounds of the African night.

Activities:

Guided walks and game tracking, games drives into and around the Masai Mara Game Reserve, picnics and sundowners at scenic view points, flycamping in the area and visits to a local Masai manyatta.

TS

Mpata Safari Club
Mapata Safari Club, Box 58892, Nairobi
☎ *(2) 217015, FAX: (2) 217016*

This luxurious, upmarket Japanese club hotel sits high on the edge of the Oloololo escarpment with panoramic views across the Mara Plains. The club is named after a Tanzanian artist S.G. Mpata, whose paintings enjoy great popularity in Japan. Mpata was voted the best lodge in the Mara recently by KATA (Kenyan Association of Travel Agents).

A melding of Japan and Kenya, the Mpata Safari Club is the most pricey place to stay in the Mara area. There is an emphasis on elegance and sophistication, personal attention and luxury. Each suite has its own private outdoor jacuzzi—bubbles in the sun and the world spread out below. The Kenyan chef has been trained in Tokyo and offers world-class international cuisine. The unusual furniture, conceived by a Japanese designer was made by Kenyan craftsmen. Typically, each group of clients is hosted by one of the club's upper management team (Japanese or English speaking) who customizes the clients' stay, joins them for some meals and generally sees to clint well-being. The hotel staff are almost exclusively Kenyan and bring a relaxed and friendly style to the operation of the club.

The architecture of the Mpata Safari Club is most unusual. Guests stay in separate concrete structures well-spaced along the top of the escarpment. There are 10 suites and 12 deluxe units, each with interlocking curves separating bedrooms, bathrooms and verandas. The chief feature of the deluxe rooms is the panoramic sweep of the Mara you can see from your bed. The suites have similar views and are larger with a lounge, kitchenette and, best of all, a jacuzzi. The units are reached by stone pathways meandering between indigenous bush and trees which help to soften the towerlike concrete structures.

The soaring main clubhouse has several levels, huge windows and wonderful views. Natural materials have been used—stone for steps and floors, wood for tall posts and beams. The center of the clubhouse is a large circular shaft open to the sky and the elements with lush tropical vegetation at its rocky base. A library nook has a fireplace, a diverse collection of books in both Japanese and English, and the only comfortable, curl-up seating in the club. A spacious bar looks out over the vast view. Way below is the Mara River, the distinct circular shapes of Maasai manyattas, and the golden expanse of the Mara plains stretching to purple hills. Above, the forever sky.

Not only does the Club's name honor art, but throughout there is a flavor of the artistic and the unusual. The long wood reception counter is a carved masterpiece of curves and bends, inspired by the Mara River, which winds and shimmers far below. Fantastical African sculptures surprise and intrigue, colorful Mpata paintings hang in the suites, and everywhere there are fun, whimsical, improbable chairs—chairs which invite photography rather than sitting—giant carved wooden chairs with lethal looking protrusions, feminine little skirted chairs for straight backs—hardly two the same.

Gourmet meals are served in style in the dining room where wooden posts rise to the roof high above, large wooden chairs make a dramatic statement, and more enormous windows face the view. Menus are printed in French, and nouvelle cuisine is so attractively presented that you are reluctant to disturb the artistry. But do! It rewards the palate as well. Special dietary needs are catered to, including a taste for Japanese cuisine.

With a ratio of about two staff to every client, you are made to feel very special and very welcome. Besides receiving a great deal of individual attention, you find fresh flowers in the room, a thick white toweling gown to wear to the jacuzzi, and a hot water bottle to greet you in bed at night.

There are a variety of activities to choose from. You can go on day or night game drives in one of the Club's Land Cruisers, you may choose to have a bush breakfast or sundowners on the escarpment, you can accompany a Masai naturalist on a bush walk learning about the birds and plants you encounter, you can hike to the bottom of the escarpment and up again (with an armed escort), you can swim in the attractive swimming pool or you can take to your jacuzzi and the view.

Since the Masai Mara National Reserve is about a 40 minute drive from the club and because there is so much to tempt you on the grounds, we recommend that you spend several nights at Mpata (pocketbook willing).

Although Mpata Safari Club was designed to cater to its Japanese Club members, bookings can also be made within Kenya, and management is keen to encourage an international mix of upmarket clients. To try and boost a low occupancy rate, Mpata Club has been offering discounted packages to Kenyan residents.

From the Visitors Book:

"Best food I've tasted in a long time, could steal the furniture, gorgeous location, super service."

"Room with a view!"

"You could spend the night in the jacuzzi admiring the stars."

Off Notes

The vistas are breathtaking, but the animals are far below and it is a long drive down for close-up viewing... Even if you have a yen for your own outdoor jacuzzi with a marvelous view, it requires many, many yen to stay there.

Olkurruk Mara Lodge

African Tours and Hotels, Box 30471, Nairobi
☎ *(2) 336858, FAX: (2) 218109*

The new Olkurruk Mara Lodge has a spectacular site high on a rocky cliff at the top of the Oloololo escarpment. There are panoramic views over the plains and the meandering Mara River far below. This location was used in the Denys Finch-Hatton funeral scene in the film *Out of Africa*.

There are 19 thatched guest rondavels designed to create the feel of an African village. *Olkurruk* means pied crow in Masai, and the theme is carried through in the handmade bedspreads and rugs as well as in eye-catching leather wall hangings which depict local myths about the pied crow.

The public rooms have been simply and attractively decorated using natural local materials. There is an indoor/outdoor dining area, a cozy circular lounge with an open fire in the center, and the *Out of Africa* bar which has the best view of those vast distances. Beyond this bar juts a large rocky overhang where you can sit and feel suspended in space over the Mara. With binoculars you can pick out herds of elephant, or see a distant clutch of combies (mini-vans) perhaps crowded around a kill. In the early morning you might watch a colorful hot air balloon drifting below you.

Unfortunately, there are many places in the lodge where that marvelous view is obscured by vegetation. Several rondavels which would otherwise have magnificent outlooks, face bushes instead. We were told that it is frequently windy at the edge of this escarpment and that the vegetation acts as a windbreak. At this height, it can be cold at night. In the rainy seasons, it is often misty, with poor visibility.

The rooms are cozy and snug. They are more appealing in the evening than in the heat of the day when they seem a little dark and enclosed. There are pale reed walls, handwoven rugs on the painted floor and an unusual fabric ceiling which is gathered tentlike up to the peak of the rondavel. Bathroom walls are made of rough dark timber, and there are showers with plentiful solar-heated water. Decor in the rooms is imaginative and appropriate, but it is already showing some signs of wear.

It is a long haul down into the Reserve, and half or even full-day game drives are more popular than the traditional shorter game drives, offered by most lodges in the Reserve. Olkurruk operates six Land Cruisers for game drives, and an airstrip has been recently constructed nearby. There is 24-hour electricity and an electric security fence.

Keekorok Lodge

Block Hotels, Box 47557, Nairobi
☎ *(2) 335807, FAX: (2) 340541*

Dating from 1965, Keekorok Lodge is a large and busy lodge located at the well traveled crossroads within the Masai Mara National Reserve. It can accommodat almost 200 guests including many minibus tour groups. Keekorok is popular amon those who prefer solid walls to tents and for its location. It is one of the easier Mar lodges to reach from Nairobi by road. The lodge is sited on a shallow rise where yo can see for miles, and the sky stretches—beyond the horizon—to infinity.

With whitewashed walls in clean contrast to high-peaked black rooflines, th lodge is laid out to give all main rooms and most guest rooms a wide open view c the Mara. The main hotel building is usually a hive of activity. There are notic boards announcing activities, a lecture room, a busy gift shop and a comfortabl lounge surprising in leather and tartan. The dining room is open to the terrace– allowing for fresh breezes and that view. The large stone terrace has heavy woode chairs and tables, and overlooks mowed lawns and a swimming pool made private b bougainvillea bushes. Below are the tall trees and lush growth at the edge of th Pololet River. Beyond all of this stretches the golden vastness of the Mara plains.

Keekorok, which means place of black trees in the Masai language, is named fo the trees at the river's edge. A high wooden walkway has been built here, and allow close-up views of the plants, trees, birds and other wildlife that live along the rive At one end, a small thatched sundowner bar overlooks a river pool with resider hippo. There are no fences around Keekorok, and it is not uncommon to see ele phant and buffalo wander on to the perimeters of the grounds—always under th watchful eyes of the *askari* on guard.

Accommodations

Although Keekorok has over 70 rooms, the different wings have been laid out t minimize a sense of crowding. Rooms are simply but nicely furnished, most wit tub and shower. Some have double beds and minibars. Many rooms have views o the Mara, and from most new wing rooms and the VIP House, there are eve opportunities for early morning game viewing while lying in bed or from your pri vate terrace. *Our Favorites*: #41 (a corner room which overlooks the water hole) #52–59 (for great views), and the VIP house (Kissinger stayed here, so can you!).

Special Facilities

Game drives (there is only one hotel van, most visitors are with tour buses or in private vehicle), early morning ballooning (by arrangement), Masai dancing, natu ralist slides, lectures on Masai culture, pool, video room, conference room, souveni shop, airstrip, petrol station.

Safari Journal — Tuesday, after dinner

After dinner coffee on the terrace .... pinch me,
this is _Africa_! There's some nice scent in the air
and the Maasai dancers have left for their village.
Everything seems much quieter. The moon and the
stars are amazing. Even in the dark we can see
some buffalo and that elephant we've seen come
and go all afternoon. We can hear the people
at the next table talking about the lion cubs
they saw today and about international politics
all at the same time.

Off Notes

Can be crowded and noisy with tour groups... You can hear balloons inflating for early morning flights.

Mara Serena Safari Lodge

Serena Lodges and Hotels, Box 48690, Nairobi
☎ *(2) 710511, FAX: (2) 718103*

This popular lodge is set high on a ridge within the Reserve. It commands magnificent uninterrupted views down across the Mara plains and over two water holes. The Mara Serena's unique architecture and decor suggest a fantasy Masai *manyatta*—rounded spaces, earth tones, natural furnishings, and tribal touches.

A swimming pool has been positioned to take advantage of the wonderful view. Well-tended luxurious flower beds line the paths to the rooms which extend in a row from the main lodge. There are almost 80 rooms—small, enclosed, and rather claustrophobic. They all face views but have small windows and no balcony. The rooms are brightly colored in yellows and oranges with full bathrooms en suite. Mineral water is provided in the bedrooms each night.

The public rooms are harmoniously decorated with lights in hanging pots, spears in window treatments and tribal motifs on walls. There are some thoughtful touches such as refrigerated platters keeping the buffet fresh, complimentary champagne at breakfast, internal windows framing tropical plants, and an outdoor bird feeder near a stone seating area. The lodge offers a variety of special activities such as breakfast at the hippo pool, wildlife films, Masai dancing, balloon safaris and bird walks.

Special Facilities:

Gas station, airstrip, 4-wheel-drive game vehicles, 24hr. electricity generators, nurse, souvenir shop.

Off Notes

At this height, and surrounded by concrete, you feel rather removed from the bush.

Mara Simba
Box 84334, Mombasa
☎ *(11) 311093, FAX: (11) 316474*

Built on the Talek River, this newest of the Mara Lodges has 36 guest rooms. Guests stay in double story bandas built out of wood and stone. There are six rooms per banda and each has an en suite shower and toilet and a private veranda facing over the river. The rooms are spacious and can easily accommodate an extra bed.

The grounds of Mara Simba are a combination of natural vegetation and landscaped gardens of indigenous plants. Well-lit pathways link guestrooms with the main lodge which commands a view over a bend in the river. The decor incorporates ethnic design elements from the Masai people. There is a reception lounge, a guest lounge, a bar, dining area and a souvenir shop. Guests can relax on the large open verandah fronting the lounge and dining area, or cool off in the swimming pool.

Because of its position, Mara Simba is able to offer guided game walks and night drives outside of the Reserve. A naturalist presents talks of wildlife and ecology of the Masai Mara.

Visitor's Quote:

"The lodge is nicely done and the staff were very friendly. But when you look across the river, you usually see goats, not wild animals."

Getting there:

By plane or by road. The lodge is 7 kms from the Sekenani gate.

Masai Mara Sopa Lodge
Kenya Holiday Management Services Ltd., Box 72730, Nairobi
☎ *(2) 337410, FAX: (2) 331876*

The Masai Mara Sopa Lodge is built on a high ridge in the southeast corner of the Masai Mara National Reserve. The best thing about this lodge is its spectacular terrace view across a valley, with wildlife visiting a small water hole below.

To enter the lodge you descend steep stairs into an enormous round lobby and lounge leading to the dining area, another huge space. All of this is capped by a tall thatched roof that is amazing in size. Surprisingly, these huge rooms are quite dark, perhaps in keeping with the Masai manyatta decor—curving walls and the floor shades of rusty red. The open terrace with the far-reaching view is a relief from the heaviness of the main rooms.

The 60 double rooms and 12 suites are lined up along the ridge in connected thatch-topped rondavels reached by a rock-paved path, and all of them face the view. Unfortunately, the private verandas are not very inviting, but room windows do face the view. Furnishings and bathrooms are adequate, but rather tired.

The swimming pool and sports area needed maintenance when we visited. The lodge has a disco farther down the slope.

Special Facilities
Balloon safaris, conference facilities, boutique and sundry store, minibars.

Off Note
The whole lodge was in need of a thorough cleaning.

Paradise Mara Camp
Paradise Safaris Ltd., Box 41789, Nairobi
☎ *(2) 229262, FAX: (2) 228902*

The Paradise Mara Camp at Hippo Point is on the banks of a bend in the Mara River just beyond the northwest corner of the Masai Mara National Reserve. This thatch and stone built lodge overlooks a well-populated hippo pool and offers morning and evening game drives which are included in the tariff.

There is a thatched lobby which opens to the river. An adjoining Lookout Bar and dining veranda is built right over the water. Hippos bellow and splash below. At night a leopard is baited across the river.

Guests stay in two-story huts built right along the riverbank. Each room has a thatch-shaded veranda overlooking the river. There are mosquito nets and adjoining shower bathrooms. Some family suites are available.

Indian vegetarian delicacies are a specialty of the lodge. The head chef presides over separate vegetarian and vegan kitchens. There is a swimming pool, and a campfire is lit at night.

We did not visit this lodge, but we hear that it is used by large tour groups.

The Nguruman Escarpment

Visiting the Nguruman Escarpment gives access to a changing panorama of unspoiled African bush. The Nguruman Escarpment forms the western wall of the Rift Valley and affords stupendous views of the Rift, as well as views of Lakes Magadi and Natron. This trip is seldom made by tourists. The challenging dirt tracks are rough, and an experienced guide is advisable.

Ol Donyo Laro

Ol Donyo Laro, Box 44924, Nairobi

Ol Donyo Laro is one of the best bush experience in Kenya. It is certainly the most exclusive. Ol Donyo Laro, which means Mountains of the Buffalo in the Masai language, is a private wilderness sanctuary in the Nguruman Escarpment.

In this totally unspoiled piece of Africa, you are shamelessly spoiled. The natural scenery is stunningly spectacular—to do it justice would take pages of superlatives, a coffee-table book of soul-inspiring photos. There you are, the only people in this vast and beautiful tract of wilderness—Africa "as she was." As to the blissful luxury—you stay in small and tasteful camps, the food is sublime, the service superb, and there are such unthinkable extravagances as a floodlit tennis court high on an escarpment, an

pool where, as you swim, you have unsurpassed views over the Rift Valley. There
re beds with real down duvets, beautiful books on Africa in your tent and mahogany
oors.

Throughout your Ol Donyo Laro experience, you will enjoy loving attention to
etail and quality. You will be impressed by the ingenious way the camps have been
esigned and built to harmonize with the natural surroundings. You will marvel at
e foresight and engineering which made all of this possible. This is a place visited
y the rich and famous—it is also a place loved by those who know and care for
frica.

Ol Donyo Laro is not just a single camp, but an entire experience which takes you
om one carefully placed camp to another. Each gives you a different taste of bush
fe: vistas vary, vegetation changes, climates fluctuate. Even the ambience of each
amp is different. You are constantly delighted and surprised.

Only one group of up to 10 are ever accepted at Ol Donyo Laro at any one time.
he group has exclusive enjoyment of this sanctuary for their reserved time: a mini-
um of four days and nights. For most people, the experience begins when you are
et by your guide in Nairobi. Although there are landing strips near the camps,
uests are strongly encouraged to make the four-wheel drive passage from the city
nd the smooth tarmac of the Magadi Road to faint and rough tracks leading into
e wilder African bush.

Leaving Nairobi, you pass the Ngong Hills and plunge down into the Rift Valley
nd on to Lake Magadi. In the still heat you cross this otherworldly soda lake—
npossible pinks, drifting flocks of flamingos, and reflections of clouds and the deep-

est blue. Ahead, the Nguruman Escarpment rises dark, the green of its steep slope folding into sharp ridges and peaks. Each turn reveals another quiet glade, a different unsuspected vista—you feel you are on a return journey into Africa.

Ol Donyo Laro extends through 2134 meters from the Rift floor into the valley hills and rain forests above. The fortunate guest has the opportunity to enjoy this varied environment and can be assured of the utmost privacy, exclusivity and security. Guests are carefully screened to ensure that the natural ambience will not be disturbed.

Your host and guide will lead you into the complex and multileveled experience of Ol Donyo Laro. There are three fixed camps and a mobile fly camp. How you move among these is customized for your group.

You may spend a night in a wilderness fly camp, sleeping in a tent close to the earth. There is a campfire and night sounds of Africa are all around. Sometimes the fly camp is set up in arid scrub bush, sometimes in the high rain forest.

At **Kisidai**, the jungle camp, trees and bush surround each customized tent. It is hot, green and humid; there are enormous tamarind trees, and the sounds of birds are everywhere. The mess tent is near a stream and a small dam has slowed the water to form a natural swimming pool among the trees. Dougie tells us plans are afoot to create a lounge and perhaps a sleeping area or two in the spreading tops of towering fig trees.

The timber and canvas tents are spacious and sturdy, with screening on all sides to give the feeling of staying among the trees. Each has a well-designed bathroom with hot and cold running water and flush toilets. The shower has an innovative huge showerhead—lots of hot water and pressure. The water here and in all of the camps comes straight from mountain springs and is drinkable. At Kisidai, you notice leaves, butterflies, trees and plants, the minutiae of the surrounding life with glimpses of the high Ngurumans through the trees.

Ol Duvai Camp is much higher up, right on the edge of the escarpment with views over the Rift Valley. The vistas are vast; you can see across to the opposite side and south into Tanzania. Dominating the view is Shombole, its high volcanic peak and dry eroded sides clearly etched above the hazy golds of the Rift Valley floor. Lake Natron lies silver and pink below.

The heart of Ol Duvai is an open-sided tented lounge and dining area. There are yards of safari green canvas rising to a vaulted ceiling, chunky pale wood furniture and sculpted stone seating comfortable with cushions. All is natural, low-key and well-made. Closer to the escarpment edge is a raised swimming pool made with rounded stones set in cement. As you swim in the mountain spring water, you can see across the Rift.

A stone path winds to a thatched gazebo on a little point with the world spread below on three sides. Guests often breakfast here. In early morning sunshine they sit and watch as mist forms below and slowly rises to eye level. During the day dozen of dust-devils whirl in tall columns on the Rift floor. Sometimes at night, a flock of flamingos might fly just overhead—floating silhouettes in the moonlight.

At Ol Duvai guests stay in customized "tents" which combine canvas ceilings with stone walls. Plenty of screens allow for views and breezes, and keep out the bugs. All is spacious and comfortable and the bathrooms boast many mirrors and more big showerheads. There is an airstrip at this camp, as well as a tennis court—floodlit, of course, for cooler night play.

Laro is the highest set camp. As the most luxurious, it is usually saved for last. Through a gateway of travelers palms you enter a perfect world. You stay in imaginative comfort in tropical gardens. Behind rise steep hills; to the side plunge forested gorges; in front, the awesome spectacle of the Rift.

You pass under a bougainvillea arch, through an open tent door—in front of you is the swimming pool with nothing beyond it but lounge chairs and the whole Rift Valley—just you and that view.

You take off your shoes to enter the drawing room. The mahogany floor gleams; there are mirrors and bookcases, groupings of sofas and chairs, bowls of flowers and old brass. Here is Victorian elegance touched by Africa—the walls are canvas, the roof a soft furry thatch and one entire side is completely open to the bush and the view.

You climb mahogany stairs to the broad veranda of your tent raised high on sturdy poles. The furniture is handmade, there are bouquets of fresh flowers and oil lamps of etched glass and brass. The bathrooms are lined in African mahogany, the voluminous bathsheets are deep-piled, and there is even a toothbrush with Ol Donyo Laro stamped in gold.

Before dinner, guests gather around a campfire close to the escarpment edge for quiet talk and tall tales, drinks and hot snacks. At night the romantic "drawing room" is lit by an extravagance of large candles. Elegant tables are set for gourmet meals. Always the service is smooth, friendly and unobtrusive.

Nothing was spared in creating these beautiful and high quality camps. This is particularly amazing when you consider the intricate planning and engineering required in this rough and isolated terrain. The many kilometers of roads were hacked through the bush, cleared and contoured by hand. Water and electrical systems were custom designed to meet the needs of each camp. A base has been set up where fresh fruits and vegetables are grown. The steep roads to reach Laro meant that all materials and furnishings had to be painstakingly carted by four-wheel drive vehicles.

This wilderness sanctuary is huge. Some of the camps are more than an hour's four-wheel drive apart. The going can be rough and dusty. Encephalitis-free tsetse-flies may invade the vehicle and lead to a frenzied bout of slapping and mashing. You ford fast-flowing rocky streams, brave "impossible" inclines, marvel at evidence of animal passage and note the airborne color of birds and butterflies. This is what you came for—the unspoiled Africa.

Other Offerings

Flying trips to Masai Mara, Samburu, Mt. Kenya...

Off Notes

Game is there. You hear it, feel it. But you seldom see it.

Melepo Hills

Sirata Suruwa

Bush Homes of East Africa Ltd., Box 56923, Nairobi
☎ *(2) 571647, FAX: (2) 571665*

In the middle of greater Masailand, 90 kms south of Nairobi, lies Sirata Suruwa, the tented home of the Rainys, an American naturalist family.

Sirata Suruwa is the focus of "a unique conservation effort that links the Rainy's knowledge of wild animal behavioral ecology to the cultural ecology of Maa speaking people." The original Rainy nucleus has expanded to include 5000 acres of their neighbor's land, all now joined in a conservation effort. In only two years they have seen a fivefold increase in wildlife and have virtually stopped wildlife poaching!

There are three spacious tents for guests, each with a sitting and sleeping area and an en suite long-drop loo and safari bucket shower. The tents are set up in the natural bush and well spaced for privacy. There is a rustic sitting and dining area with open sides, a thatch roof and safari chairs. From its position on the side of a hill, there are spectacular views across the Rift Valley. The camp is at 6000 ft. so evenings can be chilly.

These rolling Melepo Hills afford vast views. From the summit you see forever looking across the Rift towards Lakes Natron and Magadi, purple ridges in the distance, eagles soaring overhead and an endless sky. You can go for escorted game walks in this hilly grass and thornbush country. In some seasons over 30 wild species can be seen here. Sirata Suruwa means "Glade of Elands" in Maa and there is a herd of over 80 eland which is seen regularly.

When you stay at Sirata Suruwa you can also become involved in the conservation effort by joining a morning animal count or adding to individual recognition records. As well as walking, you can go on game drives, visit a neighboring Masai settlement, or just simply relax in peaceful solitude.

Surata Suruwa is a convenient stop en route to Tanzania.

Getting There:

By road: 1-1/2 hours from Nairobi or Namanga (Tanzanian border).

Amboseli National Park

Amboseli National Park was Kenya's first established game park. Since 1948, millions of international guests, including Hollywood film companies, have been drawn to the park by the magic of Mt. Kilimanjaro—the snow-capped mountain reaching to the sky above, with wildlife grazing under flat-topped thorn trees below.

Despite its proximity to the mountain, many tourists today are disappointed with Amboseli because of its dusty dirt roads and the barren expanses caused in part by the overuse of humans and animals. Years of abuse by tourist vehicles have left off-road vehicle tracks where there had been grasslands. Prolific herds of elephant have broken and destroyed trees—creating stark and stunning weathered sculptures on the landscape.

AMBOSELI AREA

Much of Amboseli is dry and desertlike. In fact, about a third of the park i taken up by Lake Amboseli, a seasonal soda lake which, at certain times, ap pears to be a dead, flat wasteland. Indeed, *amboseli* is Maa for "salt dust." I dramatic contrast to these dry "desert" areas of Amboseli are riverine forest and swampy areas bright green with primordial clumps of vegetation.

In Amboseli, more than in any other park of Kenya, you are guaranteed t see many elephant. Elephant herds are easily visible across rolling grassy sa vannas, usually grazing their way to and from major feeding grounds o water holes.

Although Amboseli has major problems, it is heartening to consider th regenerative forces of nature. Remains of trees left by elephant are returnin

utrients to the soil. According to scientists, the water table of Lake Am-
oseli is rising. Because there is water in the lake more often, there are also
lamingos to be seen. These factors, combined with needed efforts by Ken-
an authorities and conservationists to control "tourist erosion," may help to
give Amboseli the opportunity for recovery. Off-road driving is now forbid-
len.

Many still enjoy coming to Amboseli. Always, there is the possibility of
eeing the mountain. Enjoyment of Amboseli National Park is in the eye and
understanding of the beholder.

Amboseli Serena Safari Lodge

Serena Lodges & Hotels, Box 48690, Nairobi
☎ *(2) 711077, FAX: (2) 718103*

The Amboseli Serena Lodge is the nicest and most interesting lodge in Amboseli
National Park. The rounded terra-cotta shape of the lodge resembles a Masai dwell-
ing, and wildlife and Masai themes are repeated throughout the hotel.

To enter, you walk across a wooden bridge over running water, a pleasant contrast
to the hot dusty roads of the park. Hanging gardens and water lilies contribute to an
impression of a return to Eden. Rounded spaces, walls, windows and doorways combine with a certain cool dimness to take you away from the straight sharp edges of
modern life. The emphasis is on smooth, natural harmony with the environment and
the wildlife in it.

Whimsical wall-sized paintings of wildlife delightfully decorate interior walls.
Hanging lights are shaded by the irregular shapes of hollow Masai gourds, adding
interest to the ceiling. At check-in you receive your Masai war-club with key
attached—"to fend off monkeys," the receptionist says with a smile.

The passage leading to rooms is open to the sky and traverses thick tropical gardens. The bedrooms are small. However, large wall-sized windows either look towards Mt. Kilimanjaro or towards the water hole visited by herds of wildebeest, antelope, or elephant. Bedroom walls echo the wildlife outside with another animal mural. The bathroom is modern, but the wall is curved, and a Masai spear holds up the shower curtain. The decor uses natural materials in unusual ways to suggest the Masai way of harmonizing with nature: cut sticks frame the beds, a Masai club is the door handle, hollowed gourds are the bed lights.

The pool, main bar and outdoor terraces overlook the surprising green grass and bush of the water hole. There are no fences. Guests have many opportunities for game viewing, even at night, when elephant families graze just a few meters away under floodlight.

To reach the dining area you cross an indoor bridge over more running water with floating gardens and water lilies. The dining area is broken up into several adjoining rooms of different sizes, making for pleasant and intimate service. Floor-to-ceiling windows give the feeling of eating in the gardens, though the main dining room is dark, and monkeys can be uninvited "guests."

Quotes:

"Once in a lifetime dream come true. Endless elephants."

"We enjoyed our cocktails with the gnus."

"A monkey came right into the dining room and stole a piece of my pineapple."

Breakfast (with complimentary champagne) and lunch are served buffet-style, and dinners are served at a table with candlelight. For an extra fee, you can choose to participate in the Masai Exotic Dinner, served every other night in the terrace below the wimming pool. Waiters in Masai *shuka* serve barbecued meats and traditional foods, nd there is an open bar.

The lodge invites guests to help preserve and restore the ecology of Amboseli by lanting a tree in the 25 hectares of grounds surrounding the lodge. For those intersted in Masai culture, Masai customs are explained informally in afternoon lectures n the Conference Room, and Masai dancers appear at the nightly campfire.

The clientele often includes tour groups, guests usually stay for only one night, nd for many it is their first experience with animals in the wild.

Safari Journal

Thursday

I went down to the open grassy terrace. I was just enjoying the breeze when this gorgeous lady elephant ambled right into the spotlight in front of me, delicately pulling and munching the low, lush grass... Other people came up, but the elephant didn't twitch an ear. She was only about ten feet from me ~ I just couldn't believe it. Sharing after dinner coffee with an elephant!

ccommodations

Bedrooms are small. There are 86 with twin beds and 10 with double beds. All have modern bathrooms with combination bathtub and shower. Rooms with double beds are smaller and have no large window. *Please note*: Best water hole views, #45–51. Best Views of Kilimanjaro, #23 & 24. Good Views of Kilimanjaro, #4–26.

pecial Offerings

Game drives, bird walks, binoculars, swimming pool, jogging path, playground, small airplane flights over Mt. Kilimanjaro by arrangement, folk singing guitarist at night, lectures on Masai culture, library room, souvenir and sundry shop. Resident nurse, gas station, conference room.

ff Notes

The rooms seem very small. Seeing Mt. Kilimanjaro is a memorable part of the Amboseli experience, but there is little opportunity to see it from the public areas of the Amboseli Serena.

Ol Tukai Lodge

Bock Hotels, Box 40075, Nairobi
☎ *(2) 540780, FAX: (2) 545948*

SOUTHERN KENYA

This is the newest Block Hotels property, and lies in the heart of Amboseli National Park. The authors have not yet visited this lodge, but from the description and photographs it sounds very pleasant. An impressive wooden walkway across green lawns and between acacia trees leads guests to an airy reception area which has been artfully designed using natural materials.

Guest stay in chalet-style, single story blocks which have been built using local gum trees and pale slate. There are a total of 80 good-sized rooms each with a sitting area, a giant mosquito net enclosing the twin beds, and en suite bathrooms with showers. Rooms have a good view towards Mt. Kilimanjaro or over the wetlands.

There is a large and attractive swimming pool with shady areas to sit and a pool bar for snacks and drinks. Guests can watch animals from the open-air Elephant bar which looks over the wetlands, play board games in the lounge, or use the library which commands a lovely view of Mt. Kilimanjaro. You can go on bird walks in the property or attend a lecture given by someone attached to the elephant research station.

Other services:

24 hour telephone service, two rooms designed to accommodate the disabled, pre-booked game drives, Masai dancing in the evenings.

Amboseli Lodge

Kilimanjaro Safari Club, Box 30139, Nairobi
☎ *(2) 227136, FAX: (2) 219982*

This is an older lodge located in the park. Its 118 double rooms are full of tour groups, and the lodge has seen better days. However, it has a nice lounge and terrace with views of Mt. Kilimanjaro. The best rooms are #5 & 6 and #30 & 31 for views of the mountain. It has lovely green lawns and a large swimming pool. A new reception building is under construction. The lodge shares an off-putting entry with its sister lodge, the Mt. Kilimanjaro Safari Club.

Kilimanjaro Buffalo Lodge

Kilimanjaro Safari Club, Box 30139, Nairobi
☎ *(2) 227136, FAX: (2) 219982*

This older lodge was built in 1973 and needs refurbishing. It can accommodate 200 and is very often full of tour groups. It is outside the Amboseli National Park, about a 20-minute drive from the nearest gate. It is also near a Masai village. You have a fantastic wide-open view of Mt. Kilimanjaro from rooms #80-90, the Hemingway Tower Bar, and the swimming pool. The decor combines lava stone with dark wood and high ceilings. Room rondavels are spread through grounds. It is near the Kenya departure point for climbing Mt. Kilimanjaro.

Special Offerings

Light plane ride over Mt. Kilimanjaro, camel rides, bush banquets, day trips with picnics to Chyulu Hills, Taita Hills and Mzima Springs, bird walks.

Mt. Kilimanjaro Safari Club

Kilimanjaro Safari Club, Box 30139, Nairobi
☎ *(2) 227136, FAX: (2) 219982*

This older lodge resembles a large tented camp, but without canvas. There are approximately 100 double rooms in concrete and thatched cottages and a newer "K" Wing with cottages built of wood. Unfortunately, each room practically touches the next, and work is in progress on the water table which has caused flooding in some cottages. There is a pleasant dining room, but only the new rooms in "K" wing are appealing with many windows, private terraces and bright fabrics. Rooms # K-9, K-10, and K-12 have fantastic views with terraces opening out to green lawns and Mt. Kilimanjaro. This lodge is frequented by tour groups and shares the off-putting entry with the Amboseli Lodge.

Tortilis Camp

Tortilis Camp Limited, Box 39806, Nairobi
☎ *(154) 22551, FAX: (154) 22553*

This select camp of 15 tents offers a special blend of rustic style and luxurious comfort. It is without question the nicest place to stay in Amboseli. When you arrive at Tortilis (easy by plane and a long, dusty, bumpy road by vehicle) you walk in to the spacious lounge and dining area. You feel you need go no further. Beautifully thatched roofs soar overhead, the sides are open to the breeze and to the wrap-round view. Dominating the horizon is snow-capped Mt. Kilimanjaro rising massively out of the acacia plains. Animals can be seen browsing in the scrub land and converging on a small waterhole. Below, nestled under large spreading acacia tortilis trees, are the thatch-covered tents. There is the welcome green of watered lawns and a blue swimming pool beckons.

A stone path winds down the hill (a hot walk in the midday sun). The tents are wonderful—spacious, cool and with an oversized large veranda where you could easily while away an afternoon just enjoying your private view and listening to the hundreds of birds which have flocked to this green oasis. The tents have been cleverly arranged so that each has a view and you are not aware of your neighbors. There are large comfortable beds and pleasant en-suite bathrooms. Solar panels provide the hot water and electricity.

We found the meals at Tortilis to be exceptionally good—fresh, tasty and varied with an emphasis on delicious pastas. Some of the vegetables and herbs are grown right in camp.

Tortilis is placed just outside of the park (near the Kitirua gate) and guests are able to go for guided game walks. We went out early in the morning with an extremely knowledgeable and friendly Masai guide. The ground between the trees was depressingly dry and dusty but we were treated to Kilimanjaro clearly etched against a morning sky and the thrill of getting close to giraffe, Grant's gazelle and zebra. A large herd of elephant kicked up dust in the distance. We saw scores of elephant at close range later in the day when we went for a game drive in Amboseli Park. For those who do not come with their own transport, Tortilis has 4-wheel drive vehicles and drivers. Guests can also arrange to go for hilltop cocktails at sundown.

The owners, Stefano and Max Cheli and Liz Peacock, are known for providing high quality, personalized safaris. They have kept the camp small to ensure that each guest is looked after in a very special way. The camp is managed as a conservation project and the owners work closely with the Masai people and the Kenya Wildlife Service.

> *"Tortilis Camp is the only one of its kind in Amboseli. We offer our guests the chance to experience the real Africa. Sleeping under canvas and waking up to spectacular views, our guests can enjoy something special, a bit of luxury and seclusion away from the bustle of the main lodges." (Liz Peacock, owner)*

Kimana

Near Amboseli National Park lies a 25,000 hectare Masai group ranch called "Kimana/Tikondo." In 1994 a section of this was demarcated to become the Kimana Community Wildlife Sanctuary. Elephant, buffalo, lion, leopard, giraffe and plains game are found here and hippo frequent the wetlands area.

Kilimanjaro Camp

Cottar's Safari Service Box 44191, Nairobi
☎ *(2) 884508, FAX: (2) 882234*
e-mail: Cottars@form-net.com

This is a small and rustic hosted camp. Five tents are well spread out under huge acacia trees near a running stream which is sometimes home to hippo. A central mess and dining tent is near the hippo pool and a lookout affords views of Kilimanjaro and is a popular spot for early morning tea or sundowners.

Tents have en suite hot showers and flushing toilets. Lighting is solar powered.

Activities that can be enjoyed here include guided game walks and tracking, night game drives, game drives in Kimana, Amboseli or Chyulu, flycamping in the area and some excellent birdshooting. Game drives, park entrances, and transfers from the local airstrip are included in the price.

From the Visitors' book:

"I could stay here for two weeks or more."

"Walking through the bush is the only way African nature and wildlife should be enjoyed."

Off notes:

The generator at nearby Leopard Camp sometimes adds to the night noises.

Kimana Lodge

Kilimanjaro Safari Club, Box 30139, Nairobi
☎ *(2) 227136, FAX: (2) 219982*

This undistinguished lodge is located between Amboseli National Park and the Chyulu Hills. Catering mainly to tour groups from the coast, it has 112 double or triple rooms in several wooden units crowded together in a small garden/parking area. However, the attractive bar/dining room is light and airy, with the lounge and terrace overlooking a waterfall. There is a swimming pool.

Kimana Leopard Camp, Ltd.

Kimana Leopard Camp, Ltd., Box 16004, Nairobi
☎ *(2) 732125, FAX: (2) 732462*

A cut-rate tented camp for tour groups, this camp is on the river. The tents are gnome-sized with metal beds and flush toilets. Signs abound warning guests to "watch out for leopard" and that "guests must pay for breaking furniture"!? A leopard is baited nightly.

Chyulu Hills

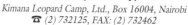

The Chyulu Hills are a beautiful rolling ridge of volcanic mountains, dating back four or five centuries. This makes them some of the youngest mountains in the world. On the eastern side of the range is the black Shaitani Lava Flow, an evil-looking wasteland of lava rock created when the Chyulus were born. The lava flow is near the Chyulu Gate of Tsavo National Park West.

Ol Donyo Wuas

Richard Bonham Safaris Ltd., Box 24133, Nairobi
☎ *(2) 882521, FAX: (2) 882728*

Perched on a ridge in the foothills of the Chyulus is Ol Donyo Wuas, Richard Bonham's exclusive hideaway. The setting is superb. The land falls away, stretching for miles in green and golden waves with strange shaped hills and flat-topped acacia trees for accent. Beyond and above towers the whole Kilimanjaro massif with the famous snow-capped peak unbelievably high in the sky. It is clear that this site was carefully chosen for the view.

Richard Bonham built his home here in the middle of Masai country and has added thatched rondavel-style cottages for guests. There are seven cottages for otal of fourteen guests. The main room is a large separate stone building with a high hatch roof. It is open on one side to frame the compelling view. There are comfortble stuffed chairs and couches in faded florals, an inviting fireplace, shelves crammed with books and music, and intriguing animal pictures on the walls. This room serves s lounge, dining room and bar area. It has a lived-in atmosphere—a place to feel at ome, put your feet up, help yourself to a drink.

The cottages are well spaced among bushy trees. They have been artistically decoated with local furniture, fabrics and handicrafts, and each has a veranda and firelace. There are mosquito nets, solar powered electricity and en suite bathrooms with hot showers and flush toilets.

Safari Journal — First Day

The elephant was only yards away. A huge bull with awesome tusks. I stepped carefully over the dead branch, crouching under the leaves. i watched for Richard Bonham's hand signals, feeling totally confident in his experience, his gun, and his dog. What a thrill! i looked down ruefully at my city clothes. We had just arrived, gulped down tea, when Richard, who had flown in minutes before, hustled us out to track down the elephant he had spotted from the air. The object — to take identity photos of the elephant to try to determine where he had come from. Count me in any day!

One of the cottages is extra large and has two bedrooms and a shared bathroom—ideal for families. Our favorite cottages (there are now five of them) are built on stilt and won our private award for rooms with the best view in Kenya. There is also a small sitting area which, like the bed, faces the marvelous view of Mt. Kilimanjaro. The high roof comes almost down to floor level and a wide opening has been cut in the thatch to frame the view. No glass here between you and the immensity of Africa.

No glass or walls either between the long-drop and the view! Sheltered behind by trees and built at the edge of the ridge is the long-drop toilet, magazines piled at the side and one of the most spectacular views imaginable in front. Although there are toilets and showers in each cottage, the long-drop is recommended when convenient because all water has to be brought up from the pipeline below.

Ol Donyo Wuas means "The Spotted Hills" in Masai and is situated miles from any major settlement. To reach it you drive through open veld dotted with plain game towards the impressive Chyulu Range, a younger volcanic range running between Amboseli and Tsavo National Park. During the rains the Masai move in to this area. You can often see young Masai herders with their cattle at home among the wild animals. The land which Richard Bonham leases is part of a 100,000 hectare Masai Group Ranch.

Chip and Sandy Cunningham are the hosts of Ol Donyo Wuas and they share Richard's love of the animals and the bush. Sandy has a long history in the hotel and restaurant business and handles the accommodation and meals. Chip is a commercial pilot and safari guide who, with his Masai guides, will take you on game drives, walk or to ride horses in the hills.

You may be surprised by a bush breakfast—eggs and bacon cooked in the open and served under a tree with a mountain view. It is a joy to go on a game drive in Richard's cutaway Land Rover with a high bench seat built in the back. Again, there is nothing between you and the enormity of the scene: the game, the mountains, the tremendous sense of distance and sky. There are many options, lots of flexibility, and no other tourists to clutter up the scene.

Chip Cunningham inspires great confidence with his wealth of experience in the bush and is a fund of information about animals. Richard continues to organize unusual safaris and spends his time each year between Ol Donyo Wuas and the Selous Game Reserve, leading exclusive walking and boat safaris in the remote and unspoiled areas that he operates in. Sand Rivers Selous is his latest lodge—eight cottages built of local materials overlooking the Rufiji River with the same charm and atmosphere of Ol Donyo Wuas.

Special Offerings

Horseback riding, horse safaris (meeting fly camps each evening), day and night game drives, walking safaris, bird shooting available July to October, airstrip.

Off Notes

Don't go if your main object is to see the Big Five or laze by a pool.

SOUTHERN KENYA

Tsavo National Park, East and West

Tsavo National Park covers more than 20,800 square kilometers. It is Kenya's largest national park and is split into Tsavo East and Tsavo West by the busy Mombasa/Nairobi Road and the railroad.

During the last century, **Tsavo West** has been through changes connected with the great elephant herds. Thick forests were gradually turned into grasslands by elephant grazing patterns. By 1960, the elephant population was up to at least 50,000. Because of poaching, they were reduced to only 5000. Now the grasslands are changing again to new forest and scrub. Poaching has been a major problem in this park, and the black rhino population was reduced from about 7000 in 1969 to less than 100 in 1981. Thanks to today's conservation efforts, poaching has largely been contained.

Tsavo West's approximately 9000 square kilometers also include the Ngulia Mountains and the Ndawe Escarpment, all part of the same volcanic upheavals that created the Rift Valley, Mt. Kilimanjaro and Mt. Kenya. The volcanic ridges give rise to the underground river systems forming Mzima Springs, an incredible outpouring of crystal clear water which forms a series of pools. The luxuriant growth at its edges is in marked contrast to the dry harshness of the surrounding terrain. There is an underwater viewing chamber from which you can often see hippo. Mzima Springs is the source of much of Mombasa's drinking water.

In Tsavo West, the combination of rocky hills, high viewpoints and dry scrublands creates a harsh beauty—a certain drama.

Tsavo East, far less visited than Tsavo West, is approximately 11,000 square kilometers of varied bush, arid flatland and desert. Most of the area north of the Galana River is closed to the public for security reasons. Much of this part of the park is the Yatta Plateau, a lava flow 300 kilometers long. Oases along the Athi, Tiva, Tsavo and Voi Rivers relieve the dry scrublands.

A handful of tented camps—some permanent and some mobile have been established in Tsavo East, making this vast wilderness more accessible for the adventurous traveler. The authors have not visited these camps, but believe most would provide an "authentic" African camping experience—far from fleets of mini-buses and hordes of tourists. Some of these camps offer game walks—because of the security issue, armed KWS (Kenya Wildlife Service) antipoaching rangers accompany the walks.

Tsavo West and East combined have 2000 kilometers of dirt tracks, some of which serve as firebreaks, all of which are important in the continuing fight against poaching. Despite this network of tracks, wildlife is not easy to see because of large distances, thick scrub and high grass. However, the stunning landscapes and the sense of isolation felt in this vastness can put you in touch with a part of the real Africa.

Tsavo West National Park

Finch Hattons Safari Camp

Future Hotels, Box 24423, Nairobi
☎ *(2) 604321, FAX: (2) 604323*

This luxurious tented camp in the Tsavo West National Park is named after Denys Finch-Hatton, the enigmatic adventurer who was immortalized by Karen Blixen in *Out of Africa* and led royalty on safari in Kenya. Finch-Hatton did things in style. He brought Mozart and crystal into the bush. So does this new upmarket camp which has been lovingly planned by owner Peter Frank, previously a regional director with Hilton Hotels Ltd. Peter lives on the site and acts as host.

Finch Hattons Safari Camp is built at the edge of three hippo pools which are fed by natural springs. Surrounding the camp is the vast, dry expanse of thorn scrub and volcanic lava which characterize this rather hilly section of Tsavo. Mt. Kilimanjaro forms a majestic backdrop—visible from many parts of the camp.

There are 35 very luxurious tents widely spaced on both sides of the hippo pools. The tents are raised on wooden platforms and face towards the water. Each has a spacious and shaded veranda with a Lamu-style day bed and chairs. The tents are extra large and airy with many big screened "windows." They have wooden floors, rich kilim rugs and high quality beds and mattresses. There are minifridges in each tent and the en suite bathrooms have stone floors, oval mirrors and showers.

The main lodge, with its open terrace, looks over a hippo pool towards Mt. Kilimanjaro. There are lava-stone walls, and a high and intricate thatched roof. The camp has been decorated in keeping with its name—old-fashioned, British and high-class. There are leather couches, brass lamps and writing desks. On the walls are prints of old safari photos, and there is a fireplace with a big chimney. Guests are required to dress for dinner—no shorts. There is Mozart and crystal.

The camp is not fenced, and animals are free to wander in the grounds. A battalion of busy *askari* escort guests to and from their tents. Elephant have been seen on the camp paths, and at night hippo pass the tents to graze. (The proximity of wild animals means that children are not encouraged as guests.) The natural vegetation has been retained, and the camp paths pass through lava rock and bush. Some tents are under tall trees. There are bridges over the stream, a raised walkway and two special observation areas. At night the hippo pool is discretely illuminated. The farthest tents are quite a hot hike from the main lodge, and stocked minifridges will be most welcome.

A kidney-shaped swimming pool is surrounded by natural rock and has been elevated to keep out the wild animals. Thoughtful and thorough planning has gone into this camp. Peter Frank spoke of proper sewage systems, solar heating, and a "clinical" kitchen with white tiles and walk-in freezers. He wants to emphasize good food, and plans to hire exceptional chefs.

Special Offerings

Pool, souvenir and sundry shop, minifridge in tent, safety deposit, observation areas, game drives.

Ziwani Tented Camp

Prestige Hotels Ltd., Box 74888, Nairobi
☎ *(2) 338084, FAX: (2) 213387*

Ziwani is a pleasant tented camp on the western boundary of Tsavo West National Park, not far from the Tanzanian border. It is in an undeveloped part of the Ziwani Sisal Estate, on the edge of a small natural-looking dam in the Sante River. Clumps of papyrus grow in the dam, tall trees fringe the far banks, and lawns extend from the lodge to the water. Birds are everywhere—ducks swim past the papyrus, a fish eagle perches on a fallen tree trunk, a large marabou stork putters about in the shallows. There are monkeys playing in the trees, and you can sometimes see hippos and crocodiles in the water. At night, bait is put up for a leopard on the far side of the dam. When it is clear, you can see the snow-covered peaks of Mt. Kilimanjaro high above the trees.

Ziwani has 20 tents and an attractive dining and bar area with views across the dam. This open-sided structure has a makuti roof and local "twig" chairs painted green. There is an inviting bar counter and hanging clay pots with plants. The effect is natural, pleasing and functional.

The original 16 tents are fairly close together. They are set far back from the river and have unremarkable views. From some you hear the relaxing sound of flowing water. The tents are on large cement slabs which provide generous verandas. Large *makuti*-thatched roofs keep the tents shaded. There are woven mats on the canvas floor and many "windows" to let in air and light. The furniture is made of pale wood, and there are high-quality mattresses on the twin beds. Immediately behind each tent is a private bathroom with a long-drop toilet and a safari shower. Since there is no electricity, hurricane lamps are used instead.

Four new tents have been added across the river. These are extra large and can accommodate a third or even fourth bed if necessary. They have electricity run from the camp generator and modern en suite bathrooms with flush toilet and shower with hot and cold running water.

The lunch we had was delicious, with a variety of freshly "home-cooked" dishes. Since there is no electricity, all meals are prepared on charcoal, and metal trunks are used for baking. Guests have a full English breakfast and eat a barbecued dinner at night on the lawn by a campfire.

At Ziwani you can go on night game drives or guided walks where you are likely to see hippos at close range in some of the river pools. You can also go on game drives in Tsavo West National Park. Most visitors are tourists from the U.K. who are driven to Ziwani from the coast. For this amount of driving and to appreciate the natural beauty and peace of Ziwani, it's worth coming for more than one night. There is an airstrip right next to the camp.

Kilanguni Lodge

African Tours & Hotels, Box 30471, Nairobi
☎ *(2) 336858, FAX: (2) 218109*

This lodge is worth a trip because of its magnificent setting in the heart of Tsavo West Park with views of the Chyulu Hills and the snowy peaks of Kilimanjaro. First built in 1962, Kilaguni was the first luxury lodge in Kenya.

The main lodge building is newly rebuilt and inviting with tall thatch roof and one whole side open to the view and a waterhole which attracts large numbers of zebra, buffalo, elephant, impala, baboon and warthog. Beyond the rustic reception area, the dining room and bar/lounge share the open-sided view.

> *"During dinner we watched a hyena waiting for our scraps below the railing. Hornbills and weaverbirds came to the table looking for crumbs. Even eating at this lodge is a wildlife experience." (Guest Quote)*

The 53 guest rooms are simply furnished and have full private bathrooms. Each room's veranda overlooks the waterhole and Mt. Kilimanjaro. All the rooms are undergoing renovation, and a separate VIP cottage and a new wing of superior rooms are under construction.

The meandering wings of the lodge set off lovely interior grounds filled with rock gardens, bougainvillea and other colorful tropical plants. The rock gardens are home to nearly tame hyraxes playing hide-and-seek among the rocks along the pathways and near the swimming pool. The pool is also scheduled for repainting, but is still operational with the "adams" and "eves" dressing room signs appropriate in this eden-like setting.

Best Accommodations

Rooms on the second floor (#14–20) for best view.

Other Facilities

Gift and sundry shop, airstrip, conference room.

> ### Authors' Tip
>
> *You can arrange with reception to join a guarded caravan through the Chyulu Hills road if you are traveling that way to Amboseli the next morning.*

Ngulia Safari Lodge

African Tours & Hotels, Box 30471, Nairobi
☎ *(2) 336858, FAX: (2) 218109*

Located in the Tsavo West National Park 290 kilometers from Nairobi, Ngulia Safari Lodge has a spectacular site. The top of a rocky outcrop has been carved into two flat terraces for the lodge buildings and swimming pool. One side of the site is a sheer cliff dropping off to the Yatta Plateau below. The two-story stone lodge rises at the edge of the cliff to overlook a grassy water hole. Game from the surrounding hills are frequent visitors day and night.

You walk through reception and up to the open-sided view terrace and dining room, which echo under high ceilings with excited guests lining the balustrade to see animals at the water hole below. Bait is left each evening for rhino and leopards, and the water hole is floodlit for night game viewing.

The 52 guest rooms are located on two floors to one side of the lodge. All have twin beds with mosquito nets, balconies and en suite bathrooms. The bathrooms are very tired and bear testimony to the fact that this lodge was built in 1969. Extra beds are available for families.

There is a small, but sparkling swimming pool in the rock gardens at the side of the dining room. Nearby, a breathtaking covered viewpoint teeters at the very edge of the cliff where the view is unbroken and without measure.

All guests are on full board, with breakfast and lunch served from the buffet. Dinner is served by candlelight.

Ngulia Safari Lodge caters to a mixed clientele of international tour groups.

Quotes:

> *"Very exciting day—changed flat tire in front of lions. 10/10 for view, service, and food—even saw the leopard at night."*
> *"Es ware alles "super" hier."*
> *"Very beautiful view, but you need new bathrooms."*

Off-Notes

It is dangerous to take walks from the lodge. There are no vehicles, so you need your own for game drives.

Hunters Lodge
Mada Holdings, Box 40683, Nairobi
☎ *(2) 221439, FAX: (2) 332170*

This landmark on the road to Mombasa is 145 kilometers from Nairobi. The lodge was opened by the famous game warden, John Hunter. Today it is best known as a rest stop en route to and from the coast. There is a petrol station and a restaurant. The lodge has 20 very basic rooms. There is a dam with a bridge and a garden with peacocks.

Tsavo East National Park

Tsavo Safari Camp

Kilimanjaro Safari Club, Box 30139, Nairobi
☎ *(2) 227136, FAX: (2) 219982*

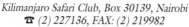

Near Mtito Andei, this restful camp is a good overnight stop en route to the coast. Twenty-seven kilometers into the hot dryness of the little-visited Tsavo East National Park, the Tsavo Safari Camp is a green oasis on the Athi River. To get there, you park your vehicle in the camp lot and take a very short trip across the river in a rubber boat.

Tsavo Safari Camp has been in operation for 28 years and was originally a hunting camp. Today 30 tents and six bandas (for those who don't like canvas) are set close together in a row along the river. They are well-shaded by mature trees. Small gardens of indigenous flowers and exotic plants are scattered in amazingly green lawns, a sharp contrast to the dry and dusty scrub in the park beyond. After your long drive, the camp swimming pool is a refreshing treat.

The focal point of the camp is the stone and thatch bar/dining area open on two sides to garden and river. Lionel Nutter is the long-time host—he creates a warm and personal atmosphere. Everything is very relaxed and casual. The bar has become a popular watering hole for British Kenyans who might even fly in just for the afternoon.

There are hundreds of resident birds—the camp is a real hornbill heaven. Take your chair down to the riverbank to watch the birds at sunset.

It is not easy to see game from this camp. A dik-dik here, a dik-dik there and the occasional oryx or jackal. If you're lucky you might see kudu. Since you leave your vehicle on the other side of the river, you must book and pay extra for game drives, which can be rather expensive. Another special offering is a trip up to the Yatta Plateau for sundowners and to watch the sun set behind Mt. Kilimanjaro.

Accommodations

The tents are comfortable and simply furnished. They all have large shower bathrooms with solar heated water and flush toilets. There are five family tents with extra beds.

Special Facilities

Swimming pool, game drives.

Voi Safari Lodge
African Tours & Hotels, Box 30471, Nairobi
☎ *(2) 336858, FAX: (2) 218109*

Voi Safari Lodge sits high on a red rock bluff overlooking a busy water hole and a large expanse of Tsavo National Park East. The entire lodge curves along the edge of the cliff so you get that marvelous view from everywhere—dining room, terrace, pool and bedrooms.

The lodge itself is not luxurious, but it is remarkable, even spectacular in several ways. Natural rock has been used effectively in walls and floors with interesting gourd lamps in the lounge/bar, which is open to air and birds. The wooden animal carvings over the bar are often accented by the real thing when baboons peer in through the roof skylight.

You walk on bare red rock through rock gardens to the viewpoint and the swimming pool at the edge of the cliff. During the five minutes before noon, we saw three cape buffalo, eight elephants and numerous baboon and antelope from the viewpoint.

Each of the 50 double rooms has one entire wall of windows, either two or three twin beds and a rather tired bathroom with telephone shower.

The lodge is located in Tsavo East National Park, 338 kilometers from Nairobi and 161 kilometers from Mombasa. It is very popular with tourists and is often used as a lunch stop en route between Mombasa and Nairobi. There is an airstrip three kilometers away near Voi town.

Returning from the lodge to the Mombasa Road, we saw a herd of more than 75 elephant.

Baobab House and Nyika Safari Camp

Ian MacDonald Safaris Ltd., Box 24957, Nairobi
☎ *(2) 882030, FAX: (2) 533529*

Baobab House

This double-story thatched house is situated on the banks of the Mtito River overlooking Tsavo East National Park. On a clear day you can see Mt. Kilimanjaro. There are four ensuite bedrooms, a spacious upstairs veranda, a bar, lounge and dining area. The house is fully staffed.

A large swimming pool is surrounded by lawns and gardens. The bird life is prolific and you can take walks along the river or up to Holly's Rock for sundowners. From Baobab House you can take trips to both Tsavo East and West, drive to Amboseli, go to Mzima Springs or go white water rafting on the Athi River.

Nyika Safari Camp

This tented camp is close to Baobab House and is also set on the banks of the Mtitio River. There are six tents each with an en suite bathroom with hot and cold water, shower and flush loo. Guests at the tented camp also have access to the Baobab House swimming pool. With a minimum of four people, non-Kenyan residents can stay on a full board basis. Residents can opt for self-catering.

The authors have not yet visited Baobab House or Nyika Safari Camp.

Tsavo Inn

Mt. Kilimanjaro Safari Club, Box 30139, Nairobi
☎ *(2) 227136, FAX: (2) 219982*

This small inn at Mtito Andei, is an easy stop on your way to Mombasa. It is right on the main Mombasa Road and about three hours from Nairobi. There is a restaurant and a pool in a garden setting. The 30 rooms are very basic—no frills.

Galdessa Safari Camp

Box 15095, Nairobi
☎ *(2) 890635, FAX: (2) 891307*

Galdessa camp is built on a curve in the Galana river and shaded by tall doum trees. Away from the river the land is hot, dry and dusty with sparse scrub and thorn trees. It is refreshing to come to the comfort of Galdessa.

There are eight tent/*bandas* —basically canvas walls with a thatch roof, a wooden floor in the bedroom and a stone floor in the bathroom. Three of the units are larger with their own separate sitting room. One of these is by the river and the other two are at either end of the camp—guaranteeing extra privacy (ideal for honeymooners). The tents have running water and flush loos, but guests are treated to a proper safari bucket shower. The large mess tent is comfortable with big white sofas and a view over the river.

Galdessa combines the adventure of an authentic African bush experience with great style and luxury. There are no fences, and wild animals are free to wander around camp. You are bound to lie awake thrilling at the sound of the African night a heartbeat away through canvas walls. You can go for game walks with an armed ranger and enjoy the excitement of a night game drive. You might choose to go fishing by the Lugards Falls or simply relax in this supremely peaceful place.

As for the style and luxury—gourmet meals are served under the stars, on the banks of the river, or as a surprise out in the bush. Your laundry is done, you bed is turned down, your shower water is heated, your drinks are iced...What more could one ask?

The owner, Pierre-Andre Mourgue d'Algue, who lives in London, divides his time between international banking and African conservation. Pierre is very eco-sensitive, and has helped to reintroduce black rhinos into the park. Solar power lights the lamps in your tent and there is no generator—just the sounds of nature.

Guests can fly into the airstrip at Lugards Falls.

Tiva River Camp

 This is a small, mobile tented camp on the banks of the Tiva River in the northern section of Tsavo East National Park. The camp is managed by Patrick Reynolds who has 20 years experience operating wildlife safaris.

There are five tents and it is possible to arrange for exclusive use of the camp. Tents are basic with two single canvas beds, camp chairs and a veranda. Guests share a traditional safari bathroom facility. The evening meal is cooked on an open campfire.

Staying at Tiva River Camp allows for guided nature walking in a remote and vast wilderness. Guests can "fly-camp" near waterholes to see which animals come to drink. The camp can be reached by air charter.

Epiya Chapeyu

Alpha Tauri Ltd., Box 14653 Nairobi
☎ *(2) 749796, FAX: (2) 750035*

Epiya Chapeyu, an Italian owned tented camp, is located next to the Galana river about 9 kms from Lugard Falls. There are twenty tents each covered with a makuti-roof. There is hot and cold running water and flush toilets. A generator supplies electricity for lights.

The cuisine is typically Italian. There are 4-wheel drive vehicles for hire. Most clients are with tour groups driving from the coast for a one night safari stop.

Other Tented Camps In The Area:

Satao

A luxury tented camp at Mkwaju with 19 tents.

Westerveld

Tented Camp, where the Athi river becomes the Galana.

Makoka

Tented camp on Tiva River, seven tents.

Kingfisher

On the Galana (see Kingfisher Lodge page 335).

Taita Hills Wildlife Sanctuary

Hilton Hotels in the Wild

The privately owned Taita Hills Wildlife Sanctuary is 17,000 hectares of rolling savanna accented by dramatic rocky outcroppings and small plateaus. Because there is plenty of water, many animals shelter there, and large herds of elephant and other plains game migrate to the sanctuary from Tsavo each year.

Hilton International holds a long lease on the land and has built a trio of safari lodges to harmonize with this beautiful setting. These include the Taita Hills Lodge, the Salt Lick Lodge for overnight game viewing and The Tents, a tented camp hidden in the forest along the banks of the Bura River. All are run according to high Hilton standards of luxury and service. Visitors are an international mixture of tour groups, businessmen and small private safaris arriving every day by road or by air.

Hilton is also responsible for managing the sanctuary and ensuring the safety of the animals. For this reason, there are 18 game wardens on Hilton's Taita Hills staff. Because the sanctuary is privately managed, there are very few vehicles on game drives. The wardens keep track of the animals to guard them from mishap and poaching. The wardens also pass the word to drivers, which can make game drives very exciting and satisfying.

Taita Hills Lodge

Hilton International, Box 30621, Nairobi
☎ *(2) 334000, FAX: (2) 339462*

You enter the Taita Hills Wildlife Sanctuary through the impressive Taita Hills Lodge. It is here that you check in to all three lodges. It is possible to arrange a stay that includes meals or even nights at each of the different lodges.

The Taita Hills Lodge resembles a fortress and was built with sandbags of World War I cemented together to form the tall three-story ramparts. However, the rather stark outlines of the lodge are softened by dark green veils of creeper, and the walls enclose elegant public rooms leading to lawns, tropical gardens and a swimming pool.

Once you enter the fortress, you find yourself in the spectacular two-story tall central room that is the heart of the lodge. Windows reaching from floor to ceiling give light and beautiful views of gardens and the plains beyond.

Inside, there is harmony and creativity—a blending of African themes and natural materials. There are tables made with African drums, stone settees and carved panels and batiks of Masai life.

This dramatic room is particularly memorable for the wonderful hangings and furnishings especially designed and handwoven by the Nairobi-based Weaver Bird company. Wall-sized tapestries depict African wildlife and Masai themes. The woven rugs, curtains and cushions are rich and elegant—complementing the polished stone and wood of the room. A stunning stone fireplace soars for two stories from a sunken conversation area. A small bar serves drinks and snacks. Bamboo fan-back chairs are set in the window nooks.

The 60 guest rooms are uniform double rooms with twin beds and full en suite bathrooms. More Weaver Bird woven rugs and fabrics give the rooms some bright colored style. All rooms have a small balcony. Some look over the sanctuary plains with good views of wildlife or distant mountains. There are also two suites available with nicely decorated sitting and dining areas.

Lunch and dinner are served in the large Chala restaurant. In the evening there is often live music or entertainment by traditional dancers. The breakfast buffet is set up in a sunny room which looks over gardens and lawns on three sides and is reached by a rock pathway through the lovely central garden. This room is often used for conferences, and business services are available.

Champagne breakfasts, barbecue lunches and elegant "Out of Africa" dinners can be arranged in the bush on request.

Special Offerings

Day or night game drives in 16 minivans, balloon safaris, swimming pool, minigolf, camel rides on grounds, tennis courts, soccer or football field, darts, basketball court, video films, conference facilities, business center, and private airstrip.

Salt Lick Safari Lodge

Hilton International, Box 30624, Nairobi
☎ *(2) 334000, FAX: (2) 339462*

Salt Lick Safari Lodge is an all-night game viewing lodge. (See section on Night Game Viewing Lodges.) This lodge is especially memorable for its imaginative structure. A complex of rondavels sits on stilts over a series of water holes. These two-story towers, topped by peaked thatch roofs, are connected by open-air bridges—creating an African fantasy reminiscent of a medieval fortress.

You walk across a drawbridge which will be pulled up at night. The curved walls, the natural stone, the horn trophies, the air of general excitement and commitment, all predict an unusual experience ahead. You climb the stairs to the dining room and terrace, then find your room by traversing the outdoor walkway connecting the room towers. The curved rooms are amply comfortable with twin beds, easy chairs and ensuite bathrooms. Those on the top floor have the advantage of a dramatic soaring thatch roof. Most rooms have large windows and you often see animals from your own room.

Salt Lick Lodge has been built with game viewing in mind—you can see animals in all directions and from many vantage points. Unlike most of the other night game viewing lodges, which are built in forested areas, Salt Lick commands some spectacular open views. You might see elephant while on the walkway from your room. There are game viewing terraces on the ground and upper levels, and you can cross through a carpeted underground tunnel to a blind that puts you among the animals. Fantastic!

The lounge has an unusual free-standing stone fireplace—you can pop in for a quick warm-up during your night game vigil. Candlelit dinners are served buffet-style in the ring-shaped dining room. The stone chimney from the ground floor lounge fireplace lances through the central space to the high peaked roof above like a sleek piece of modern sculpture. Hot and cold drinks and snacks are available all night long. It is FUN to be locked up in Salt Lick.

Hilton Safari Camp

Hilton International, Box 30624, Nairobi
☎ *(2) 334000, FAX: (2) 339462*

Perfectly at home in the thick forest on the banks of the Bura River, 24 forest green tents are a slice of Eden under canvas. Green shade and the refreshing sound of rushing water envelop every tent site with coolness and privacy. Birdsong and the flit of bright feathers are everywhere. Each tent has twin beds with forest green Hilton blankets, safari chairs, verandas and ensuite bathrooms with flush toilets. You go back in time for your wood-heated hot water and the soft glow of hurricane lamps at night.

Pathways through the trees and wooden bridges over water wind from site to site in an undefined circular way. They lead back to the heart of the camp, the fanciful James Stewart House, a natural tree sort of house, constructed for the movie *A Tale in Africa* starring Jimmy Stewart, as you may have guessed. It is the gathering place, where you can have small snacks and drinks night or day. You dine with the sounds of Africa around you and the stars overhead—often a Kenyan barbecue and other ethnic dishes are served buffet-style. Night sounds are terrific, you hear lots of animals over the water and bird sounds. However, an electrical fence and spear-carrying night guards ensure that you sleep securely.

Lake Jipe

This volcanic lake straddles the border with Tanzania. The shore is flat and thick with reeds, making it a haven for birds. Grogan's Folly, a run-down castle in the medieval style, was built by Ewart Grogan, a shady entrepreneur who planted the sisal on the plantation where the castle stands. Beyond Lake Jipe are the North Pare Mountains of Tanzania.

Lake Jipe Safari Lodge

Lake Jipe Safari Lodge Ltd., Box 31097, Nairobi
☎ *(2) 227623, Telex: 25508*

This lodge is in Tsavo West National Park close to Lake Jipe. Due to annoying lake flies, the lodge has been built at quite a distance from the shore, and you cannot see the lake from the rooms. If you can brave the mosquitoes, however, the pool area does have a spectacular view of the lake and the Pare Mountains in Tanzania.

Except for the pool, this lodge lacks charm. The lounge and dining areas are in a huge rondavel, tour group stickers on windows mar the view, and the food is below average. Accommodations are in thatched rondavels which are crowded together, have no verandas and offer little privacy. There is a public veranda with a view, but, because of the mosquitoes, it is not always furnished, and you may have to arrange for chairs to be carried out.

You must drive to reach the lake. It is beautiful on Lake Jipe—the views of the mountains are superb, but the boats and service used for these trips are not. Friends who went out complained that the boat was leaky and that they were not provided with drinks.

THE KENYAN COAST

THE KENYAN COAST

The harsher beauty of most of Kenya's interior is tempered by the soothing south-sea-island delights of Kenya's coral coast. The lush, tropical bush of the coast is brilliant with many birds and fragrant and/or colorful blossoms of frangipani and hibiscus. The vivid colors of bougainvillea and stands of graceful palms frame long stretches of white coral sand lapped by the gentle warm water of the Indian Ocean. It is hot and humid, but the pace is languid. A Swahili proverb much-used at the coast says it all: "*Haraka haraka haina baraka*"—or, literally, "haste, haste has no blessing."

Stretching 480 kilometers from Somalia in the north to Tanzania in the south, the Kenyan Coast has been known to the world since A.D. 110 when a stop at the port of Mombasa was recorded by a Greek explorer named Diogenes. Ptolemy, another Greek, included details of the Kenyan coast in his A.D. 150. "Map of the World."

Since then, Arabs who had come to trade settled, intermarried, and mingled coastal tribal and Arab ways. They created a new Swahili language and culture which is still very much alive today in Old Town Mombasa and on Lamu and Wasini Islands. They built beautiful cities embellished with carvings and monuments, and they valued fine arts and crafts.

Portuguese explorers and traders brought a garrison to Mombasa at the end of the 16th century and built the formidable Fort Jesus, which still stands. In the 19th century, British interest in exploration and in abolishing the slave trade led to Kenya coming under British influence. There are still British colonial monuments and ruins along the coast.

Now the Kenyan coast is known for its fine beaches and resorts and generally even-tempered weather. The hot and humid weather is pleasantly cooled by the monsoon trade winds blowing off the Indian Ocean. Despite the winds, the beaches are protected with approximately 240 kilometers of coral reef. Although you can often see white breakers beyond the reef, the water on the shore side is usually quite calm—better for windsurfing than for surfing. Swimming between the reef and shore is also generally safe from strong currents and protected from nasties such as shark. The water ranges from 27–35 degrees centigrade.

The beauty of the coral and the amazing colors and shapes of these tropical fish invite goggling or scuba diving. The national marine parks and reserves off Shimoni, Mombasa, Watamu, Malindi and Lamu protect these marine treasures. Kenyan reefs have been favorably compared with those of Australia and the Red Sea.

THE KENYAN COAST

There are many ways to explore the Kenyan reef. On certain beaches you can swim and even walk out to the reef through tidal pools. Some hotels maintain glass-bottom boats. You can snorkel from these or from other smaller boats. Private boatmen are eager to take you to the reef and sometimes even to rent equipment. Prices are negotiable. Snorkeling is fun and easy, even for novices—a beautiful and memorable experience. Try it!

There is a big tidal variation along this coast. On some beaches high tide leaves only a narrow strip of sand, and in places the water reaches right up to the edge of hotel property. At low tide the water sometimes recedes back beyond the reef, leaving would-be swimmers high and dry. However, almost all hotels have their own swimming pools, and it seems that the majority of guests are just as happy to nab a beach lounger by the pool or in the shade of a palm tree to work on their tans and relaxation.

On the most popular tourist beaches, there are many hawkers trying to sell their wares. Informal displays of carving, jewelry, and bright cotton kanga are set out along the sand; a small shack professes by its sign to be a "Massage Parlor"; and women want to braid your hair with beads. As you stroll the beach, you are likely to be approached by friendly but persistent vendors. Some hotels employ security guards or police to try to discourage these hawkers. It is inadvisable to walk along the beach displaying wealth with fancy jewelry or cameras.

Although the climate is generally easy to take all year long, the monsoon winds blowing across the ocean determine the seasons. The kaskazi is northeasterly and lasts from October to March. November is usually the month of occasional rains during the *kaskazi*. The kusi is the stronger and colder of the two winds, lasting from April until September. During this wind, rain is to be expected from May until June. Even during the months of "rain," however, there are often fine days at the coast. Hotel rates are usually lower at this time of the year. Some of the hotels catering primarily to overseas tourists even close.

Over the course of the year, especially during the *kusi*, a great deal of seaweed is washed up on to the Kenyan beaches. The amounts and location of the weed can vary from day to day, affected by the winds and currents. There are occasions when there is so much seaweed that it is difficult to walk on the beaches or to swim in the ocean. Several hotels employ staff to rake and bury the seaweed in the sand—this helps, but it is still waiting for you in the water! Seaweed afflicts some beaches more than others. For example, Watamu on the North Coast is badly affected, while Diani on the South Coast is somewhat less so.

Sport fishermen from all over the world come to Shimoni in the south, where big game fishing for marlin and sailfish is at its best in the Pemba Channel. However, many of the big resorts along the coast can give expert and novice fishermen an unforgettable day "hunting the big ones." On the North Coast, Watamu and Malindi are the "in" places to go, and there are many fishing tournaments.

Beyond the sybaritic beach experience, you can still see wildlife in nearby forested areas such as Shimba Hills National Reserve, Arabuko-Sokoke Forest and the Tana River Delta. Travel agents, specially trained hotel staff, and homestay hosts can help you arrange safaris into these areas.

In all ways the island of Mombasa is the hub of the Kenyan Coast. It is a major seaport. There is an international airport, the train from Nairobi brings many visitors to the Mombasa Railroad Station, and Mombasa is where the road from Nairobi meets the coastal highway. Mombasa, separates the North Coast from the South Coast.

The **South Coast** is reached by crossing on the Likoni Ferry. There are a string of resorts on a series of beaches, the best known and most developed being Diani Beach. South of Diani is less developed.

The **North Coast** has concentrated groupings of hotels near Mombasa, Malindi, and to a lesser extent, Watamu. Farther north towards the Somali border are the islands of the Lamu Archipelago. The ancient Swahili town of Lamu is well known and often visited by tourists.

The Kenyan Coast is a popular destination for package tours from Europe. Resort management and clientele often reflect specific nationalities, with German and Italian predominating.

There is a sophisticated infrastructure of resort hotels ranging from the luxurious to the more basic. Many hotels offer similar services, facilities and activities. The hotels range from the exotic (high-thatch roofs, whitewashed arches, Lamu-style furniture) to the more prosaic (cement accommodation wings, balconies angled towards a possible sea view, plastic loungers).

There are also some resorts with private villas or condos (complete with cook, if desired), as well as opportunities for more personalized homestays. You can even opt for the romance of staying in a grass shack on the beach. In addition there are private homes which can be rented through agents. However, as these require self-catering, they are not covered in this book.

Mombasa

Mombasa City Codes ☎ *11, FAX: 11.*

Mombasa, the second largest city in Kenya, is on Mombasa Island. It is a steamy, tropical, low-rise city with asymmetrical streets, a languid pace, and a diverse and intriguing population. Mombasa is mostly a Swahili town. Women chatter by in dark *bui-bui* or wrapped in brilliant multicolored *kanga*. There are dozens of intricate mosques and temples, pungent open markets, mazes of narrow lanes crowded with street stalls. Mombasa is a port and a commercial center, not a resort town. It is rather seedy and romantic, not slick and efficient. There are no beaches in Mombasa and the hotels tend to be modest and somewhat old-fashioned. Tourists in Mombasa have mostly been "bused" in for shopping and sight-seeing.

Mombasa has a long and complex history, best appreciated by a visit to **Fort Jesus** and the **Old Town**. Fort Jesus, begun by the Portuguese at the end of the 16th Century, dominates the entrance to Mombasa Harbor, and commands good views over the Old Town. The fort is now a national monument and houses an interesting museum. The Old Town is a maze of narrow streets, mosques and crowded buildings, some with impressive carved doors or intricate balconies.

The Castle Hotel

The Castle Hotel, Box 84231, Mombasa
☎ *(11) 223403, Telex: 21008*

This city hotel is centrally placed in Mombasa Town and harks back to an earlier era. There is a big open dining veranda with whitewashed pillars, tiled floor and potted plants. This is a good spot for a cool drink and watching street life. Tour buses bringing sight-seers into Mombasa often use the Castle Hotel as a drop-off and pickup point. This adds to the bustle and activity of the open veranda and also signals an increase in drink prices.

The 60 rooms at the Castle have few frills and are rather worn. There are high ceilings with fans, and the furniture is tired and old.

New Outrigger Hotel

New Outrigger Hotel, Box 82345, Mombasa
☎ *(11) 20822, Telex: 21368*

This hotel is above Kilindini Harbor, with views over the water. There are palm trees, tropical shrubs and a swimming pool. Rooms have balconies facing the sea, air conditioning, and telephones. The hotel is under Belgian management, features French cuisine and a beach.

Manson Hotel

Manson Hotel, Box 83565, Mombasa
☎ *(11) 222420*

This is a newer business hotel in Mombasa. We did not visit but hear it is adequate.

The Oceanic Hotel

The Oceanic Hotel, Box 90371, Mombasa
☎ *(11) 311191*

Advertised as the "largest hotel on Mombasa Island," this multistory cement hotel is near the Likoni Ferry and overlooks the Likoni Bay. It is not a "beach hotel." The style recalls the 1950s and the hotel is large, rather shabby and run-down.

Polana Hotel

Polana Hotel, Box 41983, Mombasa
☎ *(11) 222168, FAX: (11) 314505*

This high-rise hotel has 140 rooms including junior suites. Rooms are air-conditioned with bath, shower, minibar, radio, TV and telephones. The hotel has a conference room for up to 200 people, a casino, and offers car rental, theater bookings, laundry service, in house parking and excursions. The hotel is described as being "in the heart of Mombasa Island, in walking distance to all places of interest and business locations in the town." The authors have not visited this hotel but suggest it would be of more interest for business travel than tourism.

South of Mombasa

Heading from Mombasa to the south coast, travelers must take the Likoni Ferry. This is usually a hot and colorful experience with little stalls lining the road as you wait for your ferry and a stream of pedestrian traffic in various garb passing your window. There are bags of cashew nuts for sale, fresh coconuts as a thirst quencher—lots of noise and color.

The coastline which extends from Mombasa down to the Tanzanian border is generally less developed than the north coast, the exception being the long stretch of Diani Beach which has many tourist hotels.

You will not see the ocean from the road which heads south. Sign-posted roads off to your left lead to the various beaches. In the case of the less developed beaches you will find yourself driving down winding dirt road under tall coconut palms. You pass little settlements—thatched houses made of coral rock and dried mud, children and chickens in the road, women draped in bright kanga.

Shelly Beach

This is the first beach after the Likoni Ferry. The beach is narrow and rather uninviting.

COAST: MOMBASA & SOUTH

Shelly Beach Hotel

Shelly Beach Hotel, Box 96030, Mombasa
☎ *(11) 451001, FAX: (11) 451349*

The hotel sports a great deal of concrete. The beach looks unappealing. Plastic loungers surround a crowded pool and there is little shade. The hotel has many facilities to offer and seems to be full of inexpensive package tour groups. Shelly Beach Hotel is close to the ferry and to Mombasa Town.

Tiwi Beach

Tiwi is a relatively quiet stretch of beach bordered by private homes and rental cottage complexes. These cottages, some of which have communal pools, are typically self-service. There is a camping site which edges the beach and is popular with overlanders. There are fewer foreign tourists here and not as many vendors trying to sell their wares.

Minilets

Minilets. Box 96242, Mombasa
☎ *(11) 51059*

Minilets is a series of individual thatched chalets built on a cliff overlooking Tiwi Beach. Nestled in colorful gardens, the chalets each have a private open-sided veranda and are linked to the restaurant and bar by paved paths. The chalets are basic, having neither fans nor hot water. A few chalets have kitchenettes but most guests use the restaurant and the beach bar. There is an interestingly shaped swimming pool and a scuba-diving base.

Tiwi Villas

Box 86775, Mombasa
FAX: (11) 51265

Individual cottages, pool and restaurant.

Tiwi Sea Castles

Box 96599, Mombasa
☎ *(127) 51220, FAX: (127) 51222*

Separate cottages set in gardens. Each has kitchen, en suite bathrooms and private veranda. Pool and restaurant. Only steps to the beach.

Travellers Beach Hotel Tiwi

Smart Tours and Travel Ltd., Box 42830, Nairobi
☎ *(2) 449640, FAX: (2) 449642*

This large hotel is only partially finished. Part of the hotel has opened, but more is planned and it is likely to be some time before the full complex is completed.

We have not visited Travellers Beach Hotel Tiwi, but know the site—a beautiful spot with lovely sandy beach and not far from Tiwi river mouth.

The promotional material for the hotel promised much: 208 spacious rooms with air-conditioning, overhead fans, hair dryers, 20-inch TVs and minibars. There is mention of banquet and conference facilities, two executive suites, a 24 hour coffee shop, five restaurants, five bars, two tennis courts, stables for riding and water sports. Much is made of the spectacular swimming pool which "meanders downhill" and the wonderful view from the main restaurant. Computer and communications systems and Internet connections are listed. It all sounds very ambitious. Check before booking.

Diani Beach

This is the most popular and the most sophisticated beach south of Mombasa. There are many hotels, shops and services. The beach itself is a long stretch of white sand fringed by palms and other indigenous bush.

Although there are many hotels on Diani Beach, most of them are low-rise and are set in quite large properties with gardens and trees. There are also many private homes along the Diani beachfront. Therefore, although this is a popular and busy tourist spot, you do not feel overwhelmed by cement and people. There is still a nice sense of nature, most of the hotels have a laid back, relaxed atmosphere, and in certain places you can still walk along the beach where there will not be throngs of people.

Many hawkers are on Diani Beach selling their wares. There are opportunities for windsurfing, diving and snorkeling. You can take small boats out to the coral reef—less spectacular here than farther south at Kisite Marine National Park or north at Watamu and Malindi.

There is quite a variety of accommodations to choose from. You can be personally hosted in a private home where you are the only guests, you can stay at a sophisticated, gleaming hotel with several restaurants and evening entertainment, or you can select a relaxed, low-key family-style hotel. There is a golf course and you can take microlight trips.

The Indian Ocean Beach Club

Block Hotels, Box 40075, Nairobi
☎ *(2) 540780, FAX: (2) 545948*

The Indian Ocean Beach Club is possibly the most upmarket hotel on Diani Beach and probably the most expensive as well.

It definitely has the best setting on the beach. Located at the northernmost part of Diani, close to the winding Tiwi River mouth, the club looks over wonderfully clean golden sands and good surf. There are enormous old baobabs, and right next to the club, nestled in a forest of these ancient trees, is a 16th-century Arab mosque.

The club has been designed as a Swahili village, with clusters of whitewashed cottages arranged on both sides of the large main buildings. There are 100 rooms, all of which face the Indian Ocean. Some cottages are single-storied with makuti-thatched roofs while others, housing a few rooms, are double-story with flat roofs in the Swahili-style. The main building, with its grand red-tiled roof and wooden shutters, is more reminiscent of colonial Kenya. The overall effect is a rather busy mélange of architectural styles.

The public rooms are simple and elegant. "Spices," the large and airy upstairs dining room, seems to have no walls, just a series of arched-top windows lined in wood. Instead of glass, there are wooden shutters, opening to reveal glorious views of palms, white sand, and blue ocean—all only steps away. Below this restaurant is an open-sided breakfast area and a large free-form swimming pool with water flowing over the edges.

The Indian Ocean Beach Club does not intend to be just another hotel-on-the-beach. Arriving guests are greeted with scented towels and then, instead of queuing up at a long reception counter, will be ushered to chairs at individual welcoming tables. There are message boxes outside of each room and a 24-hour valet service. Many watersports are included in the tariff such as windsurfing, sailing, goggling, and there are guided bird walks up the Tiwi River. In addition to the large main pool, three small plunge pools are scattered around the grounds.

The rooms also evidence quality and detail. There are king-sized Lamu beds, cushioned window seats, nice stone-tiled floors, dark mangrove beams set in white ceilings, and the hotel logo of a fish painted on the tiles above the bath. There are also fancy extras—direct-dial telephones, hair-dryers, and air conditioning which automatically turns off when you open the door. However, the rooms are disappointingly small, and the bathrooms astoundingly compact. The rooms feel cozy and somewhat enclosed rather than spacious and airy. The arrangement of the cottages is such that some rooms are very close together—ideal for families or groups.

To an appreciable extent, it is the club's location which makes it so special. The baobabs are truly awesome—enormous bulges in undreamed of shapes—hundreds of years old. They provide interest and focal points to the grounds which are still rather lacking in shade or color. Because there is a gap in the reef, waves are able to reach the shore, and even at low tide, the water is deep enough for swimming. This is quite unusual along this coast. With exposed sandbanks and indigenous vegetation, the gentle meandering channels of the Tiwi River add a special interest. Children were leaping down sheer cliffs of sand into the river, then floating gently upstream in the clear ocean water of the incoming tide—great fun.

Special Offerings

Free sports facilities (tennis and squash) including green fees at the Nyali Golf Club, unlimited water sports (extra charge for deep sea fishing and scuba diving), free courtesy shuttle bus to Likoni and Diani, fully equipped conference room with air conditioning, gift boutique, beauty center, children's club.

Staff Notes

Cottages are close together... Rooms are cozy rather than spacious... Some lack of privacy in ground-floor rooms.

Ocean Village Club

Going Places, Box 14776, Nairobi
☎ *(2) 447479, FAX: (2) 446402*

A wonderful alternative to the big bustling hotels on Diani Beach is the exclusive and low-key Ocean Village Club. The grounds are a shaded garden of Eden with huge indigenous trees, jungle-like vines and a profusion of brilliant flowering shrubs and creepers. Just beyond is the glare of white sand and the sparkle of the ocean.

Guests stay in small cottages (white stucco and arches) tucked amongst the gardens. The 26 cottages each have a spacious entrance/lounge area and either two or three bedrooms all with bathrooms ensuite and individual air-conditioning. Although the bedrooms are not especially large or bright, they have all been attractively refurbished and the bathrooms given a quality finish in marble and granite.

Each cottage has its own large veranda—a perfect shady place to escape the heat c the day or enjoy a sundowner.

Ocean Village projects an image of quality and relaxed elegance. The main recep tion area near the ocean is a gleam of polished marble under high thatch. Gold plate and utensils shine on red tablecloths in the open-sided a la carte "Sails" Restauran We enjoyed a romantic seafood dinner there with an ocean breeze and a full moo rising over the water. Waiters wearing long flowing robes added to the sense of th exotic.

The buffet meals in the main dining area were above average and the smaller siz of Ocean Village meant that guests did not have to queue for food as much as in th bigger coastal hotels. At lunch guests can also eat at tables by the attractive swim ming pool or in the "Sails" Restaurant with its great views of sand and sea.

Beach loungers are arrayed on the sand under tall palm trees. Only a low coral wa separates you from the public beach so you can relax in the shade watching the pass ing beach parade of suntanned tourists, persuasive touts and plodding camels. State of-the-art neon windsurfers skim the water and timeless wooden dhows bob in th shallows.

For some years this hotel was almost exclusively patronized by French clientel The majority of the guests are still from France although Ocean Village is als becoming popular with the Kenyan ex-pat community.

Special Offerings:

Tennis court, table tennis, pentague, and volley ball. Snorkeling, Scuba Diving an Windsurfing. Safaris and day excursions.

Accommodation:

68 en suite bedrooms.

Off note:

If your party does not fill a cottage, you may be sharing the entryway and verand with strangers.

Alliance Hotels on Diani Beach

Three Alliance Hotels make up a large resort near the southern end of Diani Beach. Each of the hotels has its own personality. When you stay at one of the hotels, you may choose to use the restaurants and facilities of all three although there is a surcharge to dine at Safari Beach. A shuttle bus connects the hotels if you'd rather not walk.

Jadini Beach Hotel

Alliance Hotels, Box 49839, Nairobi
☎ *(2) 337501, FAX: (2) 219212*

This is our favorite of the three Alliance Hotels. The hotel has many windows and is open to sea breezes. You can see the ocean from practically everywhere.

The hotel's many restaurants and public areas seem to line the beach. Walking round Jadini Beach Hotel gives the feeling of moving along a lively and colorful boardwalk with the beach and ocean always in view. The pool is small but sparkling. It is surrounded by white plastic loungers and overlooks the beach.

There are several places where you can eat. The main restaurant is large and bright with windows on three sides looking out to sea. White tile floors and colorful blue and pink fabrics lend a cheerful appearance. There are ceiling fans and a special area with child-sized furniture. Nearby is an ice cream parlor and a lobster bar. You can also choose to go to restaurants in the other Alliance Hotels.

Jadini Beach Hotel can accommodate 172 guests. The bedrooms face the ocean and have large sliding windows and high ceilings. They are attractively decorated, up-to-date and feel spacious and full of light.

Safari Beach

Alliance Hotels, Box 49839, Nairobi
☎ *(2) 337501, FAX: (2) 219212*

The Safari Beach Hotel is touted as the most deluxe of the Alliance Hotels. However, staying there does not give the feeling of being near the sea. The bedrooms are behind the main reception area with no ocean views and quite a walk from the beach. Even the public rooms only offer glimpses of the ocean.

The most impressive part of the hotel is its lobby—spacious under high thatch. Nearer the beach is a pleasant and good-sized pool where you can have snacks and indulge in ice creams.

The 186 rooms are located in separate two-story thatched rondavels set well back among trees in the hotel's extensive grounds. The rooms are generous and fairly comfortable with the usual modern conveniences and especially nice bathrooms. However, furnishings are rather faded, air-conditioners are tired, and a swim is a long walk away.

There is a well-equipped Sportsman Club built far from the beach, behind the accommodation rondavels. It has a small pool, three tennis courts, a squash court, and modern machines for body building. You can slake your thirst at the Sportsman's snack bar.

Off Note

There was a strong "whiff" of mildew when we visited the Island Grill à la carte restaurant.

Africana Sea Lodge
Alliance Hotels, Box 49839, Nairobi
☎ *(2) 337501, FAX: (2) 219212*

This is the most basic of the Alliance Hotels, with a variety of accommodation styles including small individual rondavels set close together and very far back from the sea. The rooms are clean with en suite bathrooms, but with unimaginative decor. Renovation has begun. The pool is very small, and white plastic loungers crowd its perimeter. There is a dank disco, though dancing to live music poolside at the Jadini Beach Hotel is the bigger draw.

As well as 158 rooms, the lodge also boasts a six-bedroom Directors' Cottage with private living room, terrace, garden and fully-equipped kitchen, complete with cook if desired.

Lagoon Reef Hotel
Reef Hotels, Box 61408, Nairobi
☎ *(2) 214322, FAX: (2) 332702*

Lagoon Reef is near the southern end of Diani Beach. This hotel feels slightly more intimate than some of its larger neighbors. The hotel, situated on 20 acres, has

pectacular grounds and an interesting pool. Near the beach is a huge 50-year-old
aobab tree which attracts many monkeys. The free-form pool, built like a lagoon,
as an island with jungle vegetation. Tropical gardens cascade down the long slope
owards the beach.

The lobby, with its high thatch roof is cool and exotic. There is the sound of water
nd interplay of light and shadow. Wooden bridges lead over large lily ponds, and
here are bird songs from a small aviary. The main dining room is at the same level as
he lobby—the ocean and pool are a long way down a rather steep slope. This hill has
een nicely landscaped and paths meander down towards the pool. At night the gar-
ens are illuminated.

There is more informal dining near the swimming pool. An open-sided bar right
t the edge of the beach overlooks the ocean. Across the road, built in the forest, are
vo hotel tennis courts.

ccommodations

There are accommodations for almost 300 people in thatched blocks, three stories
high. All rooms have balconies and big windows, and most have garden or pool
views. There are fans and air conditioning. Mosquito nets are available on request.
There is a choice between superior, standard and family rooms. *Our Favorites*: the
superior sea-front rooms on the top floor. Like its neighbors, Lagoon Reef attracts
tour groups.

Kaskazi Beach Hotel

LTI - Kaskazi Beach Hotel, Box 135, Ukunda
☎ *(127) 3170, FAX: (127) 2396*

The Kaskazi is one of the newer large hotels on Diani Beach. Its luminous white marble, graceful arches and established gardens suggest a magical palace right out of the Arabian Nights:

> *"Aladdin asked the spirit of the lamp to build him a palace near the sea...the next moment a magnificent white building with beautiful arches and cupolas emerged from the dry coastal land, the sound of the fountains filled the air, and there were people and music every-where..."*

Like the tale, the hotel's decor is light, bright and airy. Jewel-bright cushions, drapes and upholstery accent the intricate wooden shapes of Swahili-style furniture. There are touches of stained glass, patterned brass and cool tiling.

The open-air reception sets the scene with towering high thatch roof, a vast expanse of white tiled floor, and a scattering of rich color in upholstery and decorative tiles—exotic, elegant and airy. Even from reception there are tantalizing views of the blue ocean framed by white arches. A winding marble stairway follows an indoor waterfall to the colorful Lamu Lounge. Just beyond are rock garden dining terrace overlooking a large free-form swimming pool, the romantic ruins of an old mosque and the sea.

The graceful proportions of the mosque's arched window have been reproduced in the balcony arches of the guest rooms, which rise in tiers on three sides of the terraced rock gardens. Most rooms have some sort of balcony sea view. Children are welcome.

Breakfast buffets and dinners are set up in the table d'hote restaurant or on the terrace. The Aladdin Grill is an elegant restaurant for more romantic à la carte dining, and there are snack-bars at poolside and beach. A weekly program is announced which includes nightly entertainment such as tribal dancing, acrobats, games and dancing to the hotel's resident band. On some evenings dinner is set up and served around the floodlit pool. Music is played on and off during the day, volleyball arranged on the beach, and watersports often enliven the pool.

Kaskazi has a somewhat more sophisticated and elegant atmosphere than many of the other hotels on this beach. We visited this hotel when it was still new and looked sparkling—we hope it wears well over time. It was too soon for Kaskazi to have established a reputation, but it is certainly visually beautiful.

Accommodations

There are 193 rooms at Kaskazi. Each room has one double and one single bed, small en suite bathroom, air conditioning, ceiling fan, minibar and telephone. Some rooms have connecting doors. There are wonderful views in Central Rooms #432–440, in South Wing Room #331, and in North Wing Room #358.

Special Offerings

There are air-conditioned conference facilities, two floodlit tennis courts, and centers for sea sports at the beach. There are plans for Kaskazi to operate as an all-inclusive club resort, similar to Club Med.

Staff Notes

The main dining area is very crowded when the hotel is full. Furnishings, although bright and attractive, are not particularly high quality. This stretch of Diani Beach is rather narrow and rocky, and is not especially good for swimming in the ocean.

Leopard Beach Hotel

Leopard Beach Hotel, Box 34, Ukunda
☎ *(1261) 2111, FAX: (1261) 2113*

This hotel was built in 1974 and combines modern lines with African high-thatch architecture. Its rooms and suites are at the top of a rocky cliff with public areas at different levels leading down to the beach.

The small beach has interesting rock formations and tall palms. You need shoes to protect your feet from the coral bottom when swimming.

A unique feature of this hotel is that you only see one level at a time, it is large but seems small and intimate. The pool is lower down on the cliff, built into a terrace

which juts out with good views of the small bay. A disco is also cut into the clif
Rock gardens and lily ponds combine cool color with beckoning corners and nook

The cuisine is billed as international with Italian flavors. Meals are taken in a ver
large dining area where some tables overlook the sea.

Standard rooms are very tired. The reason for choosing this hotel would be to sta
in one of the very reasonably priced, beautifully located, and commodious suite
Wonderful choices are Master Suites #1 and 7 (especially #7!), each with private si
ting area and terrace with magnificent sea view and private garden (can rent wit
master bedroom only, or with additional double bedroom).

Other good choices are Jr. Suites #15, 16, & 18 which share a sitting area and te
race. Cottage #19/20 (two double rooms connecting) is also a good possibility
These all have minibar; TV in English, Italian and German; and excellent privat
bathrooms (with bidet) for each bedroom.

Two Fishes Hotel

Two Fishes Hotel, Box 23, Ukunda, Mombasa
☎ *(1261) 2101*

The most remarkable feature of this large hotel is the unusual swimming poo
meandering through the lounge area and out into the grounds. There are bridge
over the narrow channels of water and a slide leading to a lower pool. A few larg
painted plaster animal figures are scattered in the gardens. The hotel seems popula
with children and has a low-key, informal atmosphere. The main lobby and loung
area look dated with furnishings in orange and brown, and amateur murals on th
walls. When we visited, the hotel was less than spotless.

The 199 rooms are located in three-story thatched buildings. Some rooms ar
close to the beach and have ocean views.

Diani Reef Grand Hotel

Sonotels Kenya Ltd., Box 61753, Nairobi
☎ *(2) 227571, FAX: (2) 227585*

This hotel was built in 1981, and it is huge! It is a rambling complex of 30
rooms, seven restaurants and many lounges and public rooms. There are two swim
ming pools, a romantic lagoon with pedal boats, and a beachfront terrace wher
there is dancing every night under the stars. There is also a disco, a casino, a shop
ping arcade, a children's playground, a gymnasium, video room, beauty shop and
conference hall for 300.

The beach area is wide and very pleasant. Breakfast is served buffet-style in a roo
floating on the garden lagoon with ocean views. There are tropical flowers, rock ga
dens and the familiar but beautiful tall swaying palms.

With a choice of seven restaurants, you can select among French, Italian, Polyne-
sian, Middle Eastern, African, Indian Ocean and International cuisines. The choice
is more exciting than the food. There are also two floodlit tennis courts, air-conditioned squash court, archery range, bocce, and a fitness track.

Accommodations

Older rooms are too-much-used and tired, but due for redecorating. All have air
conditioning, minibar, radio, telephone. The newer Deluxe Wing is better and is
closest to the sea. Ask for rooms #720/721 & 925–927. Rooms #820, 924, and
923 form suites, but can be reserved as doubles.

Off Notes

Several of the public rooms are fighting mildew problems and have a very musty
smell.

Diani Sea Lodge

Welcome Inns Ltd. Kenya, Box 37, Ukunda
☎ *(127) 2114, FAX: (127) 2287*

This is advertised as a "bungalow hotel" with 135 Swahili-style bungalows set far
back from the beach in established gardens. All have a terrace, shower and AC. Some
have an extra bedroom. Closer to the beach is a ten-room apartment with sea views.

The main building has shops, a disco, a bar and a restaurant which looks towards
the kidney-shaped pool and the sea beyond. There is also a toddlers' pool, a children's playground, and a pool bar which serves snacks. Sports options include tennis,
table tennis, minigolf and billiards as well as the usual selection of watersports and
activities. Shady lawns with wooden loungers stretch down to the beach.

The hotel is run by German owners.

Diani Sea Resort

Welcome Inns Ltd. Kenya, Box 37, Ukunda
☎ *(127) 3081, FAX: (127) 2287*

This new resort hotel is part of the German Welcome Inn-Hotels. The architecture is very plain, with the central wing distant from but facing the sea, and two side
wings angled towards it. The hotel has 340 beds, standard and family rooms, and
several suites. The dining area is at the top of a long sloping central garden. Exposed
pathways shimmer in the sun.

Rooms are spacious with air conditioning and private bathrooms with showers.
Light-giving French doors open to a terrace or garden. The pool at the foot of the
central garden area has an island and water slide. There are sports and resort facilities.
This hotel has yet to develop any character, but at least it is new and clean.

Leisure Lodge

Leisure Lodge, Diani Beach
☎ *(127) 2011*
or book through travel agents in Germany

This large resort on Diani Beach is a classy Hotel-Club-Casino combination specializing in catering to a tour-group clientele from Germany. Leisure Lodge has hotel section which is closer to the ocean, as well as a more exclusive Club set in gardens far from the beach.

A huge reception area leads into a glitzy shopping arcade, followed by a Casino. Beyond are terraces, bars, and restaurants, some with sea view. There is red tile underfoot and the cooling peaks of high thatched domes above.

The hotel has more than 200 double rooms in several multilevel blocks stretched along the property to one side, some with good sea views. All have air conditioning and en suite bathrooms. There is one hotel swimming pool.

Although farther from the sea, the club is very exclusive and more upmarket than the hotel. Entry to the club is carefully restricted. The 116 rooms are more luxurious with elegant decor. There are 16 deluxe suites and two swimming pools. Pretty walkways pass over lily ponds. There are lawns, colorful flower beds and a dining terrace. The golf course has been recommended.

Special Offerings

Guests of both hotel and club share resort facilities: casino, restaurants, beach lounger rental, windsurfing with lessons, a PADI Diving School, four floodlit tennis courts, a golf course, horse riding on the beach or inland, beauty salon, massage parlor, and bus service to Mombasa.

Golden Beach

Golden Beach, Box 31, Ukunda, Mombasa
☎ *(127) 2625, FAX: (127) 2321*

This is a huge concrete highrise with 138 rooms. There is little charm and loud decor—it feels rather like a convention center. Although the beachfront is extensive, the buildings are far from the beach. There are many sports activities, a big pool and gardens. The hotel is frequented mainly by German tour groups.

Robinson Baobab Club

Robinson Baobab Club, Box 84792, Mombasa
☎ *(1261) 2026*

Built in 1974, this is one of the oldest hotels on the beach. It can accommodate 300 people. The clientele is predominantly German, and bookings are made in Frankfurt. The hotel has a magnificent site high on a rocky promontory, well-treed, and with views down over the ocean. There are some nice touches—a waterfall by the lobby, interesting Lamu furniture, dining tables next to big open windows with sea views. However, closer inspection reveals drawbacks—there is a maze of rooms, heavy doses of mildew, and loudspeakers broadcasting rousing music.

Southern Palms Beach Resort

Southern Palms, Box 363, Ukunda, Mombasa
☎ *(127) 3721*

This is a new beach resort going up near the northern end of Diani Beach. Southern Palms will have 180 rooms in three-stories. There is to be a large pool, sports and conference facilities and nightly entertainment. Rooms will have Swahili-style decor and balconies facing the sea. They will also have air conditioning, mosquito nets, and large double beds. An extra Lamu-style divan will add to the Swahili theme.

Trade Winds Hotel

African Tours and Hotels Ltd., Box 30471, Nairobi
☎ *(2) 336858, FAX: (2) 218109*

This hotel can accommodate approximately 200 people. Public rooms and old wing rooms have sad decor and are substandard. A newer wing with Arab-style windows is set farther back from the beach. There is a large but poorly maintained swimming pool and a nice beachfront.

THE KENYAN COAST

Diani House

Diani House, Box 19, Ukunda, Mombasa
☎ *(127) 2412, FAX: (127) 2391*

Diani House is a coastal taste of colonial Kenya. Located about halfway along Diani, this pleasant home with grassy slopes rolling down to the beach is a nostalgic reminder of what the Kenyan coast was like before the mushrooming of resort hotels. Sitting on the cool veranda with dogs at your feet, you feel transported back in time.

When you stay at Diani House you are hosted by Annelise (Lulu) Archer and John Clark. This lively young couple helps you to feel completely relaxed and at home, and they will organize activities or outings to suit. They have a boat for fishing, snorkeling, or visiting nearby islands. You can also windsurf. Side trips to the Shimba Hills National Park for game viewing or into Mombasa for shopping or sightseeing can easily be arranged.

Safari Journal — last, late evening

At dinner there were candles, music wafting out of the living room, and a selection of wines. There was a pleasant breeze, a bushbaby ran along the edge of the veranda and we could sense the ocean through the night. Conversation flowed. Could have spent a week just talking to John and Lulu, to hear more about their wonderful and diverse experiences growing up in Kenya — from game safaris to movie sets.

Diani House can accommodate a maximum of eight guests. The bedrooms are spacious and simple. Lulu has decorated them with individuality using Kenyan furniture, fabrics and crafts to make them colorful and attractive. There are bookshelves piled with books and scattered rugs—the ambience is casual and homey rather than luxurious. There are fans (no air conditioning) and each bedroom has a large bathroom en suite. In place of glass, there is dark meshing over the windows, but from the veranda outside there are nice views down over the garden towards the ocean.

The almost five hectares in size grounds are impressive with palms, baobabs, and bougainvillea are also a refuge for all manner of birds and small wildlife. There are colobus monkeys in the trees, a bushbaby helps itself from a feeder, and everywhere there are birds.

Fresh home-cooked food is served with an emphasis on the wonderful seafood and tropical fruits available. Meals are casual and usually enjoyed alfresco on the long veranda.

Nomad

Nomad, Box 1, Ukunda, Mombasa
☎ *(127) 2155, FAX: (127) 2391*

Nomad is a return to basics on Diani Beach. You pass new shopping malls, disco
and highrise hotels and then turn down a long, winding dirt road shaded by old
trees: a staggering contrast. Guests have a choice of staying in one of the three new
large family cottages or in the older small bandas. The setting is idyllic—only grass
and tall palm trees between you, the beach, and the ocean beyond.

Staying in the bandas at Nomad is like camping on the beach—except the "tents"
are made of sticks. The cottages, on the other hand are bright and spacious with sliding glass doors on to private verandas and the beach just steps away.

Nomad began as a restaurant 15 years ago, and is still a popular place to eat. The
food is simple and excellent. There are two restaurants. The main restaurant (high
thatch roof, sides open to views and breezes) serves à la carte meals in the evening,
with an emphasis on seafood. On Sundays there is a curry and Jazz lunch.

The ultracasual "Nomad's Beach Bar" is basically a *makuti* roof supported by a
tree trunk with sand underfoot. Customers are often in swimwear, and the ocean is
only steps away. The menu ranges from sandwiches to wonderfully fresh seafood
platters. The Diani Boutique adds color and activity to the scene.

Nomad is popular with British Kenyans. It has a relaxed and friendly atmosphere.
The staff have been there a long time, there is a loyal repeat group of guests, and children are welcome. As the manager said, "This is the exact opposite of a package tour
place...there are no jumping Masai for entertainment...here you can completely
relax, you don't even have to talk to anyone else." The only pool is the Indian
Ocean. Deep sea fishing is available, and there is a diving school.

Accommodations

Nomad can accommodate a maximum of 50. The three family cottages each have
one double room and a family suite which can sleep four. Two cottages have an
upstairs garret which can sleep two. Rooms are bright and attractive and are
equipped with an electric kettle and a large mosquito net enclosing both beds and
a fan. Bathrooms are large and modern. The bandas are small, basic and dark—some
are family units with a very small second bedroom. Each has a bathroom en suite.
There is electricity, but no fans. Even if you don't stay at Nomad, at least stop by
for a meal.

Galu Beach

Situated south of Diani, Galu Beach is less built up, with fewer hotels and
no shopping malls. There are dirt roads and indigenous bush. The beach is
smaller and more private than Diani, and has fewer beach vendors or boating
activities. Coral rock means more difficult swimming along some portions of
this beach.

Neptunes Hotels on Galu Beach

Neptune Village, Box 696 Ukunda, Mombasa
☎ (127) 3061, FAX: (127) 3019

Side by side are two Neptune resorts—the older "Neptune Cottages" and the bright new "Neptune Paradise." Between them they have over 250 units in two-story rondavel-style cottages with very tall peaked roofs—they look like a gnome's village come to life!

Since the plots are very deep, it's a long walk to the ocean. The cottages are set back in gardens, or overlooking the pool rather than the sea.

Neptune Paradise, the new and smaller resort, has a clean "decorated" feel to it. There are scores of chairs and loungers in pastel hues with coordinating fabrics, the bar is built in the shape of a boat with bar stools to look like dolphins. The open-sided beach bar and the thatched dining area are built close to the beach, and there is a big pool with a swim-up bar. Music plays, and there is a TV and table tennis under thatch. Images of Florida and ice-cream parlors come to mind.

Accommodations

The rooms are clean, attractively decorated and well-equipped with minibars, phone, radio, tables and chairs. Most rooms look into the backs of others. Those closest to the pool have the best views and the most noise.

Pinewood Village

Protea Hotels, Box 190, Ukunda, Mombasa
☎ *(127) 3720, FAX: (127) 3131*

Pinewood Village is a new complex of 20 townhouses in the coastal forest near the end of Galu Beach. These two-story white villas are compactly arranged along narrow grounds stretching to the beach. Staying at Pinewood Village is more like renting your own condominium than staying at a traditional ocean resort hotel. You have a living room and a fully-equipped kitchen with staff to cook and clean. Privacy and individuality are combined with the security of being part of a complex.

Set well back from the sea, the villas have views of coastal bush rather than the ocean. They share a lovely curved swimming pool which has a swim-up thatched bar. Landscaped steps beyond the pool give way to gardens and lawns, then Galu Beach.

The villas are solidly built and attractively furnished, giving a sense of quality and attention to detail. Fresh whitewash dominates—a dramatic contrast with the dark ethnic furniture and bright fabrics. Arches abound. The effect is clean, spacious and uncluttered—more aesthetically pleasing than comfortable.

Upstairs, however, all is comfort. Big beds with ceiling fans above are encased in voluminous mosquito nets. Again there are pleasing fabrics and bright whitewash. The bathrooms are elegant with tiles imported from Italy. With central air conditioning, the bedrooms are also the coolest rooms in the villa. (There are fans, but no air conditioning downstairs.) The bedrooms open on to large terraces where you might glimpse colobus monkeys in the trees.

Each villa also has its own direct dial telephone. Some villas have connecting doors which allow a larger family or group the opportunity of sharing a doubled living space with four to six double bedrooms upstairs.

A cook steward is assigned to each villa and, if you choose, will cook and serve all of your meals. Supplies can be purchased at the mini supermarket in the main building. Fresh seafood and vegetables are on sale at the resort's own small open market. There is a charming restaurant and bar in the main building which is reached by a wooden bridge over a lily pond. There is a half-board option.

There is a certain thoughtfulness at Pinewood Village—accommodation for drivers and ayahs is included in the tariff, kitchen staples are placed in your villa, and cold beers can be purchased at the store.

Other Facilities

Floodlit tennis court, squash court, games room, conference facilities, air-conditioned video/TV room, and a terrace which can be used for conferences and parties. The management will organize tours to Mombasa, sea sports, and shopping or entertainment trips to Diani Shopping Center, only eight kilometers away.

Chale Paradise Island

Chale Paradise Island, Box 4, Ukunda, Mombasa
☎ *(127) 2127, FAX: (127) 3319 Msambweni*

This small island south of Galu Beach is astoundingly beautiful with a lovely natural sandy bay, dramatic rock formations and a great variety of indigenous trees. Chale Island is now being developed, though many had hoped it would become a protected reserve. The developer is full of vision and energy—he sees Chale Paradise Island as a luxury tented health spa. The tents will be large and full of antique Lamu furniture, the rough rocks will be covered with sand for barefoot walking, the pure natural sulphur mud will be amazingly regenerative. There was talk of masseurs, health food and attentive service. It seemed a pity that the tents were being constructed cheek by jowl, that day trippers were expected, and that the development tractors were driving over coral. What price tourism? Update: Chale Paradise Island is advertising bookings and on-site birthday and wedding ceremonies.

Msambweni

A bumpy dirt road leads past palm groves and mud houses to Msambweni. This is a relatively unspoiled stretch of beach edged primarily by private properties. There are rocky outcrops, low cliffs and patches of coral on sandy bays.

Club Green Oasis (Formerly Black Marlin)

Club Green Oasis, Box 80, Msambweni
☎ *(127)52030*

This spread-out resort bakes on a cliff. The beach below is rocky, disappointing and small. The clientele is mostly German and French tour groups. The sea-view pool schedules adult water polo and exercise. There are horses for riding. Accommodations are a series of rather scruffy small villas and rondavels scattered in huge lawns. The Barracuda Villa Rooms #110, 111, & 112 would make up for a lot just because of the private sitting room and wonderful view!

Update:
We hear that parts of the hotel have burned down and that it has opened under a new name: Club Green Oasis.

Seascapes Beach Villas

Seascapes Limited, Box 45541, Nairobi
☎ *(2) 744033, FAX: (2) 743966*

Seascapes is ideal for people who want to escape hotels, but still want the option of eating meals in a restaurant instead of cooking. In a dramatic cliff-top setting, 16 thatched double-story Arab style villas share a central swimming pool. Each white villa has three large double bedrooms with bathrooms en suite, a lounge-dining area, a fully equipped kitchen and sun-balconies. There are fans, but no air conditioning. Sea breezes are free to blow through the unglassed windows. Each villa comes with a cook and cleaner.

The setting of Seascapes makes it unique. The wide expanse of beach is far below down many stairs. Although it is quite a hike, once you are on the beach, there are no crowds or beach vendors, just long stretches of sand. The villas are well spread out on 12 acres of landscaped grounds. Stone paths lead through lawns. There are palm trees and bougainvillea.

The swimming pool is fairly small and has an adjoining bar and bistro/snack restaurant. There is also a shop where you can purchase groceries and produce for your cook to prepare. Tennis and squash are free to villa residents. At Seascapes you have a sense of privacy, although you can be communal around the pool and bar. The best villas for the view are #1 and #11.

Funzi – Shimoni – Wasini

After Msambweni the coast road passes open green swamps, tall palm trees, then fields of sugar cane. About 80 kilometers south of Mombasa is Shimoni, known for game fishing and coral caves. In view of the shore is Wasini, a narrow rocky island with no roads and no running water. On the island is a small Swahili village, exposed coral gardens, some Muslim ruins, and the Wasini Island Restaurant with a reputation for wonderful seafood. Day-long dhow trips to the island give you a look at Swahili culture and a gourmet lunch.

The snorkeling in this area is superb. Boats can take you to the Kisite-Mpunguti Marine National Park—magnificent coral reefs less visited than those further north. You can use your own snorkeling equipment and hire a small local dhow to get to the reef. Or, you can go to the other extreme and splurge on an outing with Shimoni Aqua-Ventures Ltd. where equipment, expert underwater guiding and instruction, and even a fabulous five-course seafood lunch are included. (Contact **Shimoni Aqua-Ventures** at Indian Ocean Beach Club ☎ *(127) 3730 ext 179*)

Pemba Channel Inn
Pemba Channel Fishing Club, Ltd., Box 86952, Mombasa
☎ *(11) 313749, FAX: (11) 316875*

The Pemba Channel is world famous for some of the best big game fishing in Africa. The Pemba Channel Inn is small, delightful and very personal. It is the capable manager, Sandra Ruysenaars, who gives the inn its special character. Her warmth and good humor put her guests at ease, her cooking is outstanding, and she has made this once rather spartan fishing lodge an attractive and comfortable place to stay.

The inn is built on the high banks above the channel. There is no proper beach, but there is a pleasant view of water, boats and Wasini Island. The Tanzanian mountains seem to loom just at the end of the water. You can cool down in the large, beautifully tiled swimming pool.

The Inn has a central clubhouse—large and sprawling with open sides. There are overstuffed chintz cushions on wicker sofas, bowls of shells, and freshly picked flowers. Marlin trophies, photos and lists of amazing catches add substance to enjoyable conversations recounting special experiences fishing or snorkeling in the channel.

A feeling of professionalism and purpose touches everything connected with the big game fishing here. The teamwork and the experience of the all-Kenyan boat crews help Pemba Channel boats to bring in more catches over 500 pounds than any other boats on the Kenyan coast. There are three boats, each of which is fully equipped for three people to fish at a time. Each boat has tackle in the 130, 80, or 50 lb. class. An experienced fisherman always goes with the boat to give advice or to instruct novices. Children under eight years are not allowed. There is an eight-month fishing season from August to the end of March. Being in the lee of Pemba Island, the seas are normally calm.

THE KENYAN COAST

The ship-to-shore radio crackles! You know firsthand the fortunes of each deep-sea fishing boat right up to the moment of weighing in the catch. The understated pride, the world-class significance of what is done, laces everything at the Pemba Channel Inn with a fizzing excitement.

Pemba Channel Inn can accommodate a total of 14 guests in a series of simple white bandas scattered on the grounds. The rooms are bright and spacious with cheerful fabrics, a standing fan, and mosquito nets. The en suite bathrooms have huge showers with welcome water pressure. Sandra has made the rooms personal with magazines, baskets of toiletries, and flowers. Each banda has a small veranda—some with views over the water.

Thanks to Sandra's culinary skills, dinners at Pemba Channel Inn are memorable adventures in gourmet dining, often served on the terrace under the stars. You have the feeling that everything is done for your personal delight—especially the individual chocolate souffle!

Just minutes away from Pemba Channel Inn is a colorful coastal market which is spread out on the site of the old British colonial outpost. Nearby, you can examine some of the terrible "black holes" of the slave trade, which are still said to be haunted.

Please Note

The Inn is closed April–July 31. Reservations which include fishing boat booking will bump bookings for lodgings only.

ff Note
No real beach.

Shimoni Reef Lodge
Reef Hotels, Box 61408, Nairobi
☎ *(2) 214322, FAX: (2) 332702*

Best known for its PADI Diving Center, this small lodge mainly attracts divers. It s built on the high banks of the Wasini Channel, and the bar and restaurant overlook he water. The atmosphere is very casual and tranquil. There are ten rather run-down ottages with thatched roofs, fans and private flagstone verandas. There are grassy reas, trees and a free-form swimming pool that has seen better days.

Sea Adventures Ltd.
Sea Adventures Ltd., Box 56 Shimoni
☎ *Shimoni 12*

If you plan to go big game fishing for more than one day, you can stay with the Iemphills. Pat Hemphill and his son, Simon, have years of fishing experience, and perate two boats equipped for big game fishing. They specialize in light tackle fishng and offer special "kids days."

Guests stay either in the Hemphills' home or a guest cottage. There are four dou-le rooms, and meals are taken with the Hemphill family. Rates include fishing.

Funzi Island Club
Funzi Island Club, Box 90246, Mombasa
☎ *(11) 225546, FAX: (11) 316458*

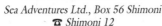

The canoe speeds up and heads straight at a wall of mangroves. The instinct is to luck, but suddenly you are in a narrow waterway overhung by trees—dappled light n the water, the splash of jumping fish. Land on sand and race up the hot midday lope to the cool dark welcome of a big thatch banda.

Shades of Graham Greene: A wonderful antique Victrola is scratching out a une—a call to dance on the straw matting in bare feet with chilled wine in hand. There are giant polished mangrove root tables, fish trophies mounted on makuti valls, visitors books and photos of guests having a good time. Out in the bright glare lonkeys plod, pulling water for the tents. Dogs tease. All seems rather a mirage, a tep out of time, blurred and softened at the edges.

Funzi Island is peace and privacy at a price. There are only seven tents—wonderful vhimsical tents set far apart—large and light-filled. There are kingsize Lamu beds vith tie-dye covers made by your hostess, Robina. In front of the tents are big shaded veranda areas and water-filled footbaths for sandy toes or birds. There are many delightful and ingenious touches such as the large tree nuts used to operate the bush shower.

Although the tents themselves are wonderful, they do not command any special views—sand and scrubby bush—no panoramas over water. We visited on a very hot and rather airless day and did not spend the night, so have no sense of whether breezes provide sleeping comfort.

Funzi Club is best known for fishing. One or two day fishing trips can be arranged in Funzi Club's "Jungle Cat," which is equipped with tackle, fighting chairs and an experienced crew. Beyond the reef are big game fish—marlin, sailfish and yellow fin tuna.

However, you don't have to like fishing to enjoy yourself here. Your host, Tony Duckworth, is a knowledgeable ornithologist and can lead bird walks as well as canoe trips up the river estuary and between the mangroves. He gloats, delighted at having spotted a white-backed night heron. (Mean something to you birders?)

If you're not much into fish or fowl, you might prefer to lounge (with drink and food at hand) on the "African Queen" in the middle of a peaceful bay, or land on a sandy spit of beach for a picnic and a swim. The choice is yours—no timetable, no set agenda. All just very languid and lazy.

There is a minimum of a three-night stay at Funzi Club. Robina commented that some people leave in tears, and an entry in the visitors' book read "Robinson Crusoe refuses rescue." The lunch we had was excellent—lots of ultrafresh seafood and great salads. To quote Tony, the price includes "Full board and drinks on the sideboard." We regretted that we could only spend a few hours at Funzi Club—didn't get to test out the Lamu beds or enjoy more of the wry humor of our host.

Funzi Club also offers a selection of day trips for people who have lodging elsewhere. The Club closes over the low season months. Funzi Island is 60 kilometers south of Mombasa along the main coast road.

Shimba Hills National Reserve

The Shimba Hills run parallel to the coast south of Mombasa. It takes less than an hour to drive from Mombasa up into this hilly reserve. At 500 meters above sea level and covered by beautiful forest, the Shimba Hills National Reserve is a refreshing contrast to the coast. There is not a great deal of game in the reserve although there are elephant, buffalo and giraffe. The park is best known as being the only place in Kenya where you might see the rare sable antelope.

Shimba Hills
Block Hotels, Box 40075, Nairobi
☎ *(2) 540780, FAX: (2) 545948*

Shimba Hills is a pleasant overnight game viewing lodge (see section on Night Game Viewing Lodges). It is nestled in the Shimba Hills Game Reserve only miles from the tropical scenery of the Kenyan Coast. Compared with the sticky humidity at sea level, Shimba Hills is cool and refreshing—welcome jungle greens after the glare of sand and sea. After you leave your vehicle, a lush scenic walk leads you into the stunning open treehouse ingeniously built into the forest—three rooms even have trees growing through them!

Every aspect of the building is designed to be in harmony with nature. The dining room is a covered veranda overlooking the floodlit pond—you can watch game during dinner. Walkways and balconies provide picture perfect views of exotic trees, birds, monkeys, and even herds of elephant drinking at the waterhole below. The trees are labeled for the fledgling botanist. To minimize the mosquito population, the pond is home to a school of Gambusa Fish.

Typically, you arrive at Shimba Hills in time for tea, a sundowner game drive, or chance to enjoy jungle life and sounds at one of the three bar areas. The most uniqu is the Jungle Bar at the end of a long, winding wooden walkway. At night floodlight illuminate the waterhole.

Shimba Hills can accommodate up to 80 people. All rooms have standing balco nies facing the water hole. The rooms, although small, are light and cheerful with bi windows and nice fabrics. There are ceiling fans and ample electricity. Guests shar clean, bright communal toilet and shower facilities which are constructed of woo and stone.

Weddings have also been held at Shimba Hills, with the ceremony performed a the end of the Jungle Bar Walkway. The bridal suite is very large with an outstanding view of the water hole, ensuite dining area, and private bathroom.

Accommodations

There are 24 doubles, five triples, and two self-contained suites. All the doubles and triples have twin beds. The suites have double beds and ensuite bathrooms. All rooms have ceiling fans and mosquito nets are provided on request. The rooms are sprayed, and there are screen and glass windows. Suites are #19 and #20. The rooms with trees growing through them are #22, 23, and 16. No children under 7 are allowed.

Special Offerings

Sundowner game drive, pre-dawn game drive, souvenir and sundry shop.

Off Note

Not noted for abundance of game.

Sable Valley

Bush Homes of East Africa Ltd., Box 56923, Nairobi
☎ *(2) 571647, FAX: (2) 571665*

Sable Valley is a privately owned game sanctuary adjoining the southern end of Shimba Hills National Park. Dick and Rosemary Knight live in the sanctuary and provide accommodation for two guests (plus two children) in a self-contained cottage. Guests have access to a swimming pool, a good library and two willing bridge partners. Wholesome, home-cooked meals are offered, with many of the ingredients coming from their small farm.

The Knights have a lifelong love of the wilderness and an interest in conservation. They are involved in the re-introduction of species that were known to be in the Shimba Hills but disappeared through hunting and poaching. Fiona Alexander, an ornithologist, is also resident in the sanctuary and will take guests out bird watching.

Guests can go for game drives and bush walks, and can visit areas of rain forest. Wildlife in the area includes elephant, buffalo, sable antelope and leopard as well as a variety of buck, small cats, and monkeys. If you would like a change of scenery, it is less than an hour to the beach for a day of sun and sand.

Getting There:

Two hours by road from Mombasa, 45 minutes from Ukunda. Transfers can be provided.

Shimba House

Cottar's Safari Service, Box 44191, Nairobi
☎ *(2) 884508, FAX: (2) 882234*
e-mail Cottars@form-net.com

This private hosted homestay situated on a ridge about 1000 feet above sea level, has views towards the Indian Ocean and catches a refreshing breeze.

In addition to the main house with its two master bedrooms, dining room and lounge; there are also three private guest houses with en suite bathrooms.

Shimba House is being billed as a comfortable place to relax while being close enough to enjoy both the ocean and wildlife. It is a twenty minute drive to the beach and fifteen minutes to the main entrance of the Shimba Hills National Reserve.

North of Mombasa to Kilifi

Mombasa City Codes ☎ *11, FAX: 11.*

The coastline stretching north of Mombasa is heavily developed with resort hotels. The concentration of hotels peters out as you move towards Kilifi and then intensifies again in the Malindi area. Heading north from

COAST: MOMBASA & NORTH to MALINDI

Mombasa towards Kilifi, the resort beaches are Nyali, Bamburi, Shanzu, and Kikambala.

If you want a change from beach activities you can visit the *Bamburi Quarry Nature Trail*, an impressive and heartening example of land reclaimed from a cement quarry. There is also the *Mamba Village* crocodile farm and *Bombolulu*, a handicrafts center which employs disabled people. Golfers might choose to try their skill at the *Nyali Beach Golf Club*.

Nyali Beach and English Point

English Point looks across towards Old Town Mombasa, and Nyali Beach begins the coral sand beaches north.

Nyali Beach Hotel

Block Hotels, Box 40075, Nairobi
☎ *(2) 540780, FAX: (2) 545948*

The Nyali Beach Hotel is the grand old hotel of the Mombasa coast. In 1931, the 1300-foot Nyali Bridge opened to link the Port of Mombasa with the northern mainland. After World War II, the Kenyan Government invited Harry and Eva Noon to build a hotel at the coast developing some of the prime land on Nyali Beach. Beginning with a rough clearing or *nyali*, they dealt with every problem and setback, determined to build an elegant and comfortable hotel. In December 1946, the Nyali Beach Hotel opened to become the first of Kenya's beach hotels with a reputation for hospitality and excellence that endures to this day.

Your first impression is of cool whitewashed walls and tiled floors. There are ceiling fans, potted palms, pale marble and white wicker furniture. Light streams through paladian windows to emphasize the blue-green color of cushions where hotel cats doze. A large brass samovar catches the light, and there are pots of tropical foliage. The atmosphere is easy, there is a sense of comfort and tradition. You have the feeling that you are waiting for Humphrey Bogart and Sidney Greenstreet to appear.

Although the hotel opened with only 57 rooms, today it can accommodate approximately 450 people and do it with style. Nyali attracts honeymoon couples, families with children, and tourists from all over the world. There are many choices of accommodation, 26 acres of grounds and gardens, many varieties of water sport and activities. Guests can sample aerobic workouts, beauty treatments, deep sea fishing, golf and tennis.

Marine "safaris" take you to the reef in glass-bottom boats, and you can safari to see big game in Tsavo National Park. There is the jungle environment of Shimba Hills and the lure of Old Town Mombasa nearby. In fact, Nyali Beach is perhaps the closest resort hotel to the shopping, sightseeing, and restaurants of Mombasa.

There are two swimming pools, one olympic-sized with a huge outdoor terrace overhead. The other is the appealing Lagoon Pool, free-formed, near the beach, surrounded by lush tropical flowers and palms—a perfect place to enjoy the sea view from a wooden terrycloth-cushioned lounger. With a drink and seafood bar nearby, you can easily spend the day.

Variety is the spice of life at Nyali Beach Hotel, and that applies to the seven eating areas. The cuisine varies from the gourmet splendor in the oceanside Mvita Grill to the open-air fruit bar and Parrots' snackbar at the beach. A wonderful breakfast is served every day in L'Orangerie with active chefs preparing eggs and pancakes to order!

The hotel issues a daily entertainment and sports program. Two shopping arcades boast seven boutiques and shops for every possible need. For romantic nights, you can dance at the Nyali Blues Disco or even under the stars on an outdoor terrace within sight of the sea.

Accommodations

There is a wide range of accommodations from luxury suites to elderly cottages in slightly overgrown gardens. Wings of rooms and cottages are spread through the grounds. Some guests stay in the main building which has spacious older rooms. In the most recent addition, the "new wing," there are three luxury suites and 54 superior ocean view rooms.

All rooms have modern bathrooms with both bathtub and shower, air conditioning, mosquito nets on request, telephones, fridges and 24-hour room service.

Special Offerings

Conference facilities, a games room, library, customized weddings, organized children's activities.

 ## Silver Beach Hotel and Silver Star Hotel

Prestige Hotels Ltd., Box 74888, Nairobi
☎ *(2) 338084, FAX: (2) 213387*

Previously part of the German chain of African Safari Club Hotels, Silver Beach Hotel and Silver Star Hotel are now being managed by Prestige Hotels Ltd. These sister hotels lie next to each other on Nyali beach in their own cove. Guests may use the gardens and facilities of either hotel. The authors have not visited these hotels.

In both hotels all rooms are en suite with showers, and have a balcony or terrace. There are individual air-conditioning units and room safes for rent.

Special Offerings:

Evening entertainment, Starion Night Club, two floodlit tennis courts, table tennis, darts, pool table, beach volleyball, windsurfing, scuba diving center, fitness center, laundry service, safari excursions, medical clinic, gift boutique.

Silver Beach Hotel:

There are 100 twin-bedded rooms facing towards the sea. Forty-eight of these actually overlook the beach.

The main hotel restaurant is indoor-outdoor style and there is also a pool side area for snacks and lunches. There is a lounge bar and a patio bar and two swimming pools. The large pool is made available for games while the smaller pool is closer to the ocean.

Silver Star Hotel:

There are 123 twin-bedded sea-facing rooms, each with a balcony or terrace. Rooms are ensuite with showers and have individual air-conditioning units.

There is a main restaurant serving buffet-style breakfasts and dinners, and a deck restaurant for snacks and lunches. There are three bars. A large free-form swimming pool with a patio terrace and sunbeds overlooks the ocean.

Mombasa Beach Hotel

African Tours & Hotels, Box 30471, Nairobi
☎ *(2) 336858, FAX: (2) 218109*

This is a larger hotel with five-story accommodation blocks facing the sea. It is built on an attractive rocky point with old trees. Many stairs lead to the beach. There are three conference centers, a shopping arcade, five restaurants, and a waterpark with slide. The pool is surrounded by a concrete terrace with plastic lounge chairs. There are many recreational choices. The rooms are bright and airy, and many have good sea views.

Reef Hotel

Reef Hotel, Box 82234, Mombasa
☎ *(11) 471771, FAX: (11) 71349*

The Reef is a large resort hotel which can accommodate about 350 guests. There is no sense of the ocean from the main rooms or pool. The layout is rather confusing with many passages and paths before you reach the beach. There are rows of rooms and lots of concrete. The hotel offers a plethora of facilities and activities: bingo, videos, conference facilities, hair salon, fitness center, tennis, several restaurants, organized pool activities, water sports. The rooms have air conditioning and fridges. A range of room types are available, including a five-bedroom villa with private pool.

The Tamarind Village

The Tamarind Village, Box 95805, Mombasa
☎ *(11) 471729, FAX: (11) 472106*

The Tamarind Village in Nyali is a beautiful and luxurious condominium complex which looks over the harbor towards the Old Town of Mombasa. It shares a driveway with the Tamarind Restaurant, justly famous for its wonderful seafood and setting.

The Tamarind Village has 22 privately-owned apartments. About half of these can be booked through central management. There are one, two, and three bedroom apartments, each with a private entrance, enchanting views, and outdoor terraces. The apartments are serviced and have fully equipped kitchens. As well as the option for self catering, the Lido Bar near the pool serves breakfasts and light lunch dishes. Room service to the apartments can also be arranged. And, of course, you can always splurge next door at the Tamarind Restaurant.

What makes the Tamarind Village so special is its lovely site and exotic and luxurious appearance. It is built in Swahili style and has a series of arches, open-sided walkways with tantalizing water views, and open grillwork walls in Moorish designs. All is in startling, sparkling whitewash alive with the exuberance of bougainvillea spilling over balconies and peeping into corridors. The complex is built along the side of a hill in six levels—balconies jut out at different heights, some shaded by thatch, others by log beams letting through slants of sunlight. Although this is a large, multilevel building, the interest and variety in the layout and design make each apartment personal and unique. There is a clean simplicity, an exotic elegance about the place.

The apartments vary in size, but all have master bedrooms, with bathrooms en suite. There are telephones and air conditioning. Since they are privately owned, there are different styles of decor, and some are much nicer than others. We found

#41,#45,#54 and #65 to be well-appointed and comfortable. Each apartment has a terrace and some have lovely views down across the water. A few have private outdoor jacuzzis.

Safari Journal — afternoon . . .

This is the life! Here I sit in a cool jacuzzi, with a glass of champagne. Below me is the Mombasa harbour with a few dhows, sails slack in this still heat and the water looking incredibly blue. There are about ten of us lounging, joking, and toasting in this oversized jacuzzi ~ a wedding party. It seems the perfect activity in this beautiful and luxurious place. I pinch myself and take another sip.

The landscaping and swimming pool deserve special mention. Paths wander down through flowering rock gardens and lawns, creepers climb up walls and drape over balconies. The large contoured pool is glorious, with a swim-up bar, unheated jacuzzi and great views over the harbor. Next to the pool under a thatch roof is the sit-up Lido Bar with a selection of snacks and light dishes.

Other Facilities

Air conditioning, telephone connection to 24-hour switchboard, fax facility, fully serviced apartments, swimming pool with jacuzzi, nearby stores.

Bamburi Beach

This is the next beach up the coast. It is a busy strip full of large and small tourist hotels.

Whitesands

Sarova Hotels, P.O Box 30680, Nairobi
☎ *(2) 333233, FAX: (2) 229388*

Accommodating up to 700 people, this is the largest resort hotel on the Kenyan Coast. This low-rise complex is widely spread out on well-maintained and spacious grounds. There is a clean and exotic flavor to Whitesands—yards of cool white marble, rows of arches and a wonderful use of water. Public areas seem to float on aquatic gardens, bridges cross meandering swimming pools, and birds dip into lily ponds, shattering arabesque reflections.

There is an attractive wide beachfront with lawns and tall palms. Many of the rooms overlook the ocean and beach.

Whitesands gives the impression of being a well-maintained and efficient operation. There are many standard resort facilities and activities, as well as some more unusual offerings such as Swahili lessons and events like coconut tree climbing. There are three attractive swimming pools and a fun water slide. A separate entertainment pavilion doubles as a late night disco. Whitesands is a popular conference center.

The lounges and dining areas are in four separate open-sided pavilions with colorfully decorated pillars and ceilings. Although accommodation blocks separate them from the sea, the public rooms overlook aquatic gardens and are reached by stepping stones and bridges. The full-board meals are repetitious buffets—commingling smells and long lines. For a change of pace, there is a coffee bar, the pool grill, and an à la carte restaurant. The wonderful Tamarind Restaurant is only a short cab ride away.

Accommodations

The rooms have air conditioning, nice bathrooms, and private balconies. Many have lovely views and are only steps from the beach. Double beds, larger triple rooms, and suites can be requested. There are 70 executive rooms with color satellite TV. Set way back from the sea is a sumptuous VIP cottage. *Our Favorites*: # 1036 and 1037—quieter, ground floor, close to beach.

Other Offerings

Watersports, tennis courts, games room, fitness center, children's playground, business center with secretarial services.

Severin Sea Lodge

Severin Sea Lodge, Box 82169, Mombasa
☎ *(11) 48500*

This is one of the larger hotels on Bamburi beach. It has a rambling layout and some unique features such as a dhow restaurant moored on a little stream, and a conference center which resembles an Islamic mosque. There are two swimming pools and a high thatched rondavel bar which sports game trophies.

The rooms are in two or three story whitewashed bungalows with thatched roofs. The rooms are better than average—all with mini-bar, telephone, and air conditioning. The 90 new comfort rooms, each with one double and one single bed, have Lamu-style furniture and nice bathrooms with double sink and hairdryer. Most rooms are set back from the sea, but standard rooms 400 and 402, and comfort rooms 177 and 178 have good ocean views. There is a busy entertainment program from water polo to jazz bands.

Off Note

There is no beachfront at high tide.

Bamburi Beach Hotel

Bamburi Beach Hotel, Box 83966, Mombasa
☎ *(11) 485611*

This hotel has a small beachfront and is crowded with package tours. There are many sports activities and a night club.

Kenya Beach Hotel

Kenya Beach Hotel, Box 95748, Mombasa
☎ *(11) 485821*

This is a narrow garden complex of 100 rooms in two and three-story blocks. The beachfront is not very wide. The hotel is Swiss-run and clean. There is a large pool, an extensive cement terrace and open-air dining close to the beach.

Ocean View Beach Hotel

Ocean View Beach Hotel, Box 81127, Mombasa
☎ *(11) 485601*

Concrete and run-down. Sunbathers on plastic loungers crowd the constricted lawns facing the beach. There is a scuba diving center.

Neptune Beach Hotel

Neptune Beach Hotel, Box 83125, Mombasa
☎ *(11) 485701*

THE KENYAN COAST

This is a family hotel with 80 rooms. A pleasant entry leads to a long and narrow plot busy with shops, Disney ice cream bar, sun loungers, and colorful furniture. There is a thatched bar by a circular pool. Undistinguished rooms are set back from the beach.

Plaza Hotel
Plaza Hotel, Box 88299, Mombasa
☎ *(11) 485321*

A highrise on a thin plot. There are slow elevators and tired wall-to-wall carpeting. Pool.

Travellers Beach Hotel
Travellers Beach Hotel, Box 87649, Mombasa
☎ *(11) 485121*

This newer hotel is divided into two sections to skirt a private beachfront property. The hotel is long and narrow. There is a white and clean lobby with a high roof, stream, and swimming canal which connects with the pool. There are lines of shops, several restaurants, and many sports. Fully equipped rooms have a double and one single bed and a TV. There is a rather unreal shopping mall atmosphere about this hotel. It's a long way to the sand. There is a small, but fully equipped health club and squash court.

Shanzu Beach

After the long straight stretches of Nyali and Bamburi, there is a more intimate curve to Shanzu Beach. Even at low tide there is usually enough water for a swim here. There are major hotel properties on this beach.

Mombasa Serena Beach Hotel
Serena Lodges and Hotels, Box 48690, Nairobi
☎ *(2) 711077, FAX: (2) 718103*

Imaginative arabesque architecture makes the Serena Beach one of the most interesting hotels on the coast. The buildings are a delight of whitewash, arches, and grillwork. There are lush garden courts, and a spectacular arrangement of pools. Water is a major theme of this hotel. A free-form swimming pool sparkles in the sun, there is the sound of fountains, and cool garden pools compliment white marble and colorful flowers. Beyond, the sea laps the beautiful white sand of Shanzu Beach.

The reception area sets a striking mood for the hotel. The high white ceiling has contrasting mangrove beams, and there is an entire wall of elegantly carved and arched wall niches. Lamu-style furniture with bright cushions and hanging brass lanterns continue the Swahili motif.

Although the hotel has space for more than 300 guests, its spacious grounds and rambling low layout mean that you never get the feeling of being in a large busy hotel. The management limits the size of tour groups. All the public areas look over lawns and tall palm trees towards the sea.

Serena Beach Hotel has been accepted as one of the "Leading Hotels of the World." There is something extra special about the appearance of this hotel and the services it offers. The public rooms and dining areas are particularly lovely. A host of water sport activities are included in the tariff. Champagne is poured at breakfast, and afternoon tea served on the beach.

There are several restaurants. The elegant Fountain Restaurant has white arches, cool dripping fountains, and intricately carved Lamu furniture. The restaurant spills out on to a terrace overlooking the ocean. Right on the beach, is the less formal

Jahazi Grill which specializes in charcoal-grilled seafood and barbecues. Here you can eat with sand underfoot or climb to the open upper level which is built like a dhow with sails overhead. There is an air-conditioned piano bar with complimentary hot hors d'oeuvres at the cocktail hour.

The new pool at Serena Beach is lovely. Situated in the center of the hotel grounds, it is truly a focal point—eye-catching when you come out from reception. Free-form in shape, this tiled pool has cascades, and the water flows over the edges. There is also a wading pool and swim-up bar.

Safari Journal — Arrival

Through the whitewashed Arab archway, I can see brilliant bougainvillea and palm trees, graceful and tall next to a series of blue-green pools. Water cascades down from the lagoon-like swimming pool, and beyond that I can see the white foam of the waves breaking on the reef. I can't wait to explore!

Accommodations

Guest rooms and suites are in separate whitewashed buildings which are only two or three stories high. They are rather charming, with thatched roofs, carved balconies and various shaped arches. The rooms are located in the grounds on both sides of the main buildings.

The older section is closer to the sea and has smaller rooms. This section was designed to represent an old Swahili village. Some rooms are tucked behind others. The new section, although built further back from the sea, guarantees a glimpse of the water. These rooms are bigger with far superior bathrooms.

There are several suites and some family rooms. Two VIP suites are especially luxurious with private jacuzzis. There are both twin and double bedded rooms.

All of the 166 rooms are furnished in Lamu style, and although the decor is interesting, the old wing rooms are small and rather cramped. Swahili arches frame mirrors and windows. Each room has a balcony and en suite bathroom with tub. There is air conditioning, a minibar, hair dryer, and direct dial telephone. *Our Favorites*: #221 in New Wing—corner room with great sea view and sunning balcony. Front rooms in old section have good sea views (#116 and 121 sleep four).

Special Offerings

Swimming pool, watersports center (windsurfing, sailing and snorkeling free to hotel guests), scuba diving, deep sea fishing, dhow cruising by arrangement, four floodlit tennis courts, air-conditioned squash courts, minigolf, pool table, table tennis, conference room, hairdresser, free shuttle bus to Mombasa.

Off Notes

All standard bedrooms feel somewhat cramped, too small for the grand reputation of the hotel.

Hotel Intercontinental Mombasa

Hotel Intercontinental Mombasa, Box 83492, Mombasa
☎ *(11) 485811, FAX: (11) 485437*

This hotel is somewhat unique on the Kenyan coast. It is more formal and glamorous than the laid-back tropical hotels more commonly found on these beaches. The Intercontinental features wall-to-wall carpeting, elevators, and an indoor piano lounge. Men arrive in business suits—it is not a place to wander around with sandy feet.

It has been well decorated—tasteful and with an eye to quality. The lobby is impressive with its high, huge atrium, marble floors, and fountains. There are 192 rooms on four floors. The carpeted rooms are comfortable, and are equipped with every modern convenience: telephone, color TV, minibar, air conditioning. You are reminded that you are at the beach when you open the sliding glass doors onto your private balcony which is angled to give you a good view of the wonderful pool below and a glimpse of the sea.

The large pool has water flowing over the edges and a swim-up bar. It is set in lovely grounds filled with gardens and palm trees bordering the beach.

Accommodations

In addition to the standard rooms there are two presidential suites, one executive, and six junior suites. Best Sea Views: Standard rooms # 340–343, 312–315, 411, and 439.

Other Offerings

Many restaurants, conference facilities, banquet halls, a casino, and a sports center with health spa.

Oyster Bay Beach Hotel

Oyster Bay Beach Hotel, Box 10252, Bamburi, Mombasa
☎ *(11) 485531, FAX: (11) 485963*

Perched on a rocky cliff, this new hotel of 35 suites overlooks an attractive lagoon-shaped pool and the ocean beyond. The beach here is very small. An elaborate jetty for watersports is under construction.

The hotel's clean modern architecture is dazzling white next to dark rock, bougainvillea color, and blue-green sea. Curving balconies provide a large shaded terrace with a sea view for each suite. There is Lamu-style furniture, and sitting rooms have fans. Bedrooms have air conditioning and nice private bathrooms with bidet. Two bedrooms per suite are possible.

The dining room is on a terrace above the pool, a seafood grill is in the planning, and there is 24-hour room service. The pool is surrounded by rock gardens with a waterfall and swim-up bar. Resort activities are planned.

The African Safari Club

African Safari Club, Box 81443, Mombasa
☎ *(11) 485906/7/8, FAX: (11) 485909*

North of Mombasa there is a chain of very clean, very safe, high standard hotels owned and operated by this German travel company. In all the hotels, the public rooms tend to be spacious and dramatic. Accommodations are in simple and basic rooms, each with small bathroom including shower, toilet and basin. The hotels have an attractive choice of restaurants, shops and sports facilities, with some of these being shared by two or more hotels. Each has a swimming pool and some kind of beach access. They are fanatic about security and usually have larger-than-average well-fenced grounds. If you enjoy a real German atmosphere and cuisine, these hotels will please.

The hotels are Bahari Beach with sister hotels Silver Beach and Silver Star at English Point; Coral Beach, Palm Beach, Shanzu Beach, Paradise Beach, Malaika,

Dolphin, and Flamingo Beach at Shanzu; Club Sea Horse and the nearby Manarani at Kilifi Creek; and Watamu Beach.

In addition Mara Buffalo Camp in the Masai Mara and Masai Safari Lodge near Nairobi National Park are part of this chain.

Reservations can be made through one of their European offices or by contacting African Safari Club in Mombasa.

Kikambala Beach

Kikambala is a long straight beach, 28 kilometers north of Mombasa. We found no hotels on this beach which we would especially recommend.

Le Soleil Beach Club

Le Soleil, Box 84737, Mombasa
☎ *(1253) 2195, FAX: (1253) 2164*

This is a modern condominium-style complex which operates as an "all-inclusive" beach club. It is built on a narrow plot with most of the rooms set back quite a distance from the ocean. Le Soleil is a family resort with standard rooms, suites, and three bedroom villas. There are equipped kitchens for self-catering and a choice of restaurants. The large pool has a swim-up bar. The rooms were less spacious or well-furnished than expected. Included in the club membership price are water-sports, games, entertainment, meals and local drinks.

Club Sun and Sand

Mombasa Sun and Sand, Box 2, Kikambala
☎ *(125) 12621, FAX: (125) 12133*

This is a sprawling thatched resort with tall palms and lots of bougainvillea. It has become Kenya's largest all-inclusive club where food, local beverages, water sports, and games are included in the price. There is a choice of three specialty restaurants, a supervised mini-club for children and nightly entertainment. Deep sea fishing and motorized water sports are available at an extra charge.

The hotel caters to large package tours (queues for meals), has a conference center for 200, and offers many sports activities. There are two pools, one is seawater. Accommodations are in small cottages with thatched roofs and air conditioning. Some have nice sea views. The hotel looks tropical and exotic, but is rather run down.

Thousand Palms

Club Thousand Palms Ltd., Box 84 Kikamabala via Mombasa
☎ *(125) 32165, FAX: (125) 32161*

A very ordinary package-tour hotel. The public toilets were dirty when we visited.

Whispering Palms Hotel

Whispering Palms Hotel, Box 5, Kikambala
☎ *(125) 12004, Telex: 21018*

This hotel is rather a hodge-podge with heavy concrete structures as well as thatch. There are three small pools, peeling paint and pay-as-you-go sports. It caters to package tours and has a cut-rate atmosphere.

Mnarani Club

Mnarani Club, Box 1008, Kilifi
☎ *(125) 22320, FAX: (125) 22200*

Perched on cliffs and facing eastwards to the Kilifi creek and Indian Ocean, the Mnarani Club has a lovely position and is treated to a constant gentle ocean breeze. After a change in management the Club has been recently refurbished, and reopened its doors in December 1996.

THE KENYAN COAST

The authors have not visited this hotel since it reopened, but we have heard favorable reports and seen enticing photographs. Peter Brainch, who has taken over, is well respected in the travel business in Kenya and is dedicated to making Mnarani Club a very special place. The attractive brochure describes how the Club has been decorated in a brilliant array of coastal colors and exudes a relaxed and informal atmosphere. There is mention of quality touches: Egyptian Cotton sheets, mosquito nets specially treated against insects, and the use of matured timber in room decor.

One of the most stunning aspects of the hotel is the new 750 sq. meter freeform swimming pool. Your first view of the pool is as you enter the hotel and pass the members bar—through wide windows you see the pool with its disappearing horizon merging into the creek and the ocean beyond—a seemingly unbroken stretch of water continuing from the hotel to the horizon. Peter describes this as the "wow" view—everyone who sees it for the first time exclaims "Wow!"

A high dramatic thatch roof extends the full-length of the main building. Walls are brightly whitewashed and the hotel has been simply furnished with quality items and an eye-catching blue and yellow color-scheme. Star shaped lights hang from the thatch, hand-blown blue glass is used in the dining room, finials on the mosquito-nets are brightly painted—a nice attention to detail.

Focus is being placed on simple, high quality meals. Alasdair, the general manager, wants "none of the dreaded safari buffets." Instead there will be quasi a-la-carte menus with Mediterranean and Swahili flavors, home-made chutneys and Kilifi oysters. Breakfast and dinner are served in the main dining room which also has that wonderful view of pool and creek. A new seafood and pasta bar has been created at beach level.

Peter kept emphasizing the Mnarani goal to be "very simple" but "very good." He is also keen to create an atmosphere—something fun and "slightly wacky" to hark back to Mnarani's earliest days as a club focusing on watersports.

From the club, steps take you down the cliff to a small sandy cove below. There are thatched sun-shelters on the beach, a small shop and the jetty. Because you are inside a deep-water creek, and so close to the ocean, it is possible to indulge in all manner of water-related activities: sailing, windsurfing, water skiing, scuba diving, snorkeling and big game fishing. You can try your hand at sailing a traditional Arab "ngalawa," take PADI instruction, or go for a creek safari with a picnic and enjoy the many bird species who make Kilifi Creek their home.

There are a total of 84 guest rooms, and guests have three accommodation options. There are the ocean view Rooms which are in double storied thatched buildings; the ocean view Cottages which are bungalows and very close to the swimming pool; and the smaller creek cottages which are tucked further away and can offer a less expensive alternative for families whose children want their own room. Bedrooms are simple and bright with colorful furnishings and natural wood finishes.

All rooms have bath or shower, fans and/or air conditioning, safes, and direct dial telephones. There is a squash court and a TV/video room.

Mnarani is an informal member's club and offers special rates and services to members. Nonmember guests are welcome on a temporary membership basis.

Kilifi

Kilifi Creek is a major break in the coastline between Mombasa and Malindi. Before 1991 there was no bridge spanning this wide creek, and travelers crossed by car ferry. There are few hotels in Kilifi, but many interesting private homes. It is a popular sailing and boating center.

Baobab Lodge
Baobab Lodge, Box 40683, Nairobi
☎ *(2) 222229, FAX: (2) 332170*

This small and casual lodge is built on top of a rocky cliff overlooking the ocean at Kilifi. Rondavels are scattered around a nicely shaded property. There are 26 attractively decorated rooms with Masai murals on the walls and spacious verandas. Most rooms do not offer sea views.

There is a lovely pool with a swim-up bar and views over the ocean, but there is not much of a beach. Steps down through the rocks and past baobab trees lead to a small cove with more coral than sand underfoot. The lodge offers diving, and owns a glass-bottom boat. You can walk to the reef at low tide. There is a relaxed and low-key atmosphere—a dart board hanging on a tree, private shady places to lie and read, and a cool, open-sided dining area under high thatch.

Kilifi Bay Resort Hotel & Village
DEINSA S.A., Box 3092, CH 6901 Lugano
FAX: [41] (91) 228490
or
Box 156, Kilifi
☎ *(125) 2511, FAX: (125) 2225*

This Italian hotel can accommodate 85 and is typically booked in Europe. Designed and decorated with flair, it feels spacious and exotic. There are high thatched roofs, large open air verandas, carved Lamu-style furniture, and lush and colorful tropical vegetation. Public buildings are set well back from the beach and look over the pool and past palm trees to the ocean beyond. Accommodations are in three-roomed bungalows, some close to the beach. Stone steps lead down to a long beach with a thatched shelter for shade. Invigorating music was being played for scuba diving lesson in the pool.

Takaungu House

Bush Homes of East Africa Ltd., Box 56923, Nairobi
☎ *(2) 571647, FAX: (2) 571665*

On a private curve of beach, far from the hotels of Mombasa and Malindi, is Takaungu House. Located south of Kilifi, the house is named after the neighboring small village of Takaungu—supposedly the oldest slave port in Kenya.

Phil and Charlotte Mason are your hosts. Guests stay in a very old slave trader's house with thick whitewashed walls, giant roof beams, and shutters on the windows. It is close to the ocean. The Masons themselves stay nearby on the property in a newly constructed Arab-style house.

Takaungu House is special because of the wonderful setting, the atmosphere of tranquillity and timelessness, and the delightful hosts. The small bay is edged with dark rocks and has golden sand seldom marred by human footprints. The big old baobab trees and the hoary stone ruins bear silent witness to history, Africa, and inspired imaginings. The house was recorded on a map drawn on the HMS *Stork* as he passed in 1844.

We ate a delicious home-cooked lunch in the cool of the old house. A horse peered through the door, blocking the bright light which shimmered in from the heat and ocean outside. He reluctantly obeyed Charlotte's entreaty not to enter. You can ride horses when you stay with the Masons. You can also use their boats. Phil operates a boat yard, and you may choose to join him sailing on their yacht, scuba diving, or perhaps explore the nearby creek in their dingy—have a barbecue on the beach of an island. There are three guest bedrooms, each with functional bathrooms. The house is comfortable and lived-in—lots of books, slip-covered couches. There is a very small swimming pool. The Masons can arrange to pick you up from the air-port—Mombasa, or Malindi. The tariff includes all food and activities except deep sea fishing. They close for May.

African Rainbow Sea Safaris

Box 25, Kilifi
☎ *(125) 22478, FAX: (125) 22478*

THE KENYAN COAST

Mirella Ricciardi, the accomplished photographer and author, has opened her Kilifi home to paying guests. From October to March Mirella will host guests herself and can arrange for alternate hosting at other times of the year. Mirella is a strong minded woman with a penchant for ambiance, lively conversations and good cuisine.

There are actually two houses, perched high on the banks of the Kilifi Creek. Steps lead down to a small private sandy beach, and massive baobab trees add a timeless feel. Between the two houses Mirella can host up to 10 people.

The newer house has an impressive high-thatched roof with a large opening through which bougainvillea spills. Below is a wide veranda. There are no windows—just big arched openings and metal grillwork. There is an artist's touch everywhere—carvings on wooden pole supports, relief designs in the plaster work. This house has two bedrooms downstairs and a sleeping loft up a ladder. The other house is an older coastal home with a spacious living/dining room with lovely views of trees and water. There are two en suite bedrooms and a Mediterranean style pergola overlooking the water.

There is a swimming pool and guests can take to the creek in rubber dinghies. From this base, guests can also arrange to take a sailing and goggling safari in a 50 ft catamaran.

Kildini

Kesana, Box 39672, Nairobi
☎ *(2) 749062, FAX: (2) 741636*

This spacious and airy Arab-style house belongs to Michael and Jean Skinner (who own Juani Farm in Molo). Kildini has three double bedrooms and can cater for up to six people. The house is surrounded by delightful gardens, and there is a swimming pool. Steps lead to a private beach on Kilifi creek.

The Skinners can host your stay and show you neighboring points of interest. The house can also be rented with house staff on a "self-service" basis. We did not visit Kildini, but did see photographs of this very attractive and exotic-looking house. Apparently it is right on the creek, not far from the new bridge.

Watamu

Watamu, south of Malindi is best known for the Watamu Marine National Park—a spectacular coral reef alive with tropical fish and only a short boat ride, or energetic swim at low tide. The beach is really a series of wide sand bays separated by rocky outcrops. The area is distinctive with its craggy rock islands dotting the bays. Dark and jagged with narrow necks, they invite exploration. At low tide it is possible to walk out to many of these strange isolated formations. Crabs skitter out of sight, and impossible shapes have been culptured by the sea. Rock pools ring the islands revealing their treasures of hells, seaweed and bright fish each day when the tide is out.

The coastline is more interesting than some of the popular long sandy tretches such as Diani Beach south of Mombasa. Watamu has only a handful of hotels, but there are many private beachfront homes. At certain times of year, (especially May until the end of September) a great deal of seaweed is washed on to the Watamu Beaches.

There is much to see and do in the Watamu area:

Watamu Marine National Park
This is one of the better places on the Kenyan coast for snorkeling.

Big Game Fishing
Many people come to Watamu for the big game fishing.

Mida Creek
Peaceful daily dhow trips are offered on Mida Creek. This broad stretch of water lined by tidal mud flats and mangroves is home to a multitude of birds and is a noted migratory stop. These dhow trips are operated through Ocean Sports, but any Watamu hotel can book them for you.

Gede Ruins
This Swahili city was mysteriously abandoned in the 14th century. Today you can wander through the 18 hectares of these interesting and thought-provoking ruins. Sightseers can also visit the Giriama Village nearby to see drumming and dancing.

Arabuko-Sokoke Forest
This is the largest remaining stretch of lowland coastal forest in East Africa. It shelters rare trees and animals and is of particular interest to birdwatchers.

Watamu Village
Explore this fishing community—many souvenir sellers.

Hemingway's
Hemingway's, Box 267, Watamu
☎ *(122) 32624, FAX: (122) 32256*

Hemingway's is an intimate, privately owned hotel built right at the edge of the beach—the ocean can be seen from most rooms. The impression is one of pristine whitewash and spacious stone terraces. There are two sparkling blue swimming pools, and a multitude of very tall coconut palms continually wave in the breeze. The hotel exudes a casual "upmarket" elegance. It is known for deep-sea fishing and is also a romantic and relaxing getaway, popular with honeymooners. What makes Hemingway's special is its attention to detail, service and pampering touches. You

will be delighted by the vases of roses everywhere, the welcome basket of strawberrie
in your room and the interesting menus.

A newcomer to Watamu, Hemingway's was built in 1988 on the site of the ol
"Seafarers" Hotel. The hotel was raised nine feet so that it would look down on th
sea. From the beach there is a fortresslike wall giving a rather forbidding aspect to th
hotel, but when you are above, on the terrace or sitting in the dining room, you hav
lovely views down over the ocean and across the bay with its intriguing rock forma
tions.

The bar, dining room, and reception area are in huge white rondavels with dra
matic soaring thatched roofs, so distinctive of the area. The main dining room has
sunken central area for buffet, band and dance floor. Tables are arrayed around th
raised circumference as well as in a "minstrel's gallery" on a higher level. Tables nea
windows have lovely views. Candlelight dining is outside on the terrace during th
gentle *Kaskazi* (seasonal northeast wind) from late November to Easter. During th
rest of the year, when the stronger *Kusi* blows, all meals are served in the main res
taurant.

Hemingway's places an emphasis on dining. There is elegance in the starche
tablecloths, fresh flowers at each table, and candlelit dinners. As well as a set menu
there are à la carte choices. You can also be served unusual and tasty snacks at pool
side. We had breakfast crepes smothered with strawberries and yogurt—a real trea
Afternoon teas are included in the tariff.

The bar is a large and pleasant room with big doors opening out to the ocean terrace. It sports impressive fishing trophies such as a 750 lb. blue marlin. There is a friendly sit-up central bar and comfortable rush chairs around tables. The feeling is airy, natural, and uncluttered. The hotel's intimate nature combined with its popularity among British Kenyans and fishermen means that the bar is a place where new friends are made and fishing tales are swapped over many a drink. We were reminded by the manager that the name Hemingway's conjures not only images of Africa and fishing, but of drinking as well.

Many clients come to Hemingway's for the deep-sea fishing. The hotel owns several twin-engine boats and charters others. Full-day and half-day fishing trips are offered for both novice and skilled fishermen from August to May. The main billfish are sailfish and marlin.

Quotes:

"The original dream for Hemingway's was freezing cold drinks, really good food and sport." Garry Cullen, managing director.

"It's a class act all the way" A happy American fisherman returning from a deep sea fishing trip with his family. His young son was handed a framed polaroid photograph of the family with the fish they'd caught. Staff were asking which fish they would like prepared for their dinner.

Accommodations

The hotel has a capacity for 175 guests. There are two wings: an older sea-view wing which has double rooms, and a brand new "superior" wing which includes triples and suites. The bedrooms of the older wing are disappointingly small for a hotel of this caliber. They are, however, close to the ocean, and afford the best sea views. The new wing is two and three-stories high and angles back from the beach. You can see to the ocean beyond the gardens and swimming pools.

Safari Journal — Friday

We sit in comfort on the stone patio in front of the bar.
Below, the big blue Hemingway's sign hangs above
the fish weighing area. The tension mounts; the crowd
is full of camaraderie as many binoculars focus on the sea.
The deep sea fishing boats rock over the waves
flying catch flags. Six white flags... six fish over 30 lbs,
one black flag ... one Kingfish. The bar will be lively tonight!
Yesterday, honeymooners from London caught
a big sailfish ~ the sail an incredible, deep iridescent blue,
the novice fisherman all smiles

I can't wait ~ my husband and eleven year old son
have been out since 6:00 a.m. Their first fishing trip ever.
Did the seasick pill work? Hope my son caught something.

All rooms have air conditioning, mosquito-nets, fans and a safe for valuables. All of
the rooms except the suites have a balcony and a shower. The suites have bathtubs
in addition to showers and a large sitting area instead of a balcony. Sliding glass
doors open the rooms to light and air and distant sea views. Superior rooms have
bar fridges. *Our Favorites* for being closest to the sea—old wing #103–109 (ground
floor) and new wing #145 (ground floor), #373 (top floor). Even in the bedrooms
at Hemingway's you are treated to many thoughtful extras—there is a poem and
rosebud on your pillow at night and a bottle of Hemingway's mineral water next to
your bed.

Special Options

Fishing (deep sea and inshore), snorkeling trips in a glass-bottom boat, windsurfing,
diving, dhow trips on Mida Creek, free trips to Malindi for shopping and to the
nearby Gede ruins, free transfer to and from Malindi Airport, day-room facilities

with shower (extra charge), video room, conference center, small boutique and sundry shop.

f Notes

Limited shade, terraces get hot... Old wing bedrooms are small... Small, barred windows and fussy curtains tend to hide the wonderful views from the old-wing bedrooms... Remember that during the off-season the beaches can be full of unsightly seaweed. Rough seas will mean that deep-sea fishing is suspended.

Turtle Bay Beach Club

Turtle Bay Beach Club, Box 457, Malindi
☎ *(122) 32080, FAX: (122) 32268*

Turtle Bay is a larger family-style hotel which operates on an all-inclusive resort stem similar to a Club Med. Included are meals, snacks, most drinks and a range of orting activities (watersports as well as tennis, mini golf , etc.) This hotel is appealg for its relaxed ambiance, its range of activities for families, and the pleasantly aded area overlooking the beach and ocean.

The focal point of the hotel is the pool area. The large rectangular pool has a divg board. To the side, and sheltered by makuti thatch, are table-tennis, darts and ooker. There is also a giant chess set with wooden African playing pieces. A atched bar and restaurant at poolside serves a snack and à la carte menu. It is opended and has views of the ocean through a stand of palm trees. Stretching from the ool to the beach is an area well-shaded by mature palms and other indigenous trees here guests can lie on padded lounge chairs placed on the sand. There are pleasant a breezes, lovely views of the beach and ocean and shelter from the hot sun.

The hotel is built on a slope—there are winding paths and series of wide cement eps. Low-rise accommodation blocks are reached through tropical gardens vivid ith bougainvillea. Some rooms have good ocean views, but most are set further ack, only glimpsing the sea through palm trees. The main dining area is open to rdens and fishponds—but has no sea-view or sea breezes. The food tends to be

rather unremarkable—generous safari buffets predominate. There is evening ente
tainment ranging from bingo nights in the large and rather functional lobby loung
to acrobatic performances around the pool with the night sky and waving palms f
an added touch of the exotic.

Children (ages 4–12 years) can join the Children's Mini Club with various acti
ties and programs (videos, swimming, painting etc.) under supervision.

Water activities at Turtle Bay include windsurfing and scuba diving. Glass-botto
boats make the short trip out to the marine park for snorkeling. We hear that the
is now an expert who will accompany you on your snorkeling trips, pointing out a
explaining items of interest as you swim along.

This hotel is popular with families and is also booked by European tour groups
predominantly German.

Accommodations

There are 154 rooms, all with private balconies, ceiling fans and en suite bathroom
Most rooms are in fairly large low-rise white structures. There are also deluxe roor
which are somewhat larger and newer. These rooms are in smaller thatched thre
story units. *Best Sea Views*: Deluxe Rooms #43, 44 and 45. Beach Block #1–5.

Ocean Sports

Ocean Sports Ltd., Box 100 Watamu
☎ *(122) 32288, FAX: (122) 32266*

Ocean Sports opened in 1957 and was the first hotel at Watamu. This small fa
ily-run hotel is popular with British Kenyans. The hotel is ultracasual and relaxed
bare feet and first names. It appeals to families and does a lot of repeat business.

As its name suggests, there is an emphasis on ocean sports. There is a diving scho
and opportunities for deep-sea fishing. The bar is alive with fishing tales and hea
with fishing trophies. (It boasts more impressive catches than its upmarket neighbo
Hemingway's, but has been at it a lot longer.)

The bar and dining rooms have good views over the ocean, and there is a lar
outdoor terrace just steps off the beach. A good basic seafood menu is offered. The
is a smallish pool and many paths winding among colorful bougainvillea. Oce
Sports offers dhow trips on Mida Creek. Tennis and squash are also available on t
premises.

Ocean Sports has character. It is low-key and has an established air—quite a co
trast to some of the glitzier, more uniform large hotels which cater primarily to pac
age tours from Europe.

Accommodations

A series of cottages are built along a small hill behind the main hotel. There are 2
standard rooms and four air-conditioned rooms. The rooms are basic and quite sp
cious, each with a private bathroom. There is a charming lack of uniformity. On

cottage is a quaint little double story "house," another has four double rooms and a large shared veranda. Afternoon tea is served on your private veranda. Some cottages glimpse the sea through vegetation.

ff Note

Rooms are quite far from the sea and across the parking area.

Blue Bay Village

Blue Bay Village, Box 162, Watamu
☎ *(122) 32626, FAX: (122) 32422*

This is another Italian hotel with architectural and decorative flair. It has wonder-l soaring thatch, fresh whitewash, and opulent use of Lamu furniture and rich fab-cs. This hotel has an unusual central "courtyard" which is spacious and open to the y. It is dominated by a pool and surrounded by boutiques, a restaurant, lounge eas and a simply beautiful high-roofed lobby. The restaurant serves Italian cuisine d has a window wall overlooking the ocean.

You walk on to the beach through a large carved door. Built at the edge of a bay, ue Bay Village uses two beaches. If one is marred by seaweed, the other is usually ean white coral sand. Beach loungers are arranged on the sand and a volleyball net vites some exercise.

Accommodations are separate thatched cottages in verdant gardens. Most do not ve ocean views. Although the clientele is almost exclusively Italian, this hotel can e booked in Kenya.

Barracuda Inn

Barracuda Inn, Box 59, Watamu
☎ *(122) 32061 Telex: 21347 BARCDA KE*

The Barracuda Inn is an Italian managed "village" resort with 64 rooms. There are high thatched roofs and whitewashed walls. Guests stay in cottages which are built in rows running back from the beach. Barracuda Inn is on Blue Bay Lagoon (around the corner from Blue Bay Village). Guests tend to congregate around the large swimming pool. Sports offerings include tennis, squash, gymnastics and ping-pong.

Temple Point Village

I Viaggi Del Ventaglio,
Via de Amicis 43, 20123, Milano, Italy
☎ *5818644 (Milano)*
or Box 296, Watamu
☎ *(122) 32057, FAX: (122) 32289*

This is a stylish thatched village with two swimming pools and accommodations for 180. You must either book through Italy or take your chances as a walk-in guest. The two-story cottages have ceiling fans, mosquito nets, Lamu furniture, and are attractively decorated in the Swahili-style. There is a dramatic view of the Indian Ocean from the bar and restaurant. Unfortunately, rough coral rock prevents guests from ocean swimming in front of Temple Point, but hotel boats will take you to a private sandy beach nearby. There are tennis courts and watersports, a dhow and a bathing beach on Mida Creek.

Mrs. Simpson's

Mrs. Simpson's, Box 33, Watamu
☎ *(122) 32023*

Mrs. Simpson has been hosting guests at her rambling and informal beach home for nearly 20 years. She has lived in Kenya since 1923, and at her advanced age is still active in marine conservation.

There is room for seven people on a full-board basis, but Mrs. Simpson often takes more, and somehow finds everyone a bed, mosquito net, lamp and sheets. In her words, she "runs the house as a party." The guests are a mixed group of families, researchers and young world travelers who are happy with basic but friendly accommodations. They all eat together with Mrs. Simpson, and afternoon tea is a communal affair. As Mrs. Simpson says, her house "is not a smooth place"—showers are cold, some share bathrooms, and some guests even sleep on the roof.

Her trained staff can take people goggling or birding in the Arabuko-Sokoke Forest, and guests can rent the house sailboat. The house is very informal and full of old worn furniture and books. Guests were complimentary about the meals and especially enjoy the company of Mrs. Simpson, who is a keen naturalist.

Malindi and Vicinity

Malindi city codes ☎ *123, FAX: 123*

Malindi is the second largest city on the Kenyan coast. There are trendy outiques and shops, many restaurants, and a colorful outdoor market. It is mous for the Malindi Marine National Park and deep sea fishing. Many of he beach resorts have a significant Italian influence.

Most of the hotels are strung out along the beachfront to the south of Ma-ndi's town center. Those closest to town resemble city hotels. There are lso many hotels which are further inland and have no beach access. We did ot visit all of these hotels.

Indian Ocean Lodge

Savannah Camps and Lodges, Box 48019, Nairobi
☎ *(2) 331191, FAX: (2) 330698*

This prestigious lodge in Malindi accommodates guests in sumptuous Arab-style ouses. The lodge has four acres of private property and is built on a promontory verlooking the ocean. There is great beauty and a sense of the exotic about this nusual and exclusive lodge. Your first impression is of wonderful color contrasts— rilliant white arches against a vivid profusion of bougainvillea and the deep blueness f the Indian Ocean gleaming beyond. Timeless baobabs twist with ponderous race.

Indian Ocean Lodge offers something similar to a private homestay since your osts, Peter and Joanna Nicholas, live here and are familiar with the surrounding area d its history. The difference is that the lodge looks more like a perfectly arranged useum than a "worn at the corners" family home. You want to stop and admire the vely Swahili furniture, the carpets, the wall decorations.

The lodge guarantees exclusivity. A maximum of only eight guests are accommo dated at a time. The guests stay in spacious quarters with four-poster beds, sittin areas, and private patios or balconies. All has been tastefully decorated in keepin with the Arab style of the buildings. There is an indoor-outdoor feel about th lodge—open arches, outdoor stairways, breezes blowing and bright clear ligh streaming into rooms. The whitewash dazzles the eyes.

There is a swimming pool within the walled property, and you must climb dow many steps to the sea. A boat belonging to the lodge can be used for fishing or snor keling. The rates include your hosts collecting you from the airport and driving yo within a 40 kilometers radius for shopping or sightseeing. They will also accompan guests to tennis, golf, squash, windsurfing, or scuba diving. Deep-sea fishing can b arranged at an extra charge. Full board rates include alcohol, soft drinks and dail laundry.

The atmosphere and ambiance of a privately hosted stay depend to a large exter on the hosts. Unfortunately, since we could not arrange to spend the night or sampl the food at the Indian Ocean Lodge, we can comment only on the physical nature c the lodge—which is truly outstanding.

Malindi Beach Club

Malindi Beach Club, P.O. Box 868, Malindi
☎ *(123) 20928, FAX: (123) 30103*

The Malindi Beach Club stresses privacy and a Swahili atmosphere in its 24 new renovated rooms. With its private beach fronting Malindi's marine park, you ca sample all marine sports, take advantage of nearby disco and casino, play golf or ten nis, go for morning horse rides along the beach, or just enjoy palm-shaded court yards and terraces, some with a sea view.

The peaceful harmony of an Arabian village is suggested by an irregular groupin of white two-story structures, accented by arches, black grillwork, and balconies. Til pathways meander through shaded gardens and into courtyards. There are two salt water swimming pools, a club house, bar, piano and barbecue. The restaurant men features fresh seafood and Italian cuisine. The Swahili theme is accented inside wit fine antique pieces of brass, chests and oriental carpets. All is well coordinated ar tastefully done.

The rooms have Swahili decor with tile or wood floors, air conditioning, mosquit net, refrigerator-bar, telephone, and private bathroom.

Kilili Baharini

Francorosso International Spa, Via Veneto, Rome, Italy
☎ *(06) 4457055*

The unique layout of the Kilili Baharini gives it an intimate and personal atmo-
here. The spacious thatched villas are arranged in groups of three or four around a
nall swimming pool. There are a total of three such groupings, each with its own
orivate" pool. Nearer the ocean is a larger communal pool and a dining and bar
ea.

The landscaping is exotic with many trees and flowering shrubs. The villas are
versized, with loads of veranda space and Lamu furniture colorful with kanga cush-
ns. A high platform above the veranda is reached by ladder and is yet another pri-
te space to relax. The place has flair and offers an exotic and unique concept. Most
ents are Italian.

Kingfisher Lodge

Kingfisher Group, Box 29, Malindi
☎ *(123) 21168*

Kingfisher Lodge is the Malindi home base for the exclusive family-run business
hich also includes luxury tented safaris and big game fishing. The extended Paul
mily (British Kenyan) are experienced hosts, guides and fishermen.

The lodge is 3 kilometers from Malindi harbor and beach. It is in a peaceful spot
d can accommodate 14 people in 7 doubles. The original four deluxe cottages are
t in beautifully maintained gardens around a sparkling swimming pool. These
atched cottages have spacious bedrooms with air conditioning and ceiling fans.
he additional three doubles are in the form of a private villa which has its own gar-
n and a large veranda. There is a sitting room and the bedrooms each have an
suite bathroom.

Delicious home-cooked meals are served in the open-air dining rondavel next to
e pool. Many optional excursions are available from the lodge: bird watching,
mel and horse riding, snorkeling and diving, golf, tennis etc.

Kingfisher also operate five fully-equipped crewed charter boats for deep-sea fish-
g. Sailfish, marlin, swordfish and tuna are found off Malindi. Kingfisher Safaris
erate their own exclusive tented camp in Tsavo East on the Galana River—a two
d a half hour drive from Malindi.

White Elephant Sea Lodge
Turisanda: International Tour Operator,
Via Poerio 2/A 20129 Milano

Classy and elegant, this smaller lodge caters almost exclusively to Italians. It ca
not be booked within Kenya, but if there is space, they will accept walk-ins. Beautif
furniture and unusual artwork distinguish the White Elephant. There are huntir
trophies on the walls, elephant hide covers the reception desk, and beautiful views (
flowers and water are framed by carved doors and windows. An aura of nostalgia ar
refined taste pervades. You may wish you spoke Italian.

There are 40 spacious rooms with Lamu furniture and air conditioning. Rooms (
not have sea views.

The Driftwood Beachclub
The Bunson Group, Box 45456, Nairobi
☎ *(2) 337604, FAX: (2) 723599*

Like its name, the Driftwood has been around for a long time, gaining charact
and some forgivable grunge. It has recently been refurbished and three adjoinir
cottages with a private pool added. This low-key and personal family-style hotel is

ng-time favorite of British Kenyans. It is known for its relaxed and friendly atmo-
here, popular bar and good food. The attractive dining room and bar are open to
eezes and sea views, and the beach is only steps away.

Accommodations are in individual bandas. The rooms are rudimentary. Some
ave sea views and air conditioning. Rooms closest to the ocean are #21, 22 and 25.
here are two luxury family villas, a pleasant pool and a diving center.

Appreciate the Driftwood for its character.

Silversands Villas

Silversand Beach Cottages Ltd. Box 91, Malindi
☎ *(123) 20407*

This is a small, Italian run hotel on a long, narrow plot. The hotel can accommo-
ate 62 guests in a series of cottages and larger family villas. Although most of these
e some distance from the beach and breezes, they are surrounded by gardens.

The rooms have parquet floors and Lamu style furniture and each has a private
atio. There are ceiling fans and air conditioning, and there are bidets in the bath-
oms. Reserve the "Malindi" villa if you want to be closest to the beach.

Two swimming pools are in the central garden area along with a large makuti-
oofed restaurant with adjoining bar. Especially appealing is the natural thatched bar
d restaurant built right on the beach—checked cloths on the tables and sand
nderfoot.

Kivulini Beach Hotel

Kivulini Beach Hotel, Box 142, Malindi
☎ *(123) 20898 Telex: 21335*

This hotel is built on the edge of a rocky cove with an attractive walkway by the
a. The clientele is predominantly Italian. Accommodations are 36 thatched ron-
avel cottages with private verandas. Kivulini Beach hotel has eye-catching wooden
rniture, a free-form swimming pool and a well-stocked gift shop. The hotel is
out five kilometers from town and reached by a sandy road through natural bush.

Coconut Village

Coconut Village, Box 868, Malindi
☎ *(123) 20938, Telex: 21459*

Coconut Village is an Italian resort with flair. There are two-story thatched beach
llas with Arab style furniture. Some rooms have sea views. The pool and restaurant
e set back from the beach. There is a casual atmosphere and nightly entertainment.

Eden Roc Hotel
Tropicana Hotels Ltd. P.O. Box 350 Malindi
☎ *(123) 20480*

This large city-style hotel in Malindi town has been recently renovated and loo
fresh and clean. It caters primarily to inexpensive German package tours. There a
sea views from the lobby and some rooms. It is a long walk through gardens, dow
terraces and past two swimming pools to the beach.

African Dream Village
African Dream Village, Box 939, Malindi
☎ *(123) 20442, FAX: (123) 20119*
or Pan Travel Viaggi Turistici, SA 6900, Lugano, Switzerland
☎ *(091) 232043, FAX: (091) 226286*

Set in natural tropical gardens, the large African Dream Village can accommodate approximately 120 guests in a high-thatch complex on the beach near Casua-
rina Point and the Malindi Marine Park. Public rooms and restaurants are airy, a
semi-circular swimming pool curls around a swim-up bar. Rooms are air-conditioned with private bathrooms. There are many sports activities, a disco, and a conference center. This hotel caters primarily to tour groups from Europe.

Blue Marlin
Blue Marlin, Box 54, Malindi
☎ *(123) 20440 Telex: 0987/21410*

This city hotel on the Malindi beach front has 145 basic rooms with air conditioning. There are sports facilities and two pools. It is a long walk through the
grounds to the beach.

Bougan Village
Bougan Village, Box 721, Malindi
☎ *(123) 21205, FAX: 5242139 (Italy)*

This large Malindi resort on 16 acres is quite a distance from the beach. For
guests who want the beach experience, there is continuous bus service as well as a

beach snack bar. Rooms and bungalows are located in gardens and have en suite bathrooms and Lamu-style furnishings. The thatched club has a restaurant, two bars and a swimming pool. There are two tennis courts in the park. The influence here is Italian, with disco dancing at night.

Dorado Cottages

Hotel Bldgs. Ltd., Box 868, Malindi
☎ *(123) 20252*

Pretty thatched whitewash cottages are closely spaced in bougainvillea gardens around two pools. There are currently 22 cottages and more are planned. Each cottage has a living room, bedroom and kitchen with refrigerator but no stove. Two extra beds can be added. There are fans. Full-service dining is in an older house overlooking the beach. The beach access is down a hill from the site. The cottages do not see the ocean. It is under Italian management and caters to tour groups.

Lawfords Hotel

Lawfords Hotel, Box 54, Malindi
☎ *(123) 20440*

See "Blue Marlin." This is next door, run by the same company and even more down-market.

Palm Tree Club

Palm Tree Club, Box 180, Malindi
☎ *(123) 20397 Telex: OVERTURCO 21214*

This large Italian resort is right next to the Malindi golf course about 600 meters from the ocean. There is a shuttle for continuous transportation to and from the beach.

The circular construction of the main building surrounds a large swimming pool. Double rooms overlook the pool or are located in separate cottages on the extensive grounds. Tall thatched roofs ensure coolness, and there is an interesting combination of Lamu-style furniture, zebra-skin rugs, African wood carvings of tribal fetish statues and bouquets of tropical flowers. Each room has a full bathroom.

In addition to a restaurant with à la carte menu, there are sports facilities for tennis, golf, and bowling. Riding stables on the grounds provide horses for the resort riding school or for free riding in the forests or on the beaches. Italian films are shown regularly.

Scorpio Villas

Scorpio Enterprises Ltd., Box 368, Malindi
☎ *(123) 20194, FAX: (123) 21250*

This is a maze of large cottages set close together. The ocean is nowhere in sight but can be reached by hiking along a small footpath. The cottages are furnished in Lamu style and have equipped kitchens with fridges. There is a restaurant and three swimming pools.

Stephanie Sea House

Stephanie Sea House, Box 583, Malindi
☎ *(123) 20720*

A primarily Italian resort, Stephanie Sea House has 80 beds. A pool and raised restaurant overlook the beach and ocean. Cottage rooms are set far from the sea and close together. There is high thatch and Lamu-style furniture.

The Tropical Village

The Tropical Village, Box 68, Malindi
☎ *(123) 20256, FAX: (123) 20788*
or Pan Travel Viaggi Turistici, SA 6900, Lugano, Switzerland
☎ *(091) 232043, FAX: (091) 226286*

The Tropical Village is another Swahili-style hotel on the beach which caters to European tour groups. There are tropical gardens, whitewash and thatch, Lamu furniture and a free-form swimming pool. The "village" accommodates approximately 60 in several double story buildings.

A focal point is the large open-sided restaurant serving seafood and Italian specialties. There are many sporting activities and nightly entertainment.

Malindi to Tana River

Up the coast from Malindi (and south of Lamu) are two unusual and more remote places to stay. One is a tented camp sheltered by dunes, and the other offers grass shack beach accommodation. There is also a large Italian resort complex under construction—Angel Bay.

Che-Shale

Che-Shale, Box 857, Malindi
☎ *(123) 20676*

At Che-Shale, the accommodations are a step above camping, the food is superb, and the location a remote and sandy beach. It is romantic and rustic. Built on a deserted beach, 20 kilometers north of Malindi, Che-Shale is reached by 4-wheel drive or you can ride there from the Kibokoni Riding Center.

Accommodations in ten small *makuti*-mat shacks are spread among the sand dunes. The location is bright and hot with little natural shade or ground cover. The sand underfoot can burn, and eyes crinkle in the glare.

The cool makuti restaurant serves world-class seafood with a gourmet Italian taste. We enjoyed deep-fried seaweed, fresh cracked mangrove crab, and char-grilled sea fish. The bar is interesting and comfortable with Lamu beds, brass accents, and huge floor cushions covered in kanga cloth.

It is pleasant to swim in front of Che Shale—the beach is sandy and deserted, and at certain tides sandbars stretch out into the ocean. There are plenty of opportunities for long walks and bird-watching, and fishing and sailing can be arranged. The wide beach curves to a rocky point where you can snorkel. At low tide it is possible to take a 4-wheel drive vehicle along the sand to discover and explore even more remote bays.

Accommodations

Each makuti shack has a double bed and basic bathroom with chemical toilets and safari pull shower. There is an electrical generator which provides light for the tents until midnight. A shaded veranda in front of each shack has a daybed—private and peaceful. *Shack Choices*: # 9 & 10 for sea views, # 5 for bird-watching, # 1 for honeymooners, and #3,5,9 for triple occupancy.

Off Notes

Hard to book through local Italian owners in Malindi... Tour group day-trippers can come for lunch at a separate restaurant... Angel Bay Resort, a large Italian complex with shops and condominiums, is being constructed nearby.

Che-Shale closes from the end of April to the middle of July.

Tana Delta Camp

Bush Homes of East Africa, Box 56923, Nairobi
☎ *(2) 571647, FAX: (2) 571665*

Tana Delta Camp is a unique and unusual experience. It takes time and resolve of purpose to get there. When you finally arrive, you feel privileged to be in such an isolated and unspoiled place—a mixture of beach and creek, sandy beaches and mangrove-lined waterways and only a handful of other guests.

Tana River Delta is a small, tented camp where a branch of the Tana River meets the sea. The camp, sheltered behind high sand dunes, looks out over a broad stretch of river. Climb over the dunes, and on the other side, surf pounds onto miles of deserted sandy beach.

It is not simple to get to Tana River Delta. Most guests are met in Malindi by the camp vehicle and drive north for over three and a half hours through thick thorn scrub and doum palms. You might see topi, buffalo, waterbuck. When you reach a tributary of the Tana River you transfer to the "Tana Queen" and putter down the river for another half-hour in this converted dhow. The terrain changes from savannah to mangroves and salt bush. You pass hippos and crocodiles, and there are masses of birds. It is very hot.

You round a corner into a broad stretch of the delta and head for the camp, well camouflaged under thatch on a bushy sand bank. There are only seven permanent tents. The heart of the camp is an open-sided rondavel which includes lounge, dining area and bar. The tents are quite close together, but natural bush has been left between them for privacy. Each tent has its own veranda, some have a glimpse of the water, and those set further back are hotter and have bush views.

A new mess with panoramic views over the ocean and the delta has been built. Meals are served here. There is an emphasis on seafood—crab and swahilifish in coconut milk.

There is lots to do at Tana Delta Camp. You can explore the waterways in motorized fiberglass canoes—fish, marvel at all those birds, or even go to the main mouth of the river where there are fishing villages. You can visit the raintree forest on the Tana which was a location for Lucas Film's *Young Indiana Jones Chronicles*. You are guaranteed to see hippos in the river, and this area is a favorite nesting site for crocodile.

This is an ideal place for walking. You can walk for miles along deserted ocean beaches, or head inland to open acacia woodland. You can go walking in the dunes with a tribesman and look for birds and game such as the rare Tana River bushbuck. You are certain to see baboons. This area used to be a hunting block, and apparently here are still elephant and lion not far away. Over 200 species of birds are found in the area and there is a bird feeding table at camp.

There are some therapeutic mud-flats where you can immerse yourself in mud before being taken into the sea for a wash-off. A thatched shelter has been built on the surfing beach, and a cold box might be brought there so you can have a refreshing drink before tackling the feet-burning sand on the dunes. Being so close to the river delta means that the sea can sometimes be muddy.

Quotes:

"It was absolute magic going over the top of the dunes and seeing mile after mile of beach without another soul... I loved the total pristineness of it... I didn't know beaches like that existed anymore."

Accommodations

The tents have en suite bathrooms with flush toilet and showers. There is a local, coastal flavor to these comfortable tents. Bright *kanga* fabrics have been used in the decor, and the beds are made from mangrove poles. Large netted windows let in light and the occasional sea breeze. Tents #1 and 4 have a glimpse of the Tana River.

Other Offerings

Arrangements can be made for deep-sea fishing. There is an airstrip for charters (shortens the trip by two hours).

Off Notes

The main drawback of Tana Delta Camp is also its main advantage—its remoteness. You have to make time for Tana Delta... The drive from Malindi is rough, dusty and bumpy... It can be very hot, and a swim is a hike away... Mosquitoes are a seasonal problem.

Please Note

The camp is closed in the low season.

Lamu and North

In this northernmost coastal area, the emphasis is on exploring Swahili culture in the streets of Lamu or at the sites of historical ruins or monuments. You can also return to nature—explore a coral reef, sail on a dhow, or stay in a romantic grass shack on a secluded beach.

To reach Lamu Island you must cross by boat. There is no motorized transport on the island. Visitors tend to stay either in Lamu Town for closer contact with the Swahili culture, or in the nearby fishing village of Shela,

COAST: MALINDI to LAMU & NORTH

where there are better hotels and access to a swimming beach. You can als elect to stay in beach resorts further away or in private homes.

Lamu Island – Lamu Town

As an interesting and historic city of Kenya, Lamu Town attracts many vi itors. Situated on Lamu Island with only donkeys and dhows for transpor this ancient town has narrow winding streets, open sewers, historic mosque a fort, colorful markets and many eager local guides.

There are not yet any hotels which we would strongly recommend in Lamu Town. However, if you choose to stay in the town, here are some possibilities which came to light during our research:

Petley's Inn

Petley's Inn, Box 4, Lamu
☎ *(121) 33107, Nairobi,* ☎ *(2) 29612*
e-mail: Baraka@tt.gn.apc.org

This old, well-known hostelry is on the waterfront near the museum. It is steeped in Lamu tradition. The hotel became quite run down, but was acquired by new owners who closed the hotel for complete refurbishing. The hotel has 11 bedrooms and a three-room family suite. Some rooms have air-conditioning and others have ceiling fans. There are traditional Lamu four-poster beds and private balconies. There is a small swimming pool taking up most of the second floor, a rooftop restaurant and a pub on the ground floor.

Lamu Palace Hotel

Lamu Palace Hotel, Box 83, Lamu
☎ *(121) 33272*

This is a fairly large new hotel on the waterfront. The advantages of this hotel are its proximity to downtown Lamu and the fact that it has air conditioning throughout. It has a Lamu-style decor. There is a restaurant with an extensive menu. The bedrooms seem small and enclosed.

Stone House

Island Hotel, Box 179, Lamu
☎ *(121) 33290*

Stone House provides bed and breakfast in an 18th century house. The house derives its name from Lamu's historic stone houses with their Swahili Islamic architecture. The rooms are all doubles and have Lamu furniture, a telephone and a private bathroom. The house has its own water supply—a boon in Lamu town. There is a restaurant which offers seafood and Swahili delicacies. Stone House is advertised as being "small" with a "serenely quiet and private" atmosphere and "personal and friendly service." We hear that mattresses are rather soft and that some ground floor rooms can be noisy. No alcohol.

Yumbe House

Yumbe House, Box 81, Lamu
☎ *(121) 33101*

Yumbe House is in an old-style building deep in Lamu Town. It is quite basic and has the feeling of a well-set-up youth hostel. Rooms have private bathrooms and can hold up to three beds. There is a rooftop lounge with city and harbor views. Breakfast is included. There are fridges in the rooms and friendly, helpful management.

Lamu Island – Shela

You have a nicer choice of accommodations at the fishing village of Shela a short dhow ride from Lamu Town, and the site of its closest swimming beach. Although Shela Beach is good for swimming and some watersports there has been danger from thieves and thugs.

Peponi Hotel

Peponi Hotel, Box 24, Lamu
☎ *(121) 33029, Telex: 21471 PEPONI*

For many years people visiting Lamu have passed the word: "Peponi's is the place to stay."

The hotel is right at water's edge in Shela Village, a few kilometers walk, or pleasant 20-minute dhow ride away from Lamu Town. This privately owned hotel has been in the hands of a Danish family, the Korschens, for 25 years.

Part of the appeal of staying at Peponi is arriving by water. Most guests fly to Lamu Airstrip on Manda Island and then board the hotel's large wooden dhow. Immediately you are transported back to a slower, more peaceful time. You chug past Lamu Town, then by beautiful gardens and villas. After landing, you walk along a sandy beach to reach the hotel.

You are dazzled by whitewashed terraces, blazing bougainvillea, and tall waving palm fronds. There is color and life in the busy open-air public bar, the riot of exotic flowering shrubs, and the bustling boating activity in front of the hotel. On the other hand, peace and relaxation are found in the residents' section of the hotel with its quiet and established air. There is a solid, timeless feel about Peponi—nothing slick or nouveau. It invites indolence: reading, sitting on deck chairs admiring the view, sipping a drink on the terrace, just watching boats…. It lives up to its Swahili name. *Peponi* means place where there is coolness, rest and relief from trouble…

There are only 25 rooms at Peponi Hotel, and the atmosphere is intimate and low key—no sense of bustling, mass tourism. There is an interesting layout of rooms. On one side of the main building, a row of rooms faces a lawn with tall palm trees and a low stone sea wall clothed with bougainvillea. There is a more unusual arrangement on the other side of the hotel, where rooms are at different levels and reached by meandering paths between flowering trees. Some rooms are up narrow flights of open-air stairs, others are tucked below, overlooking sand and water. All rooms have a private veranda with comfortable chairs and pleasant views. The newer rooms have been attractively decorated with bright carpets, modern art, and cane furniture. The older rooms are simply and solidly furnished, dim and cool with high ceilings and "casablanca" fans—echoes of a colonial time.

The dining room is simple and elegant—predominantly white with dark wood furniture. Colorful old Dutch plates and bowls brighten the white stucco walls, and there are attractive Lamu chairs with woven string backs. A wall-size painting of an intricate Swahili arch adds an exotic touch. Along one entire side of the room are windows with French doors leading out to a comfortable terrace overlooking the water. In addition to the formal dining room, there is an outdoor grill restaurant with raked sand underfoot and a tangle of bougainvillea overhead. The hotel specializes in seafood and has both a table d'hote as well as an à la carte menu. The drunken prawns were a treat!

After a day's sight-seeing in Lamu Town climbing up narrow and pungent streets in the heat, peering into dark shops, squeezing past donkeys and absorbing a sense of history and the exotic, it is a pleasant relief to return to the tranquillity, beauty and security of Peponi…and a cold drink—the lime juice is wonderful.

Accommodations

The 25 rooms vary somewhat in size. There are high Lamu-style beds (king, double, or twin), en suite bathrooms, 24-hour electricity, mosquito netting, and ceiling fans. The four newest rooms are nearer the water and seem brighter with a more colorful and interesting decor. *Our Favorites:* New Wing: #24, #25. Old Wing: #19, #20. Also check out the view from the room they call "Top."

Safari Journal
Sunday begins . . .

Lars, the second generation manager owner, told me Peponi's was "the sunrise place." And it is. I came down from my room above the white roof top terrace just at dawn when the birds started calling. Everything is so quiet and peaceful. The water is like glass. The air is still and the light a bright haze. The little dhow across the way with its brown triangle sail leaves hardly a ripple as it glides out to sea. Even this early you can feel the heat starting to build and swell. The California couple swim just in front of the main building. They stroke straight out, cutting through the calm water, right through the moorings of the hotel boats. She turns against the current ~ I see her stroking, but the current holds her still. Then they turn to swim back. The steward just arrived with my early morning coffee ~ rich and freshly brewed...

Bathing Beach

A short walk around the rocks from Peponi leads to a long beach backed by dunes. This is the closest bathing beach to Lamu Town and dhows bring visitors here. Hotel guests are warned not to take anything valuable to the beach because of thugs and thieves.

Local Tour Guides & Boatmen

Local residents are always available for hire at the hotel's outdoor bar to guide you through Shela and Lamu Town or to take you where you want to go by boat. Their knowledge is worth it, and so is their protection from others wanting you to hire them!

Hotel Dhow Service to Lamu Town

Free 9 a.m. shuttle with return at noon. Takes about 15 minutes.

Walks

Transportation on Lamu Island is by foot, by donkey, or by boat. The walk to Lamu Town takes about 40 minutes with interesting views of water traffic and villas along the way. Walk along beach. Explore Lamu Town or Shela.

Water Activities

Through the hotel you can arrange to go snorkeling, waterskiing, or deep-sea fishing. For a special treat, enjoy a lobster feast on a dhow by day or moonlight. There is a windsurfing concession at the hotel beach.

Off Notes

Too much "local color" at the bar can be wearing on guests seeking tranquillity... Watch out for strong currents in the water... Swimming from the hotel beachfront seems uninviting during the day due to boat traffic.

Note

The Peponi Hotel closes in May and June.

Kijani House

Kijani House, Box 266, Lamu
☎ *(121) 33235, FAX: (121) 33237*

Kijani House is a small garden hotel with four double and three triple rooms spread among three charming Swahili houses. The houses have traditional coral walls with high makuti roofs. They are surrounded by large tropical gardens full of flowers.

The grounds go down to a jetty where fishermen secure their boats after fishing, and a walk along the water is very picturesque. It is possible to walk the three kilometers to Lamu Town, or to walk 300 meters up the beach to Peponis Hotel, then farther on to Shela Beach.

There are nine superior and three standard bedrooms. The rooms are spacious with high ceilings. Mellow Lamu-style wooden furnishings complement the pristine white of walls and linen. Four-poster beds support a canopy of mosquito netting, and copper vases full of flowers are on antique bureaus. There are ceiling fans for comfort, and full bathrooms. There are more Lamu-style wooden chairs and loungers on each private terrace.

You eat with other guests at communal tables in an open-air dining area shaded by the cool thatch roof. There is also a bar and lounge area under thatch. There are two well-kept freshwater swimming pools on the property convenient to guest accommodations. The Swiss management can arrange for excursion trips by motorboat, dhow, four-wheel drive vehicle, or airplane. Ask for Room #1 or #3 for best view of the water.

Island Hotel
The Island Hotel, Box 179, Lamu
☎ *(121) 33290*

The Island Hotel is located in the heart of the village of Shela. It is basic and clean, though some of the 14 rooms are not very private since some walls do not extend to the ceiling. All rooms have private bathroom and fan. There is Lamu furniture and some outdoor terraces. There are nice views of Shela rooftops from the top-floor restaurant, which is partly open to the sea breezes. The wonderful penthouse is worth the extra cost.

Private Houses in Shela Village

By far the nicest accommodation option on Lamu is to stay in one of the privately owned Swahili-style houses in Shela Village. You take over the entire house which could be three to four stories with open courtyards and roof terraces. You are looked after by local house staff and a cook. The houses are built right in the village of Shela, so you get a feel for the community. You hear the muezzin's call to prayer, you pass women hidden beneath floating black bui-buis, you share narrow passageways with donkeys. There are bright whitewashed walls and brilliant bougainvillea. Shela is small, and it is an easy walk to the beach or to catch a dhow into Lamu town. You can arrange to go snorkeling or on a romantic sunset cruise.

Lamu is a Muslim Island—guests staying in private houses are advised to bring their own wine, spirits and any pork products they desire. Butter and cheese can be difficult to find in Shela.

Three private houses are described here. Others are available and it seems that more will be opening. Check them out.

Shela House and Palm House
Box 39486, Nairobi
☎ *(2) 445013, FAX: (2) 445010*

Guests have been coming to Shela House for some years. Palm House opened in November 1996. Staying in either house is pure bliss. They are breathtakingly beautiful, totally relaxing and very exotic. You feel special and pampered from the moment you arrive by dhow from the airport and are greeted at the jetty by the welcoming house staff. They carry your bags and lead you through narrow streets to the house.

Step through a beautifully carved door into paradise. There are courtyards open to the sky and filled with flowering creepers, beautiful Swahili furniture, bright exotic fabrics.... everything done to perfection. You will never want to leave.

In both houses the kitchen, dining and a living area are on the lower level. Climb up smooth steps to explore the various floors above—bedrooms with Lamu beds, sunny outdoor passageways, cool areas for sitting and reading, bookcases filled with books. Walls are bright whitewash, the floors are a cool yellow and windows have no glass to impede the breeze. Everywhere is a view worth a picture—whether it is looking down into the central courtyard, into the narrow streets below or out to the blue of the sea shining beyond the white minaret of the nearby mosque.

The top levels of the houses are open-sided, thatched roof terraces which catch the breeze and offer panoramic views over the village and the water beyond. There is a bar with fridge— ice and cold drinks. This is the place to read or sleep away the heat of the day on a Lamu daybed or in the hammock, the place to gather for sundowners and listen to the evening call to prayer, the place to come to after dinner to look at the impossibly bright stars, the place it's especially hard to leave when you have to return to the real world.

The staff in Shela and Palm house look after your every need—setting up for drinks before dinner, doing laundry if needed, keeping the house spotless. There is a cook and two house staff in both Shela and Palm House. The cooks are superb chefs. We have eaten unparalleled meals—ginger crab, coconut fish curry, succulent lobsters. Fishermen bring their catch to the door and you can select what you would like. The staff will discuss with you what you would like to eat and go shopping on a daily basis, keeping a tab for your account. It is possible to arrange to get alcohol from nearby Peponi Hotel if you don't bring your own.

There is a secluded shady garden where you can have barbecues, and a pool is planned.

You'll feel that you don't really want to leave the house but there is an endless almost deserted beach for lovely walks and swims, and there are dhow owners eager to take you sailing, snorkeling or to ancient ruins under giant baobabs. You can catch the Peponi Hotel boat into Lamu town for the morning, you can wander around Shela village just enjoying the charm and the exotic nature of the place.

A comparison between Shela and Palm House:

Palm House

Palm House is newer, has larger bedrooms, and a better view from the roof terrace. Palm house has four bedrooms, all en suite. There are three rooms with double beds and one with twin beds.

Shela House

Shela House, being older, has more interesting nooks and crannies and more of a sense of history. It has two separate roof terraces—ideal if more than one family/ group is sharing the house. There are five bedrooms each of different size and character: three doubles, one twin and one single. All have ensuite bathrooms.

Shela and Palm house each rent for $300 per day—this price includes accommodation and house staff. Food is extra.

Two other houses are currently being built by the same owners.

Garden House

This will be a three level house with two bedrooms—ideal for parties of four people or less. It is being constructed at the edge of the garden shared by Shela and Palm House. Price will be $150 per day.

Beach House

Currently being built right on the beach next to Peponi Hotel, it is planned that this house will be the most luxurious of the group. There will be five double bedrooms, terraces on each level and a swimming pool. Price per day will be $600.

Kisimani House

Mr. and Mrs. Rob de Boer, Box 24711, Nairobi
☎ *(2) 882409, FAX: (2) 882409*

Originally built in the early 18th century for the Caliph of Zanzibar, Kisimani has been carefully restored and extended. Exquisitely detailed vidaka (intricately carved plaster work) around the old harem section of the house serves as an exotic reminder of its history. A heavy carved Lamu door; a baraza, the traditional outdoor sitting area for conducting business; squared and painted mangrove beams—all contribute to the museum quality of this Arabian Nights house.

There is an open central courtyard, miscellaneous cool terraces and verandas, and a crows-nest on the fourth level with a superb view taking in the channel, the ocean and even distant Lamu Town. There are pillars and arches brilliantly whitewashed, masses of vivid bougainvillea, a cowrie shell wall, and carved Swahili-style furniture. You feel you have stepped into some exquisite and exotic world—a haven of peace and beauty.

On the first floor is the eating terrace which is open to the sky and shaded by bougainvillea. Comfortable cushioned benches are built in along the parapet wall and there is a hammock. On the third level, carved veranda beds shaded by a makuti roof, offer lovely views over Shela and the Channel—views framed by waving palm fronds.

Spread among the various levels of Kisimani House are four bedrooms each with a bathroom. By far the nicest and grandest bedroom is the Harusi or honeymoon room which you enter through its own carved door and which has an enormous bed with pillars and a ceiling fan within the mosquito net. There is a sitting area and private terrace with a view into the courtyard.

You are cared for by a cook who is adept at preparing all manner of seafood and some exotic Swahili dishes. He will do the shopping and keep the accounts. There is also a houseman to clean, do laundry etc.

Staying in Kisimani house is totally relaxing and pampering—a holiday in itself. However, there is a marvelous beach just a short walk away and the interesting and exotic Shela village and Lamu Town to explore.

Kisimani House rents for $200 per day for 2–4 people and $300 per day for 5–8 people. This price includes accommodation and house staff. Food is extra.

Off note:
> If several couples share the house, there are bound to be disagreements about who gets the honeymoon room.

Johari House
Box 41822, Nairobi
☎ *(2) 891510*

Another beautiful private house in Shela. It is very close to Kisimani and similar in several respects. The house is of historic interest with vidaka (intricately carved plaster work) around the old harem section on the ground floor. There is Lamu style furniture, open terraces, a partially covered outdoor eating area, and comfortable cushioned places to sit. There is a cook who prepares primarily seafood meals and again, it's just a short walk to the beach. It caters comfortably for six guests.

Beach Resorts Near Lamu

North of Lamu are a choice of romantic beach resorts known for secluded beaches, watersports and total relaxation.

Kiwayu Safari Village

Kiwayu Safari Village, Box 55343, Nairobi
☎ *(2) 503030, FAX: (2) 503149*

Kiwayu is on the northern part of Kenya's coastline near the Somali border and 120 kilometers from Lamu. There is an airstrip just minutes away. You can fly direct from Nairobi or from Lamu.

Kiwayu Safari Village was our favorite place on the Kenyan coast. It combines great natural beauty with exotic accommodations, marvelous food, and perfect peace and privacy.

The setting is superb—the "Village" nestles under a tall stand of coconut palms on the white-sand beach of a sparkling secluded bay. Although situated on the mainland, it feels as though you are on a private island. At the far end of the bay, more tall palms signal the presence of a local village, but other than this, there is no other sign of human habitation.

Across the water is Kiwayu Island, the waves breaking white against dark rocky cliffs—such a contrast to the gentle lapping of sea on golden sand at your feet. This place was originally a hunter's camp, and elephant used to come on to the beach, sometimes to swim across to Kiwayu Island. From elephants to models—now Kiwayu Safari Village attracts international fashion photographers—perfect models posing in perfect scenery.

Kiwayu Safari Village lines the shore. At the center of the curving beach, and just above the waterline, a long spacious lounge/bar adjoins an equally long dining area. Both have high thatch roofs overhead, grass matting underfoot, and a few wooden poles to keep the two apart. The place is rustic and natural—ideal for letting the breezes and the view be part of the scene. Do not let this description conjure up spartan images. In the lounge enormous floor cushions covered in colorful *kangas* are piled upon each other in abandon, inviting you to flop—order a cold Pimms. The tables are large logs of grey weathered driftwood, bright shells are artistically arranged, irresistible snacks are brought with the drinks. Lights are low, and you hear the sound of the waves lapping on the beach. All is delightfully decadent in this dream setting.

Guest cottages are well spaced along the beach on both sides of these public rooms. Each has been ingeniously positioned to ensure complete privacy, and the ocean is just a quick dash across the sand.

"Cottage" is too meager a word to describe these luxurious and spacious grass villas. The enormous bedroom has a bigger than king-size bed, high off the floor, spread with bright fabric and draped with mosquito netting. Outside is a private lounging area with hammocks and chairs filled with colorful cushions. There is a separate dressing area with a double sink (two enamel basins) and separate rooms for a flush toilet and a fresh water shower. Walls, floor and roof—all are made of grass matting or palm leaves. There are no doors or windows, just wide open spaces in the walls which let in the air and frame views of sand and water. Growing trees are often built right into the decor and framework of the cottages. A driftwood mangrove tree stands grey on the matting, an amusing "towel rack." There is electricity. The water is unheated—not a hardship when you return hot and salty from the beach. You are likely to find hermit crab visitors in your shower—some carrying the size and type of shell you would pay dearly for in a shell shop. The whole place is wonderfully harmonious with its surroundings—nothing jars or is incongruous.

Dining at Kiwayu Safari Village is a delight—giant crab claws, platters of lobster, perfect salads, amazing fish soup. The emphasis obviously is on fresh seafood, but if you don't care for seafood and give them advance warning, they will prepare something else.

The majority of guests spend most of their time relaxing, eating and drinking. However, included in the tariff is a whole host of water related activities from windsurfing and laser sailing to goggling and creek fishing. Deep-sea fishing is also available for an additional fee.

*Safari Journal
Late*

*We recline on fat cushions spread on grass matting.
The stars above are brilliant. We agree on Orion's Belt
but debate the Southern Cross. Contentment after dinner.
Susan ordered a bottle of wine to celebrate the last
of the bumpy rides in small boats. Joan said crab
was her favorite food, that this was the best she'd ever
tasted, and then proceeded to astound us with how much
she could put away. We are joined by a young man
in charge of describing our options for the following day.
Do we want to go snorkeling, on a picnic tea to an
island, have a windsurfing lesson, walk over the dunes
to explore lovely bays on the other side . . .
or simply laze about? Wish I had the time
to do it all.*

There are miles of unspoiled beaches to walk, washed up shells to admire and a choice of swimming in the calm bay water or the wilder surf on the other side of the dunes. There are many boating trips you can take—go to Kiwayu Island or glide between mangroves along narrow channels of water. The snorkeling is magnificent: colorful coral and brilliant fish on unspoiled reefs—best of all, there is no one else there but you!

This is a wonderfully romantic spot and is popular with honeymooners. Many guests are repeat customers. Most visitors come for about a week. Some lucky ones stay longer.

Quotes:

> "*We bring people back to nature. There are no doors, no windows, no locks, no keys.... The secret is the space and solitude...*" *Manager.*

> "*I see palm trees growing in the middle of the house.... I got shells from the beach for the cook to decorate.*" *Nine-year-old visitor from abroad.*

> "*I loved being able to step out of my room, walk just a few paces across the sand, and be right in the water.*"

Accommodations

There are 22 cottages. One is a twin cottage for two doubles. The other cottages are planned for two with one big bed standard. This can be replaced by two single beds on request, and a third bed can easily be added. Overhanging eaves and shaded verandas insure privacy as does the distance between the cottages. Grass mat shades can be lowered over windows. Most of the cottages are right on the beach, close to the water. *Our Favorite Views:* #7, 11, and 19.

Special Offerings

Deep-sea fishing, creek fishing, dhow sailing, laser sailing, windsurfing, goggling trips, mangrove trips, souvenir shop, four-wheel shuttle, airstrip.

Off Notes

Pricey to fly to paradise... No fans, no air conditioning, and no hot water for those who need their creature comforts... Hermit crabs in the shower may not be your ideal way of getting back to nature.

Please Note

Kiwayu Safari Village closes from mid-April for a couple of months (dates may vary).

Blue Safari Club

Bruno Brighetti's Blue Safari Club, Box 15026, Nairobi
☎ *(2) 890184, FAX: (2) 890096*

Blue Safari Club is an ultraexclusive island paradise. It has long been an idyllic retreat for a rich and famous international clientele who seek peace and privacy. The Blue Safari Club is a handful of luxury grass huts scattered on white sandy beaches and surrounded by tall palm trees and blue waters. It is located on the northeastern tip of Manda Island, nearest neighbor to Lamu. There are no roads—you arrive by boat.

At Blue Safari Club you are the personal guests of the Brighetti family who selected this romantic spot more than 20 years ago. Bruno and his son Marco, with their outgoing friendliness, cater to your every whim. Here you do exactly as you desire. Meals are served when you are ready; the bar is always open, you can arrange snorkeling, fishing, or sailing as the spirit takes you.

The club is limited to 20 guests, and the Brighettis prefer to entertain only one party at a time. The privacy and preference of each guest is of paramount importance to all the staff. The atmosphere is casual but reserved. There is a studied informality here—mammoth floor cushions artfully arranged and beautiful people with "chic" kangas draped over swimwear.

The heart of the Blue Safari Club is the open-sided dining area, lounge banda and bar. These casual, breezy structures, built from all-natural materials have a certain elegance and artistic flair, thanks to Bruno's wife, Gianna. Grass matting, shells and driftwood are used for decor. But, hidden high-tech is also there—you can watch a video or listen to music. Guests dine with the Brighettis. Fresh seafood and fish are part of every simple gourmet meal, and the pasta is perfect.

Quotes:

> *"I feel so spoiled. It's like having my own private island in the sun."*

Accommodations

Guests stay in small round bandas of woven grass and thatch. These are well spaced in two rows, with the preferred front row at water's edge. Smooth grass matting serves as walls and floors. Curtains and bedspreads are of bright kanga cloth and a veranda in front of each banda has Lamu-style lounge chairs with woven seats.

Each banda has a private bathroom reached through a short roofed and matted walkway. Bathrooms are simple with an open shower and unheated water. There is 24-hour electricity. Mosquito nets are lowered and bandas sprayed at night. There are fans in each room.

Safari Journal

Monday ~ beautifully Blue Monday!

Handsome Marco Brighetti, broad shouldered, tanned, and young, came to pick us up for the boat ride to Blue Safari ~ what a romantic name. After days of dirty Lamu dhows and motor boats, the Brighetti's aqua-blue fiberglass boat seemed a marvel of cleanliness. The gray morning brightened as we sped through mangrove-lined waterways, bouncing a little when we hit incoming waves. The water changed from green-gray to deep blue as we made a final sweeping turn toward a white sandy point, beautiful with palms ~ there it was ~ Blue Safari . . . .

Special Offerings

(Many of these are included in the tariff) Snorkeling and scuba diving (14 tourist-free reefs to choose from), windsurfing, waterskiing, sailing, sculling, deep-sea fishing, cabin cruiser or dhow trips, motor boats, canoes, underwater photography, bird-watching, miles of private beach, free boat shuttle to airstrip, gift shop. There is a 60-foot traditional luxury dhow for cruising and diving safaris, and a 35-foot state-of-the-art deep sea fishing boat.

Off Notes

Bandas seem small and often hot (the new fans should help)... Top row bandas lack view.

Kipangani Bay

Prestige Hotels Ltd., Box 74888, Nairobi
☎ *(2) 338084, FAX: (2) 213387*

Kipungani Bay is situated at the southerly tip of Lamu Island on the opposite side from busy Lamu Town. It is private, secluded, and extremely low-key—perfect for a relaxing and romantic getaway.

A sprawling beach lounge and bar is the heart of Kipungani. It lures you with colorful cushions, low tables and swinging beds. There is grass matting underfoot, thatch above and wide open views of sand and water and distant green.

A freeform saltwater swimming pool overlooks the ocean. As you swim you can watch dhows sail past and flocks of birds skimming the water. The spillover weir gives the feeling that pool and ocean are connected—especially dramatic when the sunset is reflected in both.

Fifteen spacious grass cottages rest casually under palm trees. Most are perched just above the beach with marvelous uninterrupted views. Behind these a few slightly smaller cottages have been built up on stilts. The guest cottages have walls and floor made from local grass matting and a high pitched thatch roof. There are no doors or windows, just more grass matting which you can roll down. There are 12 king bedded rooms and three twins.

All ground level cottages have a private veranda facing the ocean and you can lounge here on local funzi beds and chairs soft with colorful cushions. Behind the bedroom is a dressing area with handwash basin and separate rooms for flush toilet and fresh water shower. The water is unheated and there is the romance of paraffin lamps at night. Most of the cottages also have electric lights serviced by a generator.

Kipungani Bay is managed and hosted by Clemens and Nancy von Merveldt a delightful, international couple who clearly love this paradise and are enthusiastic about sharing it with their guests.

Kipungani is an ideal place to get away from it all, to slow down and relax, to imagine you are on a deserted island. If you want to do something more active than lying on outsized cushions or watching the sunset, you have many choices. There is windsurfing, sailing and snorkeling. You can also go creek fishing or simply enjoy a leisurely beach walk looking for washed up shells. Bird enthusiasts will enjoy the parade of waders and water birds and at certain times of year are treated to the spectacular Carmine Bee-eater migration. A visit to the nearby village provides an interesting perspective on local life and culture. Dhow safaris to Lamu town or deep-sea fishing can also be arranged.

Kipungani Bay has a fleet of three boats: a fiberglass speedboat, a motorboat for snorkeling trips and creek fishing, and a "Sesse" canoe. A motorized Dhow can be hired.

Kipungani Bay closes after Easter and reopens around the beginning of July.

Getting There:

Fly to Manda Island and board a speedboat for the 20 minute transfer to Kipungani.

Munira Safari Camp

Box 40088, Nairobi
☎ *(2) 512213*

Munira Safari Camp is on the small and beautiful Kiwayu Island in the Lamu archipelago. It is a rustic and romantic spot. There is no electricity and water is brought to camp by donkey from a fresh-water well on the island.

The views are superb—as is the beach, the goggling and the food. There is a six mile almost deserted beach and spectacular coral reefs close to shore. You dine mainly on seafood—lots of fresh crab and lobster.

There are four bandas to take a maximum of 15 people. The bandas are spacious and simple and made from local materials. There are makuti roofs overhead and almost everything else is made from palm matting. Each banda has an en suite shower, and there are long-drop toilets with a view.

You arrive through mangrove waterways to the Munira jetty from which you can swim. It is a steep climb up to camp. On the other side there are lovely paths through sand dunes bringing you to the beach. There are dhows for "explorative" fishing expeditions, and serious fishermen can arrange to charter a fully equipped deep-sea fishing boat.

The camp is run by Mike Kennedy and his sister, Caroline.

Getting there:

Fly to Kiwayu mainland and you will be transferred by cessie canoe. If one of the camp dhows is in Lamu for supplies, clients can be picked up and enjoy a picnic on the five hour trip to Kiwayu Island.

QUICK SAFARI GUIDE FOR KENYA

Elephants

Like most people who visit Kenya for pleasure you will have an image and an understanding of what will happen on your trip. Rather than school you in the ways of safaris, it might be more helpful to deal with the most important aspects of planning a safari. Kenya is the most popular destination with

Masai Mara the most popular park. Samburu, Nairobi and Tsavo are the number two spots. Any major trip will include three to four game areas with a few stops at smaller attractions like Lake Nakuru or Thomson's Falls.

The Northern Circuit is the most desolate and awe inspiring, however you will not see many animals and it is very hot. Samburu, Marsabit, Meru and Mt Kenya are good choices. Very few people go as far as the Turkana area. There is always danger of armed bandits, and the constant pressure from poachers and drought conditions have reduced the wildlife dramatically.

The Coastal route usually takes in Amboseli, Tsavo Shimba or Tana and is a good second choice. Usually time at a beach resort near Malindi or historic tours in Mombasa can round out a more exotic safari.

The Southwestern route is by far the most popular. Streams of minivans hit the highlights between Nairobi and their final destination the Masai Mara. Nakuru, Aberdares and Naivashu are usually put on the agenda here. Many second timers, simply skip the long minibus rides and fly directly from Wilson airport in Nairobi directly to a tented camp in the Mara.

How to Safari

Although the traditional safari was a tented hunting safari supported by large trucks and scores of porters, most people are content with the politically correct wild game park version. Most Americans will book a tour before they leave totally trusting where and when they will be shuttled around. Not all safaris are the same. To help you understand the basic choices here is a brief guide to choosing a safari:

Minibus tours

It is easy to rack up a few game parks in one trip if you are traveling by minibus from Nairobi. Ideal for first timers who want to see the country but the distances between stops can be numbing. You will have the chance to visit a couple of markets, have your picture taken next to colorful tribespeople and get to know your fellow travelers but you will be under pressure to keep up with the schedule. Many roads are pure mud in the rainy season and blinding dust when they are dry. Consider flying directly to a tented camp and picking up a camp driver (who will know the park better).

Self Drive

Many expats based in Kenya drive out to the parks on weekends. The problem is that once you are committed to driving yourself around the parks you lose the constant chatter of a well informed guide. The spectre of robbery, breakdowns and bandits also appears. Unless you know a local, not advised.

Custom tented safaris

The ne plus ultra of African travel. One step above the fixed tented camps, a custom safari can be designed to take you where and when you want to go. Birdwatchers, animal lovers or people who can afford to keep their own schedule choose this method over the package tours. Abercrombie and Kent and Downey & Kerr are the best choices. Do not confuse a custom tented safari (which is in effect staying at fixed tented sites in established venues like Kichwa Tembo in the Mara) with a custom itinerary where you and your outfitter set up your own schedule and campsites.

Hyrax

Camel or Horseback safaris

The adventurous can choose camel safaris in the northern parks complete with Samburu or Rendille wranglers or horseback adventures along trails in the central or west part of Kenya. Private ranches also offer horseback game viewing rides. These trips are usually a group affair so inquire as to how many riding partners you will have. Not designed to be too strenuous, you will be exposed to the sun and the elements for the 15–25 miles a day you cover. Cooking and all camp work are taken care of by the outfitter. Camels offer a less comfortable but more romantic version of the classic safari. The fact that people will actually pay money to sit on a cantankerous camel amazes many but some people will go to any length to make Africa romantic. I would think that romance is the last thing these travelers think about at the end of a long day being bumped and humped on camels.

Balloon safaris

Not technically a safari but a morning's outing in the major game areas. Balloon trips were started in 1988 and are guaranteed to create a memory you won't soon forget—depending on the weather of course. It will also make a sizeable dent in your wallet (about $250–$400 a person). But the memory of floating over the primeval plains of Africa capped off by a champagne breakfast will last a lifetime.

Flying tours

Although they sound exotic, flying tours use the transportation infrastructure to its greatest advantage. You will pick up a small charter plane directly on arrival and in one to three hours be in camp sipping on a gin and tonic. The camp will provide a driver, all supplies and load you onto your next charter. Flying tours allow you to go fishing for giant Nile perch in Lake Victoria or fly fishing in Lake Turkana.

Homestays and lodges

The most sophisticated of all Kenyan safaris. Arrange your trip to stay in some of the most elegant and dramatic ranches, homes and lodges. Use local drivers and wranglers for safaris by car or horse. Fly between major parks and hire transportation when needed.

Other safari ideas

Who said a safari to Kenya means watching animals from a zebra striped minibus? You can go scuba diving, mountain climbing, trout fishing, canoeing, deep sea fishing or even just lie on some of the best beaches in the world. Ask your travel agent for some ideas and get going.

What Should I Wear?

This first question is the one that all hard core adventurers ask when setting out to parts unknown.

Although situated directly on the equator, Kenya has a diverse range of climates from very hot and dry to cold and wet. We have provided the various altitudes of the parks to give a rough idea.

- Near the coast, plan on hot, sticky and wet. The Indian Ocean is very tropical and very hot. You'll be most comfortable in loose cotton, with protection from the sun.

- The Eastern region below 3000 feet tends to be hot, dry and dusty. Take a hat, cotton pants, long sleeve shirts, sunglasses and sunscreen.

- The Highlands between 3000–5000 feet has cool to hot days and chilly nights. Rain showers can be frequent. Add a sweater and a rain jacket.

- The Montane area above 5000 feet is wet and cold. Add gloves, wool hat, heavy rain gear, stronger footwear and heavy pants.

What Should I Do?

The items of special interest to Americans on safari are the "bring 'em back alive" gear.

Binoculars

Preferably 10 X 40 for birders or wide field for animal watching.

Camera with telephoto lens

The ideal lens is a 300mm f2.8 that will cost you more than your entire safari. Failing that try a 200mm f4 or ideally a 80–200mm zoom with an 2.8 aperture. What the camera salesman won't tell you is that most of your best shots at sunrise or sunset will render any slow or long lens useless.

Fast and slow film

Ideally one camera body for each would be perfect. ASA 50 or 64 film for daylight shots and 100–400 asa for dusk and early morning shots with telephotos. Do not be afraid to use color negative film or to "push" (expose film at one stop faster) a roll if need be when you get back.

Video Camera

Still shots just don't do justice to the plains of Africa. Make sure you buy a unit that has a telephoto (at least a 12X zoom). Buy a car charger or cigarette adaptor and bring at least four batteries. Use a soft bag or folded jacket as a tripod and remember that the winds will render most sound recording useless unless you shield it well with extra foam.

Handbooks

Take the two compact hardbound bibles of East African safaris: *National Parks of East Africa* by J.G. Williams and *A Field Guide to the Mammals of Africa* by Theodore Haltenorth and Helmut Diller or if you prefer *A Field Guide to the Larger Mammals of Africa* by Jean Dorst and Pierre Dandelot. Other choices include the colorful Insight Guides *East African Wildlife Safari Special* from Houghton Mifflin, the *Safari Companion* by Richard D. Estes from Chelsea Green Publishing and *Adventuring in East Africa* by Allen Bechky from Sierra Club books. Bird lovers will bring along *A Field Guide to the Birds of East Africa* by John Williams and Norman Arlott or the new *National Audubon Society Field Guide to African Wildlife*.

Goodies

Bring along candies and gum for the long hot drives and gifts for villagers like pens, baseball cards or balloons. Don't forget small creature comforts like lip balm, sunscreen and a shortwave radio. I always recommend a Walkman with tapes of your favorite classics or movie soundtracks to make your own Africa movie on location.

You can buy all of the books and goodies in Nairobi but once you're in the parks your selection is limited and you will be paying tourist prices.

What You Might Not Expect

1) There are other people there.

The plains will be dotted with white and zebra striped buses. Once a driver spots a cat or an unusual event like a recent kill, dozens of buses will converge. After a while you will realize that the magnitude of the event can be described as a "five bus leopard" or even a "12 bus kill." Use your film accordingly. If you are not a fan of rush hour ask your driver to take you to less dramatic but more reflective events like watching a hippo blow bubbles (usually a "one bus" event).

2) You can't do what you want.

You will quickly learn that your driver is in charge. You will be rounded up at an ungodly hour in the morning, given a cup of bad coffee or tea and then driven out in the chill of morning for your first game drive. If you choose a deluxe drive you can leave whenever you want. If you are with other folks you will get two drives—one in the morning and one at sunset. You will then have the entire day to sit, or catch up on the sleep you are missing. Foot or horseback safaris are only part of private ranch vacations. Night drives are forbidden in all parks. Night walking safaris are usually the best way to get shot as a poacher.

3) You will actually get bored.

After your first three or four days you will learn to be more discriminating. No longer motordriving zebras and giraffes at 5 frames per second, you will begin to carefully squeeze each shot as if you were a sniper with only two rounds. One solution is to get one photo of each new species in the first few days but then spend more time just watching. Animals actually do more than just pose for tourists' cameras if you spend the time to watch their behavior. Don't be intimidated by those amazing wildlife action postcards you end up buying in the gift shop. They are the results of wildlife photographers spending years tracking just one leopard or lion family to get those great shots.

4) There is little hardship "on safari."

Safaris through Kenya require little roughing it and even less bushsmarts. Every action, need and desire will be capably handled by your guide. Even if you are on a tented safari you will probably be disappointed that your tent comes with running water and electricity. If you really decide to rough it on a custom tent safari, it gets even less rough as every whim from digging your toilet to mixing your drink is handled by a staff of up to 12 people.

Since we have exploded some myths about being on safari, here are a few tips that will help you get the most from your cosseted experience in the wilds of Africa:

1) Enjoy Africa.

Tell your driver what you want to do. Don't be a seat warmer. If you want to just park, turn the engine off and enjoy the African wildlife, tell him. He will override you in certain instances, as in the impending charge of a bull elephant, but your driver wants you to have a good time.

Like most visitors you will develop a special memory of Africa—maybe it will be the light, the wide open spaces or the feeling of being carefree and completely happy. In any case, it is a rare person who doesn't daydream about returning to Africa once experiencing a Kenyan safari.

2) Leave before dawn.

Although most game drives leave at dawn, try to get out earlier. The early morning is the best time for game viewing not only because of the activity of the animals, but the coolness and brilliant sunrise can be the most dramatic part of the day. Starting out before sunrise ensures you are in position before dawn and you will miss the rush hour traffic of the less informed travelers. Carnivores will use the early day to hunt and will then rest in the shade until dusk to preserve fluids and lower body heat. Use the time before dawn to put some distance between you and the lodge. Then sit and wait for the magical moment when the light appears and the animals come to life. Most game drives will try to leave at dawn cutting into the dramatic sunrise and you may miss the drama of the plains unfolding. Plan for plenty of action shooting.

Gerenuks

3) Map out your day.

Do not let your driver wander aimlessly or worse yet chase other vehicles looking for photo opportunities. Tell your driver to come clean and tell you where the animals are before you go out. Many will pretend to be Columbus discovering the new world every time they see an animal. They actually spent last night swapping notes with the other drivers so make them work for their tip. Tell your driver what you are looking for and that you are not just creature counting. Most drivers will assume that you will be happy chasing willy nilly all over the park as you check each and every animal off in your guidebook.

Tell him specifically what you want and when you want to photograph. For example leopards in the early morning or lions making a kill. Although no one can promise any animal or any event, patience and planning will help.

4) Be patient.

If you truly want spectacular photos or memories, plan on spending a lot of time waiting and watching. Get up before the crowds, stay out longer, drive further, stake out a vantage point from which to watch a pride of lions go through their day. Sitting and waiting means you can watch the play unfold instead of rattling around looking for the next photo opportunity.

5) Understand the animal's behavior.

Although a game preserve is not a zoo it is not unusual to find the same animals frequenting the exact same spots in the park. For example a hippo pool has and probably always will be the spot to see hippos. You may bump into one at night as it forages but chances are if there were hippos there 10 years ago they will be there 10 years from now.

The Mara is well known for its many prides of lions—all named, researched, tracked and observed day after day by the drivers that work out of the camps.

6) Pick a good camp with permanent drivers.

You will get your money's worth by picking a camp that has permanent drivers. Most people pick up a driver and a car in Nairobi and drive in. Fly in camps like Kichwa Tembo have a stable of drivers and cars that can take you exactly to where every cheetah and every pride of lions were last seen. You may not be surprised to find out that most drivers are good actors. The look of surprise and discovery is usually feigned. What they don't want you to know is that they all know to keep the leopards and lions as "safari toppers" to give you a feeling of discovery. The reality is that in the major parks the location and number of most individual carnivores are not only well known but animals usually have names to help the drivers tell them apart.

7) Work the light.

The best light is the golden light found about one to two hours before sunset. Second best are the first glancing rays of light found 1/2 hour after the sun breaks across the horizon. Remember your automatic camera will be going crazy trying to balance backlighting, dark thunder clouds or any other dramatic high contrast shots. Bracket or give it a couple of stops over and under.

Familiarize yourself with the park and the direction of the rising and setting sun. Plan to visit areas like gorges when the sun is shining on the side you wish to photograph. Conversely don't be afraid to shoot against the light during the very early and very late stages of the day. Don't even bother to take pictures during midday unless you are clicking off photos for your sighting records. As with the great hunters, one shot, one animal should be your motto. Watch, wait and if it doesn't happen there's always postcards in the gift shop.

8) Get up close.

Most drivers will discourage you from getting close to animals. There are two reasons for this. First of all, animals are distracted from their normal eating, mating, hunting and familial patterns every day of every year by hundreds of minivans. If every visitor was to get right up close the stress would be too much. Secondly, that stress can result in some very nasty attacks by elephants, water buffalo or carnivores—not out of hunger but pure frustration by being aggravated all day.

Never, never feed any animals. Maintain at least 50–100 yards and try to follow behind. Drive slowly. Make no noises or disturbing sounds. You are there to observe not to affect nature.

Sitting patiently is always the best way to view wildlife. In some cases, cheetahs, baboons or other less shy animals will actually walk onto your vehicle to gain a vantage point.

Animals with newborn and injured or hungry animals should be given a wide berth.

What to Watch Out For

Many people have a healthy fear of travel to Africa for any reason. The fact that 800,000 visitors will make the trip to Kenya and that most make it back with no more than a sunburn or rash from their camera strap should give you a certain level of comfort.

However it is important to stress that there are dangers. And they are not from the sharp-toothed animals. The biggest danger is exposure to a variety of bacteria, diseases and microscopic germs. I always tell people that the most dangerous creature in Africa is the mosquito. Malaria is a danger and every precaution should be taken.

Take your Larium faithfully, wear long sleeve shirts and wear insect repellent especially during the last few hours of the day when malarial mosquitoes are most likely to bite.

At night use a mosquito net and coils if possible. If you are bitten do not go crazy—not all mosquitoes carry malaria. However do not scratch insect bites because they have a higher chance of being infected.

Be careful what you eat. Although Kenyans feel obligated to put on a gargantuan Western spread, there are flies, organisms and other nasties who breed in the hot temperature. Try to eat only food that has been cooked, peel fruit, do not use ice, drink bottled products or boiled tea or coffee. Many Kenyans assume Westerners eat massive quantities of food. Don't be shy about demanding that the cook reduce his output or change his menu.

It is not unusual to have diarrhea because of the heat, different bacteria and jet lag. Drink plenty of fluids, drink moderately and take mild medicines such as Kaopectate to relieve the discomfort. If the diarrhea persists, see a doctor.

Rather than tell you all the woes of travel in the tropics, I suggest you con
sult with the Center for Disease Control, your doctor and read many of the
excellent books on tropical travel available in your travel specialty book store

Dangerous Animals

Many visitors ask why some drivers will not let them leave the vehicle
when in the parks while the Masai wander around with sandals and a simple
spear. Your driver has not told you how many Masai are killed or maimed by
elephants, lions, hippo, crocodiles, snakes and other cute animals. You only
need to see how invisible a lion can be in two foot light brown grass to un
derstand the fear these predators put in the local people.

The most imposing animal is the elephant. Many times they will be agitat
ed, swinging their head from side to side and shaking their ears. If an ele
phant is not happy to see you it will usually make one false charge and then
come running head down with the business end of its tusks pointed at you
This usually happens if you are in areas that have poachers. During severe
droughts elephants will charge out of thick brush without warning.

There are also numerous poisonous snakes, so watch where you walk
Long vicious thorns of the acacia bush can pierce right through hiking boo
soles, and numerous other dangers make staying in your vehicle the best way
to enjoy your safari.

Be careful, be cautious, have fun.

—**RYP**

KENYA'S BIOSPHERES, NATIONAL PARKS & NATURE PRESERVES

Eland

Kenya is the country of choice when most people think of taking their first safari. Politically stable, geographically diverse and serviced by international airlines, Kenya has the lion's share (sorry for the pun) of North America traffic to Africa. Many will tell you that Tanzania is more dramatic, South Af rica more pristine, Namibia, Botswana and Zambia more exotic—few coun tries can offer more diversity than Kenya.

There is something classic about a Kenyan safari—the colonial elegance o the hotels and game parks, the history and romance of following in the foot steps of Beryl Markham, Isak Dinesen, Robert Ruark and Ernest Heming way. Movies have drawn thousands to live out their celluloid fantasies: *Bor Free*, *Out of Africa*, *The Lion King* and other classic African stories still con tinue to inspire a dream of going on safari in millions of Americans.

Kenya sits smack dab on the equator and yet offers a fantastic range of en vironments only a few hours apart: the sweet, hot smells of the Indian Ocea and Arab history of Mombasa and Lamu, the cool wet alpine regions of M Elgon, the dramatic forever views across the rift valley, desolate volcanic re gions, endless horizons of the Western savannas, even snowcapped Moun Kenya.

Be forewarned that there is a very high wall between the tourist experienc awaiting the Western tourist and the cultural realities of Kenya. The closes most visitors will come to the local people will be to meet a tour driver (mos likely a member of the Kikuyu tribe who lives in Nairobi). Sometimes Sam buru or Maasai tribespeople will be seen and occasionally will barter fo goods. There is little contact with the crushing poverty and population prob lems of modern Kenya. The population is exploding at an alarming rate forc ing people further afield for food and shelter. Poaching, encroachment an crime are all symptoms of this problem. Yet tourism remains the only brigh spot and potential solution to these problems. Tourism provides jobs, for eign currency and a very profitable method of supporting this country. I would be hard to imagine what would happen if there were no game parks no tourism and no hope for Kenya. So don't be ashamed to be a tourist i Kenya. You are wanted and welcome.

Most people will book a safari with a North American company who wi then contract with a local company like Abercrombie and Kent in Nairob You will be met at the airport by a smiling, professional guide who will mak your trip effortless and one of the most enjoyable you have ever experienced Every day your minibus will be cleaned and spotless, your bags carried to an from your room. Every morning, afternoon and evening there will be end less buffets of rich heavy food of what Kenyans think Westerners want to ea Your guide will laugh at your jokes and point out animals that you canno even see with your binoculars. At the end of your safari your head will b spinning with amazing sights, your camera will have gone through more fil than you shot in the last two years and you will take care to leave just a littl dust on your safari jacket to show the folks back home.

Sable Antelope

Kenya has been careful to preserve and maintain its diverse range of parks
and reserves despite strained resources. The pressure from marauding Somali
poachers, hungry farmers and opportunistic teenagers have played havoc on
rhino, elephant and leopard. Kenya has employed a shoot-to-kill policy
which has been the only way to combat the constant attacks by heavily
armed intruders. Visitors will see little of this violent interface unless they
head into the Northern regions. Towards the south and central areas there is

Kenya's Parks and Reserves

little problem and the government maintains an efficient system of par
management. No vehicles are allowed out in the parks after dark but othe
than that minor restriction there is little to remind the visitor of the constan
threat facing African wildlife. People looking for more unique and person
wildlife experiences should look into staying at private game ranches listed i
the book.

Biospheres

Kenya is home to four of the world's biospheres (there are over 27
around the globe). Biospheres are areas deemed to contain unique land
forms, landscapes and systems of land use. They are intended to provid
large protected areas ideal for scientific study of their unique qualities and in
terdependencies.

Kiunga Biosphere Reserve

A coastal preserve of 250 sq. km (96 sq. mi.) that includes offshore islands and cora
formations. Dugong and green turtle coexist with a large population of reef fish. Birds in
clude various gulls and terns.

Swimming, sailing, waterskiing and diving are permitted.

Mount Kulal Biosphere Reserve

Here the vegetation ranges from mountain forest to desert with rain forest, mist forest
grasslands, dry evergreen forest, woodlands, bushlands and saltbrush scrublands. Faun
includes giraffe, zebra, elephant, cheetah, lion, black rhino, leopard, ostrich, crocodil
and gazelle.This reserve near the southeast of Lake Turkana covers 7000 sq. km (270
sq. mi.) at an altitude of 378 –2416 m (1035–7925 ft.).

Malindi/Watamu Biosphere Preserve

The best time to visit the parks is at low tide. Snorkeling can be a wonderful chang
from the hot and dry job of being on safari. Whale Island is a nesting ground of Roseat
and Bridled Terns from June to September.

This 261 sq. km (100.7 sq. mi.) park is divided into four regions:

• Malindi Marine National Park 6 sq. km (2.3 sq. mi.)

• Watamu Marine National Park 10 sq. km (3.8 sq. mi.)

• Malindi Marine National Reserve 213 sq. km (82.2 sq. mi.)

• Watamu Marine National Reserve 32 sq. km (12.4 sq. mi.)

Mount Kenya Biosphere Reserve
Mount Kenya National Park

A 715 sq. km (276 sq. mi.) park begun in 1949 that includes glaciers, bamboo forests, alpine moorlands and a favorite of mountain climbers who like a mild challenge with an altitude range of 1600–5199 m (5245–17,050 ft.). Rich alpine and subalpine region that is the only spot of the equator where you can find snow year round. Unusual species of plants like the giant rosette plants. Home of the rare golden cat usually seen only at high altitudes. Crowned by the twin peaks, Batian (5199 m/17,050 ft.) and Nelion (5188 m/17,017 ft.). Home to the giant Mount Kenya mole rat and the Mount Kenya mole shrew. Climbing, hiking and mule pack expeditions can be booked in advance through tour operators. Includes Mount Kenya National Park.

The bunker at the 2193 m Mountain Lodge offers very close contact at the waterhole with nighttime visitors.

National Parks

Established in 1945, Kenya's National Parks are designed to protect flora and fauna from encroachment by man. Although designed to provide educational and recreational use by Kenyans, they are the primary generators of foreign income as tourists from around the world come to experience the classic African safari in comparative luxury.

National Parks feature comfortable fixed tented camps and lodges. Vehicle traffic and viewing is allowed during the daytime only. Marine parks allow swimming, sailing and waterskiing

Kenya protects about 7.6 percent of its areas in parks and reserve areas and is under the control of the very military Kenya Wildlife Preserve.

Bongo

Aberdare National Park

This park was established in 1950 in Central Province—Nyandarua, Nyeri and Muranga districts, encompass 767 sq. km (296 sq. mi.). This rich montane park with cool highlands is the home of the rare bongo, trout filled rivers, bamboo forests and sylvan waterfalls. The high altitude (1829–3994 m/6000–13,100 ft.) creates a cool alternative to the typical savanna of most Kenyan parks. The elevated viewing lodges of historic Treetops (where the guest and viewing book have been filled out faithfully each night since the fifties) and the newer Ark are the prototypical game lodges that many people think of when dreaming of an exotic safari. Built around floodlit saltlicks, visitors can do their game viewing while enjoying bloody marys in the bar. These lodges provide one of the few closeups of elephants and other game from their ground level viewing blinds. There has been a lot of pressure from encroaching development resulting in lower game counts and aggressive behavior by wildlife. The elusive bongo is best spotted in the upper bamboo zone and hypericum scrub. Eland can be found in the open moorlands. Aberdare is also ideal for bird-watchers.

Special Features: • Karuru Waterfalls—the highest in Kenya, plunging 273 m (895 ft.) in three steps.

  • 40 species of animals—lions, rhinos, forest hogs, leopards, colobus monkeys, elands, bongo, elephants, etc., and more than 200 bird species. Noted as a rhino sanctuary.

Access:	•Open the year round, 215 km (133 mi.) north of Nairobi and 17 km (10.5 mi.) from the town of Nyeri, then through the Ruhuruini, Kiandogoro and Wandare gates; 48 km (30 mi.) from Naivasha on the west, through the Mutubio gate.
Accommodations:	•World-famous Treetops, off the Nyeri-Mweiga Road; Ark Lodge, deep in the mountains; and Kiandogoro Fishing Lodge, where visitors must provide their own bedding and food—nights are cold, with temperatures often below freezing.

Amboseli National Park

Amboseli is located on the Kenya-Tanzania border at an altitude of 1155 m (3790 ft.), under the slopes of Mt. Kilimanjaro, with a size of 390 sq. km (150 sq. mi.). It is one of the oldest parks in Kenya and also suffers the most from the amount of traffic created by its success. Created in 1948, it was turned over to the Maasai in 1961, and then in 1970 a sanctuary around Lake Amboseli was created for wild animals only. In 1977 it became a national park. Five wildlife habitats range from semiarid to wetlands. Amboseli is famous for its dramatic scenery and open plains. Although the image of Amboseli is usually herds of elephants against the rich blue silhouette of 5894 m (19,330 ft.) high Mount Kilimanjaro, there are currently only about 600 elephants left in the park. The unforgettable mass of high Mt. Kilimanjaro dominates the landscape and is recommended for its scenic drama.

Special Features:	•Famous for its spectacular views of Africa's highest peak, snow-capped Mt. Kilimanjaro.
	•Two springs provide year-round water—befitting the Masai meaning of Amboseli—"place of water."
	•Thousands of water fowl and flamingos are attracted to the lakes; there are also elephants and numerous other animals.
Access:	•On-road driving must be observed on the 216 km (134 mi.) network of roads and tracks.
Accommodations:	•The only available stopping place is at Ol Tukai.

Arabuki Sokoke National Park

A tiny 6 sq. km (2.3 sq. mi.) park established in 1990, located in Kilifi.

Special Features:	•Coastal tropical forests, birds, elephants.
Accommodations:	•Malindi, Watamu Hotels.

Chyulu Hills National Park

Established in 1983 in the Chyulu Hills, the park is 471 sq. km (182 sq. mi.) in size.

Special Features:	•Many unique scenic features, including volcanic geology, and high tropical plants.

•Animal life encompasses giraffes, elephants, lions, monkeys, buffalo and crocodiles at Umanyi Springs, and a rich variety of bird life. The Western slopes outside the park are a game conservation area.

Access: •Entered via Tsavo on the west, on the Amboseli-Tsavo road, or from Makutano or Kibwezi.

Accommodations: •There are no facilities within the park, but Bonham Camp in the northwest organizes horseback trips into the Park.

Kakamega National Park

Kakamega is centrally located in western Kenya, includes Mount Elgon and Saiwa Swamp National Parks near Kitale, Ndere Island National Park near Kisumu, and Ruma National Park; was consolidated in 1985.

Special Features: •Offers a canopy of tropical rain forest, generations old, stretching from Central Africa into the Rift Valley.

•Popular among bird-watchers and nature-lovers, with 330 species of birds, and 145 that are unique to the forest. Many rare butterflies, some of which have never been identified.

•Wildlife includes many species of monkeys and baboons, over 30 varieties of snakes—for example, the deadly Gaboon viper, Jameson's mamba and the black mamba. Bushpigs, civets, clawless otters, the ground pangolin, and occasional porcupines are to be seen.

•Many huge, ancient indigenous trees; orchids in abundance.

Access: •The gate is located 2 km (1.2 mi.) off the main Kakamega-Webuye Road, 20 km (12 mi.) from the town of Kakamega.

Accommodations: •KWS self-service camp 1 km (0.6 mi.) from the Park; Kakamega Golf Hotel with many amenities; Forest Hotel in Kakamega town; campsites in the southwest part of the forest.

Kisite Marine National Park

Kisite was established in 1978 in the Kwale district on the south coast, 90 km (56 mi.) from Mombasa, 8 km (5 mi.) from Shimoni, next to Wasini, 28 sq. km (10.8 sq. mi.) of park and, and 11 sq. km (4.2 sq. mi.) of marine park.

Special Features: •The most colorful coral gardens in East Africa.

•The nearby Pemba Channel fishing grounds are world-famous for marlin, tuna, and sailfish. Colorful coral fish, dolphin, mackerel and bonito are common.

•Marine and land birds, such as fish eagle, albatross, gulls, herons, storks and ibis.

•Historic caves used by slave traders are easily accessible.

Access:	•From Shimoni there is a road of 15 km (9 mi.); also shows and motorized boats to Kisite leave daily from the Shimoni jetty.
Accommodations:	•In addition to the Pemba Channel Fishing Club, there are facilities at Shimoni, Wasini Island and Funzi Island.

Kora National Park

Kora has a common boundary with the southeastern border of Meru National Park, and stretches for 65 km along Kenya's largest river, the Tana. Comprising 1700 sq. km (656 sq. mi.), the park was designated a national reserve in 1973.

Special Features:	•The reserve became a national park in 1989 after the death of "Lion Man" George Adamson. He and his game warden brother, Terence, founded the reserve.
	•There is a great wealth of animal, bird and plant life for the discerning naturalist.
	•The river presents an area of exceptional beauty with a scattering of acacia trees and doum palms.
	•Many kinds of antelopes, along with crocodiles, giraffes, ostriches, oryx and buffalo are prevalent.
Access:	•Permission to visit the Park must be obtained from the KWS headquarters at Lang'ata, Nairobi.
	•An easy approach to the park is at the extreme eastern end at Mojo on the Tana River, where the KWS park is located.
	•Campsites.

Lake Nakuru National Park

Lake Nakuru was established in 1961, this 186 sq. km (72 sq. mi.) park is situated in the Rift Valley south of Lake Nakuru at an altitude of 1753–2073 m (5750–6800 ft.). Created as a bird sanctuary, it features more than 400 species of birds, many from Europe and East Asia. The park was expanded in 1974 to include a large savanna area to the south. A shallow blue-green alkaline lake famous for its flocks of pink lesser and greater flamingos and 450 bird species. The *tilapia grahami* fish has been introduced to provide food for the pelicans who also call Lake Nakura home.

The blue-green color is because of the presence of blue-green algae called *spirulinga*. The level of the lake goes up and down with the amount of rainfall and the color is dependent on the conditions for the growth of algae. There have been up to two million flamingos on the lake at one time. When disturbed the birds lift gracefully into the air in a solid moving pink carpet.

Nakura has proven to be an excellent and safe sight for the Rothschild giraffe and black rhino. Usually a lunch stop on most safari itineraries, there is much to see along the shore. It is an excellent spot to photograph hippo, reedbuck, Defassa waterbuck and giraffe. It is also unique for its forests of cactuslike Euphorbia trees.

Special Features:	•World famous for its countless flamingos; also 450 species of other birds.
	•High concentration of waterbuck; the park is also a sanctuary for black and white rhinos.
	•The park is a "Ramsar" site—an area of international importance where wetlands are protected; there are also two educational resource centers.
Access:	•Three gates to the park are reached by air and by road off the Nairobi-Nakuru road.
Accommodations:	•Two hotels and camp sites are situated in the park; hotels are located in the town of Nakuru.

Lake Turkana National Park

Central Island

An island park located between the northern and southern shores of Lake Turkana, only five sq. km in area; established in 1983.

Special Features:	•The island is actually a dormant volcano that occasionally emits sulphurous steam and smoke. It is a symbolic relic of the massive upheavals that occurred in the earth's crust 10 million years ago, opening a huge geological divide stretching over 3500 miles from Ethiopia's northern Red Sea coastline to Mozambique, and that is now known as the Great Rift Valley.
	•The island is uninhabited, and is famous as a breeding ground for crocodiles. Lake Turkana, which is Africa's largest Rift Valley lake, has the world's record population of over 10,000 crocodiles. The lake is also noted for being the only known location of a genetically pure species of tilapia.
Access:	•An hour's boat ride from Lake Turkana's Fishing Lodge near Kalokoi on the western shore. Kalokoi is reachable fro Kitale, via Lodwar, by air or motor.
	•The remote but world-famous Sibiloi National Park, source of the historic findings of early man, can be reached by boat or air from Kalokoi, 48 km (30 mi.) across the lake.

South Island

Special Features:	•This island, along with a third known as North Island, offer some of the most remote, ruffed and windswept spots on the planet.
	•Uninhabited except by birds, snakes and crocodiles, it is occasionally visited by fisherman and particularly hardy adventurers.
	•Volcanic vents, rising 1000 feet above the lake, emit a ghostly luminous glow at night.

Access:	•The island features a "bush" airstrip, and is also accessible by boat from Loyangalani Lodge on the southeastern shore of the lake.

Malindi and Watamu Marine Parks

This area was established in 1979 and declared a "Biosphere," is among the four biospheres in Kenya. Located on the Malindi-Watamu shoreline, 199 km (123 mi.) from Mombasa.

Special Features:	•Hundreds of species of fish, including huge groupers and rock cod, and some not yet identified, abound in a bewildering variety of shapes and colors.
	•Numerous categories of marine fauna, flora and shells, and three main types of coral.
	•Glass-bottom boats are available at the park entrance, and scuba diving and fishing are popular.
	•Big Three-Caves lie at the mouth of Mida Creek, Watami.
	•Tidal wetlands are a mecca for crustacea, palearctic waders and crab plover.
	•Whale Island features the world's largest nesting site of the roseate tern; nearby are the Gedi ruins.
Access:	•By air from Nairobi, or by road from Mombasa.
Accommodations:	•Beach cottages and hotels are in the town.

Malkamari National Park

Located in Mandera, 876 sq. km (338 sq. mi.), established in 1989.

Marsabit National Park

Marsabit was established in in 1940, the park is 360 sq. km.

Special Features:	•Mt. Marsabit is 1000 m (3280 ft.) high.
	•Lake Paradise and Little Lake, an indigenous forest and a desert combine to produce the most compelling landscape on earth.
	•Elephants and Greater Kudu abound.
Access:	•In a powerful vehicle, the road from Isiolo to Marsabit is tolerable. Another route is via Lake Turkana through the blisteringly hot Chalbi Desert on the west side of Marsabit.
Accommodations:	•Lodges are prevalent all the way form Naro Moru to Lake Turkana, with gas available in the major towns.

Meru National Park

Meru is an 870 sq. km (336 sq. mi.) park, located in the Eastern Province, north of Mt. Kenya, formed in 1966. The park's altitude ranges significantly, 1036–3040 m (3400–9970ft.). The park was made famous by the books of writer and painter Joy Adamson and later by her surrogate daughter, Elsa the lioness, the star of *Born Free*. Rarely visited, the thorny bushland with riverine forests offers the visitor a quiet and unfrequent-ed corner of Kenya. The unusual doum and raffia palm are found here as well as ostrich, gerenuk, lion, leopard and elephant. The park is hot, lonely and best visited during the dry months when the game concentrates around the northwest plains with its marshes and year-round rivers. Meru is a good choice if you are looking for gerenuk or the lesser kudu *(Tragelaphus imberbis)*. Meru is also a good spot for the more sedentary sight of giant baobobs.

Baobobs *(Adansonia digitata)* are constantly under siege by hungry elephants who will spend hours carefully stripping the bark from the trees to get at the tender pulp inside. Elephants also like to search for the nuts of the doum palm. *(Hyphaene coriacea)*.

Special Features:	• Situated on the Equator, with a great range of vegetation—forests, savannahs, and dry scrub traversed by many streams. The Tana River forms the eastern border.
	• The home of Joy and George Adamson, of "Born Free" and "Living Free" fame.
Access:	• Drive around Mt. Kenya to the town of Meru on the mountain's northern slope to within 35 km of the park's Murera gate.
Accommodations:	• Leopard Self-Service Lodge on a very attractive riverside setting—but watch out for crocodiles! Rooms have kitchens and verandahs. Linen, cutlery, gas and electric light are available.
	• Kenya Wildlife Service campsites: On the Bwathorongi River, four clearings with eight sights, each with a lockup Banda and stand-pipes, and a communal shower. Sites can be secured by paying a nonrefundable deposit for a maximum of seven nights for one party. Firewood is provided. Definitely a camper's paradise!

Mount Elgon National Park

Established in 1968, Mount Elgon is a 169 sq. km (65 sq. mi.) park on the Kenya-Uganda border. Mount Elgon is an extinct volcano. Its 4300 m (14,100 ft.) high peak is actually in Uganda. Wet montane forest and the fantasylike afro-alpine moorlands are Mt Elgon's claim to fame. Koitobas (flat topped basalt columns, like Alberta's hoo doos) and lava tube caves are also unique to this mountainous region. Elephants have entered the Kitum cave every two to three days since recorded history to dig out the salt with their tusks. Many people believe that the elephants actually dug the 200-meter-long caves since they have no qualms entering the dark caves in herds to eat the salt.

Large forests of Podocarpus and Juniper are found as well.

Special Features:	• Unspoiled mountain forest, home to over 200 elephants, buffalo, leopards, colobus and blue monkeys, the giant forest hog, water-buck and many species of antelope; over 240 species of birds.

- Four explorable caves—Ngwarisha, Makinyen, Chepnyalil and Kitum, which is known as the place of ceremonies, and extends 200 m (656 ft.) into the mountain. The latter is safe during the day, but at night the elephants enter to feed off the rich deposits.
- Mountain climbing on Mt. Elgon (4300 m/14100 ft.) at Koitobos, features a moorland and hot springs.
- The Kitale Museum is located in Kitale town.

Access:
- A signposted road network approaches to within 15 km (9.3 mi.) of the Park.

Accommodations:
- Guest House on Mills Farm, four public campsites, Kitale Club in Kitale town, and Mt. Elgon Lodge.

Mount Kenya National Park

This highland national park was established in 1949, consisting of 71,500 hectares (176,600 acres) above 3200 m (10,500 ft.) and 130,000 hectares (321,100 acres) of forest preserve.

Special Features:
- From the mountaintop on a clear day one can see Mt. Kilimanjaro to the south., Mt. Elgon to the west, Marsabit Mountain to the north, and the Indian Ocean to the east.
- A motor road goes halfway up the mountain to a popular picnic site, amid towering forests of podo, cedar and dense bamboo.
- Of interest to the botanist, rare plants grow 100 times bigger than in a garden! Big game abounds.
- Home of the Kikuyu God, Ngai.
- Best weather is from January 1 through March 15, and from August 1 through October 15; April and May are bad.
- Day trips are best made in the morning.
- Walking alone is forbidden; guides are recommended. Some not accustomed to high altitudes may experience headaches over 3300 m (11,000 ft.).

Access:
- Contact tour experts: Savage Wilderness, Tropical Ice, and Bushbuck Adventures.

Accommodations:
- Mt. Kenya Safari Club, Mountain Lodge, Naro Moru River Lodge, Bantu Lodge, Mt. Kenya Meru Bandas at Chogoria, Teleki Valley.
- Dozens of climbing huts, camps and caves. Camping is permitted at any gate, road head, mountain track, main route, or near any hut.

Mount Longonot and Hell's Gate National Parks

An extinct volcanic cone on the southern side of Lake Naivashu. Thrusting straight out of the rift valley floor, the cone is home to a wide variety of birds and wildlife. The leleshwa tree is found here in abundance—the Maasai tuck the leaves of the leleshwa under their arms to use the leaves as a deodorant. Hell's Gate, 68.5 sq. km (26.4 sq. mi.) at an altitude of 2777 m (9110 ft.), established in 1984, and Longonot, 52.1 sq. km (20.1 sq. mi.), founded in 1983, are located at Naivasha in the Nakuru District. Also known as Njorowa Gorge, Hell's Gate offers one of the most scenic and exciting walks in Kenya leading through a gorge lined with sheer, red cliffs. Fischer's Tower is a challenging rock climb and home to colonies of rock hyrax or *dassies*. Excellent for succulents, birds of prey and other bird species.

Special Features:	• Ol-Njorowa Gorge in Hell's Gate.
	• Obsidian black glass rock is found everywhere.
	• Mt. Longonot, an extinct volcano of great geological significance, is 3321 m (10,890 ft.) high, and being easy to climb, does not require complex equipment.
	• Hot springs and steam seep through vents in the solidified lava.
	• Home to more than 300 bird species, buffalo, lions, elands, leopards and antelopes.
Access:	• Via the Narasha, Olkaria or main Elsa gates.
Accommodations:	• The Lake Naivasha Hotel, the Safariland Hotel, Elsamere, Longonot Game Ranch, and two campsites in Hell's Gate. Carry clean drinking water.

Nairobi National Park

Established in 1946, 117 sq. km (45.2 sq. mi.) park in the Lang'ata area of Nairobi. One of the last bastions of the rhino just eight miles south of downtown Nairobi. Good spot for cats. No elephants due to the lack of food and danger to nearby civilization but the impressive number of large mammals and the 500 species of birdlife make this an excellent day trip from Nairobi. Primarily savanna or plains at an altitude of 1533–1760 m (5025–5770 ft.), there are areas of highland forest, acacia and riverine environments. Few people realize that the park is not entirely enclosed and that animals migrate into and out of the park with the rainy seasons. The best time to visit is at the height of the dry season. Animals will usually be found near the Mbagathi River and near the artificial dams created. If you are a birder, visit during the wet season. The park maintains an orphanage which can provide some interesting photo opportunities not available in some of the larger parks.

Special Features:	• Over 100 species of animals: rhino under 24-hour surveillance, lions, cheetahs; over 400 bird species including helmeted guinea fowl, francolins, kori, white and black-bellied bustards, quelea turacos, mousebirds and ostriches. In March and early April, European marsh and pallied harriers move northward overhead, and flocks of migrating common kestrel. Also game birds and birds of prey.
Access:	• Five gates; the main gate is on the Lang'ata road opposite the Lang'ata Cemetery.

Accommodations: • No camping sites because of the proximity to the city, but there are six picnic sites.

Ndere Island National Park

Nestled on the northern shore of Lake Victoria's Winam Gulf, a volcano-inflicted break in a 1000 km meandering shoreline. Established in 1986, the park is 4.2 sq. km (1.6 sq. mi.).

Special Features: • According to Luo legend, Ndere (meeting place) is where Miyaki, the mother of the tribe, rested after her long journey down the Nile Valley.
• Home of the impala and elusive swamp antelopes.
• Lush vegetation has attracted a wide variety of birdlife.
• Large crocodiles and hippos, with many water fowl and a rich aquatic life.

Access: • From Kisumu there is an all-weather road to Ndere.
• At Kaloka a KWS ranger post will look after your car and arrange for a sese canoe to take you to the island. The island can also be reached from the Rusinga Island Club.

Ol Donyo Sabuk National Park

In Masai and Kilimambogo, the name of this 207 sq. km (80 sq. mi.) park established in 1967 means "mountain of the buffalo." Situated 85 km (53 mi.) north of Nairobi at an altitude of 1524–2134 m (5000–7000 ft.).

Special Features: • Final resting place of the famous hunter and philanthropist Sit William Northrup McMillan.
• A paradise for hikers, sightseers, campers and nature lovers, with a clear view of Nairobi and other lowlands.
• Buffalo, colobus monkeys, baboons, bushbuck, impala and duiker can be seen; there is abundant birdlife.

Access: • Steep but motorable in a 4-wheel drive vehicle all the way to the summit, 2145 m (7035 ft.).

Accommodations: • Available in nearby Thika or Nairobi.

Ruma National Park

Situated in the Lambwe Valley, 45 km (28 mi.) from Rusinga Island Lodge, a game reserve since 1966, and a national park of 120 sq. km since 1983.

Special Features: • An uncrowded, exquisitely beautiful nature sanctuary with the rare oribi and Bohor's reedbuck, jackson's hartebeest, topi, impala, the Rothschild giraffe, and leopards. The only park in Kenya with herds of roan antelope.

- A savannah and riverine forest, with the Kanyamwa escarpment along the eastern border.

- Beautiful hills, ideal for walking, exploring, and fishing for Nile perch.

Access:
- 40 km of good road network. Can be reached from Homa Bay.

- 4-wheel drive is essential in the wet months of mid-April to mid-July.

Accommodations:
- Public campsites are at the main Kamgwage gate and Rusinga Island Camp; or at the Homa Bay Hotel in town.

Roan Antelope

Saiwa Swamp National Park

Established in 1974, located between Mt. Elgon and the spectacular Cherangani Hills, the park is less than 8 sq. km (3 sq. mi.) at 1880 m (6165 ft.). One of the tiniest national parks in Kenya and the last domain of about 100 sitatunga antelope. Swampy vegetation is also home to giant forest squirrel, spotted necked otter and nocturnal potto. The sitatunga are slowly increasing in number and spend their day half submerged in the floating plants. Brazza's monkey can be found in small numbers here.

Special Features:
- Mecca of over 370 species of birds.
- Best viewing place in Africa of the rare and unique swamp antelope (sitatunga).
- Among rare birds identified are the Madagascar squacco heron, the scope owl, the Mariquee sunbird, the swamp flycatcher and Ross's turaco.
- The cape clawlee, spotted neck otters and the DeBrazza monkey are common.

Access:
- 6 km (3.7 mi.) off the main Kitale-Kapenguria-Lodwar-Lake Turkana road.

Accommodations:
- Sitatunga Safaris—the Barnley farmhouse, 12 km (7.4 mi.) from Saiwa.

Sibiloi National Park

Located on the northeastern shore of Lake Turkana close to the Ethiopian border; established in 1973. The park measures 1570 sq. km (606 sq. mi.) and is the most remote KWS-managed wildlife area in Kenya—an arid region of doum palms and yellow spear grass on the eastern shores of Lake Turkana. A crocodile population of about 12,000 (called the largest population of crocs in the world) can be found on the crater filled Central Island. Also home to the Koobi Fora paleontological site and museum. Not very popular due to its proximity to the Ethiopian border and lack of accommodations.

Special Features:
- Most famous for discoveries in the late '60s and early '70s of fossils of early man—*homo habilis* and *homo erectus*—between one–three million years old, by Dr. Richard Leaky and other researchers, including Kamoya Kimeu. Since then, it has yielded the world's richest finds of *hominids*, 160 in all.
- The area, together with Olduvai, in northern Tanzania, is recognized as having unlocked man's earliest known origins and also as being the original area from which modern man spread to inhabit the five continents of the world over 200,000 years ago.
- Thousands of prehistoric mammal fossils and early human artifacts have been uncovered within the park's boundaries.
- Koobi Fora, site of the world-famous prehistoric museum and research base is within the park.

• Great herds of zebra, topi, lion, cheetah, leopard, kudu and other lesser species abound.

Access:
• Either by boat from Kalokoi 48.3 km across the lake on the western shore, by air or by road via Maralal and Loyangalani; or by a northern route, via Isiolo and Marsabit.

Tsavo East National Park

Divided into three parts by the Tiva and Galana rivers. The South (between the main Nairobi-Mombasa road and the Galana River). The North (centered on the Tiva River) and The Middle (centered on the Galana River). Encompasses 1.1 million hectares (2.7 million acres), and was established in 1948. Much of Kenya's largest national park is a hot waterless region with a large diversity of landscapes. Less than 51 cm (20 in.) of rain falls per year on this dry region. Whether it's the rocky gorges of Lugard Falls with its water carved rocks or the natural catchment at Mudanda Rock between Voi and Manyani, there are many dramatic sights for the explorer. Large mammals including elephant, antelope, hippos, black rhino, giraffe and eland are the primary reason to visit Tsavo. Tsavo was the original sight of the big game hunters in search of record setting ivory; Dennis Finch-Hatton and Baron Bror von Blixen popularized Tsavo. The great tuskers of yesterday began to decline due to attracted poachers and in the great drought of 1970–71 reduced the elephants to a population of under 4500. The great herds of elephants were counted at 35,000 in 1973. The rhino that are left are kept in a gated area near Ngulia Hill. Do not plan on seeing Tsavo in the usual two to three days allowed most parks. If you must choose between east and west, remember Tsavo West has the most dramatic scenery and is the best choice.

Special Features:
• Big five of the common carnivores, antelope and other ungulates, riverine animals, birdlife, lesser kudu and klipsringer.
• The greatest of all of Kenya's national parks.
• In the middle section, many rock and cave paintings.
• Ideal for exclusive camping, game circuits and walks of an adventurous nature.
• A prime field study center.

Access:
• Voi, Bachuma, Manuani, or Mtito Andei.
• North of Galana, 4-wheel drive vehicles are required.
• All roads are passable between February–March and June–October.
• River crossing points at Sala and Lugard Falls.
• All crossings subject to warden's consent.

Accommodations:
• Public campsites at Sala and Voi.
• Tsavo Inn at Mtito Andei.
• Tsavo Tsafari (via Mtito).
• Bush Whackers (via Kibwezi).
• Ndala Ranch, south of Voi.

Tsavo West National Park

Bordered by Taita Hills to the east, Tanzania to the southwest, Loitokitok to the west, Mtito Andei to the north and Athi River to the northeast. Established in 1948, size is 9065 sq. km (3499 sq. mi.).

Special Features:
- Mzima springs, Shaitani Lava flow (caves, three craters, basalt flows, lava splashes), Cheimu Crater, Tembo Peak, Roaring Rocks, Lake Jipe, Ndi Hills and graphite, marble and sulphite deposits.
- Big five, numerous carnivores, most gazelles and more. More than 150 bird species.
- Contains Ngulia Rhino Sanctuary.

Access:
- All weather airstrip at Kamboyo Park headquarters.
- Gates at Mtito, Tsavo, Chyulu, Ziwani, Mbuyni, Jipe, Maktau and Kasigau.

Accommodations:
- Lodges at Kilaguni, Ngulia and Jipe.
- Bandas at Ngulia and Kitani.
- Tsavo Inn (Mtito) and Ndara Ranch (near Kasigau).
- Special and public campsites.

Bush Duiker

South Turkana
Nasolot
Kamnarok
Kerio Valley
Kakamega

Lake Bogoria
Buffalo Springs
Masai Mara
Mwea

Losai
Samburu
Shaba
Bisandi
Rahole
North Kitui
Arawale
Boni
Dodori
Tana River
South Kitui
Shimba Hills

National Reserves

Nature and Forest Reserves

Managed by the Forest Department, these areas are not as strictly controlled but are equally as important. Most people do not realize that the most famous game area in Kenya is not a national park but a nature preserve.

Arawale National Reserve

Established in 1974 at Garissa, 380 sq. km (147 sq. mi.) in size at 85–100 m (280–330 ft.) above sea level. Hunter's hartebeest or the hirole seems to prefer the thorny bushland of Arawale on the eastern banks of the Tana River. There are no accommodations or facilities in this remote part of northeastern Kenya.

Special Feature: • Hirola (Hartebeeste)

Bisanadi National Reserve

Established in Isiolo in 1979, 606 sq. km (234 sq. mi.) in size. Dense riverine forests and swamps surrounded by arid thorny bushland. The park provides a dispersal area for animals from Meru National park in the wet season. The reserve's altitude ranges from 320–660 m (1050–2165 ft.).

Boni National Reserve

Located at Garissa in 1976, 1339 sq. km (517 sq. mi.) in area. Unique coastal lowland groundwater forest in Kenya known for its large numbers of elephants in the dry season. It is also used as a buffer to allow passage to the Dodori National Reserve where the elephants can wade out to Elephant Island at low tide.

Special Feature: • Hirolas (Hartebeeste)

Buffalo Springs National Reserve

Situated at Isiolo, 131 sq. km (50 sq. mi.) in size. established in 1985. Riverine forests of doum palm and acacia at 900–1000 m (2950–3280 ft.).

Special Features: • Giraffes, zebra, plains game.
Accommodations: • Buffalo Springs Lodge, Samburu Serena

Dodori National Reserve

Situated in Lamu, and established in 1976; 877 sq. km (338 sq. mi.). An oceanfront reserve consisting mostly of mangrove swamp, groundwater forest and lowland dry forest provides a breeding ground for topi. Linked with Boni and Kiunga Marine National Reserve. Elephants can be seen wading out to an offshore island at low tide. In the water can be found dugong and green turtle.

Special Feature: • Elephants.

Kakamega National Forest Reserve

Established in 1985 at Kamakega, 44.7 sq. km (17.2 sq. mi.). The easternmost area of Congo-West Africa equatorial rain forest was gazetted in 1985. Excellent area to discover amphibians, primates and mammals. Animals typically found in tropical areas: fruit bats, giant water shrew, colobus monkey and bush tailed porcupine are found in this unusual park. The forest's altitude ranges from 1520–1680 m (4985–5510 ft.).

Special Features: • Elephants
Access: • By Road
Accommodations: • In Bandas only.

Kamnarok National Reserve

At Baringo, established in 1983, 44.7 sq. km (17.2 sq. mi.) in size.

Special Features: • Elephants and crocodiles.
Access: • By road

Kerio Valley National Reserve

Located at Elgeyo Marakwet, established in 1983, 66 sq. km (25.5 sq. mi.) in size.

Special Features: • Elephants and crocodiles.
Access: • By Road

Laikipia National Reserve

Established in 1991, 165 sq. km (64 sq. mi.).

Special Features: • Elephants and plains game.
Access: • By road.

Lake Bogoria National Reserve

Located at Baringo, 107 sq. km (41 sq. mi.) in size, founded in 1970. Bushland and riverine forest at an altitude of 1000–1600 m (3280–5250 ft.). Primarily created to protect the Greater Kudu found on the western slopes of the Laikipia Escarpment. Thermal areas that include steam jets and bubbling springs are another attraction of this area. The water is very hot and the ground around the springs can collapse. Lake Bogoria is a shallow soda lake that is fed by the hot sulfurous springs.

Special Features: • Flamingos, greater kudu, hot springs.
Access: • By road or airstrip at Baringo Road.
Accommodations: • Lake Bogoria Hotel

Losai National Reserve

Established in 1976 in Marsabit, 1806 sq. km (697 sq. mi.) in size at an altitude of 625–1750 m (2050–5740 ft.). Thorny bushland and impenetrable forest once home to rhino.

Special Features: • Elephants and plains game.
Access: • By road or air.

Grant's Gazelle

Masai Mara National Reserve

Gazetted in November, 1974. Located 265 km (164 mi.) from Nairobi, 533 sq. km (206 sq. mi.) in area ranging from 1500–2170 m (4920–7120 ft.) above sea level. Justifiably reserved for the end of most safaris the Mara, as it is called by guides, is the capper in most safari itineraries. The Mara tends to provide spectacular numbers of not only grazers but the cats and other hard to spot animals. The Mara river and the Siria or Oloololo escarpment act like natural boundaries. The Mara also is ideal for photographers with its gently rising flatlands, scenic gorges and dramatic escarpment. The weather in the Mara is also ideal being cool at nights and warm during the day. Dramatic rainshowers sail across the sky and the last golden rays of the sun will turn the Mara into one of the world's most dramatic tableaus. The abundance of predators and wide open spaces also make it one of the few places in Africa where you have a fairly reliable chance of seeing a lion kill if you are patient.

Established in 1961, this is the premiere game preserve now famous for being the most northerly portion of the Great Migration. Between July–October the reserve is home to a quarter of a million zebras and one and a quarter million wildebeests. The Mara is also home to Kenya's largest population of lions. Very popular with tourists and feeling the pressure of too much wildlife. Established in 1961 it shares an unmarked boundary with Tanzania's Serengeti National Park. No human settlement is allowed but the Mara technically belongs to the Maasai who are traditional cattle grazers. The safety of the park and its surroundings attracts unusual numbers of large mammals and predators creating havoc for the Maasai. They complain that the animals that wander out of the park cause death and injury not only to their cattle but to the tribespeople. In the north wheat farms necessary to the sustenance of the nation are also encroaching. The final and most problematic danger may be from the tourists themselves. Hundreds of minivans range all over the park 365 days a year creating stress for the animals and a feeling of being inside a giant zoo which the Mara may one day become.

Special Features: • Plains game, the black-maned lion, wilderbeest.
Access: • By road or airstrip.
Accommodations: • Luxury lodges, tented camps/sites.

Mwea National Reserve

Located in Embu, established in 1976, 68 sq. km (26 sq. mi.), altitude 1000–1100 m (3280–3600 ft.). Thorny brushland and boabob. Few animals but buffalo, lesser kudu and elephant can be spotted.

Special Feature: • Elephants at Masinga Dam.
Access: • By road or air.
Accommodations: • Masinga Lodge

Nasolot National Reserve

Established at West Pokot in 1979, 92 sq. km (36 sq. mi.). Thorny bushland near the Uganda border. Little game due to poaching. Reserve altitude is 750–1500 m (2460–4920 ft.).

Special Feature: •Elephants and crocodiles

Access: •By road

North Kitui National Reserve

Located at Kitui, 745 sq. km (288 sq. mi.) at an altitude of 428–675 m (1400–2215 ft.), founded in 1979. Bushland and riverine forest next to Meru National Park. Good spot for hippo and crocs along the Tana River.

Special Feature: •Elephants

Rahole National Reserve

Located in Garissa, established in 1976, 1270 sq. km (490 sq. mi.). The dry thorny bushland on the north side of the Tana river was an experiment to see how local tribes could coexist with indigenous wildlife. It is known for its scenery but there is little game viewing and no facilities. Altitude 250–480 m (820–1575 ft.).

Special Feature: •Crocodiles

Samburu National Reserve

Established in 1985, 165 sq. km (64 sq. mi.). Arid hilly region with riverine forests at an altitude of 800–1230 m (2620–4035 ft.) along the Nyiro River. Across the river is its twin reserve; Buffalo Springs. Doum palms, acacia *(Acacia albida)* woodland and scrubland create the vast arid look of Samburu. This region is becoming one of Kenya's most popular stops after the Mara. The sight of the strangely branched doum palms create an unusual look to the region. The light and vast openness creates a lonely panoramic beauty. Samburu's popularity is also due to its being only 344 km (213 mi.) from Nairobi or a short air trip from Wilson airport. The permanent water supply acts like a magnet for the numerous species found here. Other animals have adapted to the waterless scrub of Samburu, for example the gerenuk *(Litocranius walleri)* who gently nibbles at the low brush. Gerenuks are always craning for the tender shoots missed by other grazers. In fact *gerenuk* is Afrikaans for long neck. Crocodiles and storks are common sights along the river. The lodge has been baiting leopards across the river for years so leopards will be common. Also the evening feeding of crocodiles affords one of the few chances tourists will have of seeing crocs slithering out of the water to feed on scraps. There is also excellent bird-watching with numerous weaver birds, the marial eagle and the blue legged Somali Ostrich.

Special Features: •Gerenuk, leopards, crocodiles, ostrich, numerous birds

Shaba National Reserve

Established in 1968 at Isiolo., 239 sq. km (92 sq. mi.). Many visitors say Shaba is more dramatic than nearby Samburu but the wildlife is sparser. Landscapes include riverine forests with acacia trees and doum palms. Penny Springs is named after Joy Adamson's leopard Penny. Adamson died here in her Shaba camp in 1980. Altitude 500–700 m (1640–2290 ft.)

Special Features: •Giraffes, zebras, plains game.

Access: •By road or air.

Accommodations: •Shaba Lodge

Shimba Hills National Reserve

Located in the Kwale region of Coast Province, and established in 1968, the reserve measures 192 sq. km (74 sq. mi.). The scenic park just 16 km (10 mi.) inland features *Brachystegia* woodland, coastal bushland, riverine forests and grasslands. Sable antelope are the main attraction here since you won't see them anywhere else in Kenya. There is also elephant, bush pig, waterbuck, reedbuck and warthog. Parklike country with open grasslands is interrupted by coastal rain forest. Roan antelope have been introduced and are doing well. Altitude 120–450 m (390–1475 ft.)

Special Features: •Famous Sheldrick Falls, 25m high. Great stands of tropical forest, rare trees and orchids, antelope, elephants.

•Leopards, elephants, buffalo; the only place in Kenya to see the rare black-maned sable antelope.

Access: •By road from Kwale, Kinango and Mariakani to the reserve entrance. Airstrip at Ukunda Road.

•From Msambweni to the west side of the reserve.

Accommodations: •Park Lodge, Shiba Lodge, deep in the forest, overlooks a water hole. Diani Lodges, self-service bandas are one km from the reserve gate outside Kwale town.

South Kitui National Reserve

Founded in 1979 in Kitui, 1833 sq. km (707 sq. mi.). Bush grasslands and acacia woods. Near the north boundary of Tsavo East National Park. Closed to tourism.

Special Feature: •Elephants

South Turkana National Reserve

Established in Turkana in 1979, 1091 sq. km (421 sq. mi.). Dense thorn bush, riverine forests are home to elephant and greater kudu. Rarely visited due to pressure from Somali poachers. Altitude 900–2270 m (2950–7445 ft.).

Special Feature: •Elephants

Access: •By road.

Baboons

Tana River Primate Reserve

Located on the Tana River, 169 sq. km (65.2 sq. mi.) at an altitude of 40–70 m (130–230 ft.), established in 1976. Rarely visited, the Tana is Kenya's largest river. A small area of riparian forest has been saved from human destruction and to protect the remaining 800 or so crested mangabeys *(Cercocebus galeritus galeritus)* a subspecies of the rare mangabey. Unusual for its population of what should be a typically West African habitat it also protects the rare red colobus *(Colobus badius)*. These are just four of the seven primates found here. The area is one of the few remaining stands of tropical dense forest near the Indian Ocean. The rare Hunter's hartebeest *(Damaliscus hunteri)* has been spotted here on occasion along with 248 bird species.

Special Features: •Maghobeys, yellow colobus monkeys, riverine forest.

Access: •By road or air.

Kiunga
Mombasa
Kisite Mpunguti

Marine Parks

The best time to visit the marine parks is during the dry seasons of January–March or June–October. The rains bring runoff which silts up the coastal areas. The winds and stormy weather can also reduce visibility and make snorkeling uncomfortable.

Kisite Mpunguti Marine Park

11 sq. km (4.2 sq. mi.), established in 1978 at Kwale.

Special Feature: • Coral gardens marine life.
Access: • By road.
Accommodations: • South Coast Lodges, CPK Guest House.

Kiunga Marine Park

250 sq. km (96 sq. mi.), in Lamu, established in 1979.

Special Features: • Elephants, dugongs.
Access: • By road.

Mombasa Marine Park

In Mombasa, 10 sq. km (3.8 sq. mi.), founded in 1986.

Special Feature: • Coral gardens marine life.
Access: • By road.

Game Sanctuaries

Salt Lick Taita Hills Game Sanctuary

Situated on the main Voi-Taita road below the Taita Hills, Salt Lick is linked by a game corridor to Tsavo West National Park. Formerly a sisal plantation, the grasslands and woodlands of the reserve cover 113 sq. km (44 sq. mi.) and now attract zebra, buffalo, waterbuck, reedbuck, impala, eland, gazelle and elephant.

KENYA'S BIOSPHERES, NATIONAL PARKS & NATURE PRESERVES

World Heritage Sites

An international group of important natural and cultural sites. These are administered internationally and have no formal protection or supervision. Fort Jesus, Hell's Gate, the Masai Mara National Reserve and Mount Kenya are examples of important sites.

Ecotourism

In 1971 the management of Bamburi Portland Cement Company approved a rehabilitation proposal for land outside Mombasa that had been stripped bare by extraction of fossils from limestone to make cement. Between 1971 and 1990 more than one million trees of different species were planted on an area of 750 square kilometers turning Bamburi into a man-made paradise. Commercial fish farming was introduced between 1972 and 1982 and crocodile farming got underway in 1990. Bamburi nature trails were introduced to the public in 1985. Many species of wildlife were introduced including crocodiles, hippos, zebras, buffalo, elands, monkeys, snakes and numerous birds. They have thrived in the environment and attracted hundreds of thousands of tourists, putting Bamburi on the map as an important coastal attraction. Phone ☎ *11-4857299* for information on the nature trail.

ANIMALS OF KENYA

For wildlife lovers Kenya has the favorable combination of vast savannas and myriad species. The end result is the feeling that you are literally watching a panoramic display of the food chain in action. Kenya's highly organized tourism industry, comfortable lodges and excellent transportation enable you to visit many different parks and ecosystems in the typical two week safari. One of the real pleasures is checking off wildlife as you dash around the parks taking in more species in a day than most North Americans see in a lifetime. There are more than 100 species of grazers alone, but all visitors will see a wide variety of carnivores, impressive animals like elephant and rhino, hundreds of birds, and myriad reptiles, insects and amphibians. We would refer you to more in depth tomes if your interest is serious wildlife study but for the casual observer here are the common residents of Kenya's major game parks. The animals are listed by their common name, scientific name and, for fun, their Swahili name (so you can impress your driver and friends back home). The following is an alphabetical listing.

Antelope, Roan

Hippotragus equinus
KORONGO

A large horselike antelope found in small herds and identified by the male's and female's thick, backswept and heavily ridged horns (the males being the larger). The roan antelope is not common but can be seen in the Shimba Hills preserve. Lighter than the smaller Sable antelope. The coat is short and smooth and the ears are long and narrow. The tail reaches the heels, the lower half tasseled.

Antelope, Sable

Hippotragus niger
PALA HALA

Owner of the most dramatic horns found on an antelope, the sable survives by using its massive horns to fend off predators. Dark colored, and found in herds of up to 30 animals. Can be found in savanna woodland and grassland. They eat grasses and only need water about once every two days. The upper body is usually chestnut brown to black with the facial mask pattern mimicking the body color.

Baboon

Papio cynocephalus
NYANI

There are seven subspecies of baboon but the yellow and the olive baboon (*papio anubis*) are the most common. Yellow baboons are the most common in East and Central Africa; the olive prefers the cooler highland areas of East Africa. Baboons are gregarious and obnoxious in many of the parks. Some sit patiently waiting for the tour buses to leave in the morning and then throw a fit if they do not receive food. They live and travel in large groups of up to 150, sleep in trees and are the favorite food of the leopard.

Bongo

Tragelaphus euryceros
BONGO

A rare and interesting antelope seen in dense forest and near water. The bongo will stand on its hind legs and dig with its horns. Solitary, shy and an impressive photo for any visitor. They are found in the densest primary and secondary forests, bushy and bamboo jungles in plains up to 4000m. At night they may leave dense cover to browse in clearings and plantations. The bongo's chief enemy is the leopard.

Buffalo Weaver

Dinemellia dinemelli (white–headed)
Bubalonis niger (red–billed)

These gregarious birds create the thousands of woven nests hanging from the acacia and baobab trees in the more arid areas. These very noisy 10" tall birds make sounds ranging from the loud falsetto croaking and chattering calls of the red–billed buffalo weavers, to the harsh parrot–like calls and chattering of the white–headed variety. They are common in Tanzania, Kenya and northeastern Uganda. Often seen in areas of thornbush.

Bushbuck

Tragelaphus scriptus
PONGO

A rather large, dull and commonly seen member of the antelope family. Bushbucks are nocturnal, solitary and will flee through the bush when surprised. Despite its size the bushbuck is a favorite prey of pythons who strangle and then can consume a smaller animal whole. Averaging about 30"–36" high at the shoulder the bushbuck can usually be found in forests, riverine thickets and bush where they have plenty of thick cover.

Cape Buffalo

Syncerus caffer
Mʙᴏɢᴏ

To hunters the wounded male mbogo is the most dangerous of the big five (lion, leopard, elephant, rhino and buffalo). Solitary male cape buffalos are known for their bad temper and unpredictable ability to charge vehicles when they come too close. Found near water the buffalo is made even more dangerous by its habit of surprising campers who seek water after dark. One hint is when walking in dense brush listen for the distinctive chirp of the ever-present tick birds.

Cheetah

Acinonyx jubatus
Dᴜᴍᴀ

Elegant, calm and determined, the cheetah can surprise many a visitor by its utter disregard of humans by using vehicles as lookouts. Leopard-size in body, they are greyhound shaped except the head which is short–muzzled, small and rounded, with ears short and roundish. The cheetah uses its speed to overtake and trip prey. Cubs are a common sight since they stay with the mother for an entire season. Lions, leopards and hyenas will often kill and eat young cheetahs; sometimes they will also attack the adults.

Crocodile, Nile

Crocodylus niloticus
Mᴀᴍʙᴀ

Although the crocodile has undergone the same persecution as his prehistoric friend the rhino, it seems that they have stabilized in fair numbers in the parks. Once hunted for shoes, belts and handbags, the crocodile is found in the lower riverine regions of Kenya. The five meter (16.5 feet) crocodiles still consume numbers of unwary Kenyans every year. They sit patiently submerged in waterholes waiting for prey to bend down to drink, then leap out of the water and drag the kicking victim to death. They literally tear the victim to pieces and then stuff the chunks in their dens at the side of rivers. Be careful approaching any river or any riverbank. Two other smaller species of crocodile are found in East Africa, the long–nosed and the dwarf crocodile, but neither is dangerous to man.

Dik Dik, Kirk's

Rhynchotragus kirki

Dɪᴋ Dɪᴋ

Kirk's is the smallest antelope found in Kenya's arid regions. (Guenthers dik dik is found in the Marsabit) They have no need of drinking water and can be found around the base of hills and kopjes. They often stand on their hind feet to get at succulent branches. The dik dik is easy to identify by its diminutive size and gentle shy demeanor. Their calls of excitement, warning and fear are a ringing "Zick–zick," hence the name Dik Dik. Mates become life partners living together with latest and previous young. Enemies include all larger predators as well as some monitor lizards and large snakes.

Duiker, Common

Sylvicapra grimmia

Nꜱʏᴀ

Found in dense brush or woodlands, usually nocturnal. Females are larger than males. When agitated will snort and wheeze. Found in many different ecosystems ranging from montane bamboo forests to arid lowlands. The bush duiker is reportedly faster than the forest duiker. It often outruns and outdodges dogs while dashing between hiding places.

Eagle, Tawny
Aquilla rapax

They are often seen along the rivers. Nests are made in the tops of trees. The tawny eagle often associates with vultures and can be seen at recent kills and around camps. They can vary between dark brown to light coffee in color (a more common sight in Northern Kenya) and have a relatively short, rounded tail, with legs feathered. Their voice sounds like a raucous, yelping cry. Found throughout East Africa but most frequently in northern Kenya.

Eland, Common
Taurotragus oryx
Pofu

The largest antelope identified by its long curving horns. Usually found grazing in the early part of the day in small herds of 5–50 animals. It avoids swamps, forests and deserts. Eland use the same water conservation measures as gazelles and oryxes to cope in waterless areas. They access high foliage by breaking off branches with their horns. Their greatest predators are lions and spotted hyena.

Elephant, African
Loxodonta africana
Tembo

The future of elephant is one of the major issues of African wildlife preservation. Facing few predators, most elephants used to die from poachers' bullets before they reached an old age. Today their wide range, massive food consumption and limited area makes them incredibly destructive on every habitat they thrive in. The great herds of the '50s are gone but the elephant is resilient. Poaching has insured that the giant tuskers of the northern part of Kenya have been genetically culled from Africa. Elephants are matriarchal and are found in close knit herds, while the old cranky bulls can be found wandering in solitude. The elephant must stay on the move to find the 250 kg of green material it needs to consume to survive every day. Elephants will push over or pull down large trees to get at the high branches. They also love domestic crops and can destroy acres of corn, bananas or sugarcane in one night. The long life (over 100 years) and wide ranging nature of elephants are a growing problem in the Masai Mara where many Masai are killed by elephants every year.

Flamingo

Phoenicopterus ruber
HEROE

Lesser Flamingos are a much smaller and richly colored species. They can be identified by the dark carmine colored bill. They consume the algae and diatoms found in the warm shallow lakes like Lake Nakura and other water areas. The greater flamingo is a bottom feeder and also eats molluscs and crustaceans. Much larger and paler than the lesser flamingo, it is easily distinguished by its paler pink bill. Both types are commonly found on alkaline lakes throughout East Africa, but are very infrequent visitors to coastal areas.

Gazelle, Grant's

Gazella granti
SWALA GRANTI

This large, commonly seen gazelle can be found going against the traditional migration patterns of the East African plains. They can be found in short glass plains during the dry season and the savanna woodlands in the rainy season. December–February and August–September is the best time for calves. They do not need to drink at water holes to survive and are usually in herds of 10–30 animals.

Gazelle, Thomson's

Gazella thomsoni

SWALA TOMI

Probably the most frequently encountered gazelle in Kenya game parks. "Tommies" are found in large groups on the Serengeti and move between the woodlands savanna and the floodplains every year. They survive well because they can feed closer to ground than the larger grazers like the wildebeest. Tommies also will go to water when available. During very dry periods they can be found in herds of over 400 animals. The young are commonly stalked by lions, cheetahs and leopards.

Genet

Genetta genetta

KANU

A nocturnal animal rarely spotted since it prefers rocks and trees as its habitat. Genets are good climbers, especially downward. They defend themselves by catlike arching of the back, erecting hair on the tail and spinal crest, and scratching and biting while on their back. They also eject an evil smelling anal secretion. Genets feed on small rodents, birds, lizards, snakes, frogs, eggs, insects, spiders, seafood and fruit.

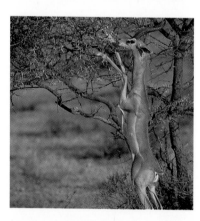

Gerenuk

Litocranius walleri

SWALA TWIGA

Found in the arid north of Kenya the gerenuk can be recognized by its giraffe-like features. It is commonly seen feeding by standing on its hind legs and nibbling at acacia bushes. One of the most desert-adapted antelopes, it prefers open landscapes. Wedge-shaped hooves, powerful lower limbs and modified lumbar vertebrae allow gerenuks to stand bipedally and graze high up more securely than other antelopes.

Giraffe

Giraffa tippelskirchi (Masai)
Giraffa reticulata (Reticulated)
TWIGA

There are three subspecies of giraffe in Kenya. The Masai with its softer pattern is the most common and found in the parks south and west of Nairobi. The Reticulated has more clearly defined patches and is darker in color. They are common in the north in more arid parks like Samburu and Buffalo Springs. The Rothschild giraffe from Uganda is the rarest and the tallest and is now only found in Lake Nakura (they were introduced by AFEW). They lose their white socks and five horns when interbred with Masai or Reticulated giraffes. Giraffes feed on acacia leaves and are able to pick between the needle sharp thorns. They feed in the early morning and late in the day. During the heat of the day they can be found sitting or standing in the shade. Males are larger than females and although adults have few predators, it is not uncommon to see claw marks and torn tails from hungry lions.

Guinea Fowl

Numida mitrata

The guinea fowl look like well dressed dowagers rushing to a linen sale. Common in bush country, arid thorn-bush areas, neglected cultivation, open parklike country and savanna woodlands. The helmeted guinea-fowl (*Numida meleagres*) is about 20" high and makes a loud cackling call. The attractive spotted plumage is offset by the bird's scabby blue head and bony horn. A series of loud, shrill cackles and a loud "kak, kak, kak, kak, kak" is the typical call you'll hear.

Hartebeest

Alcelaphus buselaphus

Kongoni

Found along the edge of woodlands and longer grasslands the hartebeast have shorter horns than most antelopes. Their long horselike faces make them easy to identify. Males are darker with more pronounced markings than females. Calves are pale tan without markings. Males often stay with their mothers until sub–adults (2.5 years) before joining bachelor herds. Found in the savanna regions, the hartebeest must drink at least once a day or feed on melons and tubers during dry seasons. Socially they mix with zebra and wildebeest.

Hippopotamus

Hippopotamus amphibius

Kiboko

Ugly, ungainly and never far from water, hippos are the overweight denizens of the savanna. Most people are shocked to discover that the hippo is the largest killer of humans in East Africa. Tourists are even more surprised to find out that hippos are commonly found wandering around campsites at night when they come up to graze. Hippos like to live in herds of 10–50 animals and spray their droppings on the rocks around the waterholes and in the water flipping their tails around in a fanlike motion to get maximum coverage. They also can be found fighting to establish dominance. Their razor sharp tusks often rip large gashes in their soft pink skin. Known to inhabit lakes, rivers and swamps with sufficient water, hippos also may be observed under ideal conditions in the crystal clear waters of Mzima Springs in the Tsavo National Park, Kenya.

Hornbills (Red/Yellow-billed)

Tockus erythrorhynchus/flavirostris
TOKOS

The gregarious hornbill is famous for being a prototypal chauvinist bird. The male seals the incubating female into a large nesting hole in a dead tree. The male then feeds the female and the young through a small opening. When old enough to fly, the offspring and the female chip their way out. These medium to large birds average between 17"–20" tall. Hornbills are characterized by their large curved bills and can be found in the Mara.

Hunting Dog

Lycaon pictus
MBAWA MWITU

A rare and colorful sight in Kenya. They run down their prey in teams until the quarry falls over from exhaustion. The pack then tears the animal to pieces. Wild dogs hunt game as small as hares and as large as zebra. Persecution, disease and reduction in wildlife habitats and populations have caused a decline in wild dog numbers, raising fears they could soon become extinct. Wild dogs often compete with hyenas who try to steal their kills.

Hyena

Crocuta crocuta
FISI

The spotted hyena is one of the few animals that can create fear in the African night. They have been known to attack sleeping humans and are fierce aggressors around camps and villages. The calls of the hyena are unique and chilling; they can make up to 17 different sounds from what sounds like insane laughter to barking to howling screams. The hyena kills live prey as well as eats carrion. It is not unusual to see them coated in dried blood skulking around campsites.

Hyrax

Heterohyrax brucei

PIMBI

Every guide will tell you that the hyrax is the closest living relative to the elephant (in bone structure only). The rock hyrax lives in communes in the many rocky outcroppings on the savanna. The tree hyrax is known for its blood curdling scream at night. Small, tailless creatures with long bodies and short legs that resemble rodents more than ungulates. Bush and rock hyraxes live in colonies composed of a male with a harem of several related females and their offspring.

Impala

Aepyceros melampus

SWALA PALA

The distinctive impala is known for its gravity defying leaps and bounds as it scurries away at the approach of predators. The impala can jump up to 10 feet high and as long as 36 feet. They can be found grazing in bachelor herds or in harems of between 20–100 females. Often confused with Grant's or Thompson's gazelle, the impala is identified by its lyre shaped horns. The horns are used to advantage when bachelor males fight for control of harems.

Jackal

Canis mesomelas

BWEHA

The jackal has a reputation for its cunning and speed. In reality the jackal is a dog and a scavenger surviving mainly by stealing carrion from vultures. It only hunts small rodents, large insects and domestic livestock. Jackels scavenge at lion and hyena kills. Leopards, with a well-known preference for dog meat, are the main predator of adult jackals and eagles are a threat to young pups around the den.

Klipspringer

Oreotragus oreotragus
MBUZI MAWE

Found on kopjes and steep rock faces. They can spend their entire lives within an area as small as 25 acres depending on availability of forage. Sure footed and sturdy they will scamper goatlike up steep rock faces when disturbed. They depend on steep, rocky terrain as a refuge against predators. Water independent, they graze on leaves, shoots, berries, fruits, seed pods, flowers, evergreens, succulents, herbs and green grass.

Kudu, Greater

Tragelaphus strepsiceros
TANDALA MKUBWA

The second tallest antelope with spectacular horns. Found in Marsabit National Reserve. Kudu live in small herds and prefer to stay in hilly areas with bush cover. Males are usually solitary. Adept at concealment, it is one of the few large mammals that thrives in settled areas. Herds typically include one to three females and their offspring but averages vary from five to up to 15 depending on the season.

Kudu, Lesser

Tragelaphus imberbis
TANDALA NDOGO

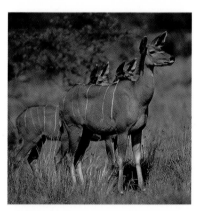

Found in pairs, the lesser kudu is smaller, has more stripes and smaller horns (only the male has horns). The lesser kudu uses thickets for camouflage, foraging on up to 118 different plant species. Herds tend to be larger in the rainy seasons. It seldom browses acacias and remains on all fours while feeding. When running the tail is fanned, raised and extremely conspicuous.

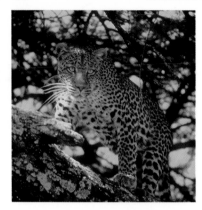

Leopard

Panthera pardus

CHUI

The crowning achievement of most safaris is the sighting of a leopard high in a tree or poised on a kopje. Leopards are shy, solitary and nocturnal animals that can be seen with some regularity in the Mara. Even though the stunning sight of a leopard is enough to attract every vehicle in the park the leopard will gaze back calmly. The sight of a rotting antelope carcass hanging in a tree is usually evidence of a leopard nearby. Leopards also like to walk around campsites late at night and are often discovered in areas of human habitation. Employing infinite patience and stealth, leopards try to get within five yards of quarry before pouncing.

Lion

Panthera leo

SIMBA

There is little to compare with your first sight of a magnificent male lion. Perhaps no other animal makes you feel glad you are in a steel vehicle. Almost invisible in the tall golden grass, lions easily stalk and kill any hoofed animal they choose. In fact lionesses can easily take down a full sized buffalo by gripping its nostrils in a suffocating death grip. They will then lovingly lick the nose and hind quarters before feeding. Lions hunt in groups with the females doing most of the dirty work. The males will slowly move the prey towards the hiding females. Many times it seems they are practicing since they lack the speed of the cheetah or the viciousness of the hunting dogs.

Lions are most active in the late afternoon and can be found sitting under trees or on rock outcrops.

Mongoose, Banded

Mungos mungo

KICHECHE

Mongooses can be seen in groups usually scattering when vehicles approach. The banded mongoose is greyish–brown and medium–sized (about 18") with transverse dark bands along its body. They prey on bird eggs, insects and fruits. They live in burrows and make a host of noises when agitated or fighting. Both sexes are territorial, repelling same-sex intruders. One male lives with several related females rearing their young communally.

Monkey, Vervet

Cercopithecus aethiops

TUMBILI

The vervet monkey is identified by its black face and smaller size (48"–56") than the baboon. Many of these inquisitive and noisy monkeys can be found around the camps looking for scraps or handouts. They are often found in riverine vegetation especially groves of fever trees which provide both safety and sustenance year-round. Vervets help propagate their food plants by dispersing seeds in their droppings. They are gregarious animals and are often found in large groups.

Oribi

Ourebia ourebi

TAYA

Found in the Masai Mara the oribi is easy to confuse with duikers. Found in pairs the oribi will bound when surprised in a stiff legged pouncing action. Oribi prefer open grassland tall enough to hide in but not too tall to see over. Settlement, agriculture and hunting have greatly reduced the oribi habitat and range.

Oryx

Oryx beisa

CHOROA

Found in arid regions the oryx or beisa has been hunted for its massive horns (some reach up to 45 inches in length) They feed at night and very early in the morning. Found in very arid regions like the Marsabit and Tana river region, they are easy to identify since both males and females carry the dramatic upsweeping horns. The oryx drinks regularly when water is available but can get by on melons, roots, bulbs and tubers for which they can dig with their sharp hooves.

Ostrich

*Struthio camelus massaicus
    (Maasai ostrich)*

*Struthio camelus molybdophanes
    (Somali ostrich)*

MBUNI

Even from a distance it is easy to spot the ungainly ostrich. The females are a drab brown and the male is all formal in his black and white plumage. The male's skin turns bright red during breeding season. Ostriches use their large feet to evade predators and can reach speeds of up to 30mph. Ostriches prefer the lush, open grasslands of the savanna plains, dry thorn bush country and semi–desert.

Python

Python sebae

NYOKA

The python is Africa's largest snake. Thick bodied reptiles, they grow to a length of 6 meters (20 ft.). They are typically found near water except in the higher regions. Pythons, contrary to popular belief, will not attack unless provoked.

Reedbuck

Redunca redunca

TOHE

A common large antelope found in the lower floodplain and grasslands. Active at night they can be seen picking at low brush in the late afternoon and dawn. Found in Amboseli, Nairobi and Tsavo the reedbuck is usually found close to water. The common reedbuck lives in monogamous pairs in territories of 86 to 148 acres. Reedbucks run in a distinctive rocking canter, well adapted to high grass and hillsides, displaying their white tails and whistling when excited.

Rhinoceros, Black

Diceros bicornis

KIFARU

The major difference between white rhino and black rhino is their lips (white is the bad translation of *weit* or wide mouthed); black rhino have pronounced triangular upper lips. Sadly you will only see black rhino in Kenya. An attempt to introduce white rhino resulted in the slaughter of the remaining five white rhinos and one ranger in Meru National Park in 1988. Many people believe the days of the rhino are numbered since there are only around 500 left in Kenya. That is down from over 22,000 in 1970. Poaching still continues (primarily by the Chinese for questionable medicinal purposes) and the price of one horn is more than most Kenyans will make in ten years. If poachers are not enough to ensure their demise, rhinos have terrible eyesight, usually run when provoked, have a heck of a time procreating, and live solitary lives.

Secretary Bird
Sagittarius serpentarius

It's easy to spot the tall gawky birds that strut purposely and slowly through the low grasslands. The 40" high bird has a conspicuous crest that looks like a tiara or halo. The leggy birds walk carefully and silently because they are after their favorite meal of snake. They are widely distributed but not commonly seen throughout East Africa on open plains, bush country and farmlands. Though usually silent, during breeding season they produce croaks and even a lion-like cough.

Sitatunga
Tragelaphus spekii
NZOHE

The Sitatunga antelope is found only in the Saiwa Swamp National Park. Their total population is just over 100 in all of Kenya. Unusual for their elongated hooves and facility in swimming, the Sitatunga are able to traverse marshy lands easily. Sitatunga feed on swamp vegetation up to their shoulders, come ashore to graze on green pastures and enter the forest to browse woody vegetation. They will stand on their hind legs to reach high flowers and males sometimes break branches with the backs of their horns.

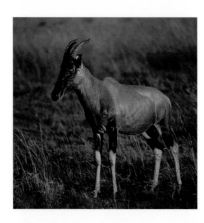

Topi
Damaliscus topi
NYAMNERA

The topi has short curved horns and a very distinctive sad face. It likes greener grasses and shoots. Morning is a good time to watch the males face off in bachelor herds. Similar to the hartebeest the topi has a rich red coat with dark hind quarters, front legs and face. Their number and habitat have been greatly reduced by human hunting and habitat destruction.

Vulture
Gyps africanus

Vultures are medium to very large birds (26"–34") with long wings, short tails and relatively small naked or down covered heads. Luckily vultures have no sense of smell. They eat what is left by hyenas and jackals (usually waiting patiently like aged undertakers in the background). Vultures actually need other predators to rip open the carcass so they can begin the job of picking and peeling what is left. You can often hear their harsh squawking croaks while they are feeding on the carrion. Sometimes after they eat they cannot fly so they will hop away and digest their meal.

Warthog
Phacochoerus acthopicus
NGIRI

Easily the ugliest hooved animal on the face of this planet. The warthog is actually a sweet lovable pig once you get to know it. They live in large burrows in termite mounds and actually have the presence of mind to enter backwards to facilitate a quick exit when disturbed. A warthog family running at full speed is a humorous sight indeed. Its puny tail sticks straight up and it is usually followed by its tiny long-legged offspring. The warthog defends it-self with its razor-edged tusks that actually sharpen against each other as it eats.

Waterbuck, Common or Defassa
Kobus ellipsiprymnus
KURU

Probably the least exotic looking savanna animal to North American visitors. These deerlike antelope have a subspecies (Defassa Waterbuck) found only west of the Rift Valley. They are usually found within a few hours walk of water and can be seen any-time day or night. Males have horns.

Wildebeast, Common or Gnu
Connochaetes taurinus
NYUMBU

The most common grazing animal on the Kenya Plains. The estimated 1.3 million wildebeest or gnus still make the great Serengeti migration each year. They need fairly fresh grasses because of the inability to crop closely and cannot stray more than 15km from water. Not known for their intelligence, gnus will never seem to make the right moves when chased by predators. Even left to their own devices they will do strange things like roll around, buck and run around in circles without any prodding.

Zebra
Equus burchellii
   (Burchell's or Plains Zebra)
Equus grevyi (Grevy's Zebra)
PUNDA MILLIA

One will ask if the zebra is a white donkey with black stripes or vice versa. The zebra is one of the more striking examples of African adaptation. Zebras prefer dry savannah to semi-desert habitats. Their stripes confuse predators when they are in a herd. Of the two species, Burchell's are the ones with the heavy bands while Grevy's have thinner, fingerprint style stripes.

Burchell's zebra are found in the east and west and Grevy's in the south and north. Both species are the favorite food of lions and hyenas.

Giraffes in Samburu

Night game viewing at Treetops

An often seen species: "minibus touristicus"

Breakfast guest at Giraffe Manor, Nairobi

Dining alfresco

Early morning tea

Hand-made artifacts await tourists

Game drive through Kenya

Masai Mara balloon safari

Samburu women

A pride of lion cubs

Tribal dance demonstration

Thomson's Falls

Early morning on the Mara